BRITISH INSTITUTE OF ARCHAEOLOGY AT ANKARA
Monograph 26

THE OTTOMAN HOUSE

Papers from the Amasya Symposium, 24-27 September 1996

Edited by

Stanley Ireland & William Bechhoefer

Published by

The British Institute of Archaeology at Ankara

and

The University of Warwick

British Institute of Archaeology at Ankara
c/o British Academy, 10 Carlton House Terrace
London SW1Y 5AH

University of Warwick
Coventry CV4 7AL

This book is available from Oxbow Books
Park End Place, Oxford, OX1 1HN

ISBN 1 898249 12 1
ISSN 0969-9007

The front cover shows the riverfront houses of Amasya
The back cover shows a frieze from the Yıldız Palace, Istanbul

Typeset by S. Ireland and G. Coulthard
Printed by Stephen Austin & Sons Ltd, Hertford

PREFACE

The present volume is in many respects the offspring of a chance meeting in Amasya in 1994 between one of its editors, the then Acting-Director of the British Institute of Archaeology at Ankara and one of Amasya's architects, a meeting that within hours was to involve the city's governor and a host of local officials. The subject of that meeting centred upon the efforts being made within the city to preserve its heritage of traditional housing. The outcome was a proposal for an International Symposium both to celebrate Ottoman house architecture, which has had an important influence upon many western architects, and also to underline the dangers faced by established urban patterns within the area that once formed the Ottoman empire. The organiser was happy to accept the offer of the city authorities to hold the Symposium in Amasya, which lies well to the east of Ankara, not only because this is one of the few urban foundations left within Turkey that still possesses a relatively intact quarter of traditional domestic architecture, including a magnificent river frontage, but also in recognition of the efforts being made to restore and maintain this as a living entity.

Traditional domestic architecture the world over has attracted increasing attention over the past decades. This interest, however, has often been powerless to halt or even to slow the pace at which such historic areas have disappeared before the onslaught of modern redevelopment, which all too often replaces the unique with the uniform, and buildings adapted to local conditions with those that take no account of their environment or the comfort of those who inhabit them. A prime aim of the Symposium, therefore, was to demonstrate the diversity and adaptive nature of traditional Ottoman architecture, to emphasise its still valid, contemporary potential for providing humane living space, and to underline the importance of preserving what remains, both within Turkey and in a wider context, not simply as islands of existence to amuse the tourist, or exhibits in some kind of museum theme-park, but as real neighbourhoods where modern life can continue to evolve.

The efforts being made in Amasya to discover a way of preserving the living essence of traditional domestic architecture, therefore, provided the catalyst for a gathering in September 1996 of some twenty architects and scholars from three continents whose work covered a vast range of topics. This in itself demonstrates the interest that Ottoman architecture generates, but if this is all the Symposium achieved, its organiser would count his efforts wasted. The enthusiasm that was so evident in those September days must now be disseminated to a wider audience, one that encompasses both the world of scholarship and the amateur in the best sense of that word, those many individuals who, in this age of mass transport, have come to value the diversity and humanity of vernacular architecture. It is the editors' hope, therefore, that within the papers which follow readers, of whatever type, will find material both detailed and general that will be of service to them.

For ease of production line diagrams have been placed at the end of each paper. Plates, in contrast, have been located together at the end of the volume.

Stanley Ireland
University of Warwick

William Bechhoefer
University of Maryland

ACKNOWLEDGEMENTS

On behalf of those who took part in the Symposium the editors first and foremost wish to express their warm appreciation for both the assistance and hospitality so generously provided by the city authorities and people of Amasya, in particular the Governor Kemal Nehrozoğlu, the Mayor Ahmet Çekin, the Ministry of Culture, and the University of Amasya. The warmth of their welcome, which contributed so much to the overall success of the Symposium, and their continued support for the project of publishing the Proceedings is something the editors, and all those involved in the production of papers, will never forget. In addition, we are acutely aware of the debt owed to the personnel of Amasya's *Riverfront Houses Project* (*Yalıboyu Evleri Projesi*) for the care they injected into the local arrangements for the Symposium and their efforts to protect the city's architectural heritage.

At the same time we owe a great debt of gratitude both to the British Institute of Archaeology at Ankara and the Centre for East Roman Studies of the University of Warwick for the support given to the organisation of the symposium, and, together with the Seven Pillars of Wisdom Trust, for the generous contributions provided by the BIAA, the University of Warwick, and the Department of Classics and Ancient History of the University of Warwick towards the costs of producing this volume.

Finally, the editors are acutely aware of the thanks they owe to those many people who have contributed to lightening their load with help and advice. Among them we would include: in Britain Josie Brown, Pauline Wilson, Helen Ireland, and Özlem Berk; in the USA Carel Bertram, and Adil & Ferhan Kilical; and in Turkey Gülgün Kazan.

CONTENTS

GLOSSARY OF MOST COMMON TURKISH TERMS

(Many more terms, some relating specifically to Amasyan terminology, are explained on pp. 93-4; see also 31 and 41 for some other local variants).

Abdestlik:	Room for the performance of ablutions
Ahır:	Stables
Avlu:	Courtyard
Baş Oda:	Principal room
Cami:	Mosque
Cumba:	Part of a room projecting like a bay window
Dolap:	Cupboard
Eyvan:	Room open on one side to a courtyard or other room
Gusülhane:	Bathroom
Hamam:	Public bathhouse
Haremlik:	The area of the house reserved for the family, servants, and female guests
Hayat:	Normally the ground floor area first entered from the street; but see also pp.31 and 93
Havuz:	Pool
İşlik:	Work room
Kışlık:	Winter room
Konak:	Mansion
Köşk:	Pavillion or penthouse
Misafir odası:	Guest room
Mutfak:	Kitchen
Ocak:	Fireplace
Oda:	Room
Odunluk:	Store (esp. for firewood)
Samanlık:	Store (esp. for straw)
Sedir:	Divan or long seat against wall
Selamlık:	The area of the house reserved for men and their male guests
Sofa:	The central room on any floor onto which all the other rooms open
Yalı:	Mansion along a sea or river shore
Yazlık:	Summer room
Yüklük:	Closet for bedding

LIST OF FIGURES

LIST OF PLATES

(All plates are at the end of the volume)

1 Bertram: Imagining the Turkish Ottoman House

3 Özgüven: Ottoman Encampment and Urban Settlement

9 McQuitty: Houses of the Ottoman Period in Jordan

10 Yıldız: Ottoman Houses in Cyprus

11 Yalçın: Ottoman House Construction in Amasya

15 Karpuz: The Architecture of Traditional Houses in Konya

16 Ülkü: Adapting a Traditional Building in Mersin

17 Bechhoefer: House and Urban Form in Amasya

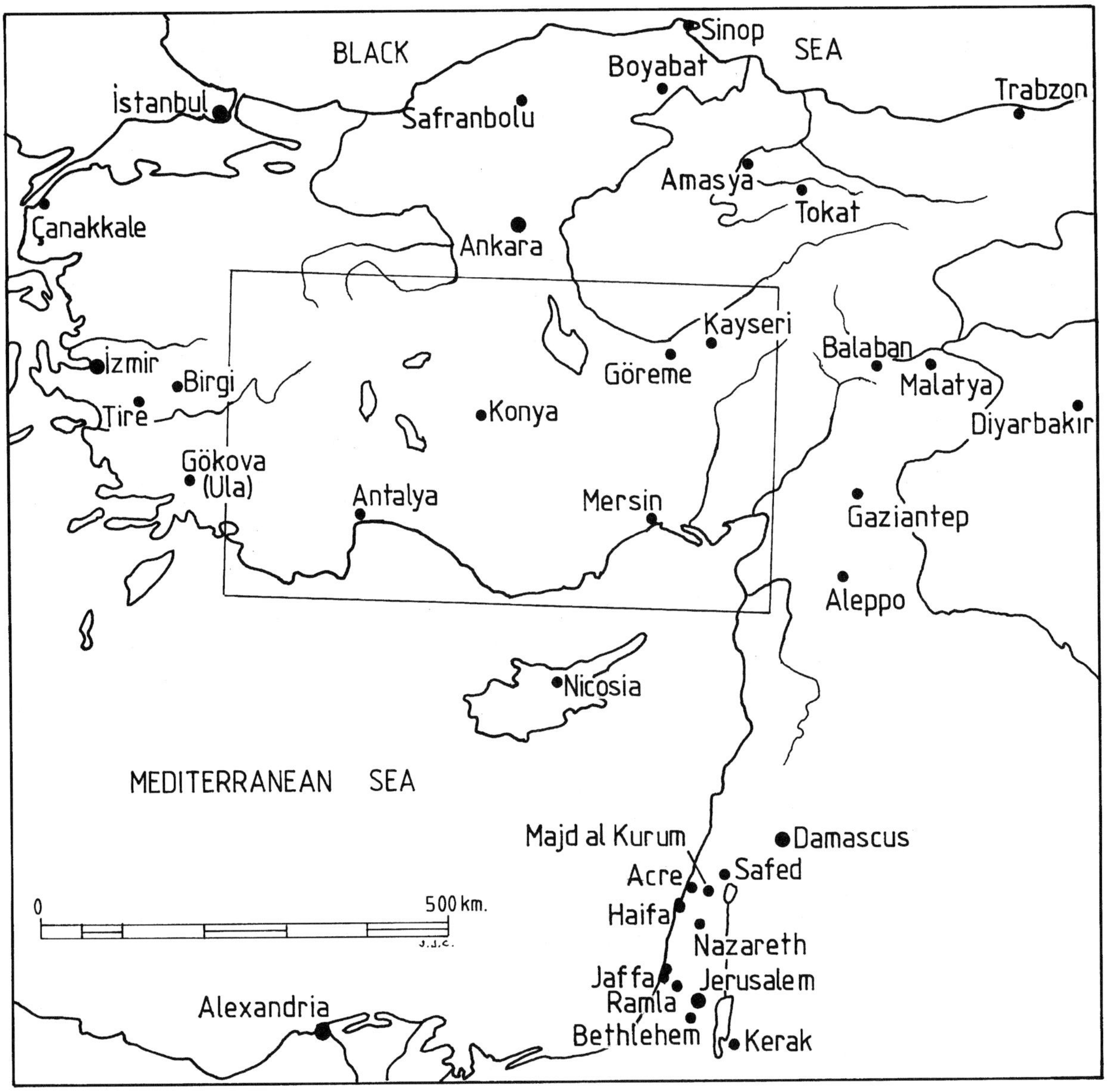

Map of Turkey and the Near East (the framed area = fig. 14.2)

PART ONE: THE OTTOMAN HOUSE IN CONTEXT

Buildings are artefacts of culture as well as individual constructions. Houses, in particular, reflect how people live together as families, as neighbourhoods, and as members of a larger society. A house may receive the loving attention of its owners and become a work of art in itself. However, a greater part of its meaning and significance comes from the ensemble of which it is a part. The study of houses, therefore, inevitably becomes the study of settlement patterns and urban form. A city is the expression of the aspirations of people to live together in a civil contract that enables culture to flourish in all its forms. To wander the streets of an Anatolian or Balkan Ottoman town or city is to experience the public and private institutions of Ottoman civilisation. This is the context in which the study of Ottoman houses takes place.

The physical context is the natural preoccupation of the architects and art historians who are the authors of the symposium papers; however, the cultural context is continually referenced as a source of motivation and inspiration. In this regard, Carel Bertram examines how the Turkish Ottoman house has become symbolic, and even emblematic, of fundamental Turkish cultural values. These houses are, therefore, a critique of Western urban planning and particularly of homogenised modern apartment blocks, even as they are simultaneously representative of out-of-date lifestyles; the confrontation of tradition and modernity is a condition of every society today and is vividly demonstrated in Turkey on a daily basis.

The remaining papers in this section describe and analyse Ottoman urban form. Maurice Münir Cerasi provides a conceptual framework for thinking about the order and character of Ottoman urban culture. He contrasts Western European urban form in which the street is the dominant pattern with Ottoman towns in which the street is merely embedded in a fabric of housing and institutional buildings. The spatial order of the house, therefore, becomes critical to the understanding of the city as a whole, and consequently significant in preservation and modernisation programs. Burcu Özgüven's paper connects aspects of Ottoman urban form to its origins in military encampments. While the relationship of house form to nomadic tents has been extensively studied, the pragmatic and symbolic aspects of settlement patterns that Özgüven discusses give insight into the Ottoman world view.

Taken as a whole, this first group of papers establishes a conceptual framework and physical context for the study of Ottoman houses. They are also suggestive of future directions for research into the contributions of the Ottomans to urban development in all regions of their empire.

1: AFTER THE OTTOMANS ARE GONE: IMAGINING THE TURKISH OTTOMAN HOUSE

Carel Bertram
University of California at Los Angeles

The Turkish Ottoman House[1] with its half timbered façade and upper stories that jut out over the street was constructed in Anatolia and the Balkans during the second half of the Ottoman centuries. Many of these houses remained, of course, after the end of the Ottoman empire, although it seems that no new ones were built.[2] Nonetheless, the Ottoman house continued to evolve in the post-Ottoman imagination, becoming a specific visual image that carried the symbolic weight of Turkey's cultural heritage. I am interested in how this visual image was constructed and how, at the same time that it was disappearing on the landscape, it came to fill the popular imagination.

Whether in central Anatolia, (pl.1.1) or Yugoslavia (pl.1.2) the old houses that filled the urban fabric of the Ottoman provincial past have become the popular image of the provincial Ottoman townscape. Turks have become familiar with them from the drawings and paintings of foreign travellers such as Thomas Allom (pl.1.3), from the turn of the century photographs such as those from Bosnia (pl.1.4) or Anatolia (pl.1.5), and from photographs published in Turkish architectural histories or travel brochures that show the houses that still exist from the pre-Republican period (pl.1.6).

In fact, in many ways, in Turkey and in the West today, the image of the Ottoman House that is presented in these drawings and photographs has come to symbolise 'Tradition', or the 'Traditional Ottoman City'.[3] For example, a book that gives the architectural history of pre-Republican Amasya has on its cover Amasya's Ottoman style river-front houses of timber (Hüsameddin 1986), (pl.1.7) even though the text of this book does not include houses at all, but rather deals with religious monuments. The contents of the book would have been more accurately represented by a photograph of Amasya's famous Bayezid II Mosque or one of the local saints' tombs. The author of this book, the historian Hüseyin Hüsameddin, finished his master work on Amasya in 1927, but in 1986 it was republished in modern Turkish and in paperback by the Amasya Municipality for the benefit of its citizens and tourists. As we shall see, by 1986 the image of the Ottoman House had come to resonate 'Historic Town' and 'Tradition'. For this reason, the cover photograph chosen by the Amasya municipality now seems an obvious choice for a town that, in large part because of its old houses along the river, views itself as a 'museum city' (Yüksel 1995). But nothing is obvious or without historical reason. In the 1960s, for example, students of the *Tatbiki Güzel Sanatlar Yüksek Okulu* (the Academy of Applied and Fine Arts) were asked to design poster images of towns like Amasya (Aslıer 1970). None of their drawings highlight houses from the Ottoman period (pl.1.8-10). One poster does show the river, the Yeşil Irmak that runs through the gorge of Amasya; it also shows Harşene Dağ, the mountain that defines its border, and makes a visual reference to Amasya's most famous crop, its apples. A second poster has an apple that engorges an Amasya that is filled with historic references such as Seljuk tombs, Ottoman minarets, and a Republican statue. A third poster offers a cut apple, ready to eat, and brings in a reference to Amasya's Seljuk history by depicting a Seljuk tomb tower. There are also houses in this second poster, but these are generic house shapes; there is in fact no recognisable architectural form.

By the 1990s, however, children in Istanbul were representing the Turkish townscape with specifically Ottoman Houses, houses that they had never lived in, or even seen (pl.1.11). How did this re-visualisation of the landscape happen? How did these houses come out of their Ottoman obscurity and into focus in Turkey? For these houses that academics are so eager to understand and historians and lovers of history are so eager to protect didn't resonate for the people who lived in them in the way that they do today. Images of these houses and city-scapes defined by residential neighbourhoods do not figure in Ottoman novels, poetry, or folksongs from the 18th and 19th centuries;[4] they are not the siting of dreams nor the subject of urban histories;[5] neither are they described in Ottoman Turkish travellers' reports: it seems that only foreigners such as Le Corbusier found them noteworthy (pl.1.12). The few 19th century city drawings by Turkish travellers such as Bozoklu Osman (pl.1.13) do not have houses as the subject. We might consider that Bozoklu Osman's rendition of Amasya, for example, has urbanism or topography as its subject, but certainly not the particularities of architecture. His drawing of Amasya is in the contemporary tradition of map-making and therefore has a generic or non-specific quality that is seductively accurate, but actually wrong. A close look indicates that nothing architectural is really identifiable.[6]

The same is true for a small painted vignette of Amasya's Hatuniye Camii (Mosque) and Hazeranlar Konağı, a great mansion built in the late 19th century at the time of Amasya's urban renaissance under Ziya Paşa (pl.1.14). This painting is on the interior walls of the Gümüşlü Camii, a mosque situated across the river from the actual mansion. When we compare the vignette to the actual scene that it must represent (pl.1.15), it is clear that the house is only schematically represented, although the choice of the subject suggests that its owner may well have been the patron of the painting. Still, we are left to understand that the late Ottoman period, the period that later came to be called 'traditional', did not define its urbanity with residential images.[7] Neither did late Ottoman period literature have many references to houses or neighbourhoods. The references to architecture during the Ottoman period are often limited to major monuments, whether as poetry that is inscribed over the doors of specific buildings, or in poetry that has abstract references, such as the following couplet that relates architecture to the cosmos:

> In a two-doored Han
> I am walking, day and night.[8]

But if the urban imagination of the late Ottoman period did not include its residential architecture, let alone have its houses as emblems of its urbanity, then how did the Ottoman house take shape in the imagination as a specific entity, with a specific resonance, finally emerging in the picture that we have of it today?

We all know that what is today referred to as the Ottoman House is an endangered species that began to be destroyed at the beginning of the Republican Period, a movement that gained momentum through the 1960s until it slowed down partly because there were so few houses left. Anatolia once had a rich stock of vernacular houses of various styles, and towns like Amasya had a thick infill of them (pl.1.16). But in the 1950s apartment houses began to pop up (pl.1.19) and the old cityscapes began to change. The Ottoman house was about to disappear.

But I would suggest that before the Ottoman house was lost to the construction of apartment buildings, it was lost to the construction of Modernism. What I mean by 'Modernism' is not merely Westernisation. Westernisation, or the importing of ideas and items from the West had begun as early as the Tulip Period, (that is, in the 18th century). But, as Tanyeli suggests, 'Modernisation' - unlike 'Westernisation' - has an ideological bent to it (Tanyeli 1996); for it demands both consciousness and desire. The desire is to *be* a certain way, to transform culturally. In the late Ottoman period Westernisation and Modernisation combined to mean a conscious desire to 'be modern'; the goal was not merely to acquire new, Western *things*, but to be a part of the culture that produced and used those things.[9]

What is interesting for us here is that in the late Ottoman Period the site of this modernisation process was the house. Physically this was the old Konak or Mansion, but its symbolic transformation was taking place on the inside. Modernisation was defined in terms of domestic objects and the importation and use of modern or 'Frenk' artefacts became the words of a cultural message. This included the clothes people wore, not just for 'show' but because they were beginning to live and work differently. 'Like our dresses, our morals and our manners became rococo' wrote Yakup Kadri Karaosmanoğlu in his book *Kiralık Konağı.*[10] For example, pianos were not merely displayed, but were important parts of upper-class life, marking a woman who played them and the house that held them as educated and refined, that is 'modern'. There was more than just display of Westernisation at issue: pianos did not gather dust in the corners, but were the centre of social gatherings; that is, the house began to be used differently as well as to look different. Rooms that had once been multi-functional were now designated by their furnishings for specific purposes such as evening soirées that included piano playing.

Another example of the way the interior of the house was changing in the interest of Westernisation was a replacement of what has been called the Ottoman 'tray culture' (Tanyeli 1996: 289-90), (pl.1.18) by one defined by the imported eating table. This meant that food was no longer eaten on the carpeted floor around a large tray that would disappear after the meal, making the room again available for a different function such as entertaining or sleeping. Rooms which had been dining rooms when the tray appeared became bedrooms when the bedding was taken from the closets. Now rooms took on designated and specific functions. In 'modern' households there was a designated dining room, and, as Tanyeli had pointed out, by the early 1920s to sit on the floor came to mean old or traditional, whereas to sit in a chair meant modern and progressive (Tanyeli 1993: 286). By making the form of the old Ottoman House inappropriate for this new culture, Modernism had begun to undermine the house ideologically before it was physically torn down. But what is especially interesting is that the old house which had not been a part of the imagination now began to come into consciousness for the first time, but as an entity with a questionable ability to be an appropriate site for Modernism.

In fact, when Atatürk took Modernism on as a stated goal for the new Turkish Republic[11], it was thought that what was needed was a 'modern' architecture to 'house' the new ideology (Yavuz 1984). A major architectural symbol of this civilisation shift was the house, because it encompassed the Republican ideology that championed a new type of family which was one that lived in a 'Western fashion'. In fact the Republican discourse on Modernism is a domestic one: it is the discourse on the nuclear family, with motherhood as a national duty and on the home as the sacred space of national renewal. The wife, not her servants or her mother in law, was to be responsible for the home, and the new kitchen designed for her (pl.1.17) was referred to in magazine advertisements, such as in the 'Home and Furniture' section of *Yedigün*, as the *kadın salonu* (the woman's room or domain; Bozdoğan 1996: 320). But women were also encouraged to work outside the home, and therefore the idealised environment was a house planned with the necessary labour saving devices of modern life, such as electric dishwashers.

Bozdoğan shows how the architectural symbol of this new Republican family was the single family home, most identifiably the cubist version of the family house (pl.1.20) with its large plate glass windows that opened out to the view. This is the exact opposite of the inward looking Ottoman house that was set above the street and enclosed in garden walls. Magazines of the 1930s were filled with these *Küçük Evler*, defining the tastes for the middle classes, and even in remote Safranbolu they said that every bride hoped for:

> A motherless husband
> A smokeless chimney
> A pressure cooker
> and a picture window (Tayla 1977)

One could say that it was this symbol, and this cubist house (although it existed more in the imagination than on the ground), that replaced the old Konak as the symbol of family life. By 1923 the traditional extended family had begun to be replaced by the nuclear family, (Duben 1991: 314) and residential space was being transformed. Now we see advertisements for intimate dining rooms for the idealised small nuclear family, suggesting, of course, that the traditional wooden 'Turkish House' was no longer adequate physically nor appropriate ideologically to represent the aspirations of a westernised élite.

Yet the fact is that it was the propagandising of this new symbol that brought the old Konak into consciousness at all, albeit as the symbol of an outdated mentality and a fading life style. In the 1930s to live in the cubic house was to live at the end of history, in the era of cleanliness and health, that is of hot water and electricity. What the government required and Modernism expected was that the new Republic's population would come out of the dark ages, an age represented by the old house, and into the light of Modernism. This metaphor of dark and light was one of the images of modern living in the 1930s.

> Whereas the moonlight reigned in the old houses...the rule of the sun is beginning in the glass enclosed buildings of today.

wrote a journalist in the weekly magazine *Yedigün* (Bozdoğan 1996: 322).

But something else was happening, too, for the old wooden house began to have a split personality: although it entered the consciousness as a symbol of the old and the out-dated, at the same time it began to represent what was wrong with modernism. Authors such as Yakup Kadri Karaosmanoğlu, although supportive of Ataturk's dream of new, modern cities, also wrote about the new cubic house with a tongue in cheek delight that left a cold taste in the mouth. In his 1934 novel *Ankara* Karaosmanoğlu writes:

> Couches like dentists' chairs, seats like operation tables, sofas resembling the interiors of automobiles, and finally, scattered all over these, some weird grotesque knick-knacks ... (Bozdoğan 1996: 325f.).

This type of satire could only make the reader conjure up an image of its opposite.

In his 1935 story, *Ev Sevgisi*, Hüseyin Cahit Yalçın makes this image of the old Ottoman house vivid:

> In a great homeland we are left as if we were homeless with no place to nest. We sold our old houses to the destruction crews, and they destroyed, with a crack and a snap, right in front of our eyes, the buildings that had formed our family history, and thus the memory of the bitter-sweet days that we once lived there; they left us to be like vagabonds in life. Perhaps we moved into apartments. Perhaps instead of those old rooms of ours, furnished with plain wood, we now have salons covered with shaggy carpets. But this is no hearth for us; it is not a 'house'. (Bozdoğan 1996: 326).

It is at this point that the old Ottoman house began to emerge into the public consciousness and take on some form, beginning its fight for its place as a national symbol. In fact it was during this period of conflicting messages that the young architect, Sedad

Hakkı Eldem, went to Paris to study Ottoman houses. By 1934 he had returned to Turkey and begun the now famous Seminar on National Architecture with the goal of teaching Turkish architects a systematic and sophisticated way to study their own history of residential architecture. But his interest was not in revivalism - in fact, like Karaosmanoğlu, he remained committed to modernism throughout his career. In fact, in the 30s and 40s Eldem saw in the forms of old houses a formal source for a new national Republican architectural style (Tekeli 1984). By the end of the 1930s Eldem had written a treatise that described these ideas for a national idiom that emphasised the value of residential forms as symbols of Ottoman-Turkish historical continuity (Alsaç 1984: 96). An example of this was Eldem's design for an Istanbul Coffee House (pl.1.21) that used Ottoman domestic forms - such as overhanging eaves and rows of windows - to create a distinctively Turkish yet modern style. This style, during the period of World War II, became known as the Second National Style and was, perhaps, the true inauguration of the Turkish House as a mental image.

Eldem went on to make a master typology of the Turkish house, and the way that its plan had developed in space and time. This was published in his 1954 work *Türk Evi Plan Tipleri* (Typologies of the Turkish House) and yet more fully in his 3 volume work *Türk Evi Osmanlı Dönemi/Turkish Houses Ottoman Period* (Eldem 1984) which also identifies the specifically Ottoman relationships of rooms, window treatments, and eaves.

The post World War II period of the 1950s was a period of 'apartmentising' (Nalbantoğlu 1981). Yet at the same time there was also a realisation that as the Turkish landscape was being modernised, Turkish culture was being put in jeopardy: a link between the values of the past and the old wooden house was emerging. It was at this point that the house began its history as a symbol of cultural survival; and it is at this point in the 1950s that students trained in the 1940s began to publish their documentation of the Turkish House, a project that continues to this day. These students had scoured Anatolia for old houses, which they lovingly drew and photographed, both inside and out (pl.1.22, 23). Even the minutest details of building and decoration were recorded, but the goal was neither to save nor to restore, merely to immortalise vanishing evidence.[12] Furthermore, this image collection and image making was part of an academic exercise, so that even by the 1960s the Turkish house as an image still lived in the imagination of the intelligentsia and was not a part of the public imagination. We saw an example of this in the city posters of Amasya where students of graphic design still chose monumental architecture to symbolise the past (pl.1.24).

What was missing, it seems, for the Ottoman House to become a symbol of the past for the people of Turkey was a way to connect it to the specific *Turkishness* of the Ottoman past. By the 1960s architects, even Eldem himself, had abandoned the National Styles, and were designing buildings in the International Style. But the concepts that had raised the Ottoman house into the academic consciousness continued at the research level. In the 1960s, the studies of typologies and room configurations that Eldem had inaugurated were analysed by scholars who had been trained with the official History Thesis of the early Republican Period. Since the Ottoman Empire had been reduced to Asia Minor, and its people were now mainly Turks, one object of this thesis was to tie the new national and ethnic identity to a specifically geographical one by deepening the roots that the Turkish people had in Anatolian soil. Scholars in this tradition, such as Emil Esin (Esin 1965) and later Önder Küçükerman (1973) posited that the Turkish room, the 'oda', which had been the centrepiece of Eldem's typology, had developed directly from the nomadic Turkish tent with a like division by gender, and with space similarly relegated for heating, socialising and storage (pl.25). It is this connection to the nomadic tent that sealed the fate of the house as the carrier of 'traditional' identity. The Turkish tent-room connection remains alive today among Turkish scholars such as Kuban who maintains that in the Hayat House 'the room is organised as a tent, decorated as a tent, and used as a tent' (Kuban 1995: 217). The nomadic roots of the 'room' fit comfortably into the methodology of the national History Thesis which had been promulgated in a period when the uncomfortable recent Ottoman past was being replaced (and therefore *not* celebrated), and when history-writing was eager to leap-frog over it into a more distant past. Certainly the idea of the room as a tent was a powerful way for the Turkish people to appropriate the house for themselves and at the same time obviate the Ottoman centuries that saw residences built by and designed for a heterogeneous population over a wide geographical area. But by the 1960s, the nation was secure with its Turkish identity and comfortably proud of its Ottoman one as well. By this time, the late Ottoman period and its houses could safely become a symbol of 'traditional time', a time now considered at the heart of Turkish culture. The graduate students who were scouring Anatolia in the 1940s and 1950s referred to the houses that they were documenting as the Turkish House (*Türk Evi*). By the 1970s the word 'traditional' had been added as in Küçükerman's *Anadolu'daki geleneksel Türk evinde mekân organizasyonu açısından odalar* (The rooms in the traditional Turkish House of Anatolia from the aspect of spatial organisation, Küçükerman 1973). The Ottoman House, fortified by its specific link to the Turkish people rather than juxtaposed to a desire to 'be modern', was ready to become the symbol of cultural survival. This move to make the Turkish Ottoman house one of the centrepieces of cultural survival was led by architects and historians such as Doğan Kuban, Perihan Balcı and Çelik Gülersoy in the 60s and 70s. In fact there was even an attempt by some architects to revive the spatial and decorative aspects of the Ottoman House, for example the homes designed by Nail Çakırhan in the Muğla area. His first neo-Ottoman House was designed in the late 60s and completed 1970 (pl.1.26). But this revival-from-scratch never became a national movement as did the move to preserve and restore the houses that did exist.

Evidence of a now widespread acceptance of the idea of the Turkish house as a cultural symbol can be seen in the 1973 Antiquities Law for the preservation of monuments (*Eski Eserler Kanunu*) that considered vernacular houses and their settings as 'cultural property'. In 1976, *Türkiye Tarihi Evleri Koruma Derneği* (The Turkish Association for the Protection of Historic Houses) was established and in 1979 the Safranbolu preservation and rehabilitation project began as a project of the Plans and Monuments of the Ministry of Old Works and Museums (Soyer 1984). In the 1970s Amasya's *Hazeranlar Konağı* (pl.1.27) was purchased by the government, which now wanted to restore this Turkish house as an image of a valuable Turkish culture. Sedad Hakkı Eldem himself suggested that each muncipality purchase a local house and restore it as a museum in order to educate the people and inspire them to value their own houses (Eldem 1980).

But this image of the Ottoman House as an inherently valuable part of the past was still part of an intellectual, rather than a popular, world view: in Amasya, as elsewhere, there were municipal vs. government court cases disputing the right of the capital to decide what each city could do with its old neighbourhoods, and the public themselves often 'voted' against restoration by acts of sabotage.[13] The *Hazeranlar Konağı*, at the point that it was being bought (pl.1.28), was being systematically destroyed with dynamite by its owner so that it could be replaced by a modern building. It is this disjuncture between the intellectual and the private conception of the Turkish house that has not been fully closed. Is the house a symbol of cultural memory, and thus public property - or is it ordinary, utilitarian property with a commodity value over which the owner should have full rights?

The Turkish house today, as it exists as an image in print, in the imagination of architects and planners and tourists, and in the few areas where it exists *in fact* on the ground, is still changing its meaning. Although the house has become cultural property because it is emblematic of a 'Turkish past', and of 'traditional time', the definition of when that time was, and of who the significant players were, is always in the process of being re-defined or re-invented.[14] For example, the Ottoman House that is restored but turned into a folklore museum invents an Ottoman Past that is frozen in the 19th century upper classes. When it is torn down and rebuilt from scratch, but with modern materials, it can become a type of false consciousness or false memory. This has happened in Istanbul with projects such as the Aya Sofya Pansiyonları, a series of old houses that were rebuilt as a hotel (pl.1.29, 30). The problem that restorationists are now beginning to face is one in which the house, even if accurately restored, can no longer serve its original residential function because the life-style that it was built for no longer exists. As offices, shops and hotels it is bound to take on a new image in the popular imagination. When we look back at this period we will ask how the Ottoman house gave a new meaning to the past. But it is just this study, the study of how images enter the imagination and how they change their symbolic weight, that reveals far more information about the present than it ever can of the past. What brought the Ottoman house into our consciousness was not its loss, but its juxtaposition with the modern. Restoration and preservation reveal how it has become, at some levels of society, an icon of cultural heritage. Whether it is an icon of a 'true past' or an imagined one is not at issue; for the visually remembered Ottoman House has taken on its shoulders the goal of providing the present with a sense of history at a time when the present is attempting to construct its future.

Bibliography

Alsaç, Ü. 1984: 'The Second Period of Turkish National Architecture', in R. Holod, A. Evin (eds), *Modern Turkish Architecture*. Pennsylvania: 94-104.

Anderson, B. 1983: *Imagined Commuities; Reflections on the Origins and Spread of Nationalism*. London.

Anon 1991: *Çevre ve Biz*. UNESCO, Istanbul.

Arik, R. 1976: *Batılılaşma Dönemi, Anadolu Tasvir Sanatı*. Ankara.

Arseven, C.E. (ed.) c. 1950: 'Türkiye'de Tanzimat Devrinden Sonra Resim', in *Türk Sanatı Tarihi: Menşeinden Bugüne Kadar Heykel, Oyma ve Resim*. Milli Eğitim Basımevi, Istanbul: 128-60.

Aslıer, M. 1970: 'Tatbiki Güzel Sanatlar Yüksek Okulu', *Türkiyemiz* 1: 137-60.

Balcı, P. 1980: *Eski İstanbul Evleri ve Boğaziçi Yalıları*. APA Ofset, Istanbul.

Berk, C. 1951: *Konya Evleri*. Istanbul.

Bozdoğan, S. 1996: 'Modern Yaşamak: Erken Cumhuriyet Kültüründe Kübik Ev', in Y. Sey (ed.), *Tarihten Günümüze Anadolu'da Konut ve Yerleşme*. Türkiye Ekonomik ve Toplumsal Tarih Vakfı, Istanbul: 313-28.

Çakıroğlu, N. 1952: *Kayseri Evleri*. İ.T.Ü., Istanbul.

Duben, A., Cem, B. 1991: *Istanbul Households, Marriage, Family and Fertility 1880-1940.* Cambridge.

Eldem, S.H. 1954: *Türk Evi Plan Tipleri.* İstanbul Teknik Üniversitesi, Mimarlık Fakültesi, Istanbul:

---- 1980: 'Türk Evini Koruyalım', *Sanat Dünyamız*, 7, 17-25.

Eldem, S.H. 1984-7: *Türk Evi Osmanlı Dönemi* (3 vols). Türkiye Anıt Çevre Değerlerini Koruma Vakfı. Istanbul.

Erginbaş, D. 1954-5: *Diyarbakır Evleri.* İ.T.Ü., Istanbul.

Erpi, F. 1987: *Buca'da Konut Mimarisi (1834-1934).* ODTÜ, Mimarlık Fakültesi, Ankara.

Eser, L. n.d.: *Kütahya Evleri.* İ.T.Ü., Istanbul.

Esin, E. 1965: 'An 18th C. Yalı, Viewed in the Line of Development of Related Form in Turkic Architecture', *Atti del Secondo Congresso Internazionale di Arte Turca, Venezia.* Naples: 83-112.

Evren, M. 1959: *Türk Evinde Çıkma.* İ.T.Ü., Istanbul.

Gökyay, O.Ş. 1992: 'Divan Edebiyatında Şehirler: I, II, III', *Tarih ve Toplum* 18: 137-40, 201-5, 265-70.

Grabrijan D., Niehardt J. 1957: *Arhitektura Bosna Put U Suvremeno.* Ljubljana.

Günay, R. 1981: *Geleneksel Safranbolu Evleri ve Oluşumu*, 456. Kültür Bakanlığı Yayınları, Ankara.

Hatemi, H. H. 1986: 'Türk Edebiyatında Mimarî', *Tarih ve Toplum* 26: 13-19.

Hobsbawm, E. 1983: *The Invention of Tradition.* Cambridge.

Hüsameddin, A.H. 1986: *Amasya Tarihi*, vol. I, (tr. of 1935 ed., A. Yılmaz, M. Akkuş). Amasya Belediyesi Kültür Yayınları, Ankara.

Kömürcüoğlu, E. 1950: *Ankara Evleri.* İ.T.Ü., Istanbul.

Kuban, D. 1995: *Türk Hayatlı Evi.* Eren Yayıncılık ve Kitapçılık, İ.T.Ü., Istanbul.

Küçükerman, Ö. 1973: *Anadolu'daki Geleneksel Türk Evinde Mekân Organizasiyonu Açısından Odalar.* T.T.O.K. Yay., Istanbul.

---- 1978. *The Turkish House in Search of Spatial Identity.* Türkiye Turing ve Otomobil Kurumu.

Micklewright, N. 1992: 'London, Paris, Istanbul and Cairo: Fashion and International Trade in the Nineteenth Century', *New Perspectives on Turkey*, 1992.7: 125-36.

Nalbantoğlu, Ü. 1981: *An Architectural and Historical Survey of the Development of the 'Apartment Building' in Ankara: 1923-1950.* Ankara.

Oy, A. 1984: 'Türkiye ve Yugoslavya arasında bir Türkü (Üsküdar'a Gideriken...)', *Folklor ve Etnografya Araştırmaları*: 393-9.

Ridvan Efendi, & Uzunçarşılıoğlu, İ.H. 1928 [1346]: *Anadolu Türk Tarihi Tedkikatından Sivas Şehri* (in Ottoman Turkish). Devlet Matbaası, Istanbul.

Soyer, K. 1984: 'Amasya Hazeranlar Konağı ve Safranbolu Kaymakamlar Evi Restorasyonları', in *Mimaride Türk Milli Üslubu Semineri.* Istanbul: 135-51.

Tanyeli, U. 1993: 'Batılılaşma Dönemi Öncesinin Türk Mimarlığında Batı Etkiler (14-17 yüzyıl)', in M. & G. Tanyeli Saçlıoğlu (ed.), *Türk Kültüründe Sanat ve Mimarlığı Üzerine Denemler.* Istanbul: 157-88.

---- 1996: 'Osmanlı Barınma Kültüründe Batılılmaşma-Modernleşme: Yeni bir simgeler dizgesinin oluşumu', in Y. Sey (ed.), *Tarihten Günümüze Anadolu'da Konut ve Yerleşme.* Türkiye Ekonomik ve Toplumsal Tarih Vakfı, Istanbul: 284-97.

Tayla, H. 1997: 'Türk Evi', *Sanat* 6; 68-76.

Tekeli, I. 1984: 'The Social Context of the Development of Architecture in Turkey', in R. Holod, A. Evin (eds), *Modern Turkish Architecture.* Pennsylvania: 9-33.

Üstünkök, O. 1989: 'Ten years with Seventeen-Ten: A Decade in the Conservation of Traditional Vernacular Houses, 1973-83', *METU International Journal of Middle East Studies* 9: 117-24.

Yavuz, Y., Suha, Ö. 1984: 'Finding a National Idiom, the First Turkish National style' in R. Holod, A. Evin (eds), *Modern Turkish Architecture.* Pennsylvania: 51-67.

Yenişehirlioğlu, F. 1989: *Türkiye Dışındaki Osmanlı Mimari Yapıtlar* , T.C. Vakıflar Bankası.

Yüksel, M. 1995: *Amasya 1995 İl Turizm Envanteri.* Amasya Valiliği İl Turizm Müdürlüğü, Amasya.

Zaknic, I. 1987: *Journey to the East: Le Corbusier [Charles-Edouard Jeanneret].* Cambridge MA.

---

[1] There are many styles of houses that were built during the Ottoman period in Ottoman controlled lands. But the terms 'Ottoman House', 'Anatolian House' and 'Turkish House' have a history of their own that I will take up in a forthcoming article. In this chapter I will use the terms interchangeably, but always referring in reality to the House that Doğan Kuban (1995: 23).calls the 'Hayat House'. This is a wooden structure that, at its most basic, had two rooms, usually divided by an *eyvan* of sorts and with a veranda, or *hayat.* The Turks enclosed this open area and the house itself for the women, and then in the 17th century cantilevered projections were added on the top storey for views. This he considers a *Turkish* rather than an Ottoman house because it developed in an area that was an ethnically Turkish part of the Empire, i.e. Northern Anatolia and the Balkans.

[2] It is interesting to speculate just exactly where, when, how and why the last Ottoman House was built. Kuban (1995: 105) suggests that the last 'Hayat House' was built at the end of the 19th century, in Osmancik, perhaps. Feyyaz Erpi (1987) would extend that date until the Republican Period.

[3] A good example of the use of the concept of 'tradition' as applied to Ottoman houses is in Balcı 1980 or Gunay 1981.

[4] Doğan Kuban (1995: 203) says that the Ottoman House, in its classical phase, was never a social insignia.

[5] See for example Hüsameddin 1986, first published 1927. City histories are a genre of books that were written at the end of the empire and the beginning of the Republic. Another example is Ridvan Efendi 1928 (AH 1346), which, like the Hüsameddin 1986, was written in Ottoman Turkish. It describes Seljuk and Ottoman public and monumental buildings in Sivas from the early middle ages to the early 19th century.

[6] For example, all the houses are represented as identical. The mosque on the left (or northern) bank could be Hatuniye Camii, except that it is not on the river front. It could also be the now lost Enderun Camii that was built in the 13th Century, but it never had an Ottoman-style minaret. If it is one of these, where is the other? There is indeed a famous hamam as is suggested by this 'map', i.e. the Yukarı Hamam, now called Sıhhi, but it is actually on the river's edge. Although there are two prominent mosques on the south bank, the most famous, the double minareted Bayezid, is not identifiable. Only the foreground bridge, the Meydan Köprüsü, bears any architectural specificity, but at the time of Bozoklu Osman there were four rather than two bridges spanning the Yeşil Irmak.

[7] Post Tanzimat painters adapted to European painting styles and techniques. Several of these have paintings or drawings of houses or street scenes, such as Osman Hamdi Bey (1842-1910), Hoca Ali Rıza Bey (1857?-1930), and Hüseyin Zekai Paşa (1860-1919), but I have not yet identified their acceptance or popular distribution (Arseven c.1950).

[8] Quoted in Hatemi 1986: 15. Besides this article, see Gökyay 1992.

[9] Tanyeli's work discusses the conceptual differences between Modernisation and Westernisation and shows how the interior of the late Ottoman House became both the real and the symbolic site of Westernisation. I have revised her data for my own purposes here, to show how the Ottoman House began to enter the public consciousness.

[10] For an interesting insight into how Western clothes were being worn and satirised in both Istanbul and provincial Bosnia, see Oy 1984. For more on Westernisation in Ottoman dress, see Micklewright, 1992: 125-36.

[11] The Republic of Turkey was proclaimed on October 29, 1923, with Mustafa Kemal Pasha, the liberator of his country, as its new president. During the first years of the Republic, he took the name 'Atatürk' and introduced many reforms aimed at modernisation and westernisation. By statute, European hats replaced the fez and women stopped wearing the veil; all citizens were required to take a surname; the Islamic calendar was replaced with the western calendar; and a new Turkish alphabet based on the Latin script replaced the Arabic alphabet.

[12] See for example Kömürcüoğlu 1950; Berk 1951; Çakıroğlu 1952; Erginbaş 1954-5; Eser n.d., Evren 1959.

[13] For a discussion of the 1973-1983 Preservation Laws and why they failed at a crucial moment to save the traditional fabric of Turkish towns, see Üstünkök 1989.

[14] The concept of re-defining and re-inventing the past for the purposes of the future is the topic of Hobsbawm 1983 and Anderson 1983.

2: THE DEEPER STRUCTURES OF OTTOMAN URBAN HOUSING FABRIC: CONSERVATION OF SPACE AND FORM THROUGH BASIC PARAMETERS

Prof. Maurice Münir Cerasi
University of Genoa

Ottoman architecture is much more than a chronological series of architectural creations. It is an architectural *koine* deeply rooted in the transformations of its urban context. The conservation of the Ottoman character of a town or urban segment, then, is not so much a question of reviving architectural style and construction techniques as of recognising the objective basic parameters and the deeply ingrained (and not always explicit) factors generating its architectural form and its deeper structures.

In a large number of Anatolian and Balkan towns the imprint of Ottoman urban civilisation is still conspicuous and worth preserving, although it has submitted to corrosive attacks in the last few decades through the action both of detractors and of those who pay lip service to Ottoman civilisation. I believe that the preservation of the general character and feeling of that very unique and original civilisation, one of the few universal form-types of urban life, is as important as the preservation of its outstanding monuments.

In the very few cases of well conserved urban fabric, orthodox conservation methods of individual outstanding houses are invaluable. I am not going to discuss this aspect of conservation, which is certainly very difficult and serious and would need, now that traditional carpentry is disappearing, fresh and inventive stimuli for the building industry. In this paper I would rather concentrate on the much more frequent case of towns or quarters where it would be more proper to channel rehabilitation (and/or redesign) of the historical nucleus or surviving areas towards a clearer expression of their traditional, and now only dimly perceivable, character.

To my knowledge no single town has maintained more than a few sparse items of any period earlier than the second half of the nineteenth century. Even the most coherent areas - those of Safranbolu are a good example for their quality and quantity - had undergone extensive modification by the turn of the century. It follows that in all these cases there is no question of ideal conservation or restoration, nor of shielding the actual situation against the enormous social and economic pressure it faces. It is more a question of giving dynamic change the right turn. We must remember that Ottoman towns had undergone fast dynamic change in all the periods of which we have documentary evidence.

Fundamentally, two obstacles have hindered the preservation of the Ottoman character in such areas. The first has been (and practically still is) the lack of good will and financial capacity: to put it brutally, almost nobody, even those who defend single Ottoman monuments or emerging houses, seems interested in the global manifestations of Ottoman urban civilisation. On the other hand, there is a prevalent hiatus - a 'black hole' - in methodology and in serious and painstaking research, which is abundant for architectural and social history, but scarce for urban culture. A descriptive, matter of fact approach dominates the scene, as if that civilisation were skin-deep, merely picturesque, as if it had no new discovery to offer. Method is the crucial point, I hold.

During the last fifty or sixty years the basic approaches to such problems of conservation, rehabilitation or redesign of the historical cores attempted or proposed have been few but quite distinct.

The claim for freedom of architectural creativity or for 'modern progress' - cultural *laissez faire* and economic liberalism marching hand in hand - has been widespread and has brought chaos in the fragile equilibrium of the Anatolian and Balkan town centres.

In other cases a mimetic approach was adopted: traditional types were imitated, but how could there be a significant repetition of artistic language, so deeply involved in techniques and social culture, when those same techniques and social culture had been superseded? As a much more refined variant, architects sought to reconstruct *some* characteristics of the traditional types and patterns: the efforts of the architects Onat and Eldem in the Forties and Fifties in Turkey are good examples of this last more sensitive approach. However, they limited their tasks to style and artistic language but not to scale, and not in the least to the urban structure of the towns, which crumbled quite as easily as if no revival had been attempted.

Lastly, I can mention an emerging tendency in Western Europe, much discussed but rarely applied: the typo-morphological approach. It is based on a few simple postulates: that a non-subjective analysis of types and patterns and a close cultural and methodological linkage of design and of historical analysis are pertinent to the conservation and rehabilitation of the historical scene; that *towns are built up of distinct parts*, in which long-term historical factors pertaining to physical structures, to building types, to architectural idioms concur to form an overall specific character; that urban factors tend to persist beyond social and economic change; that building typology and the larger town structures (morphology) influence each other; that architecture and the town's typo-morphology interact in very complex and subtle ways; and last but not least, that individual architectural design *can* and *should* be measured and judged by its relevance and fitness to the town's typological heritage and morphology. All this amounts to a very articulate, if not always complex, analysis of town structure *and* its architectural principles, which should be effected before any single line is drawn with an aim to design, redesign or rehabilitate any part of the town.

However, this approach - so fruitful in more than one historical nucleus in France, Italy and Germany - cannot be applied without modification to the Ottoman town structure. It is based on the *understanding of the deeper structure of architectural formation*, and as each architectural culture is unique, it has to be analysed with an eye to its own specific logic. Any general 'rule of thumb' would, in the end, prove to be catastrophic. In other words, the specificity of Ottoman aesthetics and of its overall urban culture *is* one of our main issues. Unfortunately for the conservation of the surviving Ottoman architectural environment, that issue has been too often seen as a mere question of reproducing Ottoman forms, which are too often considered obvious and not worth questioning. This is not so. Specificity lies in more than form (form is only the final outcome). It lies in the mechanisms and processes which precede form. If a town's street patterns and structural relationships pertain to a totally different culture or anti-culture, a generous distribution of 'Ottoman-looking' houses will no more preserve its Ottoman character than a general whitewashing.

Let us take one of the most important axioms of the 'typo-morphological' theory: that some outstanding urban elements can become form generators, in that they imprint or suggest form adaptation in other minor elements. For example, in Western 'compact' towns city walls have shaped their inner 'compact' build-up and street patterns. But this sort of interaction is very rare in Ottoman towns because of their loose texture and because both form and functional structure are the outcome of processes and traditions quite different from those of the West. Another differential factor is the result of the fact that street patterns are less important agents in urban form generation in the Ottoman urban context because the original basic unit of the urban fabric is a composite and very un-Mediterranean garden-plus-house unit. It imposes on that fabric an 'open' character, a peculiar volume distribution and ratio of wall to void, abundant greenery etc. In Western Europe the basic unit of the urban fabric is the shop-plus-house unit. In terms of density, functions, prestige and traditions this explains the organic unity of house to street and the compactness of towns even after defensive city walls were torn down. Overall street structure has given shape to large parts of the Western town. In the Ottoman town the main streets have at most influenced central areas and that only in a few cases, mainly before the 16th century in the Imperial capital towns, as was the case with the Istanbul Fatih *külliye*, which is the only Istanbul complex that effectively modelled the surrounding street and settlement patterns. If in a West European town street layout is the basis for any new or conservative design, a sort of backbone for all formal and spatial concepts, in the Ottoman town it is no more than a member part of the housing structure, a fine mesh which adapts to the main elements rather than a skeleton which conditions the other elements. Many observers of urban form have noted the Ottoman town's 'modernity', in that it recalls the modern residential quarters of the European town so contrasting with its historical parts.

Parameters of the Ottoman Town Form

In the search for the basic parameters of Ottoman town form, the peculiarity of housing patterns and house structure plays a primary role, as much as, and perhaps more than, the *vakfiye* system, the *çarsı*, and the spatial and aesthetic imprint of monumental architecture.

The main factors which distinguish the Ottoman 'core area' house[1] have been widely discussed in a very rich, if fragmentary, bibliography.[2] Each of these factors will be found in one or more of the house types of neighbouring cultural areas but their combination is unique. I shall describe them briefly.

Plan and siting. The urban fabric was composed of garden-plus-house units, originally of low density. The house is sited on the street front and is almost never placed in the centre of the not very large plot, which is more than a garden - a court not wholly enclosed by the buildings. Plan form is generated within the plot but encroaches on the street, thus conditioning its architecture: the individualism of layout and façade is the outcome of that peculiar mode of relating house to town. The peculiarity of the linkage of street patterns to building type consists of its development on an axis perpendicular to the street, articulating the volumes in a free pattern from the street *inwards*. This contrasts with the West European street-to-house relationship of continuous façade elaboration, as well as with most Asiatic or Mediterranean models, which tend to be more introverted. The latter tend also to fill up the city-block and cut out rooms within the margins of the block, whereas in the western Ottoman town, as well as in the Slavic and to a certain extent in Magyar traditional settlements, patterns are open and allow the house to be composed as an agglutination of preconceived and geometrically regular rooms. All this implies an extensive exploitation of land as opposed to the intensive use of space in the Mediterranean *hortus clausus*, in which field or plot is enclosed *a priori* and *then* built or cultivated from the given margin inwards, exploiting space fully. In the Ottoman house only the ground floor tends to adapt to the site, invariably edging up to the street front, even when this is irregular. Because of its preference for open patterns, low density and the constant search for views and good sun-orientation, the Ottoman urban morphology is ideally the result of strings of garden lots poised generally along the contours of the site.

Room conception. The Ottoman house type is articulated in three distinct space-type layers, the informal layout of ground floors reflecting street pattern, in contrast to the geometric regularity of 'room spaces'. The urban scene is composed of emergent monuments and of a series of individually articulated rooms, all other elements of the house (garden walls, out-houses, basements etc.) being mere connecting elements in the background. (This certainly was not the case in sixteenth century Istanbul where palatial forms had an important role in forming the city scene). Domestic life in an Ottoman town recalls ancient Greece, but the use of space was more complex and functionally more articulate. A garden substitutes for the court as the centre of family life and has more functional elements than the ancient Greek court contained: stables, kitchen, and bath or washrooms. Both organisation and volumetric composition recall a Far Eastern 'pavilion system' though the house proper is more compact than comparable Chinese or Japanese examples. The upper floor is an aggregate of square or rectangular rooms (*oda*), unmarked by functional specialisation; special functional spaces (water closets, baths, kitchens) are relegated to the ground floor or to out- houses in the garden. Rooms are constituted with strongly typified elements such as wide single or double layer fenestration, niches and wall cupboards, a conical small fireplace, symmetrical ceiling decoration with central focal point, and perimeter seating (*mimber*).

Timber structure. Light wooden frame structure with brick or earth in-fill or (later) wood cladding prevails. The sense of permanency is unknown and, perhaps, is not conceivable up to the *Tanzimat* reforms, within the legal, institutional and psychological context of Ottoman society. This is also reflected in:

Roofing. The house has articulated four-slope roofing with shallow slopes, adapted to room and plan composition. (The large and steeply sloping roofs embracing whole buildings seen in sixteenth century drawings of Istanbul later disappear from the urban scene). There is no equivalent of the overall shelter of wide roofs which gave psychological consistency to the west European, Alpine and west Balkan house and family life. The ephemeral sense of urban life (and of all life) in most of the Ottoman epoch is not only religious, nor is it always perceived as a menace; it is also a quality of urban life. Family life and town life are not always solid and enduring but they can be gay and enjoyable in their transience and lightness.

Foundations. A distinctive Turkish trait in urban culture is the abhorrence of deeply dug-in structures. Houses rarely have underground cellars, and foundations are even shallower than the relatively light structures would justify. Houses seem, and are effectively, poised on the ground.[3]

Some of these factors carry important consequences in composition and in the psychological significance of the house and its symbolism, and they indirectly condition urban image and town life.

The more direct effects on urban structure and design are quite obvious. Both in Europe and the Near East or in Maghrib (and even in some south-eastern Anatolian regions) the shape and space of the street determines directly the compact plot-shape and hence determines the building type. In the Ottoman house, on the other hand, form is generated within the plot (the upper floor's independent form-logic is the main input) and bursts out towards the street. Adaptation to site is delegated to the ground floor whereas the somehow free but geometrically regular disposition of the upper floor calls for links with the landscape and environment at large rather than its own plot.

The house, as a palimpsest of the family, has in this context a meaning quite different from the self-representation of bourgeois housing in western Europe. Alignments, sequence and relationship between façades, so important in the west, where façades refer to and define public space, are here merely incidental and are the fallout from developments within the plot. And yet streets *are* a referential structure (the Ottoman residential unit is not wholly introverted), but house to street linkage develops at right angles to the street axis and ultimately they give shape to house space. Also, urban morphology is the resultant form of strings of garden plots which follow the contours of the site whenever possible. Of course higher densities have modified the original layout types but façade individualism, which was the outcome of that original logic, has remained. Corner sites are the occasion for brilliant architectural solutions where the implicit individualism of Ottoman housing is at its best.

The primary parameters generating the architectural form of urban housing in the Ottoman context are the composite garden-plus-house unit, 'open' disposition, street patterns based on house plot distribution rather than on traffic-logic, volumes concentrated on the street margin of plots, volume articulation reflected in roof design and skyline, the medium size and volume of houses, the prevalence of void in wall-to-void ratio, formal and quantitative emphasis of upper floor or floors, house basement and garden walls used as a neutral base from which the individual forms of the living quarters emerge, the informal design of garden and greenery used as in-fill in the environment and the individualism of design (overall forms are never repeated) coexisting with repetition of standard elements throughout the whole (window and structural struts, cantilever roof gables, façade cladding have few standard variants). Of course this brief exposition does not account for the finer points of proportion, exact size of elements, interplay of materials and colours, too complex to deal with in this paper.

All these parameters and factors account for very peculiar plan and siting conditions. The specificity of the basic parameters I have described only too summarily will be fully understood as soon as we compare them with those of other urban cultures. As long as they are enforced, the expression of the traditional Ottoman urban fabric will live on even if materials and technology are transformed or substituted.

Contemporary Applications

It is not difficult to imagine that once the principles of formation of Ottoman towns have been understood, those same principles can be applied today both to design and rehabilitation without excessive economic or social friction, as those towns have not yet submitted to the pressure of large-scale financial operations, and land property is still of modest size. And yet I know of no really convincing example in Balkan and Anatolian Ottoman-originated town kernels where these problems of form and culture have been resolved. For the time being let me exemplify some of the wrong approaches, caused not so much by economic or social pressure as by their cultural consequences and, above all, by a lack of comprehension of the deeper character of the Ottoman art of town-building.

One blundering way of dealing with the one-time Ottoman environment is that of introducing uniformity, applied on a large scale, and monotonous repetition of one single type or shape. Such uniformity is the antithesis of the Ottoman town as a product of imaginative and individual creation. Terraced housing with linear and overly rigid alignments, too, has an overbearing impact even when its density is low. Feeling for topography was instinctive for the Anatolian or Macedonian master builder no less than for the English gardener: the instinct has been lost, but it can be rediscovered by critical awareness and rational understanding of the parameters I mentioned. Instead, planners respond with Hippodamian grids or Garden City Movement plans foreign to the local topography. With such basic errors the recourse to Ottoman-like frills - gables, *çıkma* bow-windows etc. - are to no effect at all.

But then, some will ask, can the individualistic and fragmentary modes of Ottoman town architecture meet the demands of modern functional standards and modern traffic? If the answer is that of reproducing the overall structure of Ottoman towns, the answer would certainly be 'no'. But we are not speaking of overall structure. Our topic is that of *some parts* (quarters, precincts) of towns. The town planning experience of the last few decades points to the fact that elements and parts which pertain to overall structure (e.g. traffic, transport, industry) need not be homogeneous with other parts, that co-ordination and harmony in a town plan does not mean uniformity, that living towns, no matter if planned or spontaneous, are *always* built up of many and quite heterogeneous elements and quarters. Certainly modern traffic requirements could not be met *within* a quarter of Ottoman character; but modern traffic lanes could serve such a quarter, for example skirting it or leading up to it.

One might also object that higher densities and the transition from single family housing to collective housing have rendered obsolete once and for all urban fabrics such as the Ottoman. I do not believe that those technical factors were the cause of disruption. After all, experiments and spontaneous developments in low-rise high-density housing prove, technically speaking, that they can be more satisfactory, and in the long run less expensive, than large modern blocks.

Ottoman urban society had not really solved the problems of daily life in high density intensive urban structures. Its technological models were almost rural. It needed large natural space and large natural resources to make urban and domestic life pleasant. But then, in these same societies 'modernisation' has not brought the sanitary and environmental standards or the comfort of middle-class residential areas found in the richer west European cities, and now that continuous technological or social progress in *all* sectors of life for *everybody* proves to be just another myth, presumably will not bring it. After all, those urban standards that we believe to be universally 'modern' have been actually the standards of a minority, existing for very few decades, in a small part of the world; I doubt that they will survive, even in western Europe, for as many decades and for most of the population.

To put it frankly, 'modernisation' has not always been a great success and will need some re-thinking. So much the better if it can be done with an eye for the preservation of the original character of towns. A non-disruptive rehabilitation policy has to make explicit some of the most significant assets of Ottoman urban form: open space innovation, lower densities, re-interpretation of traditional volume form and street-to-house relationship. But this is not all. We must also undertake a courageous and even drastic revision of functional standards (density, traffic admission etc.).

The capacity to stick to the spirit of the traditional character, not to its letter, or the lack of that capacity, is a matter of culture and of 'design' technology rather than of social and technological change. After the mid-nineteenth century many an Anatolian and Balkan master builder's response to higher densities and more compact volume types did not betray the meaning of their native cultures, whereas in the same years some insensitive grid-plan street design by obtuse and superficial 'Westernisation' disrupted the life and look of many Ottoman quarters.

The fabric of Ottoman housing accepted change as long as its main rules and birthrights were respected. The Ottoman house had always been open to change because it was the composite product of many cultures. After all, it was born and changed gradually, through almost imperceptible transitions, from a model wholly non-European, even non-Mediterranean, to a final product which could easily fit into a westernised or modern Levant context. The intricate relationship of vernacular architecture to cultured architecture also was dynamic and ever-changing; the two cultures fed on one another and in turn influenced each other. Local, pre-Ottoman elements, wholly Turkish Asiatic concepts, and imported innovations all wormed their way into each other to form a unique and inimitable universal type. Western influences had brought about standardisation of typology through a richer home-organisation distinction between living and functional spaces. The use of glass is one example; another example is that of better water-distribution technology, which freed the garden-court of its functional encumbrances. To the very last, however, those innovations did not obliterate the Ottoman trademark and its traditional characteristics. Adaptability to technique and new needs was ingrained in the very structure of types and forms; so was constancy to their ultimate cultural expression and to their 'feeling'. There is no paradox: the stronger the basic character of a cultural artefact the easier it can accept new forms and new positions without distortion. Ottoman culture had a curious creative approach, a greedy egocentric way of swallowing up all that came handy, with no bias as to origin, as long as it was useful for the expression of its own culture which was totally new and original despite its heterogeneous sources. Adaptability and constancy were not abstract or immanent qualities; they were brought about by the repetition of the physical and typological factors which I have described. They can still be perpetuated.

Look at the mass production of housing in Istanbul and Bursa in the fifties and sixties. Concrete building techniques, modern window panes, modernistic horizontal alternation of glass and concrete bands fitted in finely in the Ottoman scene. The horrible end of ancient urban fabric in Istanbul and other towns was not due to technology or to single forms but to incongruous urban planning, to uninterrupted masses of housing not landscaped to fit environment, to towering buildings, to over-scaling, to confusing architectural detail: gables either too large or too modest, casual colours and materials.

New Tools

All this leads to the statement that we would need *new tools* for handling the peculiar context of Ottoman urban culture. Which are they?

Technological renovation is certainly important. Light building technology is needed not simply to imitate wooden structures but also to adapt to the flexible single-room design of Ottoman town logic, to its individualistic - that is, varied and ever-changing - forms. Such technology is already available. But of course, technological renovation means also new technology for urban facilities and maintenance. For example, adaptable small calibre sewer systems do not cost more than large calibre straight and simple systems as much as we thought some twenty or thirty years ago. Maintenance work with light bobcat vehicles rather than with heavy-weight caterpillars is now a matter of fact in many European towns.

Production technology is not all; there is also a technique of concepts and ideas. Where maintaining the 'Ottoman look' of consistent parts of towns is the main issue, new analytical methods rather than new production technology are required. In other words, change is required in the quality and techniques of the architectural process itself - not so much in new ways of using (or of substituting) traditional materials, as in feeding historical data and a more subtle capacity for architectural analysis into the design process.

The main question, then, is our capacity to handle finer cultural tools. What do we mean by 'culture'?

'Good taste', 'feeling for form' or, at a different level, 'scientific outlook on conservation' are important but inadequate. Historical towns need 'cultured' architecture and 'cultured' architects with a more than instinctive or overall grasp of architectural and urban history, and with a better understanding of the main structural factors involved: the street patterns within the housing texture, the environmental significance in relation to monuments or to central place, the rules and parameters of each cultural epoch.

Besides these general questions with regard to Ottoman typology and urban morphology at large, there is also a need to understand the specific character of each individual town or quarter. It is far from easy to acquire the factual basis for such an understanding. Old maps and etchings of Ottoman towns tend to be rather vague. The reconstruction of the original layouts or of the original characteristics through archaeological and map research is invaluable. How else could we establish the form of the traditional structure, often obliterated by a century of neglect and encroachments and of senseless new streets? Unfortunately, archaeological research has concentrated mostly on single monumental buildings or *külliye* complexes and too little on standard areas to be of any immediate help in reconstructing the form of street patterns and fabric to monument relationship. It must also be admitted that traditional archaeological field-methods would not suffice anyhow and probably would not be accepted because of their cost and their interference with building activities. Ottoman towns need a wholly new and composite method of archaeological investigation.

The starting point for such investigation would have to be the analysis of town maps of any date and epoch and their comparison with ancient drawings, sketches and photographs both aerial and terrestrial. Of course, such information as might be inferred could not but be approximate, based as it is on the not very precise materials now extant. It can therefore be used only as a basis for initial hypotheses.

At this point, recent electronic techniques open new perspectives both for the co-ordination and comparison of the conclusions of diverse research teams and for the establishment of a data bank. The initial hypotheses and data would be transferred onto a computerised map, which would initially register more voids and doubtful sitings than positive information, forming a sort of dynamic archive where little positive data and much questioning would appear on a background of unfocused and changing interpretations, but it would be susceptible to growth and correction, absorbing or substituting further data and hypotheses by trial and error.

Overall tentative interpretation of the area's evolution, however hazardous, would be the next step. It is true that interpretation based on scarce material rarely produces credible answers, but it can stimulate questions on the siting and character of street patterns and housing. With some limited but strategically located drilling (looking for *débris* material layers) and much interpretation of ancient maps, we could obtain tentative answers to three questions: what was the relationship of monuments to housing in a specific area? how were housing type and technology transformed? how did the main street patterns change? Even if uncertain, answers referred to effective space would still be an improvement on most urban historians' hypotheses about the ancient state of things, based as they are on the interpretation of too imaginative maps and chronicles and on a scale too large to be of any use to the designer or urban planner.

The final phase would consist of field operations by layer perforation at strategic points selected through the previous map survey and interpretation. This would afford some knowledge of the stratification and frequency of different building materials and elements in each layer and would certainly lead to an idea of overall change. I would expect findings on the persistence of street patterns (is it true that streets were frequently encumbered, or newly opened through house demolition?) and perhaps on the dimensions and position of houses. Of course, to be really useful, such research would have to be developed over a long period and on a large number of sites but would not need costly digging campaigns on established sites.

The data thus obtained could be fed into a growing computerised data map, open over the years to the contributions of many research groups and would focus gradually, with increasing precision, on the dynamics of development of the town. It would be open to interesting interpretations as it checked the physical - architectural and spatial - image against all other multi-disciplinary findings and hypotheses such as the historian's fluid image of change, the urban historian's hypotheses of the function of single parts and sites, the architect's and architectural historian's knowledge or interpretative hypotheses of type and layout (cf. Cerasi forthcoming).

Much has been written, researched and published on Ottoman towns and Ottoman housing. Many queries on their character and structure have yet to be answered. Perhaps the time has come to link queries and material for a syncretic interpretation of those towns. No policy of conservation and rehabilitation would be coherent without such an interpretation.

Bibliography

Anghelova, R., Moutsopoulos, N.K., Pavlowitch, D.S., Pirro, T., Riza, E., Sezgin, H., Stoica, G. 1985: *L'Architecture vernaculaire dans les Balkans*, UNESCO.

Anon 1993: *Balkaniki Paradosiaki Arhitektoniki*. Athens.

Arel, A. 1982: *Osmanlı konut geleneğinde tahrisel sorunlar*. Izmir.
Cerasi, M. 1984: 'Il tessuto residenziale della città ottomana (secc. XVII-XIX)' *Storia della Città* 31/32, Milan.
Cerasi, M. 1988: *La Città del Levante: Civiltà urbana e architettura sotto gli Ottomani nei secoli XVIII-XIX*. Milan (Turkish tr., *18nci ve 19ncu Yüzyıllarda Osmanlı Kenti*, Yapı Kredi Yayınları, Istanbul, 1998).
Cerasi, M. forthcoming: 'Three Questions put to the Archaeologist for a better cognition of the Ottoman Town's Urban Texture' presented to the *1er Congrès d'Archéologie Ottomane*, Zaghouan, May 1996.
Eldem, S.H. 1984-7: *Türk Evi Osmanlı Dönemi* (3 vols). Türkiye Anıt Çevre Değerlerini Koruma Vakfı. Istanbul.
Faroqhi, S. 1990: *Men of Modest Substance: House-owners and House Property in Seventeenth-century Anatolia*. Cambridge.
Kozuharov, G. 1953: *Balgarski kasti ot epokhata na vazrazhdaneto*. Sofia.
Kozuharov, G. and Anghelova R. 1971: *Plovdivskaia Simetritsana Kasta*. Sofia.
Kuban, D. 1995: *Türk Hayatlı Evi*. Eren Yayıncılık ve Kitapçılık, Istanbul.
Megas, G.A. 1968: 'Überlieferung und Erneuerung in der Volksarchitektur Sud-ost-Europas', *Zeitschrift für Balkanologie* 6.
Moutsopoulos, N.K. 1976: 'Contribution to the Typology of the Northern Greek Dwelling', in II Symposium *Laografia tou Voreioelladikou Khorou, Komotini, March 1975*. Thessaloniki.
Peev, H. D. 1956: *Studii varhu vazrozhdenska arhitektura*. Sofia.
Zlatev, T. 1955: *Balgarskata kasta prez epokhata na vazrazhdaneto*. Sofia.

[1] What do I mean by the Ottoman 'core area'? It is an area lying west and north of the Sivas-Konya line, north of Thessaly in Greece where Ottoman urban civilisation as distinct from East Mediterranean urban civilisation (of Arab or Greek origin) predominates. The Ottoman urban system emerged with its wooden two to three floor houses, its open settlement patterns, its modest and non-monumental *çarşıs*, its unfortified not very large cities, and (with the sole exception of Istanbul) in strong contrast with the more compact - and up to the nineteenth century demographically larger - eastern urban system, from Kayseri to Syria, with its large towns which had city walls, *souks* or bazaars well articulated along main thoroughfares, well-knit and often introverted city blocks, houses focused on *iwan-eyvan* or court, mostly in stone or earth and with an aesthetic very different from that of the 'core area' houses....

[2] The sources for the study of the Ottoman house consist of a huge stock of surveys and drawings. I cannot quote them all. For each region I can recall some names: for Macedonia and ex-Yugoslavia: Deroko, Kadic, Grabrijan, Hielscher, Minetti, Nenadovic, Schulze-Jena, Tomovski; for Bulgaria: Zlatev, Anghelova, Kozuharov, Peev; for Albania: Riza, Nopcsa; for Istanbul and Anatolia; Akok, Berk, Eldem, Günkut, İmamoğlu, Kafesçioğlu, Kömürcüoğlu, Kuban, Tomsu, Özdes, as well as Gabriel, Sakaoğlu, Ünver; for Greece: Megas, Moutsopoulos.

Critical surveys can be found in Arel 1982, Cerasi 1984, Eldem 1984-7, Faroqhi 1990, Kozuharov 1953, Kozuharov, Anghelova 1971, Kuban 1995, Megas 1968, Moutsopoulos 1976; Peev 1956, Zlatev 1955; for an overall study of the Balkan area see also Anghelova *et al.* 1985, and for the photographic material, Anon 1993. For a more comprehensive bibliography on the Ottoman area proper, see Cerasi 1988: ch. 8. Kuban, 1995 contains an extensive list of works on the subject, updated to 1991.

[3] In Kayseri, Urfa, and Diyarbakır, traditional stone or earth-and-stone houses do have cellars. But it would be a mistake to attribute this solely to differences in regional building techniques, wood versus stone. Again, we note a distinctive trait of the 'core area' where Ottoman-Turkish culture and its exceptional capacity of synthesis was very selective and endorsed only those elements and qualities of local culture which were sympathetic to its own attitudes and propensity. To the East, the stronger urban tradition of Arab and Persian was left almost untouched up to the late eighteenth century by the Ottoman impact which, it is useful to remember, came some two centuries later than in Western Anatolia and the Balkans. Also, no town in the east had become a seat of imperial or princely power (as Istanbul, Bursa, Edirne, Manisa and Kastamonu did), to impose by imitation the Ottoman model of urban life.

3: OTTOMAN ENCAMPMENT AND URBAN SETTLEMENT: A COMPARATIVE EVALUATION

Dr. Burcu Özgüven
Istanbul

When we generally talk about the Ottoman palace, particularly about the Topkapı Palace, one question arises immediately: 'Why did the Ottoman Sultans, whose grandeur was so well-known in the fifteenth and sixteenth centuries, become patrons of a modest complex of small buildings, and not of tall impressive blocks, such as their western contemporaries?' Foreign visitors to the Ottoman *seraglio* were usually impressed by the court ceremonies reflecting the power of the 'Grand Seignior', the Sultan, at its peak, but they also described the pavilions of the Topkapı Palace, as ornate, but small buildings scattered over the whole area. Indeed, the Topkapı Palace was the result of a design which grew over three hundred years like a living organism, beginning with elementary pavilions, developing with the addition of further components as architectural symbols of diversifying function, and frequently changing owing to earthquakes, fires or other destruction. Particular elements of this complex give the impression of a huge village, where the pattern was fixed not by regular streets but by spontaneously erected imperial pavilions; and this seemingly irregular arrangement brings to mind another question: 'Could this type of organisation of dispersed elements simply be a continuation of the Ottoman encampment tradition?'

Ottoman institutions, such as taxation, bureaucracy and diplomacy, mainly depended on success in war. The army was among the most important factors in the administration, and above all the Ottoman Sultan was, from the beginning, a *gazi* (war-leader), whose main responsibility was to spread the Sunni faith by sword all over the world. Before going on to deal with the Ottoman army and military encampment, though, let us first examine the ancient traditions of the Turks.

Today's Turkish word *ordu* is used to refer to the army, but the early Uygurs applied the word as early as the eighth century to describe the 'Khan's encampment', then 'the imperial city' or 'Khan's city', and later the 'Khan's palace' (Sümer 1994: 30; Ögel 1985 I: 259, 261, 267-9). An example of the word, *altın-ordu*, signifies the name of the Crimean dynasty founded by Mogul tribes. *Ordu-gâh* (military encampment) had a similar meaning for the tribal federations: it was an administrative centre established by tents of the nobles, including the Khan's tent. An Arab traveller described the *Ghuzz* (*Oğuz*) troops, and observed that the Khan had seventeen noble generals, each of them commanding seventeen thousand soldiers. The *Ghuzz* encampment included the imperial tents belonging to nobles, select horses - all of them well-bred animals - and sufficient fodder to feed them. The military camp was surrounded by the soldiers' tents in such a way as to create a circle, and there were four main roads leading through these to the Khan's royal tent (Sümer 1994, 32; Ögel 1985 3: 23, 25).

We know that Turkic armies in the east and west of the Transoxiana were mainly composed of nomadic troops. In the fourteenth century the famous historian Ibn Khaldun described the nomads as follows:

> People, like the Berbers, the Turks, the Turcomans and the Slavs, are nomads (Bedouins). They use tents of hair and wool, or houses of wood, or of clay and stone, which are not (elaborately) furnished. The purpose is to have shade and shelter, and nothing beyond that ...

Ibn Khaldun (1978: 92) also describes the means of security established by these nomads:

> They have no walls and gates (around the settlements). Therefore they provide their own defence and do not entrust it to, or rely upon others for it.

Nomadic discipline and tradition was influential in the early establishment of the Turkish-Anatolian settlement, and the word 'Turk' usually included the meaning 'nomad', even in the fifteenth century. Mehmed the Conqueror, in fact, characterised three types of people in his codes: *Şehirli* (the sedentary or the urban-dweller), *Raiyyet* (the village-dweller) and the *Türk* (the nomad) (Kuban 1982, citing Kraelitz-Greifenhorst 1921-22).

Although the Turcoman tribes changed their life styles from nomadic to sedentary, traditions were still influential in their daily habits. Newcomers first erected their tents around a settlement, and then with time they became sedentary. For example, moving to mountainous areas in Anatolia as a form of transhumance is considered a continuation of the nomadic tradition, practised not only by the owners of animals, but also by other people (Kuban 1982: 154). The nomadic settings were to be accepted by the Ottoman Sultans, and applied to their palace tradition in the capital.

In this paper I would like to compare the principles of the Ottoman house to those of the Ottoman encampment, and to try to point out the common characteristics and similarities of both.

The Sultan's tent was the central feature of the camp, which in itself had a symbolic meaning for both the Seljuks and the Ottomans. During the late Anatolian Seljuk era, for instance, in the 13th century, the Sultan's tent was placed for protection at the very centre of the inner citadel of the capital, Konya. When the Mogul commander, Bayçu Nuyan, invaded the city, his prime target was the imperial tent and the other symbols of the dynasty (Konyalı 1964). The imperial tent was embroidered and furnished with precious stones. In the thirteenth century Gengis Khan's royal tent was made of gold embroidered cloth, and the so-called *Altın-ota* or *Altın-otagh* (the golden room or tent) was a symbol of power. Mogul and Turkic tribal tents were yellow and called *alachuk*. The Seljuks and Ottomans considered the tents captured from defeated monarchs as victory symbols (Goodwin 1971: 429). If the tent of an Ottoman official or commander was publicly dismantled, this gesture signified his loss of power and his fall from the Sultan's favour. In Turkish this is idiomatically described as *çadırını başına yıkmak* (pulling the tent down around one's ears) (Necipoğlu 1991: 245-8). Goodwin (1971: 429) underlines the fact that the real home of the Sultan was his tent. The tent symbolised not only wartime dynamism, but also hard nomadic discipline and self-confidence (pl.1-2). The position of the tribal leader's tent marked the centre of his domain, his capital. During the Ottoman era this tradition continued in Anatolia (Ögel 1985 1: 259). During a campaign the Sultan's tent was surrounded by a series of other tents serving as kitchen, stables, treasury etc. Rycaut (1971: 204-6), an observer of the Ottoman state in the mid-seventeenth century, described the imperial camp as 'movable habitations', and he stated that there were about two thousand tents set in no particular order, except that the Grand Seignior's appeared to be in the midst and to overtop all the rest. He went on to note that 'within the walls of this tent there are all sorts of offices belonging to the *Seraglio*'. Baron Wratislaw (1996: 166) likewise reported that the tent of the Sultan (Mehmed III), like those of his viziers and other high officials, was placed in the middle of the encampment.

Another type of building which has striking similarities with the encampment was the early modern fortification. With the introduction of firearms Ottoman strongholds were constructed to take account of developing technology, and regular troops were stationed permanently within these fortifications. 'The Cut of the Throat' or Rumeli Hisarı (European Fort), erected at the narrowest point of the Bosphorus in 1451-52, included a small village of soldiers' houses, a mosque and a cistern. Before its restoration in the 1950s old timber houses were still visible. Other fifteenth century forts, like Yedikule and those on the Dardanelles, had small settlements inside. A Fatih Mosque within the walls, a cistern, a small vegetable garden in the southern part, and probably a bakery were all elements of the Yedikule.[1] According to an anonymous drawing in the Correr Museum, Venice (printed in Anon. 1995) an irregular pattern of eighty or ninety timber houses separated by narrow paths was described as the barracks of soldiers. In 1686 Francesco Scarella depicted the same housing pattern in the Yedikule fort-village (Babinger 1961). Fifteenth century castles on the Dardanelles also had this same village character with an irregular pattern of timber houses, a mosque, cistern and bakery (Özgüven 1996). All the inhabitants of these fort settlements were soldiers whose task it was to keep the strategic routes or borders secure. To a certain degree their small villages had the characteristics of an encampment, although portable furniture and tents had been replaced by permanent features such as timber houses.

An Ottoman encampment included not only the tents of the Sultan and his servants, but also those of his high viziers, and for security reasons such military pavilions were surrounded by a wooden wall. Until the end of the sixteenth century the Sultan was, in fact, the chief commander of the army; but later on the Grand Vizier or a high commander was also allowed to lead the troops on his own. In the late seventeenth century Comte Fernando Marsigli described the Ottoman encampment as follows:

> The first step to establish a military camp was to fix an appropriate area close to a water supply and food provision.
>
> The second step concerned matters of security: the army had to create a secure area or look for a naturally secure place, one protected by a river, a canal, mountainous geography or a swamp.
>
> The third was that the territory should be capable of enclosing all the troops.

> The fourth was that they should leave some open spaces within the military camp; these open spaces were to be allocated to each group of soldiers as a common meeting area. (Marsilli 1934: 190).

Wratislaw (1996: 166) also confirms that the encampment included open spaces surrounded by tents, and that the settlement was fortified by strong wooden walls.

To Marsigli, the Pasha or Grand Vizier did not establish his pavilion unless the tent of execution had been built. Only after that did he allow his own tent to be set up, marked as it was by a pony tail hung in front, and high commanders were then allowed to follow suit. The tent of execution, in fact, signified the power of the Pasha, and without it as a symbol of authority he failed to show himself as the commander of the encampment.

Another feature of any encampment is that the Pasha and his servants together set up their camp within a circle, surrounded by an inner wooden wall (pl.6). Establishing such a wooden enclosure was, in fact, a tradition inherited by ancient Turkish nomadic armies. Like the plan of a Roman military camp, which was set out in a grid-iron pattern (Toy 1966: 38, 43-51), the Ottoman encampment also showed a centralised form of plan, with the tents of the Pashas and other commandants placed at the hub (pl.3-5). This central sector, though, also included tents devoted to a range of administrative functions: the treasury, the tents of lesser officials, the tent where the holy relics of the Prophet were kept. These relics covered the holy standard (*sancak-ı şerif*) and the holy mantle (*hırka-ı şerif*). Descendants of the Prophet prayed there day and night, and candles were kept continuously burning; on occasion, too, the Vizier attended prayers (Marsilli 1934: 195-7). Wratislaw (1996: 98) also observed *seyyids* (grandsons of the Prophet) walking with military troops. Next to the centre there was a pavilion where the soldiers were rewarded with precious goods or money.

Outside this central area the tents of the ordinary soldiers formed an irregular perimeter with meandering paths in between them. In these outer areas the Janissaries and other types of soldiers had their communal baths and toilets. There were also markets where the basic goods and foodstuffs were sold. Marsilli (1934: 200; cf. Wratislaw 1996: 165-6) explains the situation as follows:

> For defensive purposes Turks established their camp in a labyrinthine pattern. If an enemy who does not know the settlement well burst into the camp, he would be so surprised and the enemy troops would come into such a state of disorder that the Turks would be able to defeat them easily.

We can observe here some similar features shared by Ottoman civil settlements.

The Ottoman encampment was designed to represent a kind of 'happening' for ordinary soldiers. As I underlined above, various tents were allocated to various functions. The Pasha's tent was a representation of discipline within the army, which all the soldiers had to obey, just as, according to Marsigli, the tent of execution symbolised punishment. On the other hand, the treasury pavilion signalled reward. Their side by side placement represented the ups and downs of life. Allegorical messages provided by these tents would be clear to the soldiers. Within the camp there was a long street bordered by an open area which was surrounded by markets and soup kitchens, and where food was distributed. To reach this area the soldier had to walk along the street and pass all the 'allegorical tents'. The labyrinthine planning of the whole encampment could also be related to cosmological themes. The military camp, with its centre, soldiers, encircling tents and apparent disorder could be considered as a symbolic reflection of the chaotic cosmos. In some respects the tents of the Turkic tribes of Inner Asia and the Uyghurs symbolised, in fact, various visions of the moon and astrological signs (Ögel 1985 1: 267-9).

Common features between the Ottoman military encampment and the Ottoman settlement can be summarised under three headings.

1. The Philosophy of Life and its Rôle at the Centre of the Urban Settlement

According to Muslim thought the material world is unimportant and mortal. All human beings are guests in this world, and they die without exception; only Allah and His rule remain. Ottoman cities, therefore, carried traces of this Muslim philosophy of life. For instance, wealthy inhabitants were encouraged to establish religious complexes, administered by the *waqf* institution (charitable foundation), in the name of Allah. Mosques, religious schools and the tomb of the founder were all basic elements of the Ottoman architectural complex. Often a primary school, soup kitchen and a bath could be added to the group. The characteristic difference between the *waqf* complex and civil architecture is in the material used. Religious buildings, which were expected to remain until the end of the world, were constructed from stone, while houses were made from timber or mud-brick, materials symbolising the temporary nature of life. The *waqf* complex in urban settlements was often erected in the middle of the district, as the centre of the neighbourhood. And if we examine the proportions of a religious centre compared to the overall pattern of the houses, an interesting feature emerges: the dominant feature of the complex, such as the mosque or the religious school, is the predominance of the vertical, while for the urban pattern in general, the main impression is one of horizontal development.

The religious approach to life was also reflected in the military camps. According to the Ottoman *gaza* system, soldiers were voluntary messengers of religion, and they fought for Allah. Authority was symbolised by the tent of the Grand Vizier. Although no mosque or any religious centre was visible in the encampment-drawing by Marsigli, one might suggest that the Janissaries and other soldiers came together and prayed for the victory of the Ottoman army in the open area. The lack of any mosque could also be explained by the Janissaries' special religious situation. They belonged to the Bektashi order, in which prayers and other ceremonies differed completely from those of the orthodox Sunnis. But the key idea of the civil centre remained in the military encampment. The tents of Pashas, Viziers and other important persons were constructed in the centre, and the soldiers had to group themselves around these. Rycaut (1971: 204) describes the centre of the camp as follows:

> In the front of the camp are quartered the Janissaries and all others destined to foot-service, whose tents encompass their Aga or General. In the body of the camp are erected the stately pavilions of the Vizier, his Kahija or Chief-Steward or Councillor, the Reis Effendi or Lord Chancellor, the Tefterdar Pasha or Lord Treasurer, and the Kapisler Kahisee or Master of Ceremonies. These five pavilions take up a large part of the ground, leaving a spacious field in the midst, in the centre of which is raised a lofty canopy, under which offenders are corrected or executed, and it serves to shelter from the sun or rain such as attend the Divan, or other business with the officers of State.

2. The Functional Elements of Housing

The Ottoman house is like a functional machine. It answers all the user's daily needs. For example, within the traditional house the furniture, such as bedding, was put away into cupboards every morning. Other items such as carpets, kilims, *keçe* (felt carpets) and small wooden items, were all equally portable and multi-purpose (Ögel 1985 3: 157, 183-5; Goodwin 1971: 430, 441). Large copper trays, for instance, served as dining tables and the divan was used for both sitting and sleeping, both of them again portable elements. Such mobile furniture had its roots, in fact, in tribal traditions. The extended family within such houses included various groupings within it, so that each room was allocated to a sub-family. Elements, like *cumba* or *çıkma*, were also functional parts of the house. Indeed it is probable that distinct nomadic memories were influential on the style of life adopted. As a result all the materials and individual elements of the Ottoman house should be functional and simple, rather than decorative or impressive.

The nomadic tradition had to be even more influential in the daily life of soldiers within the encampment. All the materials and furniture they used were, of necessity, portable, and military life dictated to the soldier a simple, hard and uncomfortable life style, promising in return a place in heaven.

3. The Irregular Appearance of Settlements

The Ottoman city or neighbourhood constructed around a religious centre was built without a regular pattern. Travellers and foreign visitors often described the Ottoman town as 'chaotic'. Narrow labyrinthine roads, irregular streets, cul-de-sacs, all these features gave an irregular appearance to the Ottoman city. But considering other similar traditions, this type of settlement does not appear illogical.

The villages of the nomads in Anatolia and of Circassians consisted of buildings crowded together in irregular patterns - partly as protection against bandits or other hostile attacks. Their lanes meandered without apparent order. Nomads, in general, had no walls around their settlements, and this was reflected in Ottoman housing. Salomon Schweigger, a German priest of the sixteenth century, reports (1964) that the Ottomans needed no walls around their cities, and he compared this with the Spartan way of life. 'The Spartans', he says, 'did not need city walls, and were proud of their swords'. Busbecq, the famous ambassador of Austria, also states (1927) that the Ottomans were good soldiers who had self-confidence and who did not find it necessary to construct defensive walls, and he compares this with the Roman tradition of war.

This lack of defensive walls around the Ottoman city could have originated in the Asian or Middle Eastern type of irregular city pattern. The same idea could be observed at the military camp. As Marsigli describes above, Ottoman encampments had an irregular pattern, where the positioning of the tents created irregular roads and cul-de-sacs and where an enemy would usually become disorientated.

To sum up, the Ottoman military camp and the Ottoman civil settlement carried some parallel features. As the inheritor of strict rules of nomadic daily life, the architecture of civil settlement reflected distinct memories of that nomadic past, just as the later sedentary way of life, religious tradition and philosophy influenced the urban dwellers' daily habits.

The nomadic tent, then, formed the root of the traditional Turkish shelter. In Ottoman architecture three aspects of the tent could be observed:

1. Though the tent was replaced by the Ottoman house, portable and multi-purpose furniture, textiles

and wooden objects continued to be used as reflections of an original nomadic life-style.

2. Just as tents were elements of the military encampment used by the Viziers, high officials and soldiers, so fortified villages displayed similar features, but of a more fixed character.

3. The imperial *otagh* was the symbol of the Sultan during a military campaign. This nomadic tradition survived during the Ottoman era, when small pavilions within the imperial residence retained features of the old tribal tent.

From the point of view of the palace tradition, the military camp was symbolised by early Ottoman palaces like Edirne or Topkapı, and the early Seraglios reflected a symbolic version of the nomadic camp.

Bibliography

Anon. 1995: *Yüzyıllar Boyunca Venedik ve İstanbul Görünümleri - Vedute di Venezia ed Istanbul Attraverso i Secoli*. İtalyan Kültür Merkezi, Istanbul.

Babinger, F. 1961: 'Francesco Scarella e i suoi disegni di Costantinopoli (circa 1685)', *Rivista d'Arte* 35: 153-67.

Busbecq, O. G. de 1927: *The Turkish Letters of O.G. de Busbecq (1554-62)* (ed. E.S. Foster). Oxford.

Chierici, A. 1621: *Vera Relazione della Gran Città di Costantinopoli*. Bracciano.

Goodwin, G. 1971: *A History of Ottoman Architecture*. London.

Ibn Khaldun 1978: *The Muqaddimah; An Introduction to History*, (tr. F. Rosenthal, ed. N.J. Dawood). London & Henley.

Konyalı, İ. H. 1964: *Abideleriyle ve Kitabeleriyle Konya Tarihi*. Konya.

Kraelitz-Greifenhorst, F. 1921-22: 'Kanunname Sultan Mehmet II', *Mitteilungen zur Osmanischen Geschichte 1*.

Kuban, D. 1982: *Türk ve İslam Sanatı Üzerine Denemeler*. Istanbul: 153-4.

Lewenklaw, H. 1590: *Neuwe Chronica Türckischer Nation / von Türcken selbs beschrieben*. Frankfurt am Main.

Marsigli, L.F. 1732: *Il Stato Militare dell'Impero Ottomano* (new ed. Richard F. Kreutel, Graz, 1971). Amsterdam.

Marsilli, L.F. 1934: *Osmanlı İmparatorluğu'nun Zuhur ve Terakkisinden İnhitatı Zamanına Kadar Askeri Vaziyeti* (Turkish tr. of Marsigli 1732, M.K. Nazmi). Ankara.

Mundy, P. 1907: *The Travels of Peter Mundy in Europe and Asia, 1608-1667*, vol.1, ed. R. Carnac Temple. Cambridge.

Necipoğlu, G. 1991: *Architecture, Ceremonial, and Power - The Topkapı Palace in the 15th and 16th Centuries*. Cambridge, Mass. & London.

Ögel, B. 1985: *Türk Kültür Tarihine Giriş* (3 vols). Ankara.

Özgüven, B. 1996: *Barut ve Tabya: Rönesans Mimarisi Bağlamında Fatih Sultan Mehmed Kaleleri* (unpub. Ph.D. Dissertation, Istanbul Technical University). Istanbul.

Rycaut, P. 1971: *The Present State of the Ottoman Empire* (1st ed. London, 1668). New York.

Schweigger, S. 1964: *Ein newe Reyssbeschreibung auss Teutschland nach Constantinopel und Jerusalem* (ed. K. Teply; 1st ed. 1579). Graz.

Sümer, F. 1994: *Eski Türklerde Şehircilik*. Ankara.

Toy, S. 1966: *A History of Fortification from 3000 BC to AD 1700*. London.

Wratislaw, W. (Baron) 1996: *Baron W. Wratislaw'ın Anıları - 16. Yüzyıl Osmanlı İmparatorluğu'ndan Çizgiler* (Turkish tr. M.S. Dilmen). Istanbul.

---

[1] Military troops in Yedikule were described by Lewenklaw 1590: 275-6; cf. Mundy 1907: 31. Domenico Solimitano's observations were published in Chierici 1621: 3-5.

PART TWO: REGIONAL VARIATIONS IN TURKEY AND THE NEAR EAST

Ottoman houses are reflective of a lifestyle that was followed by citizens of the empire quite independently of ethnic or religious background. Therefore, it is possible to define general characteristics of spatial organisation that can be readily observed and that constitute a distinct typology. At the same time, the regional variations on this basic typology are numerous and fascinating, reflecting the multiplicity of cultures, climates and ecosystems to be found in Anatolia and the rest of the empire. These interactions are the subject of the seven papers in this section, demonstrating how the tension between a defined typology and the particular circumstantial conditions of time, place and culture gives rise to a richly varied architectural expression. The unifying force of Ottoman culture was flexible enough to allow individual variation and innovation.

Hande Birkalan discusses the houses of Safranbolu, the best preserved ensemble of Ottoman houses in Anatolia and, arguably, the standard against which other houses are judged. Her paper places the houses in their socio-economic context and outlines the spatial components of the houses in terms of domains and gradations of privacy. Typical architectural elements are described and defined by daily usage, giving a picture of how 'the house becomes the home'.

The spatial typologies developed by the distinguished Turkish architect, scholar and teacher Sedad Hakkı Eldem have become standard points of reference in the study of Ottoman houses, and these are used by Mükerrem Kürüm to describe the houses of Tire in Western Anatolia near Izmir. While conforming to basic typologies, the houses reflect the rich mix of Levantine and Anatolian influences that are characteristic of the region. Similarly, the houses of Balaban in Malatya province of south-east Anatolia described by Bekir Deniz are influenced by proximity to Syria and Iran. The adobe and wood construction is suited to the climate and geography of the area, and the houses and the urban pattern have clear affinities with neighbouring Arab and Persian towns. In a final example from Anatolia, Halit Çal investigates village houses in Boyabat, near the Black Sea. He speculates on the relationship between village and urban houses, and on the origins of Turkish houses. The account of construction methods and procedures by a local carpenter provides the kind of information that should be gathered while there are still knowledgeable craftsmen available.

Outside Anatolia Ron Fuchs describes the Arab houses of Palestine, a part of the Empire from 1516 to 1917. He demonstrates that village and city houses reflected the design of living spaces throughout the Eastern Mediterranean. Analysis of Palestinian domestic architecture reveals two basic themes - the pre-industrial all-purpose room and the 19th century central hall plan. Both these are important in Ottoman design and are realised in a variety of traditions throughout the Empire, showing affinities with Western and Eastern sources. Thus, the Arab vernacular is shown to be part of the complex cultural mosaic of the region. In a related article Alison McQuitty focuses on the architecture of the Ottoman period in Jordan, where institutional buildings were the primary expressions of imperial power. Rural houses were less directly influenced by Ottoman ideas than urban houses, although comparison with the houses of Palestine reveals common ancestries. Finally, Netice Yıldız describes the houses of Cyprus. The location in the eastern Mediterranean has guaranteed a history of multiple cultural influences on the island, reflected in transformations of Anatolian precedents introduced in the 16th century.

4: PERSONALITY AND MEANING OF GENDERED PLACES:THE CASE OF SAFRANBOLU

Hande Birkalan
Indiana University

The study of spatial experience has attracted many scholars from diverse disciplines including geography, anthropology, architecture, and history. Steeped in the expertise of their disciplines, scholars have produced several different approaches to this topic. The geographer Yi Fu Tuan, for example, in *Space and Place: The Perspective of Experience* (1977), examined the ways in which people experience these two phenomena. In his study of space and place, Yi Fu Tuan emphasises that ideas of culture are not descriptive, but they are approximations of experience. Locating his argument in human experience, Tuan furthermore concludes that place is security and space is freedom. He calls the spatial environment *topophilia*, where the dialectic relation of space and place can be learned through experience. It is in *topophilia* that people construct a certain reality, an environment of their own. As we mark our very locality, we tend to create significant places for our own use. That is how we create our *habitus,* in which the dialectic relationship of space and place becomes more meaningful. In other words, in the transformation of space to place, through our experience of making, *topophilia* gains a meaning and a personality.

Tuan's dialectic pattern is useful in understanding the essence of our everyday experience and in giving expression to our feelings, that is to say, the transformation of being alone to being with friends, being in the world to being at home, being with strangers to being with a mother. Space and freedom, place and security are mutually complementary, and the transformation of space to place depends on the relationship between the self and the environment at a given time. Human life is intimately related to things and places: the sense of belonging is fulfilled at home, that collection of meaningful objects around which family and self interact. On the other hand, the outer world is remote. When we gain certain experiences and bring our observations, reflections, and discoveries into it, space is transformed to place, world is approximated to home.

The relationship between space and place is also well presented by the Norwegian scholar Christian Norberg Schulz (1988: 31), who argues that 'the development of the concept of place, and of space as a system of places, is therefore a necessary condition for adaptation to given environment'. Schulz (1980: 33) also asserts that when people choose their spaces for dwelling, their history becomes an interaction with the landscape, the *genius loci,* where the distinction between inside and outside is of fundamental importance, and it is defined in terms of a new relationship between interior and exterior space.

Both Tuan and Schulz focus on the transformation process. In similar vein, I would like to present and analyse my data from historic Safranbolu. I will survey how history and geography, culture and tradition influenced the aura of the town, and examine the process in which the spatial environment gained its personality and meaning, both in public and domestic architecture, and especially within gendered places. In terms of theoretical framework I find the Irish scholar Emyr Estyn Evans's ideas very applicable to my study. In his work *Personality of Ireland,* Evans (1973: 66) notes that the personality of place is formed by a trilogy: history, habitat, and heritage. According to Evans, history consists of the accounts of the past. Habitat, he argues, is the total physical environment, whereas heritage can be defined as the unwritten parts of history, prehistoric past, oral traditions and beliefs, languages and crafts.

Safranbolu, a predominantly eighteenth century town in the northwestern Black Sea region, is a typical example of Turkish vernacular architecture (pl.4.1). It is typical because the elements of the traditional Turkish house are reinterpreted and realised according to the needs of the people. It is vernacular because it expresses the attitude of the architect, the materials of the habitat, and the needs of the society in relation to its cultural tradition. If we view architecture as a creative performance, through which nature is transformed into culture, then architects are the active creators who respond to an essential idea. Henry Glassie (1990: 10) observes that architects are the 'subtle engineer(s) in the organisation of human relations based on an established order'. In that framework, the building of a home is naturally shaped according to the political norms of culture and the physical environment. Using whatever material is available to him at that moment, the architect blends it with tradition. In Safranbolu lumber came from the forests nearby; architects also turned to tradition and so used mud-brick or baked brick and tiles (pl.4.2,3). The needs of society prompted the architect to build large, multi-storeyed houses with plenty of rooms, and most of these houses had large gardens. In the process of creation the architect used architectural norms embodied in both individual creation and social order. As a result, he made cultural artefacts derived from experience and a response to traditions, customs, and beliefs.

History is not the past. It is a particular story of the past which can be narrated through different media. One can look at it as a linear time, where one set of events is followed by another. In that framework, written accounts will tell us that the Turks first settled in Anatolia in the eleventh century. As they migrated from the steppes of Central Asia, they brought their rural settlement patterns, which gradually changed in response to the new conditions of the locality. Anatolia became the new 'homeland', and the conditions of this new life involved society finding new solutions for architectural patterns. Önder Küçükerman (1988: 27) notes that in the central Asian steppes, people lived in *yurts,* that is the nomad's tent, and they continually moved. Family and home were more in flux, and 'the concept of territory and feeling for a homeland was not connected with the land and this led to a very interesting abstract concept of the environment'.

In Anatolia, Turks produced new settlement patterns. However, nomadism continued, and in the later stages of development of the Turkish house, many elements were drawn from that experience. In some areas people were half-settled and they developed one or two-room shelters. Others became agriculturists, workers upon the land. The story of change given by the houses tells us that both settlement patterns had different architectural realities.

Archaeological narrative also informs us about the heritage of the town. Before the first appearance of Turks in the region, which took place at the beginning of the twelfth century, we learn from the archaeological and historical record that Persian, Lydian, Hellenistic and Roman civilisations had resided in the area.

Though there is no in-depth descriptive account of the history of Ottoman architecture in Safranbolu, we can nevertheless see from extant public architecture that several Ottoman viziers and administrative personages erected numerous structures (Günay 1981: 10). Actual documentation of public architecture, including hostels, bazaars and mosques, reveals that Safranbolu was a wealthy administrative district for production, marketing, and accommodation. For example, Cinci Hanı (lodge) was an important point on the Silk Road, as it provided accommodation for travellers, with up to sixty rooms as well as storage facilities (pl.4.6). There is no doubt that in addition to its cultural, economic and industrial relations with Istanbul Safranbolu's important geographic location on the trade routes inspired the building of lodges and hostels, especially in the seventeenth century.

In addition to the wealth which was accumulated from agriculture, craftsmanship had a great importance in the economic life of the city. *Loncas,* the local craft guilds, occupied the core of the economy, which included tanning, saddle making, light weaving, blacksmithing and coppersmithing. The census of 1894 shows that there were 1500 houses and 945 shops, some of which were in the Arasta Bazaar. In these shops were processed lumber, leather, fur and light textile materials (Yazıcıoğlu 1982: 68-75). Today as a tourist attraction the Arasta Bazaar has forty six shops which sell many different kinds of goods including kilims, carpets, several types of handicraft, embroidery, lace and light fabric weaving.

In addition to history, topography played an important role in the architectural pattern of Safranbolu houses. To a large extent the abundant supply of wood and water available helped shape the distinctive character of the public spaces in the construction of bridges and fountains. Several bridges, both large and small, were built over streams and as part of the gently rolling streets of Safranbolu, connecting streets to houses, world to home. Owing to the religious and cultural significance of water in Turkish society, wealthy families built public fountains next to their properties and provided water for public use. These fountains were decorated with floral designs, and sacred Koranic verses, which referred to human existence, connected people with their ancestors, and made a gift of the facility for future generations (pl.4.7).

Any researcher who is familiar with traditional Turkish architecture knows that in the traditional dwelling pattern of Turkish villages and towns the mosque functions as the centre of that locale. When a person first comes to a Turkish village, in order to orientate himself or herself easily, the main mosque needs to be located. This is not simply a matter of orientation, but of social organisation. The mosque is a religious as well as a social place, around which communal activities centre. Only after understanding its significance as the most significant form of public architecture, can we find a point of entry to the social order of the place, acquaint ourselves with the discourses of everyday life, and understand the relationship of individuals and groups.

In Safranbolu there are several mosques which date back as early as the thirteenth century. However, Izzet Pasha Mosque, built in the eighteenth century by the grand vizier Izzet Mehmet Pasha, is known as the main mosque. It stands out as a great piece of architecture with its beautiful exterior as well as its delicate interior decoration and plan. As it conveniently stands next to the Arasta Bazaar, most visitors are the craftsmen from it. People come and go from the coffee houses, utility stores, bakeries and grocery shops; they greet each other and have a friendly chat on their way.

Leaving the public sphere and moving into the private, we enter the realm of traditional Turkish society, where men were identified with the public space, and women were associated with the private. Men, working in the public and the material domain, built the houses whereas women engaged themselves in artistic creation and rearing children in a spiritual domain. Different activities became more substantial both in incorporating and distinguishing public, private and communal. In that respect, home became a very important place for both men and women. For men home was a means to channel themselves into the private. After coming home men socialised with their own families, and on some occasions with other families. For men home became a liminal sphere which connected them with both the communal and the personal. Home for women too had a particular significance. The concealment of the women from public space resulted in an expansion of artistic expression (pl.4.8) and, perhaps surprisingly, a subsequent active involvement in society. While men built houses in the public domain, women through their art turned these houses into homes in the private domain.

The development of Safranbolu's houses was also shaped by the extended family pattern of its society. Reha Günay notes that among the extended families of Safranbolu labour was well organised and controlled. Husbandry, agriculture, and housework were divided among the different members of the families including aunts and uncles, grandmothers and grandfathers. In Safranbolu a family could adopt a young girl and take the responsibility for her education and upbringing. When she reached the age of marriage, she was married to a selected groom and the necessary dowry was provided. This system functioned well at the time, since daughters of poor villagers found a way to better their lives (Günay 1981: 24).

In traditional daily life adults in the family would wake up very early. After performing their daily morning prayer, they would have a large breakfast. Those who worked in tanning would then go to work very early and finish their work by noon. Afternoon was saved for working in the gardens. Those who owned a store in the bazaar, on the other hand, would go to work later, because it was only by noon that business in the bazaar became of any magnitude. Women would always keep some food available for the male members of the family, since they might come back home for lunch. The males would in any case return home after the afternoon prayer. Whole families would get together at dinner. In the event that families visited each other, women, children and men would be separated in different parts of the house.

In traditional Turkish families, the eldest male member of the family represents the main authority-figure. When the son of the family married, he did not leave the house, and continued to recognise his father as the primary male person in the family. The daughter, on the other hand, always left home and lived with her husband's parents (Günay 1981: 24). When the son married and brought his wife to the new home, they moved into the room on the upper floor especially reserved for the new bride. That room, within and of itself, becomes a new home for the new bride. She can decorate it in the way she likes. Literally her room is her own, as long as she wants to keep her privacy. If she prefers a more social environment, she can spend some time in the *sofa*, an area where open interaction could take place.

As life-style in Turkish society was determined by tradition, privacy has been the major concern in the architectural design of the Turkish home. In Safranbolu a mechanical system for minding the door has been developed (pl.4.4). Those who used the *tokmak,* the door-knocker on the entrance door, would thus inform those inside of their presence. The resident would then pull a cord, which was connected to the door, from inside the house and thus open it. Watching the guest from the window of the *sofa* above, the owner of the house thus maintained security, as well as the privacy of the household.

From this entrance the Turkish house is directed towards a pattern of increment. Since the time of nomadic settlements, earth is considered as 'dirt' and sky as 'heaven'. After urbanisation the Turkish house preserved this cosmological idea. Coming from the earth and incrementing step by step, forming a niche towards God, each floor was built upon another. Each one had to be better than the previous one, reaching the perfection of the third floor. As a part of the cosmic and world view, the ground at home, 'dirt', was covered by beautiful carpets, and ceilings were decorated with interlocked star designs, which symbolised a transcendental feeling - the mortal's unity with the immortal.

The line between the private and the public is very well manifested in the ground floor, which functions as a linkage with the street. The ground floor of Safranbolu houses provides a solid basis for the structure. This floor has no windows onto the street and it has relatively high ceilings compared to the upper floors. Usually, the middle floor, the rooms of which are less high than those of the third floor, is a passage floor to that third floor, where both architectural and mystical perfection is aimed to be fulfilled. In Safranbolu houses the entrance is called *hayat,* a threshold where nature and culture meet. People take their shoes off at the stairway, leaving the dirt outside and leading their way upstairs (pl.4.5). Taking shoes off at the entrance in the Turkish home is a ritual of purification. As one enters from the outer, material world to the inner and spiritual space, the person needs to be cleansed from the so-called 'contaminated environment' in both a metaphorical and a literal sense. *Hayat,* as the threshold for purification, distinguishes kin from the distant, foreign from the domestic, dirt from the pure. About this old Turkish custom Bilgi Denel notes that taking shoes off at the entrance is done out of respect for the house and the guest as well. On the way back out from the house, as a sign of that respect, the guest would find his or her shoes cleaned, paired, and pointing outward (Denel 1989: 54).

Moving from the *hayat,* the entrance, and going to the second and third floors, we come to the actual living space - the *oda* and the *sofa* which took their forms alongside the development of the general concepts of community life. While *odas* provide a space for withdrawing, *sofas* provide a common area between rooms for wide interaction. The *odas* (rooms), are multifunctional units designed for formal talks, sleeping, sitting, and eating. They were formed by combining the environmental elements necessary for those activities. The interior arrangements are limited by definite principles created by social characteristics. These characteristics have great importance not only in the design of the rooms, but also in the maintenance of the location within structural elements.

Elaborate woodwork at the entrance of the *odas* makes an effective visual barrier, and its function is to maintain the privacy of the women. The doors are so designed that they prevent any sight of the ladies when the family gets together. Those who entered the room would be faced by a wooden folding screen. In order to come into the presence of those inside, another left or right turn is necessary. If the whole family is present in the room, the oldest person of the family would sit right at the entrance, since the upper part of the room is reserved for the most respected person.

In the traditional Safranbolu house, the distinction between public and private as well as private and communal was realised in the *harem,* and *selamlık.* The *harem* is the common area for the female members of the family in the presence of male guests, whereas the *selamlık* is reserved for males. It is worthwhile noting that the Anatolian houses did not strictly demand the separation of men and women, and the separation of genders occurred when required (Denel 1989: 51). Separate units for men and women are a more dominant feature of the larger houses where there are specific units serving either gender. In accordance with the social values, the *harem* rooms were to be modest, but they were arranged to allow flexibility of use whether for sitting, eating or sleeping.

To provide a means of interaction between *harem* and *selamlık* in the presence of guests, the wealthier houses developed an interesting system. In the small area between *harem* and *selamlık* there was a mobile platform, which had access to both parts. In this space, a *dönme dolap* (small revolving lazy-Susan) system was constructed. This is a perfect design for the houses where there is no servant present. Items were placed on the platform and passed to the other side, which allowed women to serve food and beverages to the *selamlık* without being seen by the guests.

Odas, the withdrawing units of the house, are connected to interactive *sofas.* The *sofa* is an architectural element which functions as a bridge for informal male and female gatherings within the household. Contrary to the formal design of the *odas,* we cannot speak in terms of strict gender roles for the *sofa. Sofas* are the common places of the family for daily activities. Here people get together for wedding ceremonies, prepare pastry products, and continue their informal chatting. Denel notes that the *sofa* 'is usually built to be any shape that allows the other rooms on the floor to become as close to square as possible' (Denel 1989, 54).

Traditionally speaking, in the *oda* or *sofa* there is no furniture except *sedirs* (divans). The relationship between the *sofa, sedir* and windows is notable as they bear a pragmatic function (pl.4.9, 10). The woman may engage herself in artistic activity sitting by the window on *sedirs. Sedirs,* cushions along the windows, are ideal places for the creation of art. The perfect harmony between *sedir* and window provides pleasure for the woman - she can have her daily chat, take care of the children, and at the same time, create her art. If she wants a personal moment while creating art, she can go to the *oda.* If she wants to watch the street, she can create her art in the *sofa.* The windows are important architectural elements affecting both the interior and exterior of the house. Customs and traditions conditioned the design of the house to be in accordance with the conservation of privacy. At the lower levels rooms facing a street were reduced in number and size, whereas on the upper floors, windows are more numerous and of larger dimensions.

Windows are considered to be the eyes of the house; the external environment can be perceived through the windows. As the numbers of the windows increase, it is easier to view the street from different angles, because in the Turkish house the windows are large. From the side window, the street can be controlled. The following stanza, which was collected by folklorist Ilhan Başgöz, reflects the woman's feelings about the window:

Bu evi yapan usta
Umarım olur hasta.
Bir cam bile koymamış.
Nasıl bakayım dosta?

[The master who built this house
I hope would soon become sick.
There is no window in the house.
How can I watch the street?]

Cumbas are bay windows; metal grilles or wooden shutters provide privacy. Because windows provided an opening onto the outside, the woman in the house could maintain a line of sight to connect her to the public. The windows facing the street are usually covered with the *kafes* and decorated with elegant artefacts such as lace curtains.

Women's artistic creativity was not confined to the house. Since the Safranbolu houses had very large gardens, women also worked outside. In summer looms were placed in *çardaks*, the open *sofas,* whereas in the winter they were erected in the *odas,* even in the kitchens. Women who wove fabrics for profit would always keep the looms set up. At the beginning of the century the houses which had looms were one fourth of the total houses in the town. Women would maintain a reasonable income for the family by selling the fabrics. The fabrics which were not sold were used as pillows, bed covers, sheets or other cloth.

In the urban environment of Safranbolu, women's concealment from the public led to an emphasis on artistic creativity and so to a role in the economy. In contrast with the assumptions which hold that women have subordinate or marginal positions in Islam, the data from Safranbolu reveal a traditional route to power in economic life. In this respect, women are the active agents of the personality-making process at home, where they produce beautiful artefacts which are sold in the market. In providing a space for creative art, as a key in the transformation of a house to a home, women also become active in passing down the traditional arts to the next generation as they raise their children.

From houses to the streets, from the private to the public, from the women's to the men's place, the spirit and the meaning flows. The personality of Safranbolu is due to several influences including history, habitat and heritage, as well as the artistic creation both in the inner and the outer domain. Creative sensibility of the individual, both male and female, is exhibited in different, albeit related, activities. Men make the house, women make the home.

It is home that unites people: women gather with other women and men on different occasions. Women bring the distant to the near, material to the spiritual, foreign to the kin. Home is both the private itself and the return to the private. Through the making of *topophilia,* public and private, kin and distant, material and spiritual are defined afresh and anew. Our data from Safranbolu shows that meaning and power are in the making process, through which the house becomes the home. Home is the place where a mystic resolution of the male and female was brought about; it is the communal space and the centre of the family. Home is what matters.

The author dedicates this paper to the people of Safranbolu.

Bibliography

Bektaş, C. 1987: *Şirinköy Evleri.* Bektaş Mühendislik, Istanbul.

Birkalan, H. 1992: Interview notes. Safranbolu (Turkey).

---- 1994: Interview notes. Safranbolu (Turkey).

De Certeau, M. 1988: *Practice of Everyday Life.* (tr. S. Rendall), University of California Press.

Denel, B. 1989: 'Safranbolu: Roots of Urban Form in an Anatolian Town', *Traditional Dwellings and Settlements Review* 1: 9-63.

Eco, U. 1986: *Art & Beauty in the Middle Ages.* (tr. H. Bredin). Yale.

Evans, E.E. 1973: *The Personality of Ireland: Habitat, Heritage and History.* Cambridge.

Glassie, H. 1973: 'The Structure and the Function, Folklore, and the Artefact', *Semiotica* 7/4, 313-51.

---- 1982: *Passing the time in Ballymenone*, University of Pennsylvania Press.

---- 1990: 'Architects, Vernacular Traditions and Society', *Traditional Dwellings and Settlements Review* 1: 9-21.

---- 1993: *Turkish Traditional Art Today.* Indiana University Press.

Günay, R. 1981: *Geleneksel Safranbolu Evleri ve Oluşumu.* Kültür Bakanlığı Yayınları, Ankara.

Jackson, M. 1995: *At Home in the World.* Duke University Press.

Küçükerman, O. 1988: *The Turkish House in Search of Spatial Identity.* Türkiye Turing Otomobil Kurumu Yayınları, Istanbul.

Özgüner, O. 1970: *Köyde Mimari: Doğu Karadeniz.* Mimarlık Fakültesi Yayınları, Ankara.

Pocius, G.L. 1993: *A Place to Belong.* University of Georgia Press.

Schiele, R., Müller-Wiener, W. 1988: *19.yy'da İstanbul Hayati.* Istanbul.

Schulz, C. Norberg 1988: *Architecture: Meaning and Place.* New York.

---- 1980: *Genius Loci: Towards a Phenomenology of Architecture.* New York.

Stirling, P. (ed.) 1993: *Culture and Economy: Changes in Turkish Villages*. Cambridge.

Ünver, S. 1983: *Osman Rıfat'a Göre Edirne Evleri ve Konakları*. T.T.O.K., Istanbul.

Tuan, Yi Fu 1977: *Space and Place: The Perspective of Experience*. Minneapolis.

Yazıcıoğlu, H. 1982: *Safranbolu – Karabük – Ulus – Eflani*. Özer Matbaası, Karabük.

5: TIRE HOUSES

Mükerrem Kürüm[1]
Adnan Menderes University, Aydın

House construction began in the Neolithic period when people started to have a settled form of life and within Anatolia settlement units of the Neolithic period have been found in excavations. It is clear from the remains discovered that houses were square or rectangular in shape constructed on a cell-plan and contained one or more rooms (Yakar 1991, 42-56, 108, 111; Dinçal 1984, 12-16). House plans developed as time went by. When Turks, who lived a nomadic lifestyle in middle Asia, entered Anatolia, they used the buildings they found there in accordance with their way of life and their culture. In time, however, they developed the type of house now known as 'the Turkish house' by making changes to the underlying pattern. Some scholars have advanced the idea that the source of the Turkish house is to be found in the tent-dwelling tradition of middle Asia. The present author on the other hand, while believing that this is an important factor, nevertheless seeks to stress the influence that the house-typology of those civilisations which previously occupied Anatolia has had.[2] In turn, research has shown that the 'Turkish house' affected the architecture of the Middle East and Europe in the 17th and 18th centuries. This influence began to lessen in the 19th century and finished in the 20th century. Over all, therefore, development of the houses under discussion has been influenced by factors as diverse as geographical conditions, topographical situations, local materials and religion, as well as the ethical, social, cultural and economic values of society.[3]

The best research into the topic of Turkish houses was carried out by Sedad Hakkı Eldem. According to him, the typology of the Turkish house can be divided into four major groups:

A. The type without a *sofa*
B. The type with an exterior *sofa*
C. The type with an interior *sofa*
D. The type with a central *sofa*.

In general it is true to say that this division of typology displays development over time and within each type there are many subdivisions. Within the scheme set out above the oldest house plan is that which lacks what was to become the communal living space known as the *sofa*, off which the more private apartments led. This was closely followed by the house-plan which incorporated an external *sofa*. At the beginning, *sofas* were in fact open spaces, virtually verandas with wooden columns, but later they were enclosed to become rooms in their own right. It was here that people gathered to enjoy the cool and where fruit was dried in summer. With the development of a closure to the *sofa* it became an integral part of the house interior and thus an internal *sofa*. In this case the private rooms are generally arranged on two sides of the *sofa*, facing one another. As a later development the *sofa* becomes surrounded by rooms on its other sides and is therefore referred to as a central *sofa*. As it is the upstairs sections of houses that provide the main living space, it is generally at this level that house-plans are analysed.[4]

Tire lies within of the province of Izmir (map on p.xiv) and is situated in the basin of the Küçük Menderes river on the northern flanks of the Güme Mountain, part of the Aydın-Cevizli range. It is bounded by Bayındır in the north, Aydın in the South, Ödemiş in the east, and by Selçuk and Kuşadası in the west. The name Tire survives today in many forms. Information about those civilisations that existed at Tire in the distant past is sparse, but for the period of the Aydınoğulları Principality and the Ottoman Empire one is on surer ground. It was linked to Izmir, a subdivision of Aydın province, on May 23rd 1867. It was subsequently occupied by the Greeks on May 28 1919, and it returned to Turkish control on September 4 1922.[5]

There is no certain data about when urban settlement began in Tire, but it has been an important centre holding a key position within Anatolia from the Lydian period until the present day. The earliest settlement apparently began in the south and the east of the area and in the Ottoman period, especially under Murad II, advanced westwards. Recent development on the other hand has been largely along the roads that lead north, with the result that the town centre has been protected against redevelopment.[6] Because of this Tire appears as two different cities: old Tire, remaining on the flanks of the mountain, and the modern Tire established on the plain (pl.5.1).

There are many old houses within the historical quarter of Tire. Some of these have survived to the present day by being protected, but others are in a ruined condition. We have included 54 houses in our research; four of these were inspected by Sedad Hakkı Eldem, but we have not had the opportunity to view them in person.[7] We have taken photographs of 50 houses, drawn them and recorded their dimensions. However, we were not able to make a detailed examination of some of the houses we would have liked to inspect for a number of reasons. The houses that we did examine, though, have become the basis for our evaluation.

Most of the traditional houses in Tire have been built on slopes towards the north and south, with others in an east-west alignment and some even built on level ground. Any asymmetric appearance seen on the plans of some houses arises from the specific conditions of the site. The streets of old Tire are generally narrow and paved with rough cobblestones, with small channels running down the middle in order to carry away rainwater. Some of the streets have been asphalted recently but many still retain their original character (pl.5.2).

Apart from the typical Turkish houses we also find in Tire houses that are Levantine in nature mostly built at the beginning of the 20th century. The typical Turkish house, for instance, generally has a courtyard or garden, the courtyard surrounded by a high wall; the ground floor is usually closed off from the outside, and most have a *sofa* (called locally also *hayat* or *çardak*) which overlooks or opens onto the garden (pl.5.3). In houses of the Levantine type, on the other hand, the desire for privacy and introversion has been abandoned; instead, buildings have become outward-looking and bay windows added (pl.5.4). Instead of courtyards such houses have gardens which are large and imposing.

For the most part the houses of Tire are constructed of rubble masonry and brick, internal dividing walls being fabricated out of laths on a timber frame (pl.5.2). The majority of the old houses are two-storeyed; one, three or four-storeyed houses are rarely seen. The ground floor in old Turkish houses is used for storage; the upper floor contains the living rooms. Levantine houses on the other hand incorporate living space on both floors. In general the Turkish houses have hipped or *kırma* roofs covered with channelled tiles. This is not, however, the case with houses of the Levantine type.

In most of the old Turkish houses the ground floors are naturally restricted by the boundaries of the plot, whereas upper floors have been enhanced with projections such as bay windows supported by corbels or struts. This is especially the case with those sides facing the street, which have been given a more imposing aspect (pl.5.5). The front doors of these houses are made of wood or iron and often have two leaves. Sometimes we see the entrance recessed in the shape of an *eyvan*, especially in houses of the Levantine type (pl.5.6). In old Turkish houses one first enters the courtyard and then the house, but in Levantine houses one enters the house directly from the street. It is possible to see this characteristic in all West Anatolian districts including Izmir and Bergama.

The typology of houses without *sofa*, with an external *sofa* or with an internal *sofa* are all to be seen in Tire. Exterior and interior *sofas* have been widely used, but we did not come across central *sofas* in our researches; however, this type of design may exist in the houses we could not enter. From the samples we have seen, however, it is our view that this house arrangement has not been much used in the area.

Within these broad types there are many subdivisions:

A. House-type without *sofa*
- a) Two rooms without sofa (fig.5.1)
- b) Three rooms without *sofa* (fig.5.2)
- c) Four rooms without *sofa* (fig.5.3)

B. House-type with exterior *sofa*
- a) Exterior *sofa* with one room (fig.5.4)
- b) Exterior *sofa* with two rooms (fig.5.5)
- c) Exterior *sofa* with three rooms (fig.5.7)
- d) Exterior *sofa* with four rooms (fig.5.6)
- e) Exterior *sofa* with multiple rooms (fig.5.8)
- f) Exterior *sofa* with *eyvan* (fig.5.9)
- g) Exterior *sofa* with *köşk* and *eyvan* (fig.5.10)
- h) Exterior *sofa* with two parts (fig.5.11)

C. House-type with interior *sofa*
- a) Interior *sofa* (fig.5.12)
- b) One-sided interior *sofa* (fig.5.13)
- c) Two-sided interior *sofa* (fig.5.14)

Most of the house types with exterior *sofa* found in Tire have two or three rooms leading off the *sofa* (fig.5.5, 7). In some houses the *sofa* is closed to the outside and at times serves as an *işlik* (workroom) where weaving is carried out. In the summertime much of family life goes on here. The *eyvan* (fig.5.9) is in turn a place where people can seek the cool and shade. In some cases too the *eyvan* protects rooms against cold weather. The *köşk* is one of the important rooms within the house and often serves today as a guestroom. In house-types incorporating an interior *sofa* the commonest form found is the 'two-sided interior *sofa*' (fig.5.14). Such houses mostly have four rooms.

Rooms in Tire houses, as is general in old Turkish houses, are arranged according to the needs of families. There are cupboards and a *gusülhane* (washing facility) in nearly every room (pl.5.7). By way of contrast in houses of the Levantine type additional rooms have been built as bathrooms. Some rooms have the 'main room' style of the old Turkish houses. Their doors are usually more elaborated than others (pl.5.8).

There are two methods of opening windows in Tire houses. The first one is the outward opening window, and the second is the vertically sliding sash window. Some windows retain their original wood lattices and grilles (pl.5.9). In some cases there are clerestory windows mostly used for decoration (pl.5.10).

Some of the houses in Tire are ornamented and some are not. Exterior decoration is mostly seen on the walls, gates and projections, with the old Turkish houses having less exterior decoration in comparison with houses of the Levantine type, though some of them do have plastered columns (pl.5.11). Levantine houses in general are externally more showy and ornamented, incorporating larger windows, mouldings at the edges or in the middle of the façade and plastered columns with composite capitals at the corners (pl.5.12). Supports for projecting elements are often ornamented with meanders or curved motifs. Such kinds of decoration are seen in Izmir, Manisa and Bergama.

The interiors of houses are often highly ornamented, especially the ceilings, which generally have a central rose of intricate design with plant or geometrical designs in relief as a conspicuous feature (pl.5.13). In addition to these ceilings, the subsidiary architectural elements such as wooden cupboards and clerestory windows are decorated with geometrical and plant designs (pl.5.14). Similarly, inscriptions and cypress motifs on the clerestory windows of some houses provide highly impressive features as do the columns which frame door-ways in many Levantine houses.

The number of inscribed panels in houses of the town centre is low. They do, however, indicate that the houses were built in the second half of the eighteenth century. On the other hand, where there were no inscriptions to assist dating, this could be ascertained to some degree by reference to the architectural and decorative features, as well as by the reports of those old people who preserve an oral history of the area.

Although houses in the villages around Tire show similarities to those in the town itself, for the most part they have been built in the style of provincial houses. For instance, in village houses there is not much evidence for the house-type with an inner *sofa*. The reason for this is the fact that village people use the *sofa* as a place where they work: as an *işlik* or workroom. The most widely used typology is the house with an outer *sofa*. *Köşk* or *eyvan* elements generally do not exist in these houses. In comparison to the houses in the town centre, the use of timber framing infilled with lath and plaster is more extensive. In the village houses too decoration is less used in comparison to the houses in the centre, and these houses do not have inscriptions.

Tire houses resemble the houses of western Anatolia as far as their basic characteristics are concerned. In this region, the typology of houses with inner and outer *sofas* has found a wide area of application. These houses are similar also in their construction and appearance: the houses are enclosed by high courtyard walls along narrow streets. One result of this is that at first floor level the façades overlooking the street are not widely separated from those opposite. The ground floors of the houses in this region are usually constructed of stone, the upper floors in contrast are built from wooden frames or lath and plaster work. On the upper floors, the *sofa* opens onto the courtyard or the garden with Bursa-type arched colonnades. The rooms in turn often have decorated ceilings, cupboards and doors, and are arranged in a way that will respond to the many needs of the family. In general Tire houses resemble the Muğla houses in the region, though they also have affinities with those of Kula, Ödemiş, Bergama, Soma and Birgi as far as their materials and typology of external *sofas* is concerned. The houses in other regions of Anatolia have been constructed in different ways as a result of factors as diverse as the availability of material, climate, etc. For example, wood is widely used in Trabzon and Istanbul, and stone is used more in Mardin and Urfa. In certain regions the ground floors of houses are constructed of stone and the upper floors are built with wooden frames or lath and plaster. In some places too houses incorporate inner, outer or central *sofas* and the rooms are divided into *harem* and *selamlık*. This last factor does not, however, occur in Tire. In general, though, Anatolian houses have more decoration than those of Tire and are constructed with a more mature character.[8]

The fact that, despite not retaining many of their original features, a high proportion of traditional Tire houses has survived to the present day allows them to occupy a singular position in Turkish house architecture. In addition, such houses are very important in that they demonstrate traditional Turkish house architecture in the area. That is why it is important that these houses be retained so that coming generations can understand the heritage of the past.

Bibliography

Akok, M. 1963: 'Kütahya ve Uşak Şehirlerinin Eski Evleri', *Türk Etnoğrafya Dergisi* 6 [1965]: 5-17.

Altınoluk, Ü. 1989: 'Geleneksel Türk Evi ve Yaşam', *İlgi* 56: 2-7.

Armağan, A.M., 1980: *Tüm Yönleriyle Tire*, 1. Tire.

---- 1983: *Belgelerle Beylikler Devrinde Tire*. Izmir.

Bozer, R. 1988: *Kula Evleri*. Ankara.

Çetinor, B. 1986: 'Doğu Karadeniz ve Evleri' *İlgi* 44: 15-22.

Darkot, B. 1979: 'Tire', *İslam Ansiklopedisi*, 12.1. Istanbul: 379-81.

Deniz, B. 1980: 'Malatya Türk Ev Mimarisinin Ana Hatları', *MTRE Bülteni* 11-12: 19-23.

---- 1992: 'Manisa Yöresi Köy Ev Mimarisi', *Arkeoloji-Sanat Tarihi Dergisi* 6. Izmir: 17-46.

Dinçal, M.A. 1984: 'Hititler Öncesinde Anadolu', *Anadolu Uygarlıkları Görsel Anadolu Tarihi Ansiklopedisi*. Istanbul: 11-16.

Ekinci, O. 1985: *'Yaşayan' Muğla*. Istanbul.

Eldem, S.H. 1968: *Türk Evi Plan Tipleri*, Istanbul.

Eldem, S.H. 1984-7: *Türk Evi Osmanlı Dönemi* (3 vols). Türkiye Anıt Çevre Değerlerini Koruma Vakfı, Istanbul.

Erginbaş, D. 1953: *Diyarbakır Evleri*. Istanbul.

Eser, L. 1955, 1959: *Kütahya Evleri*. Istanbul.

Eyice, S. 1986: 'Quelques observations sur l'habitat Byzantin en Turquie', *Anadolu Sanatı Araştırmaları*, 5. Istanbul: 529-42.

Göksu, E. 1986: 'Mekansal Özelliklerini Koruyan Yerleşmelerde Oluşum ve Değişim Süreci Tire (İzmir)', *Bildiriler, Ege'de Mimarlık Sempozyumu, 27-9 Mart 1985*. Izmir: 106-16.

Günay, R. 1981: *Geleneksel Safranbolu Evleri ve Oluşumu*. Kültür Bakanlığı Yayınları, Ankara.

Gürler, B. 1987: *Anadolu'da Roma Dönemi Evleri*, (Masters thesis, Classical Archaeology Dept., E.Ü.). Izmir.

Hasol, D. 1975: *Ansiklopedik Mimarlık Sözlüğü*. Istanbul.

Kömürcüoğlu, E. 1950: *Ankara Evleri*. Istanbul.

Küçükerman, Ö. 1988: *Kendi Mekanının Arayışı İçinde Türk Evi* T.T.O.K Yay. Istanbul.

Kürüm, M. 1992: *Tire Evleri*, (Masters thesis, Archaeology and Art History Dept, E.Ü.). Izmir.

Larousse 1971: 'Ev 4' in *Meydan Larousse Ansikopedisi*. Istanbul: 441-5.

Sözen, M., Sönmez, Z. 1975: 'Anadolu Türk Mimarisi', *Anadolu Uygarlıkları Görsel Anadolu Tarihi Ansiklopedisi* 5. Istanbul: 870-4.

Tanyeli, U. 1987: *Anadolu-Türk Kentinde Fiziksel Yapının Evrim Süreci (11-15.yy.)*. Istanbul.

Tokluoğlu, F. 1957: *Tire Tarihi ve Turistik Değerler*. Tire.

Tuğlacı, P. 1985: *Osmanlı Şehirleri*. Istanbul.

Usman, M. 1958: *Antik Devir Küçük Asya Evleri*. Istanbul.

Yakar, J. 1991: *Prehistoric Anatolia; The Neolithic Transformation and the Early Chalcolithic Period*. Israel.

Explanation of terms used in the plans:

Abdestlik:	Room for the performance of ablutions
Balkon:	Balcony
Banyo:	Bathroom
Baş Oda:	Principal room
Çardak:	Hall
Depo:	Storeroom
Dolap:	Cupboard
Gusülhane:	Bathroom
Hayat:	Hall
Hayat altı:	Lower hall
Havuz:	Pool
Mutfak:	Kitchen
Niş:	Niche
Ocak:	Fireplace
Oda:	Room
Sofa:	Hall
Tuvalet:	Toilet
Yüklük:	Closet for bedding

---

[1] For more detail see, Kürüm 1992. This paper was first published as 'Tire Evleri' in *Türk Kültüründe Tire*, Ankara, 1994: 139-146, and secondly as 'Türk Ev Mimarisinde Tire Evleri' in the journal *Ege Mimarlık*, 15 (1995): 56-59. The present paper represents a revised text.

[2] Usman 1958: 75-86; Gürler 1987: 86-95; Eyice 1986: 529-42; Küçükerman 1988: 62.

[3] Sözen, Sönmez 1975: 870; Eldem 1984: 28f.; Altınoluk 1989: 3; Eldem 1987: 262.

[4] For more detail see: Eldem 1968, 1984, 1986, 1987.

[5] Darkot 1979: 379; Tokluoğlu 1957; Armağan 1980, 1983; Tuğlacı 1985: 285.

[6] Tanyeli 1987: 121-122 and Göksu 1986: 109f. refer to the development of Tire.

[7] Eldem 1968: 53, 66, 69, 157.

[8] For the house architecture in other areas of Anatolia see, Akok 1965: 5-17; Bozer 1988; Çetinor 1986: 15-22; Deniz 1992: 17-46; Deniz 1980: 19-23; Ekinci 1985; Erginbaş 1953; Günay 1981; Kömürcüoğlu 1950; Eser 1955.

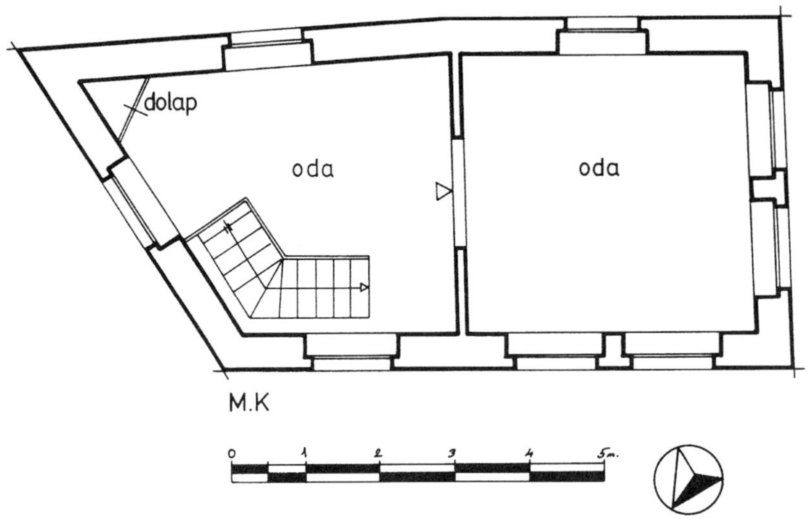

Fig. 5.1. The house of Ahmet Köse, upper floor

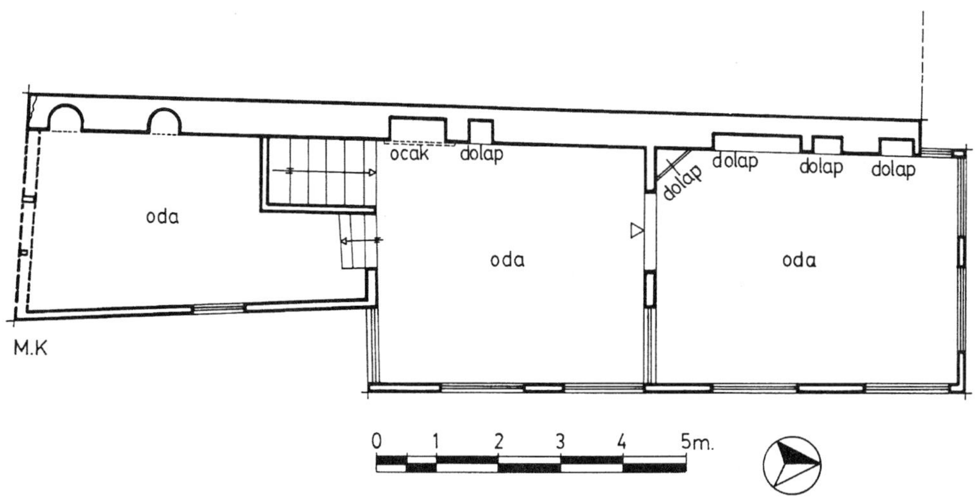

Fig. 5.2. The house of Ayşe Bedih, upper floor

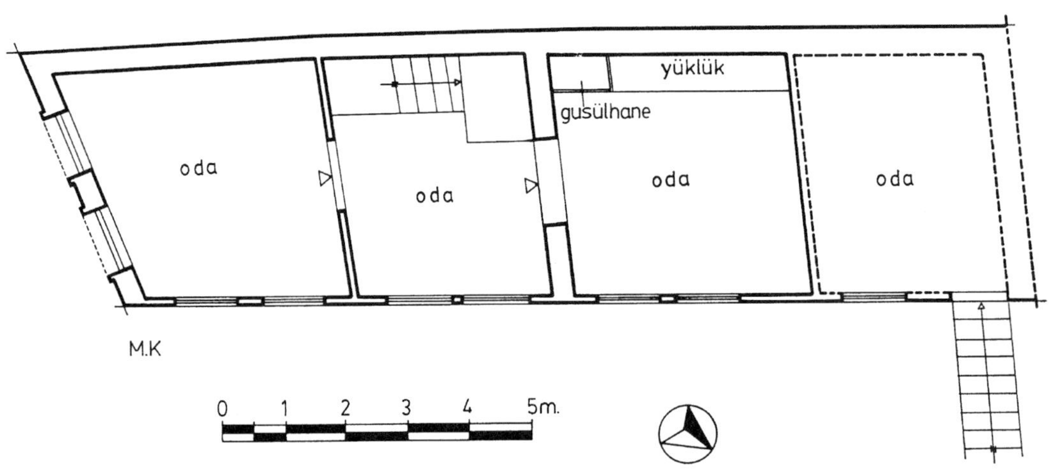

Fig. 5.3. The house of Şükrü Seke, upper floor

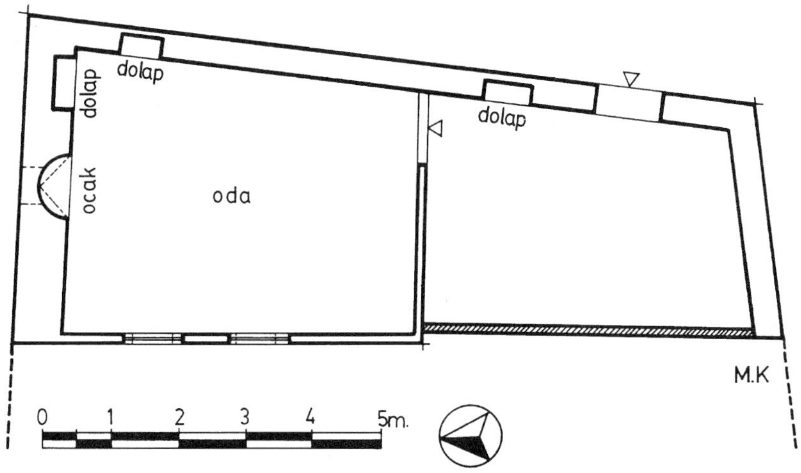

Fig. 5.4. The house of Hamide Pala

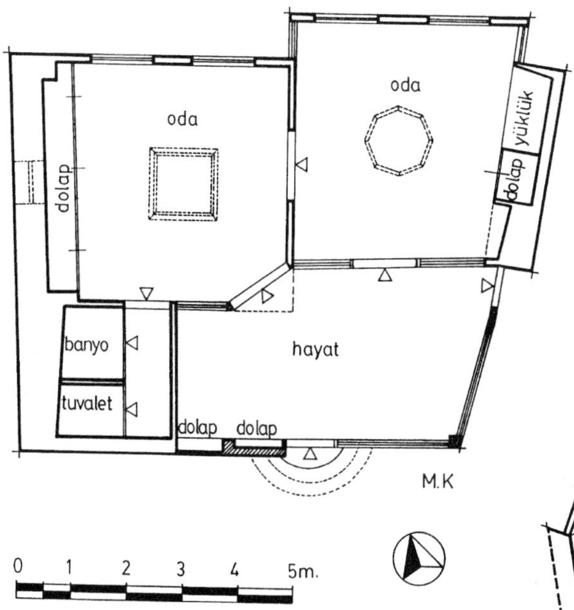

Fig. 5.5. The house of Talip Yanık, upper floor

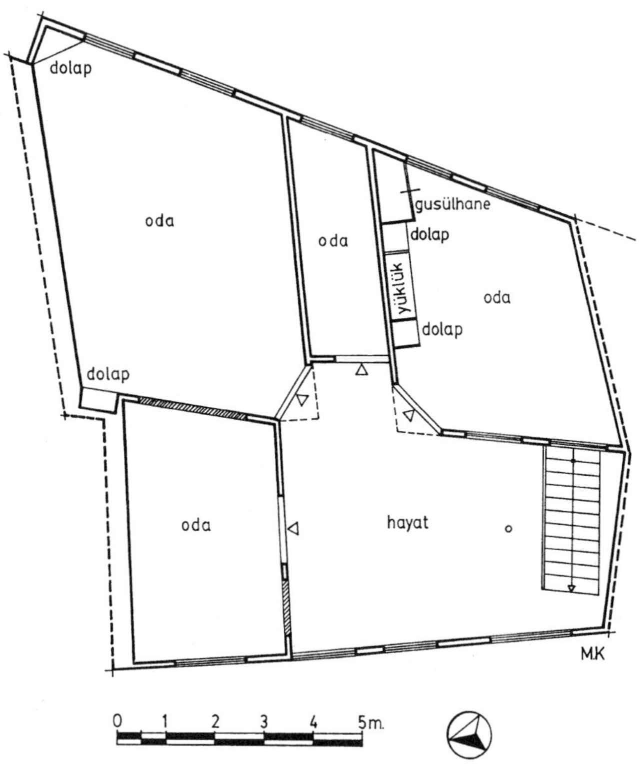

Fig. 5.6. The house of Ali Yakar, upper floor

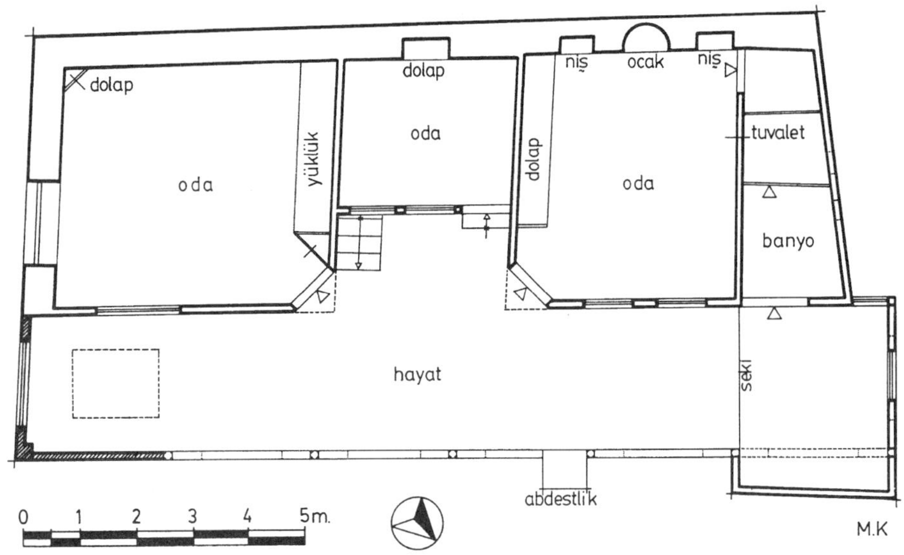

Fig. 5.7. The house of Ali Hodimli, upper floor

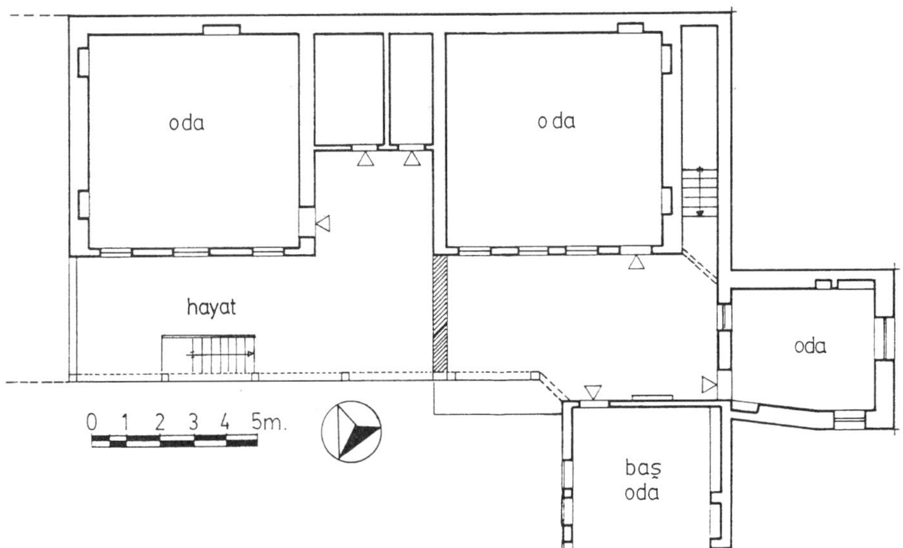

Fig. 5.8. The house of Afyonlu Sami, upper floor

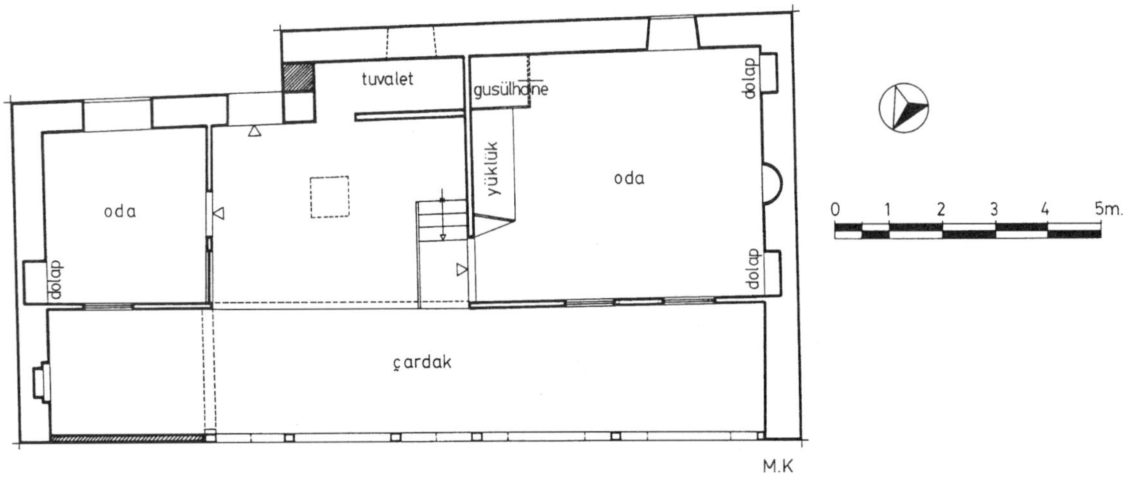

Fig. 5.9. The house of Hacı Mehmet Ali, upper floor

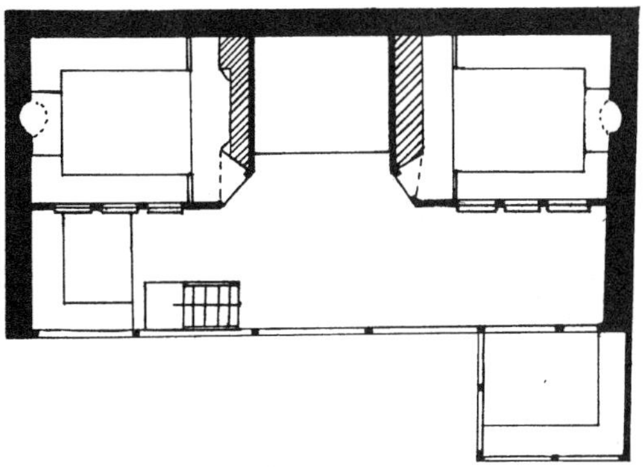

Fig. 5.10. The house of Ak Hoca Hafız

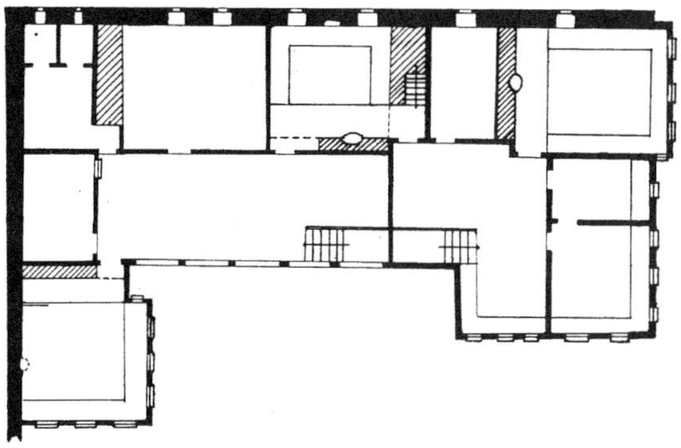

Fig. 5.11. The house of Hacı Ömer Efendi

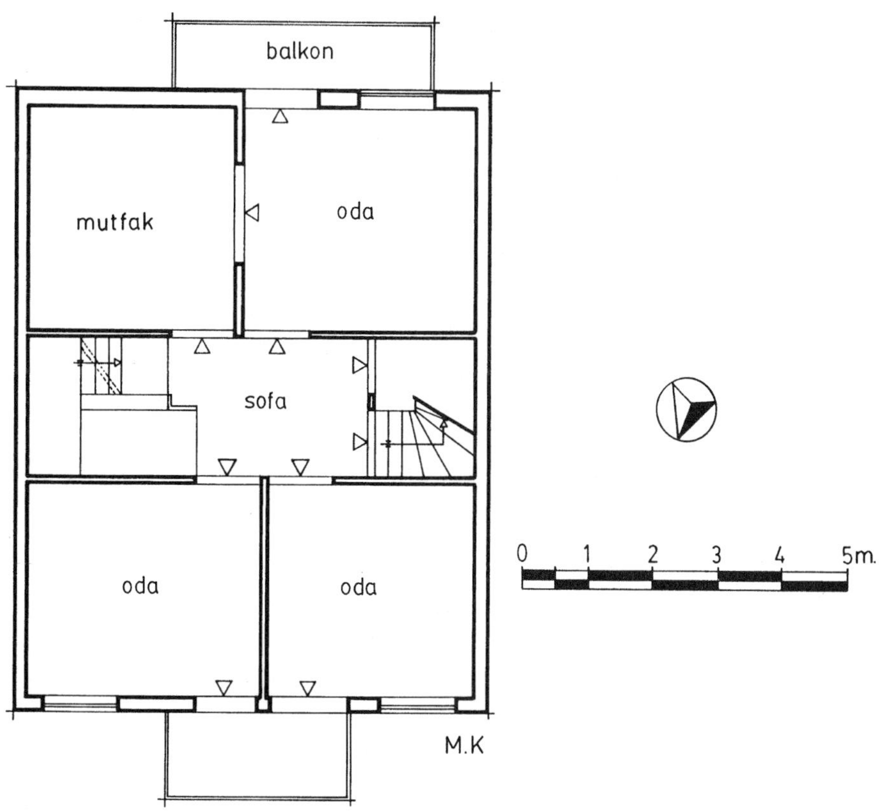

Fig. 5.12. The house of Sabit Appan, upper floor

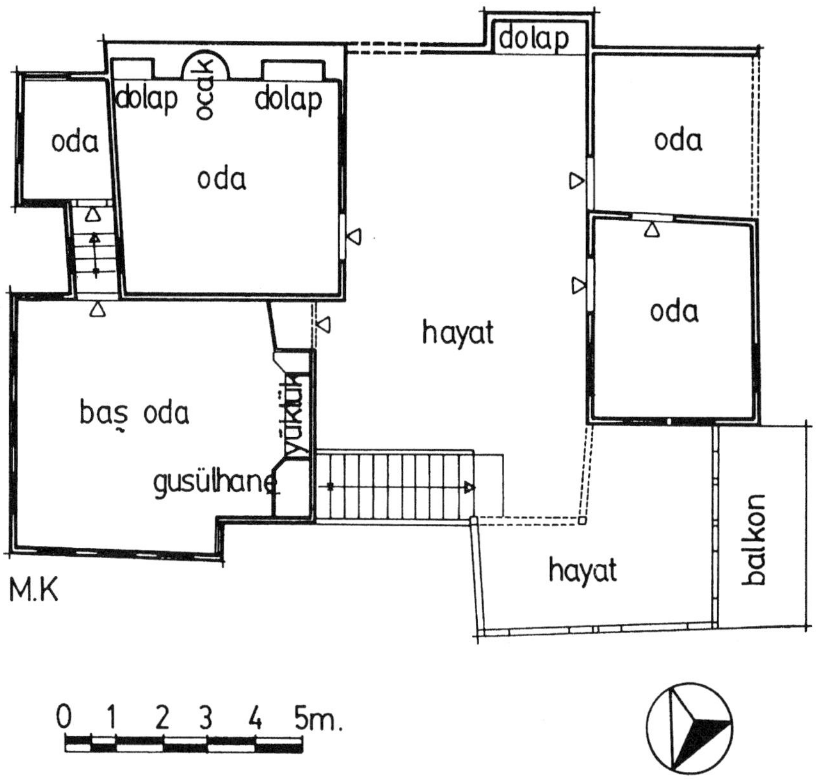

Fig. 5.13. The house of Bayraktar Ağa, upper floor

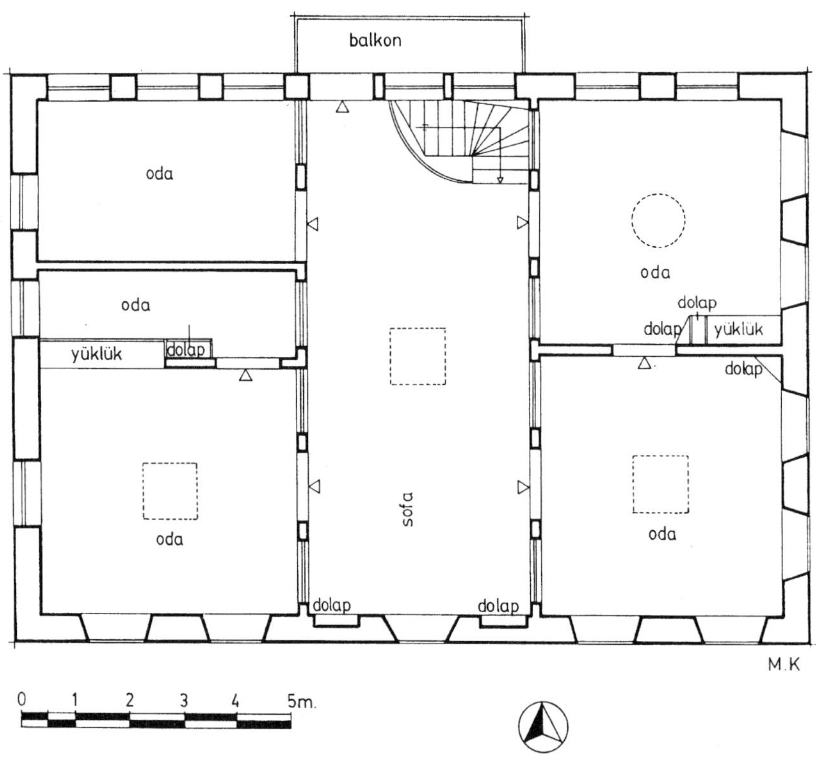

Fig. 5.14. The house of Hattatlar, upper floor

6: THE OLD HOUSES OF BALABAN

Prof. Dr. Bekir Deniz
Ege University, Izmir

Balaban is a town in the province of Malatya. It is 15 km. from Darende and 80 km. from Malatya on the Kayseri-Malatya road.[1] It occupies a position in the Upper Euphrates river-basin of eastern Anatolia, one side of which has a precipitous drop, while the other three sides are on level ground. According to the statements of elderly residents, the city was originally founded at some unknown date at Teknece, to the north-east of today's town; only later did it move to its present location.[2]

In the sources Balaban is also known as Gerimter.[3] Local tradition states that the town had been settled by someone called Balaban Bey, who allegedly lived in the 14th century, at a time when people were still living a nomadic lifestyle, and it is from him that the town takes its present name.[4] We also learn from the historical sources that there was a settlement called Balaban in Malatya, which in the 1560s, during the period of Suleyman the Magnificent, consisted of a village of 43 houses in a settled community.[5]

The town of Balaban has developed round the centre, called *çarsı* (bazaar), where shopping places crowd together and provide a focus for the daily life of the town. It is also around the bazaar that the houses of the town cluster, with the road through the bazaar meeting the Malatya-Kayseri highway at a T-junction.

The houses of Balaban present so compact an appearance that it seems at first sight as though they are built on top of one another (pl.6.1). They huddle together on both sides of the streets, which are long, narrow and winding, as well as surfaced with rough cobblestones. Down the centre, or to one side of each street, there is a small gutter to take the rain from the roofs. The projecting eaves of houses, together with balconies and bays, also provide protection for pedestrians in wet weather and give cooling shade in summer.

Sometimes, the upper storeys of houses project competely across the street, creating a kind of passageway or tunnel (pl.6.2). These passageways are called *selamlık* (meeting places) by the locals, and in a number of instances actually form the entrances to extensive cul-de-sacs, giving the impression that one is in fact entering a large courtyard. These entrances are also called *selamlık* by the local people since they meet and greet each other here as they go in and out (pl.6.3).

The houses in Balaban are built either on the street or set back from it. Those houses which actually front onto the street naturally follow its winding path. Others, however, by being set forward or back, create unexpected corners. Houses on two sides of the street may belong to the same person or to two related people, and may actually be joined to each other at first-floor level by a bridge called *geçme* by the local people. Interestingly, this may also occur where the neighbours involved are not related (pl.6.4-5).

Balaban was settled in a large and flat area. In spite of this, the houses give the impression of people snuggling up to one another. For instance, the roof of one house becomes the balcony or terrace of another. So it is possible to go all round the village by jumping from one roof to other. The fact that houses are joined together by bridges or by *selamlık* passageways shows that relationships within neighbourhoods are very sound[6] (pl.6.7).

Fountains are used communally in Balaban as in other towns of Anatolia. They are set into the walls of houses in places near to the city centre (pl.6.6). Today they have been built both in the bazaar and in more outlying quarters, and since the 1960s in houses and courtyards.

In houses fronting onto the street there are no outer courtyards. Instead, in such houses, after one has gone through the entrance, one finds a central courtyard, and it is around this that ground floor rooms and places such as the stable and storerooms are arranged. Here too in one of the corners there is usually a fireplace with a chimney-breast and an oven (*tandır*). This type of courtyard, which is invisible from outside and where daily tasks take place, is called *örtmelik* (enclosed) by the local people.

In addition to these a second type of house exists in which there is instead an outer courtyard which fronts onto the street but is surrounded by high walls. In these, features such as the barn, stable, oven, fireplace, toilet, etc. can be seen in the courtyard if one looks through the (usually) two-leaved wooden door that leads inside from the street (pl.6.8).

The materials from which Balaban houses are constructed are principally adobe and wood.[7] Generally, houses are two-storeyed, and it is onto a stone foundation some 40-50 cm high that the 70-80 cm thick adobe walls are built. The durability of the adobe is increased by inserting wooden cross-timbers within the adobe, which is made in the *yığma* (heaping) technique.

The first floors of houses in Balaban are built in *çatma* technique. In this, known locally as *ahşap çatma-çatkı*, wooden posts are nailed diagonally between corner uprights. The spaces in between the wooden frame thus formed are then filled with adobe. Even if the ground and first floor levels of the house are built in *yığma* (heaping) technique, the *çatma* technique is still used for elements such as bay windows (*cumba*) in order to be lighter (pl.6.9). Finally, the actual walls are plastered on the outside with red mud mixed with straw brought from a place called Teknece. The inside surface, in contrast, is whitewashed with a substance named *cila* brought from the same place.

There are few windows on the ground floor of Balaban houses. Those that do exist are small. For large windows one has to look at first-floor level, and these are especially large in houses built since the 1950s. There are generally two or three apertures on bay windows (*cumba*). In the older houses the frame is wooden, in the newer ones metal.

Generally, every house in Balaban has a first-floor bay window, usually above the entrance door at the front of the house. Such bays are in fact a kind of decoration for Balaban houses. As one might expect, the actual windows on the front of the bay are generally larger than those on the sides, though there are numerous instances where the front of the bay has no apertures at all, and where windows exist only at the side (pl.6.9). For the most part windows are covered with wooden shutters called *kepenk*.

Balaban houses do not have balconies as such, especially where the building overlooks the street. In this kind of house the roof of the stable and storeroom on the ground floor, which project beyond the rooms on the first floor, is used as a balcony, or the roof of a neighbouring house serves the same purpose. Here is a place that can be used either for sitting or for exercise. If needed, the space can have a more functional aspect. It can be used as a work-area: food is dried here for winter or people sleep on it in hot weather. Sometimes, there is also a one-roomed 'penthouse' called *örtmelik üstü* constructed on the roof (pl.6.1). In contrast, houses that incorporate an *eyvan* (a room-like space enclosed on three sides but open on one - often the side facing the courtyard), use this as a balcony (pl.6.8).

To form the flat roofs of houses wooden beams are placed side by side and lengthwise on the wall. Rush or reed mats are then laid on the beams to form a continuous flat surface. Onto this in turn is placed a thick mixture of mud mixed with straw. Finally a mineralised soil called *çorak* from the locality is placed on top, which is then compressed with a cylindrical stone called a *yuvarlak*. Parapets raised to a height of 40-50 cm. are added to the edges of some roofs. They are constructed out of dressed or naturally regular stone which is then plastered over with mud (pl.6.1).

There are two basic house-types found in Balaban. These are called *örtmelikli* (enclosed) and *eyvanlı* (having an outward-facing open room). Of the two *örtmelikli* houses are more common, since their arrangement seems to allow a greater degree of utility and is appropriate to the traditional life-style of the people. In this kind of house, after going through the street-door, one enters a forecourt, called *havlu* by the locals, which has a winter room off it; beyond is a generally square courtyard in the middle of the house. Around this on the ground floor are grouped rooms such as the stable, storeroom, toilet, oven and fireplace (*ocak*). From here too a staircase leads to the first floor. This part, which we can call the inner courtyard, is *örtmelik* (enclosed), and thus this kind of house is called *örtmelikli* (fig.6.1, 2). *Örtmelikli* houses are divided into two groups in terms of the locations of the rooms. In the first group there is a stable (*ahır*), storeroom (*samanlık*), often a granary or service room (*zahralık*) and a winter room on the ground floor (fig.6.1). The stairs to the upper floor of the *örtmelik* are wooden and here, on the first floor, we find rooms such as the *yazlık odalar* (summer rooms), *misafir odası* (guest room), *odunluk* (storeroom) and sometimes a second *zahra odası* (granary) (fig.6.2).

In the second group of *örtmelikli* houses the interior courtyard dominates to a greater extent. As before entry from the street through a double wooden door set in a high surounding wall brings one into a forecourt (*havlu*) beyond which is the inner court, around which are ranged the stable, storeroom and granary. From here, one climbs the wooden stairs built against one of the walls to the first floor (fig.6.4). On this upper floor are one or two rooms. One of them is used for guests, the other serves as a living room and bedroom. The surrounding parts of the courtyard on this level are used as a balcony (fig.6.3, pl.6.10).

In front of the second type of buildings, known as *eyvanlı* houses (houses with a room open on one side), there is a courtyard like the forecourt of *örtmelikli* houses, and likewise it is here that one finds things like the stable, storeroom, toilet, and fireplace. However, instead of an inner courtyard one finds an interior *sofa* (hallway) on both the ground and upper floors of these houses. On the ground floor the rectangular shaped *sofa* is called the *salon* and has rooms arranged on two sides of it. There are generally two rooms; one is the *misafir odası* (guest room), the other the *kahve odası* (coffee room, sometimes called *kahve ocaği*). The *misafir odası* is only for guests. However, the *kahve odası* is where one lives in winter and prepares coffee for guests at the fireplace which it contains. (fig.6.6).

The interior *sofa* plan is seen again on the first floor. Climbing the wooden stairs outside one finds an *eyvan* and a long corridor called the *salon* off which two rooms lead. Without going into further detail, these kinds of houses are called *eyvanlı* houses (fig.6.5).

The ground and upper floors of houses in Balaban have different functions, which change according to the house type. In the case of *örtmelikli* houses there is a fireplace built into the main wall of the house on the ground floor. There are also fewer windows on this floor, and those that do exist are small. The rooms on this level are warm since daily tasks such as cooking and heating water take place here, and it is for this reason that this area is used for living space in winter. In addition, there is a large closet for bedding in one of the walls. The main official living space on the other hand is upstairs. Here two or three rooms are generally situated above the winter room and *havlu* (forecourt) of the ground floor. One of them is a granary (*zahralık*); the other one is the summer living room and guest room. In front of these rooms there is a balcony called *dam üstü* (roof) by the local people. This balcony is above the stable and barn on the ground floor and serves as a workshop (fig.6.2).

In *eyvanlı* houses, as well as a coffee room and living room, the ground floor has a guest room at the end of the *sofa/salon*. This guest room is more imposing than the coffee room and has a large closet for bedding in one of the walls as well as small winged cupboards called *taka*, which are used for displaying small things such as ornaments (fig.6.6). On the upper floor is often another guest room and the living room. Here one generally finds a divan made of mud-brick, especially under the windows (fig.6.5).

In Balaban houses, and especially in the guest rooms, one very often finds that the floor at the entrance is lower than that in the rest of the room. This lower part, called *aralık*, is separated from the rest of the room by three Bursa-style arches called *gantarma*, made of wood and supported by wooden posts. The inner, raised, part of the room has three sections. The middle is open space and is intended for moving about; the other two are for sitting, and where they are located next to windows they are fitted with a divan ornamented with cushions and covers. Here too one finds the small ornamented wooden *taka* cupboards on the walls, while in the corner a niche, called a *çıralık* or *lambalık* and made of wood or plaster, is often to be seen (fig.6.3).

In Balaban houses, the toilet (*hela*) is located in the courtyard, and in houses without a courtyard it is next to the entrance on the ground floor. The bathroom is small and is situated next to the winter room on the ground floor or among the rooms on the first floor. Some are made in the form of a wooden cupboard (fig.6.1).

Balaban houses are not particularly imposing when looked at from outside, but their asymmetric arrangement gives a pleasing appearance to the houses in that they are irregular and follow no set pattern. However, bay windows seen on very many houses give variety to the buildings. For instance, the wooden mullions of today's windows contrast with the adobe architecture. Internally, on the other hand, *gantarmalı* (arched) cupboards, and niches made of wood and plaster represent individualising elements of ornamentation.[8]

Evaluation

In Balaban and its surroundings the construction material especially of village houses is stone in the foundations and adobe and wood for the main walls. In house architecture such adobe is seen widely in Darende, Malatya, the surroundings of old Malatya and from Harput (Elazığ) in the east westwards towards Diyarbakır, Divriği and Sivas by way of Hekimhan, Arapkir (Malatya), and Kemaliye (Erzincan). In all the above-mentioned areas, adobe is used employing the *yığma* (heaping) technique in the main walls of buildings, or spaces in wooden frames are filled with adobe and the outer surface covered with mud, just as in Balaban.[9]

A courtyard surrounded by high walls is generally found in front of buildings in traditional Anatolian-Turkish houses. Apart from this, it is very usual for the roof of the ground floor, where it projects in front of the upper storey, to be used as a veranda or workshop, especially in Diyarbakır, Siirt, Bitlis, Mardin and villages neighbouring Izmir, Manisa, Aydın, and Denizli.[10] Similar usage is also to be found in the districts around Balaban, in villages between Darende and Malatya, and in old Arapkir. As the backs of most of the houses in the above-mentioned towns are built against a mountain slope, it is normal that a *dam üstü* (a balcony formed from the roof of a neighbouring house) occurs. However, it is interesting to have such architecture in Balaban houses, which are built on the flat.

The houses of Balaban, built in such an interdependent fashion, are not found anywhere else in the region of Malatya. This architecture looks in fact as if it is unique to Balaban. Similar stone architecture can be found only in places such as Siirt and Mardin, and one is tempted to see this kind of architecture in these towns as influenced by the Arab house architecture in neighbouring countries.[11]

The location of windows in Balaban houses is the same as in the whole of Anatolia, but their shape is different. In Malatya, for instance, one finds the window shape called *gantarmalı pencere* (arched windows) with two or three interconnected arches further enhanced by the tiles that cover them. They may in fact originate from eastern Anatolia. Such arches, however, are not seen in the windows of Balaban but they do occur in the cupboards called *taka*.[12]

In the houses of Malatya and Darende the *sofa* (hallway) and *gezemek* (area for exercise), known as *köşk* (pavilions), are important elements of house design. In Balaban houses, on the other hand, the *sofa* is not so important. Instead the interior courtyard and the roofs of neighbouring houses serve similar functions (pl.6.1). One finds similar examples also in village houses between Malatya and Balaban and in old Arapkir houses. However, it is possible to come across them also in the houses of Siirt, Bitlis, Mardin, Urfa, Adıyaman and in the village houses of Izmir, Manisa, Aydın, Denizli, and Uşak. In these regions the *sofa* is often known as *çardak* and *hayat*, and the *dam üstü* as *dam başı* (top roof).[13]

The plans of Balaban houses have an interesting characteristic. In the surroundings of Darende, Malatya and Elazığ houses with an exterior *sofa* (*dış sofalı*) and interior *sofa* (*iç sofalı*), houses where the ground floor entrance is shaped like an *eyvan,* are widespread.[14] In Balaban, in contrast, one finds instead houses where the first floor entrance is shaped like an *eyvan* or there is an interior courtyard known as *örtmelik*. Something similar can also be seen in the stone-built houses of Niğde, Kayseri, Sivas, Diyarbakır, Siirt, Bitlis, Mardin and Adıyaman. Houses with this kind of interior courtyard are also to be found in Diyarbakır (Emlak Kredi Bankası 1955; Erginbaş 1953; Togay 1947; Tuncer 1971; Üçler 1942; Sözen 1971; Çetinor 1981), Urfa (Körükçüoğlu 1984; Akkoyunlu 1989), Mardin (Sayılan 1987) and Bergama (Izmir), but there are important differences between the these houses and the *örtmelikli* houses of Balaban.

The position and arrangement of rooms in Balaban houses resembles mostly those in Darende (Deniz 1978: 44-50; Sözen 1976: 19, n.3; Erdim 1975) and Malatya, which have a four-roomed scheme on the ground and upper floors of houses with interior *sofa*. Balaban houses, though, do not have the four-room plan. Instead, one finds two or three rooms upstairs, and each room is fitted with a large closet for bedding, as in Malatya houses, and a fireplace in each room on the ground floor. Also in common with Malatya houses is the small *kahve ocağı* (coffee room), especially in those built before 1950. This characteristic, also seen in village houses of Malatya and Elazığ, also occurs in the houses of Kemaliye (Erzincan) (fig.6.6).

The most imposing place in Balaban houses, as in most Anatolian houses, is the guest room (*başoda*-main room) which frequently has a projecting bay and at its entrance a *pabuçluk* (a place by the door where shoes are left on entering). This area is lower than the floor level of the rest of the room and is separated from it with two or three arches supported by posts. This feature is also seen in the village houses of Cafana, Gözene in Malatya and indicates a close similarity with the traditional Anatolian house.

There is little or no external ornamentation to Balaban houses, like those in other cities of Anatolia, though balconies, bay windows and window balustrades do provide variety to the façade. On the other hand, passageways over the streets known as *selamlık*, the entrances these can create for cul-de-sacs, and the bridges connecting the houses of close relatives give a distinct character to Balaban houses, and while there are parallels in such towns as Adıyaman, Urfa, Mardin, Diyarbakır, Niğde, Kayseri and Aksaray, none of them is as picturesque or imposing as Balaban.

Generally, the interior parts of Balaban houses are not elaborately ornamented: niches (*çıralık, lambalık*) placed in one of the corners of a room, and the wooden ceilings of bay windows give the impression of ornamental originality. Significantly, though, what is missing from Balaban houses is the wall decoration seen, for instance, in some Malatya and Anatolian houses.[15]

Conclusion

Compared to more normative Anatolian-Turkish traditional houses, those of Balaban, with their adobe construction and characteristic layouts, provide an interesting contrast, which is heightened by the idiosyncratic meandering of the streets and interconnection of structures. In some respects indeed one is reminded of the house-architecture of southeast Anatolia and Arabic countries such as Syria or Iran. Consequently, Balaban houses provide a distinctive environment for living, one that is without parallel anywhere in the vicinity, from Malatya and Darende to distant cities like Elazığ and Sivas. Among traditional Ottoman houses they have a beauty all their own, and some astonishing attributes.

Bibliography

Acun, H. 1988: 'Sivas Çevresi Tarihi Eserlerinin Listesi ve Turistik Değerleri', *Vakıflar Dergisi* 20 (Ankara): 183-220.

Akkoyunlu, Z. 1989: *Geleneksel Urfa Evlerinin Geleneksel Özellikleri*. Ankara.

Alper, B. 1985: 'Kemaliye Evlerinde Metal İşçiliği', *IV Ulusal El Sanatları Sempozyumu Bildirileri, 21-24 Nov. 1984*. Izmir: 1-3.

---- 1987: 'Yok Olan Bir Kültür Mirası Kemaliye Çarşı Bölgesi', *TAÇ* 2 (Nov.): 21-4.

Çetinor, B. 1981: 'Diyarbakır Evleri', *İlgi*: 12-20.

Çoban, B. 1976: 'Kerkük Evlerinin Özellikleri', *TFAD* (18 Nov.): 78-9.

Deniz, B. 1978: *Malatya, Darende ve Balaban Türk Ev Mimarisi* (Masters thesis, History of Art Dept., Ankara Univ.). Ankara.

---- 1980: 'Malatya Türk Ev Mimarisinin Ana Hatları', *MTRE Bülteni* 11-12: 19-23.

---- 1991: 'Balaban Evleri', *Fırat Havzası Sanat Tarihi Sempozyumu, 21-22 May 1987*. Elazığ: 105-30.

---- 1992: 'Manisa Yöresi Köy Ev Mimarisi', *Arkeoloji-Sanat Tarihi Dergisi* 6. Izmir: 17-46.

Emlak Kredi Bankası 1955: *Diyarbakır Evleri*. Emlak Kredi Bankası Yayını, Ankara.

Erdim, M. 1975: 'Adıyaman'dan Bir Kerpiç Ev', *O.D.T.Ü. Mimarlık Fakültesi Dergisi* 5 (Bahar): 69-77.

Erginbaş, D. 1953: *Diyarbakır Evleri*. Istanbul.

Erinç, M. 1987: 'Türkiye'de Vernaküler Kerpiç Mimarisi', *TAÇ, Türkiye Anıt Çevre Turizm Değerlerini Koruma Vakfı Yayını* 2 (Nov.): 36-40.

Körükçüoğlu, A.C. 1984: 'Urfa Evleri', *Türkiyemiz*, (Oct.): 25-31.

Kuban, D. 1966: 'Türkiye'de Malzeme Koşullarına Bağlı Geleneksel Konut Mimarisi Üzerine Bazı Gözlemler', *Mimarlık* 36: 15-20.

Küçükkömürcü, A.M. 1977: 'Balaban'da Bir Ev', I. *Uluslararası Türk Folklor Kongresi Bildirileri, Etnoğrafya* 5: 182-9.

Saatçi, S. 1983: 'Kerkük Yöresi Halk Mimarisinden Örnekler', *II. Milletlerarası Türk Folklor Kongresi Bildirileri* 5: 201-16.

Sakaoğlu, N. 1978: *Divriği'de Ev Mimarisi*. Istanbul.

Sayılan, F. 1987: 'Mardin Evleri', *Türkiyemiz*: 7-14.

Sözen, M. 1971: *Diyarbakır'da Türk Mimarisi*. Istanbul: 222-40.

---- 1976: 'Doğu Anadolu'da İlginç Bir Yerleşme Balaban ve Anıtları', *MTRE Bülteni*, I.T.Ü. Mimarlık Fakültesi, Mimarlık Tarihi ve Restorasyon Enstitüsü Yayını 2: 19-22.

Sümer, F. 1972: *Oğuzlar (Türkmenler) Tarihleri*. Boy Teşkilatı, Destanları. Ankara.

Togay, H. 1947: 'Diyarbakır Evleri', *Arkitekt* 16. Istanbul: 165-9, 191.

Tuncer, O. 1971: 'Diyarbakır Evleri', *Önasya* 6. Ankara: 10-11.

Türkay, C. 1979: *Başbakanlık Arşiv Belgelerine Göre Osmanlı İmparatorluğu'nda Oymak, Aşiret ve Cemaatler*. Istanbul.

Üçler, R. 1942: 'Diyarbakır Evlerinin Mimari Bakımdan Tetkiki', *Bayındırlık Dergisi*. 10-11.

Yıldız, M. 1965: 'Harput Konakları ve Evleri', *Yeni Fırat Dergisi* 3, Elazığ: 23-76.

Yinanç, R., Elibüyük, M. 1983: *Kanunî Devri Malatya Tahrir Defteri (1560)*. Ankara.

Explanation of terms used in the plans:

Ahır:	Stables
Aralık:	Lower room
Dam üstü:	Roof top
Eyvan:	Room open along one side
Havlu:	Court
Kahve ocağı:	Coffee room
Misafir odası:	Guest room
Ocak:	Fireplace
Oda:	Room
Odunluk:	Wood-store
Örtmelik:	Veranda
Salon:	Central room
Samanlık:	Straw-store
Zahralık:	Granary/food-store

---

[1] We began to research Balaban houses in 1978 with the master's thesis, *Malatya, Darende and Balaban Houses* (Deniz 1978) We set out some of our ideas in the symposium held by Fırat Üniversitesi, 21-22 May 1987 (Deniz 1991). The present paper is an expanded version of this.

[2] On Balaban houses see Sözen 1976: 19-22; Küçükkömürcü 1977: 182-9.

[3] See, İdare Taksimatı-1936, T.C. Dahiliye Vekaleti Vilayetler İdaresi Umum Müdürlüğü Yayını, Ankara, 1936: 42, 127. Sözen 1976: 19.

[4] According to the information given on 22.10.1977 by Mr. Hamit Çiftçi, a member of the town council in Balaban. Sözen 1976: 19, n.4; Küçükkömürcü. 1977: 182.

It is not known who Balaban Bey was. There was a tribe called Balabanlu among the Turkish tribes recorded in the historical sources. It is said that 'The Balabanlu tribe was dependent on the Şamlu tribe, one of the Turkoman tribes which had an important role in the settlement of the Safavid state and this tribe came into being through the main nomad families such as Beğ-dili, İnallu, Hüdâbendelu (Harbendelu), Avcı, Balabanlu, Biçerlu, Arabgirlu and Kerametlu' (Sümer 1972: 152-403). On the same subject see, Turkay 1979; Turkay (1979: 53) states that 'The Balabanlı (Balabanlu) (Balabanlar) inhabit Edirne, Adana, Kars'ı Maraş Sancağı, Malatya, Selmanlı-i Kebir Kazası (Konya Sancağı), Tırhala Sancağı, Yenişehir Sancağı (Tırhala), Sivas, Karaman, Rakka, Harpıt (Harput) Sancağı, Zağra-i Cedid Kazası (Çirmen Sancağı), Hezargrad Kazası, (Niğbolu Sancağı)'. Turkay (1979: 22) also states: 'Balaban, Balabanlar, Balabanlı (Balabanlu), Balabanlı Ekrâdi'nın Yörükân taifesinden olduğunu belirterek, Bozkoyunlu Aşiretine tabi olan Balabanlı Cemâatı, Malatya Kazası'ndan Gözene Derbendi kurbünde sakin idi.' (The Balaban Kurds come from the tribe of Yörük nomads. The Balabanlı community is dependent on the Bozkuyunlu tribe and lives in Gözene Derbendi in Malatya). The aforementioned tribe comes mainly from Iranian yörük nomads and they are from Konya, they settle and then move on. Their settlement places are Malatya Sancağı, Selmanlu-i Kebir Kazası (Konya Sancağı, Tırhala Sancağı, Erzurum, Kars, Çıldır Eyaletleri, Yenişehir Kazası (Tırhala Sancağı), Sivas, Karaman Dırama Kazası (Paşa Sancağı), Harpıt Kazası (Diyarbakır Eyaleti), Edirne Kazası, Adana, Zağra-i Cedid Kazası (Çirmen Sancağı), Karahisar-ı Şarkî Sancağı, Rakka, Ruha (Urfa) Sancağı, Filibe Kazası (Paşa Sancağı), Sögüd Kazası, Ereğli Kazası (Vize Sancağı), Hezârgrad Kazası (Niğbolu Sancağı), Karin-âbâd Kazası (Silistre Sancağı), Günyüzü Kazası (Kırşehir Sancağı).

Today, there are Balaban or Balabanlı villages also in Ödemiş (Izmir) and Ayvacık (Çanakkale) apart from those mentioned above. On the other hand, there is still a village named Gözene in Akçadağ (Malatya). We do not know whether the inhabitants of these villages come from the Balabanlı tribe and are related to those in Balaban.

[5] The name Balaban is mentioned in *Malatya Tahrir Defteri* dated 1560, but we do not know whether the Balaban in the *Defter* is the same as the one being discussed here (Yinanç, Elibüyük: 24). Based on a source in his study, Sözen (1976: n.4) points out that 'the population of Balaban increased to 750 dwellings and after a while decreased to 327'.

[6] Villagers explain that 'the reason for building the houses so close to each other is because of brigands and thieves. So the city was not able to develop'. Furthermore, the town was enclosed and had three large gates which were closed at night, so that nobody could enter late. The rear of the city was steeply sloping, so could be very easily defended from raids (according to the oral information given by Mr. Hamit Çiftçi and Mr. Mehmed Çiftçi from Balaban on 22.10.1977).

[7] On the characteristics of adobe and adobe architecture in Balaban see Kuban 1966: 15-20; Erinç 1987: 36-40.

[8] On gantarmalı kemer see Deniz 1978: 21, 43; Deniz (1980).

[9] For the house architecture of the places mentioned see, Deniz 1978, Deniz (1980); Yıldız 1965: 23-76; Sakaoğlu 1978; Acun 1988: 183-220; Alper 1985, 1987; Erdim 1975: 69-77.

[10] On the village houses of Manisa see Deniz 1992.

[11] Çoban 1976; Saatçi 1983.

[12] For further details see Deniz (1980).

[13] Deniz 1992.

[14] Deniz 1978: 41-2; Deniz (1980).

[15] On the illustrated houses of Malatya see Deniz (1980): 23, n.7.

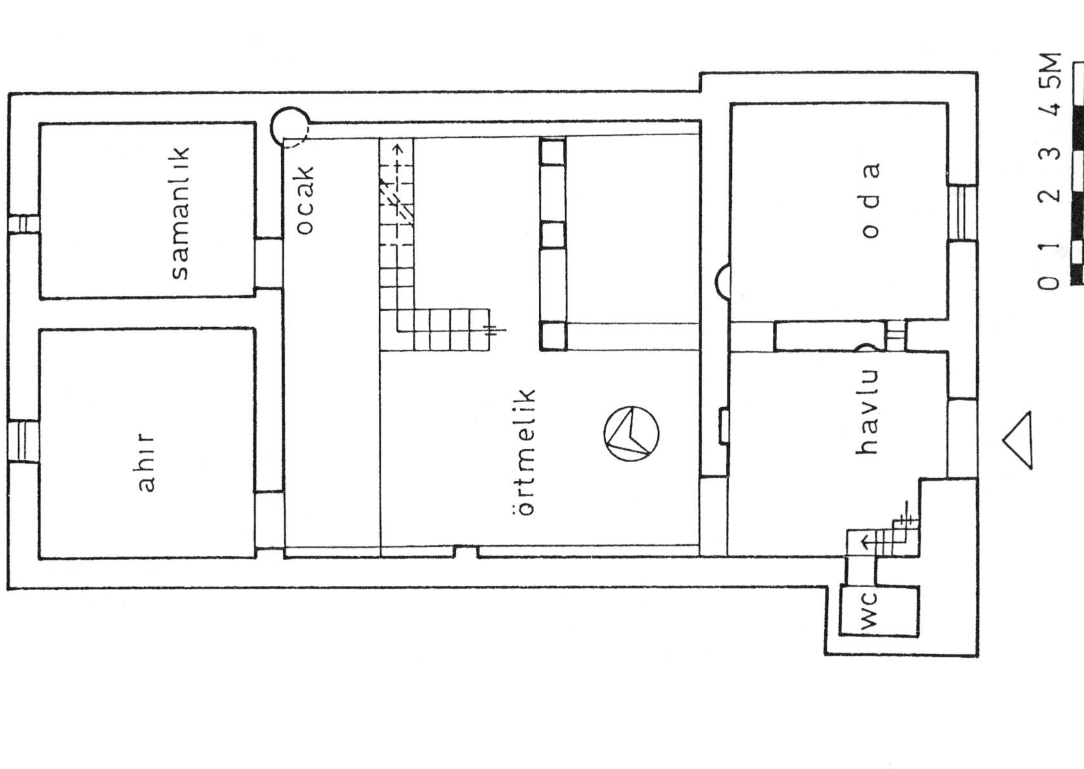

Fig. 6.1. The house of Abdurrahman Kılıçer, ground floor

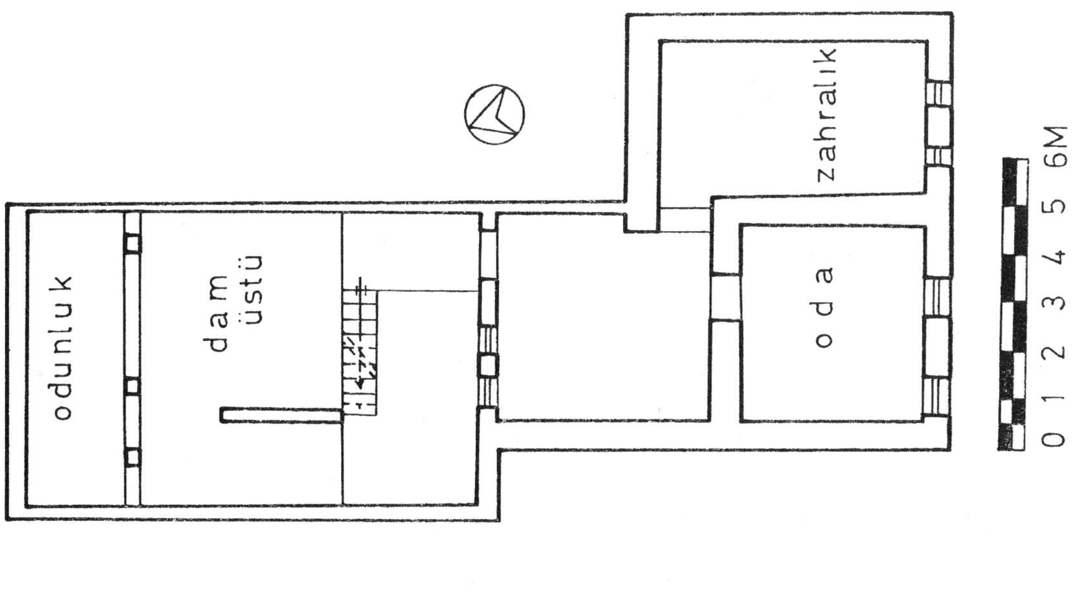

Fig. 6.2. The house of Abdurrahman Kılıçer, first floor

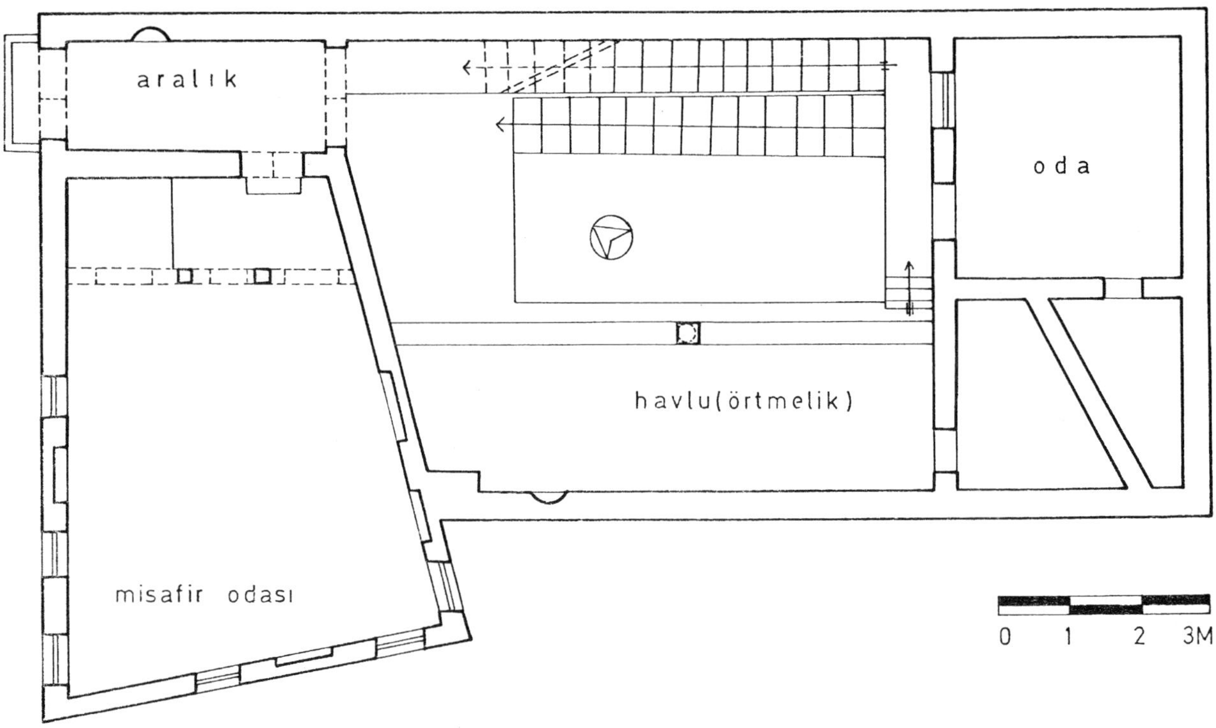

Fig. 6.3. The house of Hassan Göncü, first floor

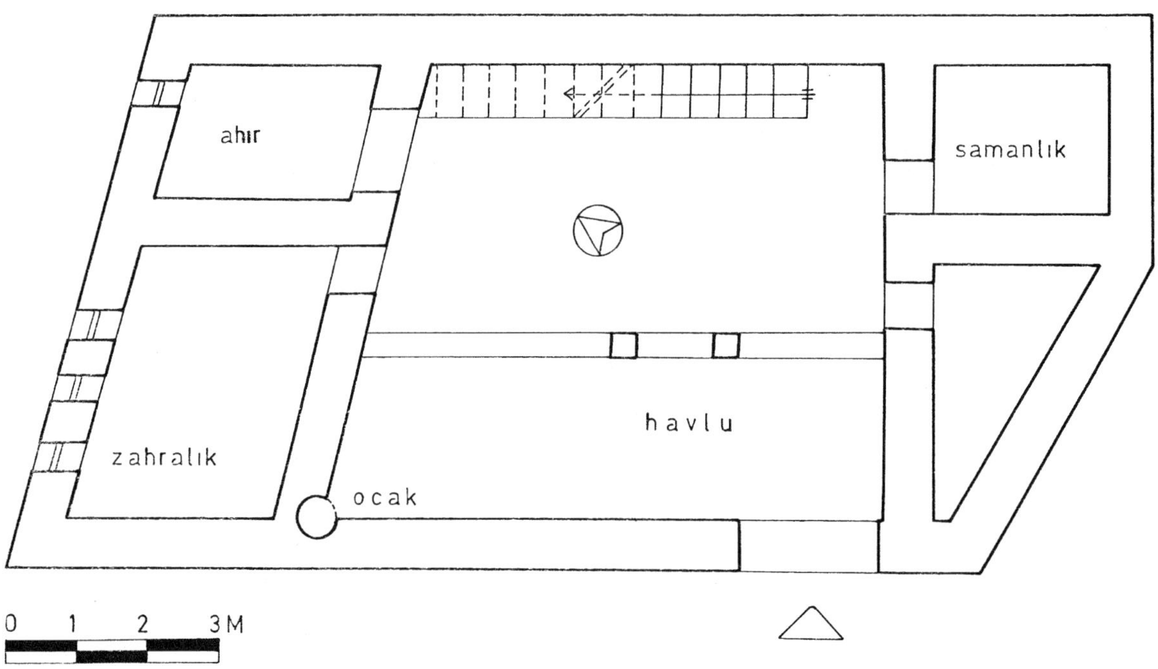

Fig. 6.4. The house of Hassan Göncü, ground floor

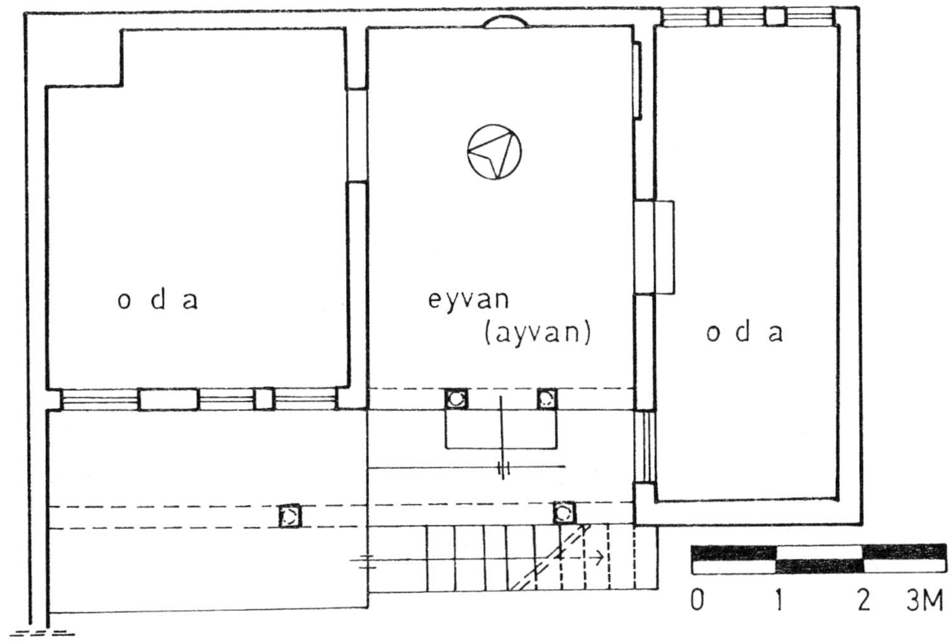

Fig. 6.5. The house of Yusuf Sevinç, first floor

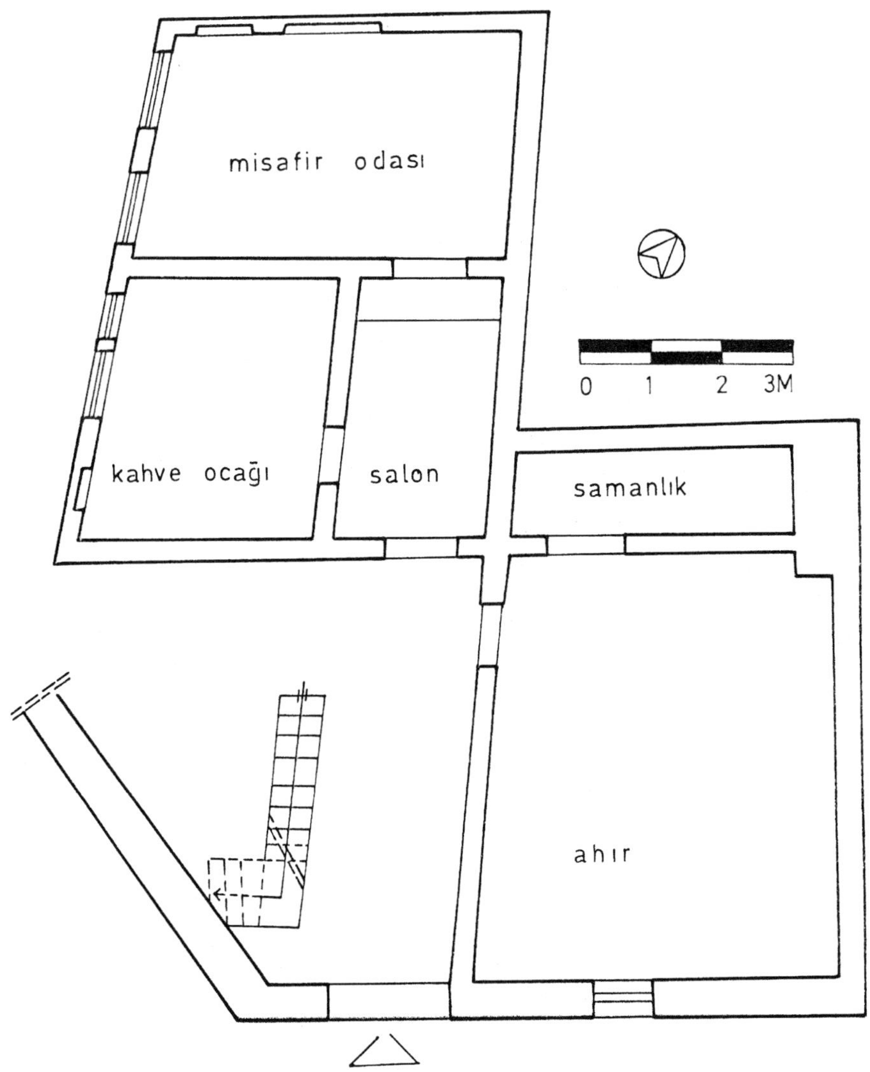

Fig. 6.6. The house of Yusuf Sevinç, ground floor

7: THE ARCHITECTURE OF BOYABAT VILLAGE HOUSES

Asst. Prof. Halit Çal
Gazi University, Ankara

Among architectural structures houses are arguably the most difficult to study. Their sheer number, when compared to other architectural structures, in addition to the fact that they are private property, makes it difficult to study them in a quantity proportionate to the total stock. A qualitative study of Turkish houses on the other hand has been going on ever since the concept of Turkish art was recognised. In this period typological analyses have been made, the philosophical basis of the concept of the Turkish house has been discussed and various views have been propounded about the role of the *oda* (room) and *sofa* (hall) in the form and evolution of houses, as well as the effects of geography and economics upon these, and the relationship of the Turkish house to the local traditions of central Asia and Anatolia.

The general principles governing the physical form and main features of Turkish houses have been extensively investigated, though we have to admit that the picture that has emerged may change as further discoveries are made. However, the studies that have already been undertaken are inevitably based on a sampling method. The exact number of urban houses in Turkey which can be defined as old or traditional is not known. The figure is estimated to be about 20,000. All the features of these houses are not known in detail and, were such a project of investigation undertaken, we might well be confronted by a rather different picture from the one we currently have.

A cause for concern is that these traditional houses are disappearing at a steadily increasing rate. Turkey is experiencing a shift away from the agricultural community to the industrial conurbation, and in this process houses are one of the first physical features to disappear. In other words, these houses are crumbling away before we have an opportunity to record those features they possess which may be different from the ones we already know about.

It should be noted that village houses have often not figured in such investigations. In a situation where it has been impossible to undertake a comprehensive study of urban houses, the village houses have all too frequently been relegated to a minor position - if they have figured at all - in generalised analyses of Turkish houses. However, it is important that village houses should also be taken into consideration in any study of the evolution of Turkish houses. For instance, in order to obtain reliable knowledge about Turkish houses in general, we need to know whether there is a difference between an urban house and a village house in the same region, and whether there exist developmental influences flowing from village to town or vice versa.

Research on village houses is so meagre as to be virtually non-existent; yet it is not possible to get answers concerning their relationship to one another unless studies on village houses in all the regions of Turkey are carried out, even if merely at the level of sampling. In this study, we will be presenting the general features of the houses in Boyabat, a country region in the province of Sinop. The plans of only 5 houses are presented here; however, the generalisations made are based on the study of many more houses.

The villages of Boyabat can be categorised into two groups: as lowland villages, where agriculture makes use of irrigation, and as upland villages set in a woodland environment, where agriculture without irrigation and cattle-breeding predominate. Bearing in mind that the difference in economic conditions may have an influence on the houses, the examples have been chosen from both groups of villages.

Design Features of the Village Houses

Almost all the houses under consideration are two-storeyed. However, a slightly different situation is seen compared to what is generally understood about a two-storeyed house. That is, the living-quarters are supported by pillars and the back of the ground floor is designed as a stable, while the front is open and looks like an extension - albeit under cover - of the courtyard, a place where agricultural tools like the plough, threshing machine and ox-cart are kept. In a corner of this space is the staircase (*basaklık*) going up to the floor above. No household work is done in this area. The stable at the rear of the ground floor is formed by filling with stone the space between the pillars supporting the first floor. In the upland villages the stable walls are also found built of wood. The stable is fitted with only one or two very small windows, and is located under one of the rooms above so that heating can also be provided for that room.

Two different arrangements are seen at first floor level, producing living quarters consisting of either a single room or a double room. In the single-room houses - locally called 'single oil-lamp houses' - the staircase leads directly into the *sofa*/hall. This is a fairly large roofed-over area in front of the *oda*/room bounded by one metre high wooden walls on three sides, which are otherwise open to the air. A projection called the 'summer house' (*yazlık*) or 'palace' (*saray*) is located on the side facing the courtyard. Here, the floor level is higher than the other areas. People sit, eat and even sleep in this 'summer house' (pl.7.1). Beside the *oda*/room runs a narrow corridor which serves as a WC and an area for ablutions. At its entrance is also the place where washing prior to prayer takes place, and washing-up is also done here (fig.7.1, 2). There are also single-room houses which are built using wooden logs from the ground up. These are the oldest type of houses.

The double-room design differs only in that two rooms lead off the *sofa,* part of which now forms a corridor between them (pl.7.2-3, fig.7.3-5). As before, the *sofa*/hall is accessed by the staircase (pl.7.4). In some instances there is a further extension at the rear of the rooms (fig.7.3), and here we find the WC located in one arm of it, with the other arm providing a storage area. In this way, the back walls of both rooms are also protected against rain and sun. The local expression for the area where the lavatory is found is *kol* (arm) or *gol* (goal). In other instances the WC is built as a projection to the side of one of the rooms (fig.7.4). The lavatories are in any case rather simple and built of wood.

The internal organisation of the rooms is very simple. Going through the door one usually finds a fireplace in the middle of the wall opposite, with a built-in closet on each side (fig.7.1-3). One of these is used to store bedding and quilts, and the other is used for bathing. On the side of the room facing the courtyard, there is a rather small window. The local expression for this window is *temek* (stable window). When glass is scarce, a hand-made piece of cloth like a head-scarf is used instead, the local word for which is *cember*. At night the windows are closed by using two internal shutters. On the wall of the room facing the window is a shelf set at about head-height and used for keeping pots and pans on. The local expression for this shelf is *sergen* (display cabinet). On the two sides not occupied by the entrance or fireplace is placed a divan.

Construction Stages of the Houses[1]

First of all, the area where the house is to be built is decided upon. The size of the house may vary depending on the wishes of the owner. However, generally double-room houses occupy a plot 9 x 10m in area, which is marked on the ground and local people call this 'taking the measure of the house'. There are no foundations to the houses. All the weight is carried by wooden pillars, and under each pillar is placed a stone. At this stage the holes where the stones are to be placed are marked out within the area, which is delineated by string. The average size of the stones is 60cm wide, 40cm long and 40cm high, and half of the stone is set into the ground. A durable kind of stone is used which may change from village to village.

The next stage is to erect the pillars on the stones: nine pillars are erected for a single-room house and twelve pillars are erected for a double-room house. The craftsmen use the terms of '9 pillars' and '12 pillars' to denote the size of the house. When the site is flat, the height of the pillars is between 180-220cm. If the wish is for the ground floor or stable to be not too high, the pillars are kept shorter. The minimum height for the stable is 180cm. If the site is not flat, the height of the pillars is varied to take account of the change in ground level (fig.7.6). The cross-section size of the pillars is between 20 x 20cm and 40 x 40cm, and the base of the pillars is shaped to fit the surface of the stone, the middle of which is hollowed out so that the pillar stays firmly in place. After the pillars are erected their placement is measured again and adjusted as necessary. In case there is a height difference between pillars after their erection, one of them is taken as the standard, and adjustments are made to the other pillars by adding a piece to the shorter pillars and cutting sections from those that are too large, so that in the end all the pillars are exactly the same height.

The next stage is to place the main beams (*kiriş*) on the pillars. The local expression for the beam is *ken*. The beams are of two different types for a double-room house, being 7m or 10m in length. Their horizontal cross-section measures 18 x 16cm or 18 x 18cm or 20 x 20cm. A total of 7 beams are used for a house with 12 pillars. After the beams are placed in position, further joists are placed over them at 50cm intervals. Their length varies according to the direction they will be placed in and their cross-section measurement is 7 x 10cm. The local expression for the joists is *döküntü* (extension). Wooden floorboards with a thickness of 2-5cm and width of 25cm are then nailed on these joists.

Following this is the construction of the actual rooms, which do not deviate much from a square in shape. The width of the rooms is generally 380cm, and their length 480cm. Larger dimensions are found but the ratio between length and breadth remains the same. In order to form a room of this size, planks - called *kandil* (oil-lamp) locally - 5cm thick and 25cm wide are used. The ends of these are joined to one another by mortice and tenon joints and in this way the room walls are built up. When the length of the planks falls short of that required, planks are joined in a way locally called *damaklama*. In this the two planks to be joined are cut at an angle of 45 degrees so as to fit each other, and a hole is made in both of them through which a wooden dowel is driven securing them together. The inner side of the planks is flat whereas the outside is slightly curved.

After the walls of the rooms have been formed by placing the planks in position, measurements are taken to ensure that the top of the wall is level. Following this, further joists (*döküntü*) 10cm deep and 5cm wide are nailed 50cm apart on top of the wall. The ceiling itself is formed by wooden cladding 2.5cm thick and 25cm wide. When the wooden cladding is nailed underneath the joists, it is called 'nailed' ceiling (*nallama tavan*), and when nailed above the joists, it is called a 'tongue & groove' ceiling (*lambalı tavan*). Thin battens cover the joints of the ceiling cladding. The ceiling joists of the *sofa* are left without cladding so that in the summer corn cobs may be hung on the joists to dry.

When a hipped roof is constructed on a double-room house, a beam is placed on the joists between the two rooms. A vertical strut with an average length of 160cm is fixed to the middle of this support. A beam 1m long and 25cm thick is in turn nailed horizontally on top of this strut; the local expression for this beam is *taç* (capital). The main structure of the roof is completed by fixing 10cm wide and 15cm deep ridge beams (locally called *salma*) to the *taç* at the diagonal corners. These ridge beams are supported at intervals by vertical struts which rest on the ceiling joists. Afterwards, rafters 5cm wide and 10cm deep are nailed between the ridge beams and the house walls. Wooden purlin strips measuring 7 x 2.5cm are placed on top of the rafters to provide support for the roof tiles. For single-room houses a simple saddle-roof is all that is required.

The bricks of the chimney are laid before the roof tiles are set in position. There are fireplaces in both rooms. The base of the fire-place is at floor level and there is a downwards gradient towards the back wall. The thickness of the soil layer which forms the base of the fire-place is between 50-100cm. On the ground floor, this soil layer is carried by a wooden tray that sits on a pillar.

In the attic there are a few steps which give access to the roof. These are covered by a small roof and the part which actually gives access to the roof is always kept open. The local expression for this part is *kuzgunluk* (raven's place) or *kedilik* (cat's place).

Materials used in building houses

Three types of materials are used in building Boyabat village houses: wood, stone and sun-dried brick.

Wood: This is the main construction material, always preferred for pillars, walls and cladding. The type of wood used is either yellow fir, larch or pine. The trees are cut down in winter so that they can easily dry. The actual height of the tree is of minor importance since it is cut into logs 10m long, unless a longer size is especially required, in order to avoid difficulties of transport in the forest.

Stone: The main use for stone in village houses is as supports for the pillars, which function as the main load-bearers. A second use is to form the wall between the pillars on the ground floor to create the stable.

Sun-dried Brick: This is used only for the fire-place and chimney. Sometimes, the fireplace and chimney are built using stone or mud mortar.

Traditions Related to Building a House

Before the construction work starts, a sheep is sacrificed if the owner is well-off. When the construction work is about to be completed and before the tiles are laid, a strip of wood 1.5m high is nailed to the 'raven's place' at the very top of the house and first the eldest member of the family, then the lady of the house and finally the other members of the family and the neighbours attach gifts to this. All these gifts are given to the craftsman who recites the following traditional invocation when each gift is being attached:

> Ustalar, kalfalar, üçler, yediler, kırklar; ustalar, kalfalar, pirler; üçler, yediler, kırklar, pir-i nebi, keremi Ali, pirimizin adı Habib-i Neccar Veli, ... ağamıza .... Efendiden bir hediye geldi, bereket versin.
>
> (literally translated: Craftsmen, builders, threes, sevens, forties; craftsmen, builders, patrons, threes, sevens, forties, the prophet, noble Ali, the name of our patron is Habib-i Neccar Veli, ... here is a gift to our Agha .... from the Master. ....)

Discussion

As we have shown, two types of design are used in Boyabat village houses depending on the number of rooms incorporated in them. These basic plans hold true no matter whether they are constructed on the plain or upland. For instance, apart from perhaps size there is no noticeable difference between the single-room houses in the village of Yukarı Arım and the upland village Asarcık Kayalı. The same is also the case for double-room houses. In these the *sofa*/hall is generally located at the front, but in the village of Asarcık Kayalı the hall is at the rear because of the nature of the terrain. These two types of layout are typical of the villages of Boyabat that we have studied, and as far as we have ascertained, the same style of house is also to be seen in the towns of Durağan and Taş-köprü. However, this design does not seem to be repeated in the rest of north-west Anatolia (Kafesçioğlu 1955), but it is only after further study of the houses in this region that we shall be able to say for certain whether the design-type is more wide-ranging or not. Why these two types of design have become a standard in the houses around Boyabat and how they came about is worth investigating. Before suggesting any answer to this, however, it is necesary to give some background historical information about Boyabat.

Archaeological research in the Black Sea region is less well developed than in some regions of Anatolia, and this is particularly the case with Boyabat. The information that is available, however, shows that the region's history extends back to the Stone Age, and the presence of tumuli, rock-cut tombs (Gökoğlu 1952; Başoğlu 1973, 1978) dating back to the 7th century BC, as well as Pontic, Roman and Byzantine remains, enable us to build up something of a cultural history. It is not known exactly when the Turks gained control of the Boyabat region. This probably ocurred at the end of the 11th century or the beginning of the 12th century during the period of the Danişmendiler (Yınanç 1976). The cultural importance of the region is that it was one of the earliest in Anatolia to come under Turkish control and has remained so ever since. Another important factor is that a large-scale movement of population has not taken place within the region. Investigation of language and art here might well, therefore, be of significant importance for understanding Turkish culture as a whole.

A caravanserai dating back to 1265 in the centre of the town of Durağan, which used to be part of Boyabat, a tomb in the village of Alan dating back to 1390 and a mosque in the village of Eğlence dating from 1273-4 are the only examples of structures belonging to the pre-Ottoman period in the region. However, we do find the names of some of the villages mentioned in documents that belong to the Ottoman period including the villages of Cuma (Erdoğan 1968: 177), recorded because of the mosque which was built by the order of Bayezid Han (his rank has not been defined), Kadılar recorded in 1859, Çaybaşı recorded in 1745, Şeyh (1733), Kovaçayırı (1851), Asarcık (1757), Boyalı[2] (1868), Gündüzlü (1863), Yortan[3] (1852), Cemalettin[4] (1708), Çeşnigir[5] (1796), Uzunöz (1792), Gölet, Söğültü and Akviran (1793), Üzümlü (1794), and the village of Darıözü[6] recorded in 1795. This information has been obtained at the initial stages of research and further investigation is being carried out. We can accept, however, that the majority of these villages were established when the region was taken over by the Turks.

With this historical background information, we are now faced with one of the main problems relating to Turkish houses; that is, whether the design of these houses existed before the Turks entered the region and they simply appropriated the design, or whether they were familiar with the design before they came to Anatolia and that it was they who introduced it. A third possiblity is that the design emerged as a result of both the pre-existing and Turkish cultures affecting one other. More specifically we can ask the question whether, leaving aside earlier civilisations, the design of these houses reflects the influence of Byzantine houses. If this is the case, what was the impact of such influence? Unfortunately available information is insufficient to provide clear answers to such questions.

According to the author of one of the most influential studies on Turkish houses, Ayda Arel, Byzantine houses did not have a noticeable influence on later houses (Arel 1982: 59-70). This would seem to be borne out by the fact that, although few traces of Byzantine houses remain in cities taken over from Byzantium (e.g. Pergamum; Arel 1982: 68), the differing lifestyles of the two peoples must have resulted in different house designs. At most perhaps Turkish occupation of pre-existing Byzantine buildings may have had some influence in the transition period as Turks rebuilt to their own specifications. Bolstering this idea is the fact that when the cities of Samsun, Izmir and Denizli were taken over, new cities were established near the earlier ones. This would not have happened if the new inhabitants had been content simply to appropriate to themselves the style already in use. In terms of villages it is known that the Turkish settlements in the Black Meander Region were not built over Byzantine villages, again suggesting a break in continuity. This may in fact have been due to a large extent to the depopulation that rural Anatolia suffered in the 11th and 12th centuries (Cahen 1979: 149). Furthermore, S. H. Eldem points out (1984: 23, 24) that influence between Byzantine and Turkish houses could only have operated on the level of construction technique and materials. He adds that no common features are observed between the houses of Byzantine notables studied in excavations and Turkish houses, and he states that it is not possible that a culture that is collapsing and a culture that is experiencing its most dynamic age can share the same type of house design. When we consider that very little information has been obtained from excavation of even brick/stone Byzantine houses in cities like Pergamum and that the houses within our research have no foundations to speak of and that the wooden material used in their construction is not durable, we can easily see that hardly any discoveries in further excavations are likely to prove that these houses bear the stamp of Byzantine influence. Yet both the Byzantines and the Turks in this region lived in the same geographical environment and climate, and had the same materials available to them. Therefore, there should be similarities between the houses they built. It is probable, in fact, that in Boyabat village houses wood was used in the Byzantine period also. However, there is simply no evidence. At best we can follow the argument of Eldem and suggest that since Ottoman architecture in general developed a different style from the Byzantine in all other structures, it is likely that this is the case with houses too.

From the question of possible Byzantine influence, let us now turn to consider the possibility of central-Asian influence. The technique of shaping the ends of wooden logs and making one end sit on another, locally called *çantı*, cannot be thought of as unique to any one community alone. This same technique must have been used in the same period in every region where trees are plentiful, from Central-Asia to Europe. We know about the existence of this technique in central Asia from Pazırık fortifications, and there should have been structures employing this technique where the Gök Turks and Huns had their winter quarters, but no evidence of it survives. Moreover, no connection can be made between the construction technique of the houses within our research region and the description given by Radloff (1994 1: 128) who visited the Altay Region in the 19th century and described a house made by the Chu-se tribe by binding logs together, or a shelter made from tree bark and logs, or winter huts made by Minusinsk Tartars using logs (Radloff 1994 2: 78, 139). He also produced a drawing of a hut made by Altays in the *çantı* technique; however, this is no different from a shelter made from logs. The connection made with central Asia in the concept of the Turkish house is based, in fact, on the room-tent relationship which will be mentioned later, the living-area raised above the ground level and the four room plan.

In studying typical Turkish house plans, the work of D. Kuban has been important for our research. Kuban (1975) points out that there are differences in the houses of Anatolia depending on the region in which they are located, but among them the original type developed by the Turks, i.e. that employing a timber frame with brick infill, is found between the Anatolian coast and the central plateau, from the region around Sivas westwards and southwards to the Aegean and the northern slopes of the Taurus Mountains, and also at certain locations in other regions including the Balkans. He adds that Turkish-type houses are formed by reproducing the pattern of room, service area and *sofa*/hall in an axial arrangement (fig.7.7).

It was mentioned above that single-room and double-room house-plans form a standard design in Boyabat village houses with no distinction between plain and upland villages. Of these, the single-room type corresponds to the first division of Kuban's typology (fig.7.7), and the double-room type corresponds to the second. Nowhere in the houses we have studied, however, have we come across Kuban's third or fourth types, though we have heard that a house with a central hall and four rooms existed in the village of Asarcık Camili, though this burnt down some time ago. We have also heard that this arrangement has been used in the village of Yukarı Oba near the town of Araç in the Kastamonu region; however, we have not been able to see it.

Arel (1982: 52) states that the central-hall/four room house-type has been widespread since the 18th century in the context of upper-class houses. A question that comes to mind is why this plan, which was used outside Anatolia before the Turks arrived there and is widely found in Anatolian structures other than houses, was not used in houses until the 18th and 19th century. Yet this is to believe that as a society progresses, it automatically abandons previous ideas and practices. In fact, societies continue to accept what went before so long as this continues to fulfil a need and perform a function. So, for instance, while we can see in the double-room plan-type a naturally generated development of the single-room house, this did not inevitably result in the abandonment of single-room houses. Those unable to afford anything else continued to have this type built. By the same token, general contentment with the double-room format for a long time made anything more complex otiose.

Every civilisation which uses wood knows the necessity of raising it above ground level to prevent decay, though the height to which it is raised has varied from culture to culture. Arel (1982: 39) states that raising the floor of the main living space on pillars or setting it on a waterproof wall indicates not only local traditions but also an Asian origin.

A rarely seen house-type in Boyabat villages are those constructed simply of logs. A shallow foundation of stones is made, and logs are then placed on the stones. Such houses are of the single-room type with the stable under the room (Başoğlu 1990). This in itself suggests that the idea of living-quarters raised from the ground has emerged by a variety of routes in the development of village houses. One point to be considered is whether the log-cabin form represents an earlier design later all-but abandoned, or whether the use of pillars to raise the living quarters above ground level is due to other factors such as the availability of materials.

The rooms in Boyabat villages are self-contained; that is, sitting, cooking and sleeping all take place there. That there is a connection between the function of the room and that of a tent (the primordial dwelling of Turks) has been maintained by a majority of researchers. In this respect it is interesting that the word 'house' is used as a synonym for the room in

Boyabat villages. In other words, each room in a house can be thought of as a house in itself. Another important point is that double-room houses with the *sofa*/hall are divided into two by a wooden partition (Başoğlu 1990, 219), which clearly shows the symmetrical development of the houses, while at the same time reminding us of the tent as a unit which can be increased by addition.

What is the relationship between village houses and urban houses? It is necessary to know about the initial settlement features in Anatolia in order to get a reliable answer to this question. It is assumed that some of the first Turks who came to Boyabat had experienced a settled lifestyle, but whether this was in villages or in cities would be interesting to learn. If they had settled in cities, it is possible that the houses experienced there would have influenced the form of housing in villages.

The houses which we were able to inspect in the urban centre of Boyabat are the ones with an inner *sofa*/hall, or a corner *sofa*/hall. The corner-hall type resembles the third stage of Kuban's typology (Başoğlu 1990: 219). However, as stated above, we have not been able to find examples of the outer *sofa*/hall type or more complex types in the village houses of Boyabat. However, these did exist elsewhere in the 17th century. The Malike House in Tire, the Germiyans House in Kütahya, the house which is behind the court-house in Bursa, the Halil Aya House in Mudanya, which dates back to 1634, the Veli Baba House in Yenişehir, and Kula houses are all examples. A further phase consists of placing the *sofa* at the rear of the house, as in the so-called House of Murad III in Bursa (Eldem 1984-7 1: 58, 69, 72, 94), or that belonging to Dr. Cevat in Kalkandelen, Macedonia.

Bibliography

Arel, A. 1982: *Osmanlı Konut Geleneğinde Tarihsel Sorunlar.* Izmir.

Başoğlu, B. 1973: *Boyabat ve Çevresi Tarihi.* Ankara.

---- 1978: *Sinop ili Tarihi.* Ankara.

---- 1990: *Boyabat Yöresi Araştırmaları.* Boyabat.

Cahen, C. 1979: *Osmanlılardan Önce Anadolu'da Türkler* (Turkish tr. Y. Moran). Istanbul.

Eldem, S.H. 1984-7: *Türk Evi Osmanlı Dönemi* (3 vols). Türkiye Anıt Çevre Değerlerini Koruma Vakfı. Istanbul.

Erdoğan, M. 1968: 'Osmanlı Devrinde Anadolu Camilerinde Restorasyon Faaliyetleri', *Vakıflar Dergisi*, 7. Istanbul.

Gökoğlu, A. 1952: *Paphlagonia.* Istanbul.

Kafesçioğlu, R. 1955: *Kuzeybatı Anadolu'da Ahşap Ev Yapıları.* İTÜ Mim. Fak. Yay. Istanbul.

Kuban, D. 1975: 'Türk Ev Geleneği Üzerine Gözlemler', *Sanat Tarihimizin Sorunları.* Istanbul: 192-211.

Radloff., W. 1994: *Sibirya'dan* (tr. A. Temir). Istanbul.

Yınanç, M.H. 1976: 'Danişmendliler', *İslam Ansiklopedisi*, 3, Istanbul: 468-79.

---

[1] Information about the construction of houses has been obtained from İsmail Biçer, a craftsman carpenter living in Saraydüzü, a town in the region of Sinop, to whom the writer wishes to express his gratitude.

[2] Başbakanlık Arşivi, Cevdet Tasnifi, vol. II, pp. 604, 803, 877, 886, 891, 933.

[3] Başbakanlık Arşivi, Cevdet Tasnifi, vol. III, pp. 2229, 2254,.

[4] Başbakanlık Arşivi, Cevdet Tasnifi, vol. IV, p.2083.

[5] Vakıflar Genel Md. Arşivi, Hurufat Defteri, no.538, p.51.

[6] Vakıflar Genel Md. Arşivi, Hurufat Defteri, no.537, p.33.

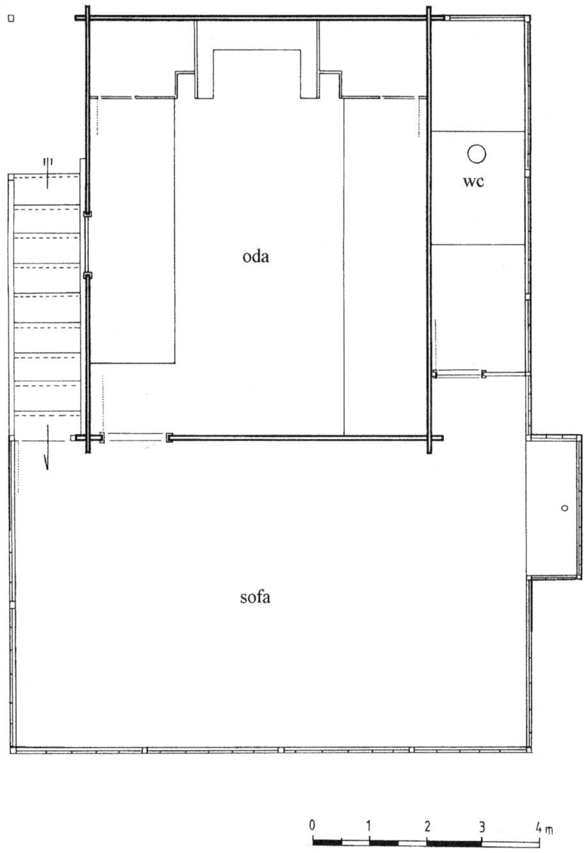

Fig. 7.1. One-room house, Yukarı Arım village

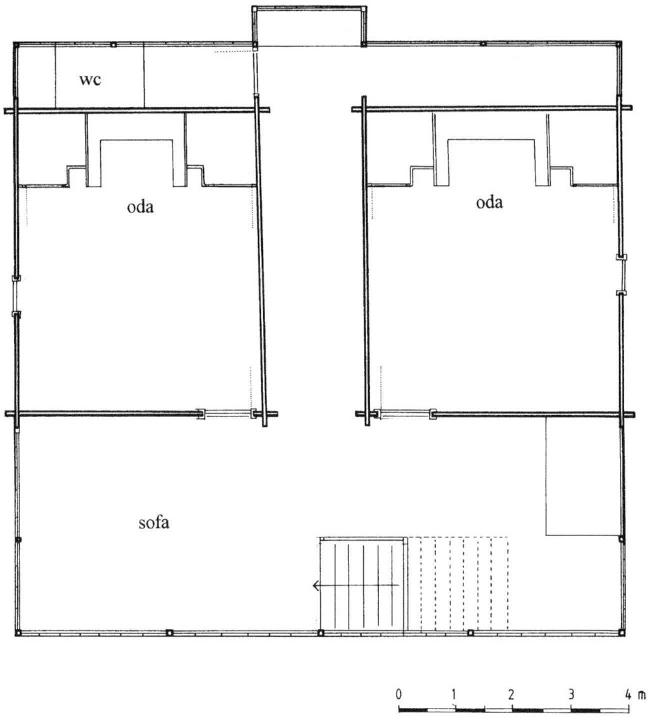

Fig. 7.3. Two-room house, Asarcık Kayalı village

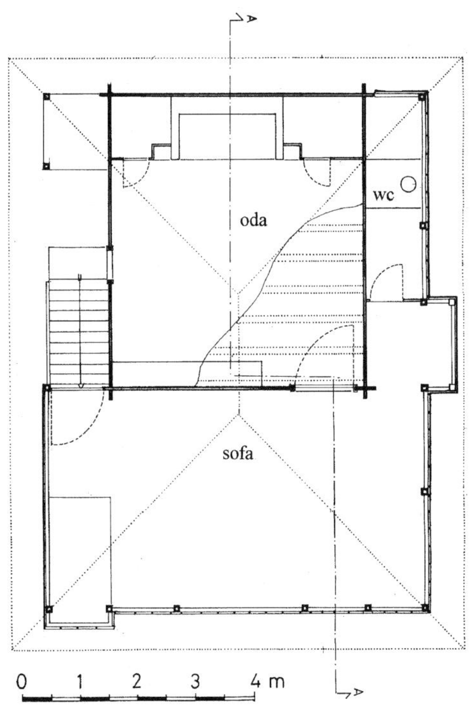

Fig. 7.2. One-room house, Asarcık Kayalı village

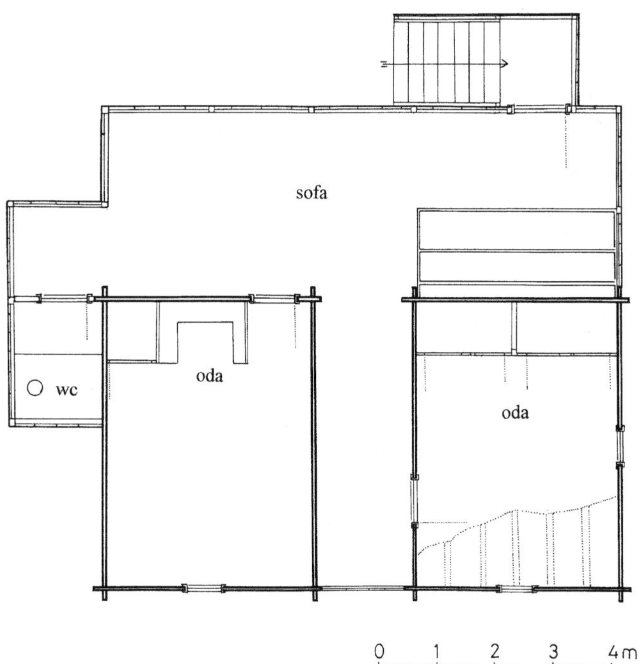

Fig. 7.4. Two-room house, Asarcık Kayalı village

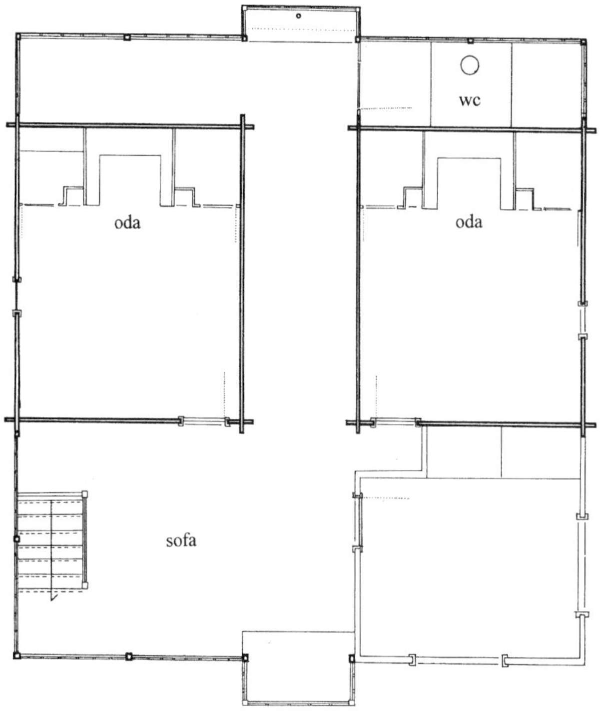

Fig. 7.5. Two-room house, Yukarı Arım village

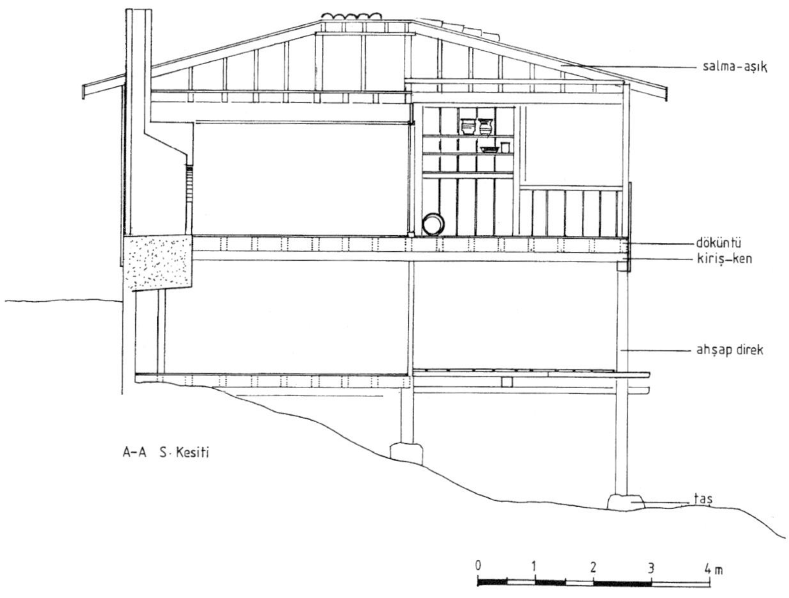

Fig. 7.6. Section through house, Asarcık Kayalı village

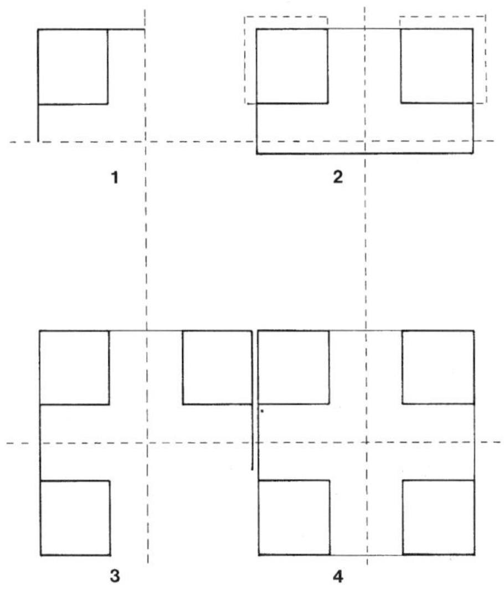

Fig. 7.7. Village house typologies

8: THE PALESTINIAN ARAB HOUSE: THE OTTOMAN CONNECTION

Dr. Ron Fuchs
Technion - Israel Institute of Technology, Haifa, Israel

Palestinian Arab domestic architecture is generally treated in the standard sources on the subject as an isolated case, having little relation to other vernacular traditions. Its origins, it is often suggested, may go back to prehistory or to 'biblical times'. Little has been done to place Palestinian architecture in a wider geographical frame or relate it to a specific historical context. However, the interpretation of the vernacular architecture of Palestine - or indeed, of any land - would be incomplete without taking into account the larger geographical, cultural and historical picture. Palestine belonged for a substantial period of its recent history to the Ottoman Empire (1516-1917/18), and the greater portion of the heritage of Palestinian Arab vernacular architecture dates from that period. Unique or provincial as Palestine may have been, it could not have remained unaffected by the Ottoman system. As we shall see, there are significant parallels between Palestinian domestic architecture and other Ottoman vernacular traditions, including those of the Anatolian heartland. Viewing the vernacular traditions of Palestine within the larger context of the Ottoman Empire is not only essential for its true understanding, it also suggests a way of gaining some insight into the unifying themes of Ottoman domestic architecture as a whole. This paper will, therefore, try to examine the affinities between Palestinian architecture and other Ottoman traditions, in the hope of achieving a better understanding of both Palestinian architecture and its Ottoman milieu.

'Pre-Industrial' Palestinian Vernacular

The Village House. In spite of a great regional diversity in building methods, and a wide variety of plan variations, the Palestinian village house followed one basic pattern, which had been observed at least as early as the eighteenth century.[1] The vivid description given here by Mary Rogers, the sister of the British consul in Haifa around mid 19th century, is one of many similar accounts:

> ... the house consisted of only one very lofty room, about eighteen feet square. The roof of heavy beams and tree branches, blackened with smoke, was supported by two wide spreading arches. The walls were roughly-hewn blocks of stone, not plastered in any way. Just within the door, a donkey and yoke of oxen stood; and I soon perceived that rather more than one-third of the room was set apart for cattle, where the floor, which was on a level with the street, was of earth, and partially strewn with fodder. We were led up two stone steps on to a dais, twenty-two inches high, where fragments of old mats and carpets were spread, and where three venerable-looking old men ... sat smoking. Their feet were naked for they had left their red shoes by the steps leading on to the dais. The sheikh took down some mats and cushions from a recess in the wall and arranged them for us on the floor. In the meanwhile ... our two horses were unsaddled and lodged in the lower part of the room ... Nearly in the middle of the raised floor the large fire ... was burning briskly.[2]

The author describes a house type that follows two general principles of spatial organisation:[3]

1. The whole house consists of one all-purpose, rectangular room where all household activities - living, sleeping, work and storage of produce - take place. The nuclear family and its dependents, sometimes as many as 25 persons, as well as their livestock, share this single space.

2. This single space is divided into two zones by means of a difference in level: a lower 'soiled' area (usually called *qa' al-bayt*) near the entrance, and an elevated surface reserved for living and sleeping (*mastaba*).

Within these two determining principles, a great variety of layouts is possible (fig.8.1a-c, pl.8.1-4). The division into levels can be achieved in a manner ranging from the vestigial to the elaborate, the area of the two zones and the level difference between them varying. The soiled area may consist of a small square near the door, 10-15 centimeters lower than the floor of the house, where visitors would leave their shoes;[4] or it may take up a sizable part of the floor area providing space for work and for stabling of animals; or, in a more developed variation, the elevated surface may be constructed as a gallery, leaving usable space underneath and requiring access by a staircase. Sometimes a gallery as well as an elevated platform are combined in the same house. A bench for sitting or reclining may run along a wall of the *mastaba*. In some cases the bench may complete a 'U' shape, i.e. a fully developed divan (e.g. fig.8.1a).[5]

Various storage elements for produce and tools were often prominent features of the interior. Grain was stored in clay containers, or more elaborately, in a system of compartments constructed of a wooden frame coated in plaster. When the opening at the bottom of each compartment was unblocked the grain would flow down into a bowl placed underneath. Niches of various sizes were installed in the walls or provided in 'cupboards' of plaster-coated wood construction. A niche or a stand for a large water jug would often be installed near the entrance. An essential feature of each living space was a large niche (*yuk*) that contained mattresses which would be unrolled on the floor when the family retired to sleep. The grain silos, cupboards, shelves and other elements were sometimes decorated with reliefs or tracery, occasionally of rather intricate design, also constructed of plastered wooden frames.

The Single-Space Village House and the Concept of the Room in Ottoman Architecture. The single-space house type was by no means unique to Palestine. Although construction, layout variations, decoration and the degree of refinement differed from region to region, village houses based on the same basic principles were common in many parts of the Levant.[6] The chief characteristic of this house type, i.e. a single all-purpose space with an elevated living platform, was reported in village houses in Jordan,[7] Lebanon,[8] and Syria[9]. Single-space houses were described in Anatolia as well: according to Goodwin, in the central region from Amasya to Kayseri, 'village houses and town houses alike were based ... on the concept of one all-purpose room where beds were spread on the floor at night and kept in a chest or cupboard in the wall by day ... further economy is achieved by connecting the stable with the family room...'[10] An elevated platform is described in the following 19th-century account of the typical village 'odah' or 'guesthouse' common in the region between 'Undzag and Erzurum': the '*odah* is a large rambling room with an irregular roof supported on rough tree-stems. In the centre, or some other convenient place, a mud platform is slightly raised ... The platform is for human beings, with the rest of the building for horses, mules, oxen, asses, and buffaloes, with a few sheep and goats probably in addition.'[11] The single-space house with the elevated platform spread as far as the Greek islands of the Aegean, where such houses, varying from the crude to the refined, are amply described.[12] In Greek houses the elevated platform may take the form of a gallery floor, an element otherwise reported mainly in Palestine.

Thus the Palestinian village house was only one variant of an archetypal rural dwelling that spread through a long stretch of the Ottoman Eastern-Mediterranean. What were the origins of the single-space village house? Of all the features of this house type, the elevated living platform, the *mastaba*, is the most essential component of its typological definition. It is the origins of this element, therefore, that most require consideration. The elevated platform is a persistent motif that appears in Islamic architecture from Iran to North Africa and from Anatolia to the Sudan. It is found in shops, khans, hammams, palaces and mosques; it may be combined with *iwans*, porches, halls or simply constitute a freestanding dais in the centre of a court; it may play a part in crude vernacular structures, or in refined palatial architecture: royal daises set in gardens depicted in Persian (and other) miniature paintings seem like rich relatives of simple wooden platforms used in domestic and public open spaces in modern vernacular structures from Anatolia to Iran. Like another pervasive Islamic motif, the *iwan*, the elevated platform may have had Iranian origins. In any case, as for Eastern-Mediterranean domestic architecture, it established itself in such centres as Cairo, Aleppo and Jerusalem by the Mamluk period.[13] It may have also appeared in Seljuk palace pavilions by the 13th century.[14] Since then it has become a standard element in the design of living apartments in high as well as vernacular traditions of Islamic domestic architecture.[15] The single-space village house proves to be but a rustic realization of a general concept of ordering a living space.

Arranging rooms - especially the better ones - as all-purpose apartments, subdivided into two zones by a difference in floor level, was customary in the three major traditions of domestic architecture of the Eastern-Mediterranean: the Syrian, the Egyptian and the Turkish.[16]

The use of such an arrangement is colourfully described in the following seventeenth century account of a visit to the pasha's residence in Tripoli, Lebanon:

> Being come to the house, the servants receive you at the outermost gate, and conduct you towards their lord or master's apartment; other servants (I suppose of better rank) meeting you in the way, at their several stations, as you draw nearer to the person you visit. Coming into his room, you find him prepared to receive you, either standing at the edge of the divan, or else lying down at one corner of it, according as he thinks it proper to maintain a greater or less distinction. These divans are a sort of low stage, seated in the pleasantest part of the room, elevated about sixteen or eighteen inches or more above the floor. They are spread with

carpets, and furnished all around with bolsters for leaning upon. Upon these the Turks eat, sleep, smoke, receive visits, say their prayers, &c. Their whole delight is in lolling upon them; and in furnishing them richly out is their greatest luxury.

Being come to the side of the divan, you slip off your shoes, and stepping up take your place; which you must do first at some distance, and upon your knees, laying your hand very formally before you. Thus you must remain till the man of quality invites you to draw nearer, and to put yourself in an easier posture, leaning upon the bolster. Being thus fixed, he discourses with you as the occasion offers, the servants standing round all the while in a great number, and with the profoundest respect, silence, and order imaginable. When you have talked over your business, or the compliments, or whatever other concern brought you thither, he makes a sign to have things served in for entertainment, which is generally a little sweetmeat, a dish of sherbet, and another of coffee; all which are immediately brought in by servants, and tendered to all the guests in order, with the greatest care and awfulness imaginable. And they have reason to look well to it; for should any servant make but the least slip or mistake, either in delivering or servicing his dish, it might cost him fifty, perhaps one hundred drubs on his bare feet, to atone for his crime.

At last comes the finishing part of your entertainment, which is perfuming the beards of the company...[17]

The elevated platform that in the single-space village house had a simple practical purpose is transformed in the urban house into an architectural convention that serves domestic ritual. Rather than separate between clean and soiled or between inhabitants and their livestock, it constitutes a symbolic gesture that distinguishes between higher and lower social status. The equivalent of the *qa' al bayt* of the Palestinian village house is termed *Ôataba* in the Syrian town house and *dur-qa'a* in the Cairene. In the Turkish house the term *sekialtı* is commonly used for the low zone, and *sekiüstü* for the living platform. A similarity exists in the basic typologies as well: as in the village house, the low entrance zone of an urban apartment could constitute a small depressed square near the door, or it could take up a wider zone along one side of the room.[18] Thus, in the Turkish house the entrance zone 'was large enough for several servants to stand in, but in more modest houses it was no more than a corner with space in which to kick off a pair of slippers [*pabuçluk*]'.[19] More elaborate spatial settings employing elevated platforms are found in apartments of the type called *qa'a* in Syria and Cairo, where one or several *iwans*, accommodating raised divans, open onto a lower central space. Houses with cross-shaped halls or pavilions like the well known Köprülü Yalı on the Bosphoros, could be cited as the Turkish equivalents.[20]

The Palestinian Town-House. If we now turn to the Palestinian town house, we discover that it shares with the village house on the one hand, and with the high traditions of the Eastern-Mediterranean urban house on the other, the same concept of room design. The ancient, pre-19th century, cores of Palestinian urban settlements - chiefly in Jerusalem, Hebron, Nablus, Ramla, Lydda and Jaffa - possessed a distinct tradition of domestic architecture.[21] Construction was based on heavy stone walls supporting vaults and domes. Sometimes the vaults of the upper apartments were constructed by an ingenious technique based on earthenware tubes held together by plaster. These domes and vaults create the characteristic roofscape of the Palestinian town, familiar from innumerable illustrations and photographs, especially of the Old City of Jerusalem (fig.8.2, pl.8.7).

The court *(hosh)* was the most basic feature of the Palestinian town house. It was accessed through a crooked corridor (*dahliz*) and in its centre there often was the mouth of a water cistern and occasionally, a small garden. Apparently there existed better-off court-houses that belonged to a single household, along large court-centred complexes where unrelated, poorer, families each owned or rented one apartment (or very occasionally two).[22]

The apartments surrounding the court were usually poorly lit and ventilated, as privacy and security did not permit windows opening onto the exterior. They were, therefore, often used as stores or shops rather than living quarters. Open staircases led up from the court to the living quarters on the upper level. Roofs served as 'upstairs courts' that gave access to the upper apartments. The inhabitants used them for performing household chores, for leisure, and for sleeping on warm nights. Privacy was protected by a high parapet that ran around the roof.

One (occasionally several) of the upper apartments was a 'best room' or *'alliya* (*baş oda* in Turkish), where the owner of the house or the master of the family resided and entertained distinguished guests.[23] The whole roof, or a fenced off portion of it, served as its private yard, and a kitchen, sometimes a bath and WC as well, were attached to it.

As a rule, the 'rooms' or 'apartments' in the Palestinian town house consisted of a single space that was conceived and equipped as an all-purpose, self-contained unit, or an independent 'house'. Accordingly, no direct connection between apartments was provided. Ideally, the standard mattress niche, concealed by a curtain, would be provided,[24] and the space would be divided into a low entrance-zone and a raised living-platform. A continuous seat - divan - ran along the three sides of the living zone (pl.8.5).

Again, Mary Rogers gives us a lively description of the interior of a house, this time of a 'best room' in a house in the town of Nablus:

> ... at sunset my brother accompanied me to his [the governor's] house. Two kawasses and lantern-bearers led the way. We were conducted into a vast open court, paved with marble, and the governor came out to meet us, and led me into the divan ... A part of the floor was raised a few inches, to form a dais, and was spread with handsome carpets, and in the centre stood a tall brass candelabrum supporting an oil lamp. In the lower part of the room a number of servants waited. They were the attendants and lantern-bearers of the several guests. Richly-dressed Abyssinian slaves handed round coffee...[25]

As in the village house, or rather, in the Syrian or Turkish domestic traditions, a full typology of apartments existed, based on the manner in which the division into two zones was realized (fig.8.3a-d). In the minimal case, a small depressed square was installed inside the door.[26] A fuller realization meant a more substantial entrance zone. As was observed in a house in Hebron, 'the room contained two levels, with the lower level used for cooking and laundry and the upper section as a living level. A closed-off storage area under the living level contained various objects and wall cupboards served for storage of bedding, clothing, and other household articles.'[27]

Usually a single-space apartment consisted of only one vaulting bay. Luxurious upper apartments could, however, consist of more than one bay. One type of a luxurious upper apartment followed an 'a-B' bay system, where 'a' was an entrance zone that occupied a strip along the short side of the room, and 'B' a living area, occasionally raised, square in plan, and capped by a pendentive dome. Some of these apartments had a vaulted entrance-porch facing the roof-court. Another possible addition was a closed balcony or *kishk* (Turkish *köşk*), hanging on stone corbels from the side of the living zone. A number of plans of such apartments from Jerusalem, Hebron and Ramla, together with their roof-courts and service rooms, have been recorded and published (fig.8.3c,4a, pl.8.5,6).[28]

The upper-apartment of the 'a-B' type is an equivalent of the Turkish room, rather than the Syrian-Cairene *qa'a*. It follows the Turkish model in the proportion between sizes of the two bays, in making the ceiling of the living zone the higher of the two bays, and in the centralizing articulation affected by the domed ceiling over the living zone. A rosette with spiraling spikes, reminiscent of the Turkish *göbek*, may decorate the centre of the dome (pl.8.8). Spatially, the entrance zone is thus subordinate to the living zone, whereas in a *qa'a* an opposite effect is created. The Ottoman character of this apartment type is best demonstrated when compared to the brick and masonry strong houses, or fortified mansions, built in eighteenth century Istanbul, especially in the Phanar.[29] These houses had an upper apartment consisting of a single two-bayed room, with a bath attached, and a dome covering the living zone. The stone *köşks* on corbels common to these houses, are occasionally paraphrased in Palestinian townhouses.

Another feature of the Palestinian townhouse that has a parallel in the Turkish house are the balustrades that sometimes separated the entrance zone and the living area.[30] These occasionally had an ornamental gate, celebrating the passage from one level to the other.[31] It is not difficult to recognize the similarity between these balustrades and the Turkish *direklik* (fig.8.4a-b). The *direklik* is a three bayed arcade that stands on the edge of the Turkish elevated platform. The central bay is a passage while the two lateral ones are blocked by balustrades. The columns defining the bays may support a beam, but the element obviously could be employed without any structural purpose. The examples cited for Palestine resemble this purely decorative, or ritualistic form of the *direklik*. Similar elements are found in other traditions within the Ottoman sphere, e.g. Greece and Sudan.[32]

The traditional Palestinian townhouse with its heavy vaulted construction could not be more different from the Turkish house with its light wooden structure, but in spite of the differences the two share the same concept of room design, and similar modes of articulation.

The 19th Century Townhouse

After the middle of the 19th century, a town house of a new type appeared in Palestine. Its chief characteristic was a central hall that cut through the whole plan from front to back (fig.8.6a-b). Living rooms flanked this hall symmetrically on each side. In the last decades of the 19th century, the 'central hall house', as we shall call it here, became the standard house-type for new urban houses in Palestine. Many such houses are found throughout the country, from the Galilee to Beersheba. Large clusters can be seen particularly in Acre, Haifa, Nazareth, Jaffa and Jerusalem (pl.8.13-16).[33]

The Central Hall House – Description. In the typical 19th century central hall house, the living floor constituted a *piano nobile*, the ground floor being reserved for storage or shops. The number of living rooms could be the minimal two, but more often these houses were spacious mansions with several rooms along each side of the hall. Initially, space for washing and cooking was not provided as an integral part of the living floor. On the façade, the whole width of the central hall was taken up by a large opening, usually subdivided into three arched bays, occasionally two or one. The central bay of the triple arcade often led out to a small balcony supported on corbels. Triple arcades, identical in design to the one on the façade, could appear inside the hall as sub-dividing elements. A tall, steep hipped tile-roof often capped the building. The ceiling that separated the interior from the attic under the tile-roof was often the object of lavish painted decoration.

A number of sub-variants of the simple central hall plan existed. The chief variations included (1) houses with loggias (*riwaqs*) running along one or several sides of the living floor (pl.8.15); (2) houses where the hall is joined in its centre by an *iwan* on each side, so as to create a cruciform central space; (3) houses where the hall does not open on the outside, but constitutes an inner space lit through clerestory windows.

After about 1900, the schematic simplicity of the plan, as well as the coherence of the late 19th century style, gradually gave way to more complex and eclectic solutions, as builders began to incorporate service spaces (kitchens, bathrooms, staircases) in the plan, to use new materials (such as concrete), and to borrow motifs from European modernist architecture. The essential arrangement of a hall flanked by rooms, however, retained its popularity in Palestine even after the Ottoman period, and could still be encountered in new construction after mid-century. Particularly interesting is its sometimes awkward adaptation in apartment-house flats.

The Central Hall House as a 19th Century Phenomenon. The emergence of the central hall house in Palestine was a distinctly new development of the 19th century. The 19th century was a period of deep change in Palestine: the legal and administrative reforms initiated by the Tanzimat in 1839, the greatly improved internal security, and the increasing exposure of the country to the West had far reaching effects on the economy and society of Palestine.[34] It was after mid-century that the impact of these developments began to be felt significantly. Population started to grow at an accelerated pace, and after about 1870 towns were expanding beyond their ancient cores. This meant a wave of new construction. It was at this period that the central hall house made its appearance in Palestine.[35] Proud new houses, with their prominent tiled roofs, cropped up outside the walls of the old towns (e.g. in Jaffa, Jerusalem), forming new neighbourhoods, or grew within the existing urban tissue itself, transforming the old townscape (Acre, Nazareth).[36]

The builders of these new houses belonged to a rising class of rich city-dwellers or 'effendis'. This new bourgeoisie owed its prosperity to the new opportunities that the growing economy now offered. The positions that its members came to hold in the newly formed local administration helped to fortify their wealth and power. Some of the new rich belonged to religious minorities that took advantage of the relaxation of restrictions over non-Moslems in Ottoman law. A large portion of profits made in commercial and real-estate ventures was invested in building spacious mansions. The grand central-hall houses with their extravagant tile roofs, so different from the introverted and secluded old urban dwellings, became a status symbol, an expression of the affluence and self-confidence of the new class.

It was the new urban elite that was most affected by the growing influence of Western culture after mid century. Its members travelled abroad, studied foreign languages and strove to give their children modern, European education (often in missionary schools). Here is a description of the manners of this Westernising elite by the author and traveller, Lawrence Oliphant, who resided in Palestine in the 1880s:

> Some of these are wealthy merchants or large landed proprietors, with incomes varying from \$5000 to \$15,000 ... As, owing to the march of civilization, the richer classes have of late years taken to travel and study of languages, persons occupying this position generally speak either French or Italian, have visited Paris, Constantinople, or Alexandria, and have a thin varnish of European civilization ...
>
> The women associate more freely than they used to do with men. [They now wear] a dress of European make, while, instead of bare feet thrust into slippers, they have Paris bottines and stockings. The men of this class also dress in European garments, wearing, however, the red fez cap.[37]

The familiarity with Western ways was soon reflected in the form of the house. The introduction of previously unavailable imported building materials had an immediate effect: roof tiles from Marseilles and sawed timber from Anatolia made possible the large roofs and the construction of thin walls; plate glass apparently from Germany and Britain permitted the construction of large windows, and glazing the triple-arcade transformed the hall into a climatically protected space, comparable to European living rooms.[38] Decorative elements (e.g. dentiled wooden mouldings decorating the contours of painted ceilings) were no doubt manufactured industrially, or copied from pattern books of Western inspiration. Another imported item was European furniture. Displaying this 'exotic' Western novelty was a source of much prestige (rather than useful necessity), as Mary Roger's account illustrates:

> On Monday, the 15th [1855], I called ... on a wealthy native of Nazareth, who had lately built a handsome house of hewn stone. He had just returned from Marseilles, where he had been purchasing furniture for it. ... Our host was the great man of his community after this trip to Marseilles, and, owing to his wealth and this famous journey, was for a time reckoned as a prophet ... He told me that he had himself designed the house and its decorations. ... His drawing room, which was something like a French *salon*, with its mirrors and marble tables, was frescoed by a native of Nazareth, who had been tutored and employed by Franciscan monks in church mural decoration. ...[39]

As time passed, the introduction of European furniture - beds, chairs, tables, even pianos - transformed domestic customs, because they undermined the multi-purpose way in which living spaces were traditionally used. Clearly the new houses accommodated an increasingly Westernised way of life. This Westernisation was, it must be pointed out, sometimes superficial. As Oliphant writes:

> [Your Oriental friend] who, when he called upon you, might have come off the boulevards of Paris, barring always the red cap, has now reverted absolutely into the Oriental. ... As he sips a matutinal cup of coffee and smokes his first narghileh of the day, there is nothing about him to remind you that he knows a word of any other language than Arabic, or has ever worn any other costume than that of his Eastern ancestors.[40]

The Central Hall House in 19th Century Ottoman Domestic Architecture. The central hall house was not uniquely, or even primarily, a Palestinian type. Palestinian examples, specifically those in the coastal towns and the Galilee, were not significantly different from those described in Lebanon, where this house type is found more abundantly.[41] Indeed, in Lebanon the central hall house has become something of a national symbol. By the turn of the 19th century, clusters of central hall houses, with their prominent tile-roofs, transformed the townscape of Beirut and the coastal towns, as well as that of many villages of Mount Lebanon. The abundance of these houses in Lebanon suggests that the focus of the phenomenon was there. Traditional 'pre-industrial' Palestinian architecture does not seem to have offered obvious starting points for the evolution of this house-type. Its introduction into Palestine during the 19th century was probably induced by the commercial and cultural dominance of Beirut, the involvement of Lebanese in commercial enterprises and real-estate investments in Palestine, and finally, by the immigration into Palestine of Lebanese merchants, and possibly of craftsmen as well. It was probably a similar process that introduced the type into Syrian coastal towns.[42]

The central hall house, as described above, could be rightly regarded as a basically Lebanese house. The use of central hall arrangements, however, was certainly not limited to the Lebanese tradition. The central hall appears to have been a basic feature that - despite great diversity in construction, detail and general architectural character - dominated 19th century house design in a wide range of traditions throughout the Ottoman Empire. Along with the central hall plan, the subdivision into a *piano nobile* over a service ground floor also proves to have been a persistent pattern, and some minor elements familiar from the Lebanese idiom - such as arcades, corbelled balconies or hip-roofs - also occurred elsewhere.

Already in the interior regions of Palestine, particularly in Jerusalem and some Judaean towns, we find local versions of the central hall house, that appear significantly independent of the Lebanese canon (pl.8.23).[43] In Jerusalem, the traditional methods of vaulted construction often persisted even when timber and tiles became available, and walls tended to remain relatively thick even when roofs were flat.[44] The triple arcade did not gain wide acceptance in Jerusalem, and a door flanked by two windows was a more common solution. Particularly removed from the Lebanese models were the 19th century houses of Bethlehem. These consisted of a *piano nobile* over a ground floor. The domestic floor, which was vaulted, had a symmetrical plan with an *iwan* or a central hall that opened on the centre of the façade through a wide, unglazed arch (fig.8.5a, pl.8.9,10).[45] Occasionally, probably in later houses, a triforic aperture was substituted for the *iwan* arch (pl.8.24). Central hall houses in Jordan too, especially in Es-Salt, have their distinct architectural character, again largely due to the preference of massive vault construction.[46]

The universality of the central hall plan is further revealed when we move away from the range of the Lebanese type. Although architectural character and stylistic details completely change, central hall arrangements appear in the Syrian interior and in Egypt.[47] A similar scheme played an important part in the Turkish architecture of Constantinople and the Anatolian provinces. Beginning in the 18th century, Turkish domestic architecture tended to adopt central hall schemes. These more introverted versions of the Turkish house may have first developed in the capital.[48] In any case, it seems that by the turn of the 19th century, the central hall plan was becoming a common solution for spacious konaks as well as for modest provincial houses (pl.8.25,26).[49] Similar arrangements were common in the domestic traditions of the Balkans, e.g. in Bulgaria and Northern Greece.[50]

In western Anatolia and the Balkans, the reliance on timber, the predilection for cantilevered projections and the occasional indulgence in Baroquish curves produced an architectural character quite different from that of the more rigid Lebanese type. The central hall was nevertheless a persistent feature of the plan. Furthermore, in those Anatolian provinces where stone was the common building material (rather than timber) the result was strikingly reminiscent of the Lebanese central hall house. Cappadocia, where stone houses often have *piani nobili* with central halls that terminate on the façades in arcaded openings, is a notable example (fig.8.7c-d). Stone houses with central hall arrangements and arcaded openings were reported on the Aegean littoral as well as in Eastern Anatolia (fig.8.7a-b,5e). Further east, in northern Iraq, houses of mud brick having a *piano nobile* with a symmetrical plan, and a wide opening in the centre of the façade often leading to a balcony on corbels, were known (fig.8.7f).[51] Central hall arrangements seem to have been known in this end of the empire as well (fig.8.7e).

The affinities between these diverse vernacular traditions were probably more than formal. The spread of the central hall plan in urban mansions apparently coincided with generally similar social developments, namely the emergence of a bourgeois class that profited from the steady modernization of the Empire. Although each region had its unique circumstances, the processes described above for Palestine had parallels in other provinces.

In Mount Lebanon, accelerated modernization began with the termination of twenty years of civil strife in 1861. The 'organic law' of 1861 not only restored stability, but also marked the end of the semi-feudal system in the Mountain. By then Beirut was becoming one of the major ports and commercial centres of the Eastern-Mediterranean. The rise of a bourgeois class and the appearance of central hall houses in Lebanon took place in the same period. Emigration was an important factor in the Lebanese scene. It began in the 1860s, and in the 90s became a mass movement. Remission of money earned abroad to emigrants' families in Lebanon and the return of retired emigrants eventually had its impact on the built landscape: according to the Lebanese historian, Philip Hitti, 'Today hardly a village or a town of the 1600 in Lebanon does not exhibit a red tile-roofed house built with money from abroad.'[52]

It would be difficult to survey here the social developments in the whole of the Empire. The case of the Cappadocian town of Sinasos, near Nevşehir, may serve as an example. Familiar themes - such as Ottoman reform, emigration, commercial success and spacious mansions - feature in an account of its prosperity in the second half of the century:

> [Sinasos] was a prosperous place in the 19th century, with a population of 3,000 to 4,000 [mostly Christians]. ... The peculiarity of the economic life and social life of Sinasos was, that the town lived half from agriculture and half from the remittances of men working in distant places. ... Within the general economic prosperity of the Greek population which followed [the Hatt-i-Hümayun, in 1856], an important position was held by the people of Sinasos, who became merchants in Constantinople. ... They prevailed in the sectors of commerce which brought them a great deal of money, and an important part of this money, we ascertain, was channeled back to their homeland ... [where] they also built remarkable mansions to which this essay refers.[53]

The Origins of the Central Hall House - Sala, Iwan or Sofa? The widespread use of central hall arrangements in Ottoman domestic architecture may be partially explained by a common response to general changes in lifestyle and domestic ritual. The different central hall traditions are unlikely to have developed completely independently of each other. A process of diffusion must have taken place, through which the basic architectural plan spread. Tracing the courses of transmission of architectural influences throughout the Empire with any degree of certainty would require an extensive investigation which is beyond the scope of this paper. Nevertheless, some discussion of the origins of the central hall is necessary, if the relationship of the Lebanese/Palestinian central hall house to the general Ottoman context is to be examined.

One possible source for the central hall plan is European models. The influence of Western culture that expressed itself, as we have seen, in daily manners as well as in the furnishing and decoration of the house may have inspired the adoption of a European house plan as well. Indeed, in Egypt (and apparently other places, e.g. northern Greece) central halls were often termed *sala*, no doubt after the Italian.[54] As for the Lebanese house-type, some regarded it as an 'unauthentic' imitation of Western models.[55] Some put it down as 'Italianate' or 'Venetian'.[56] The Venetian central hall or *pòrtego* may have exerted, perhaps, an indirect influence through Palladian villa design. Palladian planning was popularized since the turn of the 18th century through textbooks inspired by French architectural rationalism, and especially by J.N.L. Durand's writings. Simplifying Palladian villas easily produced central hall arrangements, and such stereotypic plans became by the beginning of the 19th century part of the standard technical know-how of architects and builders. Buildings erected in Ottoman provinces by European architects, engineers and surveyors, may have served as models for local builders. Conrad Schick, a German self-taught architect who was active in Jerusalem 1846-1901, actually boasted of having been the first to introduce this plan to Jerusalem.[57] Local builders could also have been inspired directly by pattern books. Illustrated text books, advocating, among other things, central-hall villa designs, existed in the 19th century even in Arabic.[58] In Egypt, the assimilation of Western design methods was promoted by a state Polytechnical School where architecture was being taught by mid-century as a part of a curriculum of Western technological subjects. The teaching of this school contributed to the assimilation of central hall arrangements in Egyptian 19th century domestic architecture.[59]

Seeking the origins of the Levantine or Anatolian central hall schemes in European villa design means assuming a process of vernacularisation and Orientalisation of a Western model by indigenous builders. No less attractive is the opposite hypothesis suggesting that the central hall plan was basically an Oriental scheme that underwent modernization and Westernisation during the 19th century.[60] This would perhaps be in keeping with the often superficial nature of the Westernisation of the provincial bourgeoisie. A persuasive case has been made for placing the origins of the Lebanese central hall house in the '*iwan* house', an older indigenous type that clearly belongs to the universal vocabulary of Islamic architecture.[61] The *iwan* house consists of a unit comprising an *iwan* (a room that opens on the exterior through the whole width of one of its sides) flanked by a room on each side (fig.8.5b).[62] The central hall differs from the *iwan* in usually having more than one room on each side. Its greater depth therefore makes the hall an independent interior space, while the *iwan* is, in fact, a large niche that serves a court or a larger space. The affinity between the *iwan* house and the central hall house is, however, clear: both are symmetrical, free-standing blocks, and both have a central space flanked by rooms. In the Lebanese central hall house a triple arcade spans the mouth of the central space instead of a broad *iwan* arch, but the two forms are, in effect, interchangeable.

The free-standing *iwan* house offered a logical starting point for a new bourgeois house. It was associated with luxurious living before the 19th century.[63] Security, the colonisation of new land outside the congested ancient cores, and possibly, change in the cohesiveness of the extended family did not invite grouping *iwan*-units around secluded courts, as was done in the courtyard houses of the 18th century from Eastern-Anatolia to Syria and Lebanon. It could now be developed into a free-standing bourgeois mansion. The *iwan* house, with its symmetrical arrangement and free-standing disposition, was more adaptable to the new ideals of house design and modern comfort introduced from the West.

The transformation and modernisation of the *iwan* house need not have taken place only in Lebanon. This house type was common through a wide geographical range. Simple houses consisting of an *iwan* flanked by rooms were found, besides Lebanon, in the vernacular traditions of Syria,[64] Eastern-Anatolia,[65] Iraq and Iran.[66] The type was also represented, although not abundantly, in Palestine and Jordan where it probably began to penetrate towards the end of the 18th century (fig.8.5a-d, pl.8.9-12).[67] In Central and Western Anatolia a mud-brick and timber version was common, in which the *iwan* arch was usually replaced by a wooden beam.[68]

Obvious transformations of the *iwan* house into central hall arrangements can indeed be found in some of these regions. A number of examples can be cited from Eastern Anatolia[69] and Lebanon.[70] The 19th century houses of Bethlehem with their prominent *iwan* arches are clearly variations on the *iwan* house.[71] The Bethlehem house in fig.8.5a is surprisingly similar to the Eastern Anatolian houses from Silvan in fig.8.5e-f. One of these houses, in which a double arcade is substituted for the *iwan* arch, is particularly interesting as it seems to demonstrate the interchangeability of the *iwan* and the arcade. Halls terminating in arcades, as in the Lebanese house, the Cappadocian house or houses such as the one from Didyma in fig.8.7a-b, could now be plausibly related to the *iwan* house.

There is no doubt that the *iwan* house played an important role in the evolution of central hall arrangements, at least in some parts of the Ottoman Empire. There is, however, another possible source for the central hall plan: the 'classical' Turkish house of Anatolia. Through its known evolution the Turkish house was based on three basic elements: the room, the *iwan* (or *eyvan*), and a wide covered deck called *sofa* or *hayat*. A diverse typology was derived by grouping rooms and *iwans* around the covered deck. In the 19th century, probably under European influence, it became common to arrange rooms and *iwans* on either side of an elongated deck, or, in other words, to create a central hall plan. Other arrangements, based on an inner, enclosed hall extended by *iwans* into a cruciform space were also common. The wide *iwan*-arch or the equivalent dominant arcade at the mouth of the hall, are missing in façades of these houses. The central halls of Anatolia would be interpreted better as descendants of the more open gallery-like *sofas*, rather than transformations of the single *iwan*.[72]

Central hall arrangements in provincial traditions such as the Lebanese house could have originated, therefore, from Turkish domestic architecture, or, at least, have been stimulated by it. The Lebanese-

Palestinian central hall house could thus be interpreted as a local adaptation of the 19th century Turkish house with its central *sofa*.[73] The use of stone rather than timber can explain the difference in architectural character. There are points in support of this theory: the Turkish house was often divided into a service floor with a domestic floor over it, and the use of tiled hipped-roofs was common (although details of construction differ). More importantly, Turkish domestic architecture could offer precedents for sub-variants with cruciform halls, inner halls, and the use of arcaded galleries (*riwaqs*). The design of the Lebanese triple arcade is strikingly reminiscent of the Turkish *direklik*, and the subdivision of the central hall by triple arcades is paralleled by similar arrangements in Turkish houses. The decoration of the ceilings in the central hall houses of Lebanon and Palestine clearly belongs - both in style and subject matter- to a similar manner of decoration that spread throughout Anatolia, the Balkans, and in fact, the whole Empire (pl.8.17-22).[74] The repeated views of Constantinople and the inclusion of Ottoman symbols indicate the cultural impact of the centre of Empire and the builders' loyalty to the central government (pl.8.19-20).[75]

Was the Lebanese-Palestinian central hall a descendent of the Italian *sala*, the Syrian *iwan*, or the Turkish *sofa*? It is likely that all three sources have some relevance. It is best to describe the evolution of Ottoman domestic architecture in the 19th century as revolving around three major poles, each having reciprocal influence on the other and each having a different impact in various provinces: the Western villa, the *iwan*-house and the 19th century Turkish house. Regional traditions, such as the Lebanese house, represent a combination of global all-Ottoman archetypes, transformed by indigenous traditions and adapted to the limitations of local materials and particular conditions. The rich traditions of Mount Lebanon before 1860, serving as a medium for the adaptation of the imported influences, no doubt contributed to the uniqueness of the end result. The heavy vaults of the Judaean building tradition gave rise, as we have seen, to different adaptations in central Palestine and Jordan. The Lebanese/ Palestinian central hall house represents, then, an indigenous tradition of vernacular architecture, possessing its specific character and idiosyncrasies, but at the same time, deriving from a number of fundamental themes common to 19th century Ottoman domestic culture in general.

Conclusion

This examination of Palestinian domestic architecture has revealed two basic themes: the all-purpose room with the elevated platform of the 'pre-industrial' age, and the 19th century central hall. Both these themes proved to be ideas of universal Ottoman importance, ideas that realized themselves in a variety of traditions throughout the Empire from Constantinople and the Anatolian heartland to peripheral provinces.

The single space of the village house with its *mastaba*, represents a rustic version of the same conventions that, in a more refined and ritualised form, dominated the ordering of living space not only in the apartments of the old Palestinian town house, but in the urban traditions of Cairo, Syria and Anatolia as well.

The central hall house of Lebanon, Palestine and the Syrian coast shows affinities with three major sources: the Western villa, the *iwan* house and the Turkish *hayat* house. These three sources represent three global influences that dominated the evolution of Ottoman traditions in the 19th century. The interaction of the three sources, modified by indigenous traditions and local conditions, produced in the 19th century a wide array of central hall traditions, of which the Lebanese and Palestinian central hall house was only one expression.

The domestic architecture of the vast Ottoman world is revealed through our analysis as an architectural heritage of great diversity within fundamental unity, the result of an equilibrium between universal themes and indigenous traditions. Such balance could only have evolved in a world where caravans travelled from town to town and steam-ships sailed from port to port, stimulating an exchange of ideas and fertilizing local creativity.

Bibliography

Aboussouan, C. (ed.?) 1985: *L'architecture Libanaise du XVe au XIXe siècle*. Beirut.

Al-Aamiry, S., Cejka, J. 1987: 'Das palästinische Haus', in G. Völger, K. V. Welck and K. Hackstein (eds), *Pracht und Geheimnis - Kleidung und Schmuck aus Palästina und Jordanien.* Cologne: 92-8.

Amiry, S., Tamari, V. 1989: *The Palestinian Village Home*. London.

Anon. 1985: *Sinasos in Cappadocia*, National Trust for Greece, London.

Antonius, Soraya 1965: *Architecture in Lebanon*. Beirut.

Asfour, K. 1993: 'The Domestication of Knowledge: Cairo at the Turn of the Century', *Muqarnas* 10: 124-37.

Aurenche, O. 1981: *La maison orientale: l'architecture du Proche Orient ancien des origines au milieu du quatrième millenaire* (3 vols.). Paris.

Ayoub, A. 1980-81: 'Habitation en milieu rural au nord-ouest de la Jordanie', *Bulletin d'Etudes Orientales* 32-33: 7-19.

Azar, G. *et al.* 1985: 'Busra: Housing in Transition', *Berytus* 33: 103-42.

Bahgat, A., Gabriel, A. 1921: *Cairo, Fouilles d'Al Foustat*. Cairo.

Bammer, A. 1982: *Wohnen in Vergänglichen*. Graz.

Ben-Arieh, Y. 1981: 'The Development of the Twelve Major Settlements in Nineteenth Century Palestine', *Cathedra* 19 (April): 83-143 [Hebrew].

---- 1984: *Jerusalem in the 19th Century: the Old City*. New York [Hebrew edition: 1977].

---- 1986: *Jerusalem in the 19th Century: Emergence of the New City*. New York [Hebrew edition: 1979].

Bishop, I.L.B. 1891: *Journies in Persia and Kurdistan* (2 vols) London.

Blaser, W. 1975: *Structural Architecture of Eastern Europe*. Basel.

Blin, O. 1987: 'La Caire XIX-XXe siècles, de la fasaha à la sala comme modèles', in *Les cahiers de la recherche architecturale* 20/21. Marseille.

Boucheman, A. de. 1930?: *Une petite cité caravanière: Suhre*. Damascus.

Burgoyne, M.H., Richards, D.S. 1987: *Mamluk Jerusalem*. London.

Camesasca, E. (ed.) 1971: *Das Haus*. Gütersloh.

Canaan, T. 1932-33: 'The Palestinian Arab House, its Architecture and Folklore', *Journal of the Palestine Oriental Society* 12: 223-47; 13: 1-83.

Carmel, A. 1975: *Geschichte Haifas in der turkischen Zeit 1516-1918*. Wiesbaden [Hebrew edition: 1969].

Carswell, J.1977: 'Onward and Eastward: Western Influenced Architecture of the 19th and 20th Century', *Art and Architecture Research Papers*, 11 (June). London.

Dalman, G. 1942: *Arbeit und Sitte in Palästina* 7: *Das Haus*. Gütersloh [reprinted 1964].

David, J.-C., Grandin, T. 1994: 'L'habitat permanent des grands commerçants dans les khans d'Alep â l'époque ottoman', in Panzac 1994: 85-124.

Davie, M., Nordiguian, L. 1987: 'L'habitat de Bayrut al-Qadimat', *Berytus* 25: 165-197.

Depaule, J.-C. 1987: 'Espaces habités de l'Orient arabe' in *Les Cahiers de la recherche architecturale* 20/21, Marseille: 8-21.

---- 1994: 'Deux regards, deux traditions: l'espace domestique perçu par les auteurs anglais et français au Levant', in Panzac 1994 2: 189-228.

Depaule, J.-C., Noweir, S. *et al.* 1984: *L'habitation urbain dans l'Orient Arabe*. Versailles.

Eldem, S.H. 1984-7: *Türk Evi Osmanlı Dönemi* (3 vols). Türkiye Anıt Çevre Değerlerini Koruma Vakfı, Istanbul.

el-Khouri, F. 1975: *Domestic Architecture in Lebanon*. London.

Farrar, F.W.1874: *The Life of Christ*. London.

Fuchs, R. forthcoming a: 'The Palestinian Arab House and the Islamic Primitive Hut', *Muqarnas*.

---- forthcoming b: 'Arab Domestic Architecture in 19th Century Haifa - Architectural Documentation', in Y. Ben-Artzi (ed.), *Collected Papers on the History of Haifa*.

Fuchs, R., Meyer-Brodnitz, M. 1989: 'The Emergence of the Central Hall House Type in the Context of 19th Century Palestine', in Bourdier, J.-P., Alsayyad, N. (eds), *Dwellings, Settlements and Tradition*, Lanham MD: 403-24.

----, ---- forthcoming: 'The Central Hall House: A New House Type in 19th Century Palestine', *Cathedra* (Hebrew).

Gabriel, A. 1940: *Voyages archéologiques dans la Turquie orientale* (2 vols). Paris.

Gonen, R., Kroyanker, D. 1993: *To Live in Jerusalem*. Israel Museum, Jerusalem.

Goodwin, G. 1971: *A History of Ottoman Architecture*. London.

Goy, R. J. 1989: *Venetian Vernacular Architecture*. Cambridge.

Greenlaw, J.-P. 1995: *The Coral Buildings of Suakin*. London & New York.

Hamilton, R.W., Grabar, O. 1959: *Khirbat al-Mafjar*. Oxford.

Hamilton, R.W. 1992: *Letters from the Middle East by an Occasional Archaeologist*. Edinburgh.

Harvey, W. 1910: 'A Native House, Jerusalem', *The Builder* 99 (July 16): 74-5.

Herzfeld, E. 1943: 'Damascus: Studies in Architecture II', *Ars Islamica* 10: 13-70.

Hillenbrand, R. 1994: *Islamic Architecture*. New-York.

Hirschfeld, Y. 1995: *The Palestinian Dwelling in the Roman-Byzantine Period*. Jerusalem.

Hitti, P. 1957: *Lebanon in History*. London.

Jäger, K. 1912: *Das Bauernhaus in Palästina mit Rücksicht auf das biblische Wohnhaus untersucht und darstellt*. Göttingen.

Jaussen, J.-A. 1927: *Coutumes palestiniennes: Naplouse et son district*. Paris.

Kalayan, H., Liger-Bellair, J. 1966: *L'habitation au Liban*, 2 vols. Beirut.

Kark, R. 1990: *Jaffa - a City in Evolution 1799-1917*. Jerusalem [Hebrew edition: 1984].

---- 1995: 'The Introduction of Modern Technology into the Holy Land 1800-1914 CE', in Th. E. Levy (ed.), *The Archaeology of Society in the Holy Land*. London: 524-41.

Kark, R., Landman, S. 1980-81: 'The Establishment of Muslim Neighbourhoods in Jerusalem Outside the Old City During the Late Ottoman Period', *Palestine Exploration Quarterly*, 112/113: 113-35.

Kark, R., Oren-Nordhein, M. 1995: *Jerusalem and its Environs 1800-1948*. Jerusalem.

Kendall, H. 1949: *Village Development in Palestine*. London.

Khammash, A. 1986: *Notes on Village Architecture in Jordan*. Lafayette Louisiana.

Kroyanker, D. 1985: *Jerusalem Architecture; Periods and Styles of Arab Buildings outside the Old City Walls* [Hebrew]. Jerusalem.

Kuban, D. 1995: *The Turkish Hayat House*. Istanbul.

Kushner, D. (ed.), 1986: *Palestine in the Late Ottoman Period: Political, Social and Economic Transformation*. Jerusalem & Leiden.

Langenneger, F. 1911: *Beiträge zur Kenntnis der Baukunst des Irâq*. Dresden.

Ma'oz, M. (ed.), 1975: *Studies on Palestine during the Ottoman Period*. Jerusalem.

Maundrell, H. 1703: *A Journey from Aleppo to Jerusalem, Easter 1697*. Oxford.

Migdal, J.S. 1980: *Palestinian Society and Politics*. Princeton, NJ.

Moutsopoulos, N.K. 1990: *Greek Traditional Architecture: Kastoria*. Athens.

Ninck, K. 1987: *Auf biblischen Pfaden*. Dresden.

Oliphant, L. 1887: *Haifa or Life in Modern Palestine*. London [new ed. Jerusalem 1976].

Otto-Dorn, K. 1969: 'Bericht über die Grabung in Kobadabad, 1966', *Archäologischer Anzeiger des Deutschen Archäologischen Instituts*: 438-506.

Panerai, P. 1982: 'Geometries et figures domestiques', *Cahiers de la recherche architecturale*, 10/11 Marseille: 126-39.

Panzac, D. (ed.) 1994: *Les villes dans l'Empire ottoman: activités et sociétés* (2 vols) CNRS, Paris.

Petersen, A. 1995: 'Preliminary Report on an Architectural Survey of Historic Buildings in Ramla', *Levant* 27: 75-101.

Petherbridge, G.T. 1978: 'Vernacular Architecture: The House and Society', in George Michell (ed.), *Architecture of the Islamic World*. London: 176-208.

Philippides, D. 1977: 'Greek Vernacular: the Interior Woodwork Decoration of the Elymbos House', *Art and Architecture Research Papers*. London 12 (Dec.): 1-9.

---- (ed.) 1983:, *Greek Traditional Architecture* (2 vols). Athens.

Pinon, P. 1994: 'Résidences de France dans l'Empire ottoman: notes sur l'architecture domestic', in Panzac 2: 47-84.

Pullan, W. 1988: 'The Palestinian House', *Eretz Magazine* 12.3 (Autumn): 33-6, 68-70.

Ragette, F. 1974: *Architecture in Lebanon: the Lebanese House during the 18th and 19th Centuries*. Beirut.

Ramzi, N. 1989: *Iraq, the Land and People*. London.

Renda, G. 1977: *Batılılaşma Döneminde Türk Resim Sanatı 1700-1850*. Ankara.

Reuther, O. 1925: 'Die Qa'a', *Jahrbuch der asiatischen Kunst* 2: 205-16.

Revault, J., Maury, B. 1975-83: *Palais et maisons du Caire du XIVe au XVIIIe siècles* (4 vols). Cairo.

Rogers, M.E. 1862: *Domestic Life in Palestine*. London [reprint London 1989].

Roman, Y. 1996: 'Overhead Art', *Eretz* 49 (Nov.-Dec.): 23-35.

Royal Scientific Society 1995?: *Architectural Heritage of the Hashemite Kingdom of Jordan - As-Salt* [Arabic]. Building Research Centre, Royal Scientific Society, Amman.

Saliby, N. 1990: 'Une maison arabe à Resafa', in P. Matthiae *et al.* (eds.) *Resurrecting the Past*. Nederlands historisch-archaeologisch Instituut te Instanbul, Leiden: 277-96.

Schick, C. 1880: 'Progress in Palestine', *Palestine Exploration Fund Quarterly Statement* 12: 187-8.

---- 1894/95: 'Die Baugeschichte der Stadt Jerusalem', *Zeitschrift des Deutschen Palästina Vereins* 17: 261-76.

Schiller, E. (ed.) 1979: *The First Photographs of the Holy Land*. Jerusalem.

---- (ed.) 1980: *The First Photographs of Jerusalem and the Holy Land*. Jerusalem.

Segal, Y. 1967: *Building in the Arab Villages in the Galilee and its Development*. Jerusalem (Hebrew with an English abstract).

Slesin, S. *et al.* 1990: *Greek Style*. London.

Stebbing, H. 1847: *The Christian in Palestine*. London.

Thomson, W.M. 1890: *The Land and the Book*. London.

Thoumin, R. 1931: 'Deux quartiers de Damas', *Bulletin d'Études Orientales*. Damascus: 120-5.

---- 1932: *La maison syrienne dans la plain Hauranaise, le bassin du Barada et sur les plateaux du Qalamun*. Paris.

Tobler, T. 1853: *Dänkblätter aus Jerusalem*. St. Gallen, Koblenz.

Tricanato, E.R. 1948: *Venezia Minore*. Milan.

Tuchelt, K. 1994: 'Notizen über Ausgrabung und Denkmalpflege in Didyma', *Antike Welt* 25.1: 2-34.

Volney, C.-F. de 1787: *Travels through Syria and Egypt in the Years 1783, 1784 and 1785* (tr. from French) 2 vols. London [reprint 1972].

Waddington, H. 1935: 'A Note on Four Turkish Renaissance Buildings in Ramleh', *Journal of the Palestine Oriental Society* 15: 1-6.

Weulersse, J. 1940: *Le pays des Alaouites*. Tours.

---- 1946: *Paysans de Syrie et du Proche-Orient*. Paris.

Yagi, K. 1983: 'Traditional Houses and Living Patterns in Syria', in A. Germen (ed.) *Islamic Architecture and Urbanism*. Damman: 343-62.

---

* Some of the following material was published in Fuchs, Meyer-Brodnitz 1989 and Fuchs forthcoming a.

1 Volney (1787 2: 335), village houses 'between Ramla and Gaza.' An even earlier allusion is given in Maundrell (1703; entry of 3 March, 1697), the village of 'Sholfatia'.

2 House in Kafr Qara, (Rogers 1862: 203-4). Cf. a house in Shafa 'Omar (*ibid.*: 136-7).

3 On the Palestinian village house see Jäger 1912; Canaan 1932-33; Dalman 1942; Al-Aamiry, Cejka 1987; Pullan 1988; Amiry, Tamari 1989; Hirschfeld 1995.

4 Canaan 1932-33: 37.

5 Cf. Boucheman 1930?: 28, fig.3; Dalman 1942: fig.43.

6 For a collection of village house plans from Levantine countries see Aurenche 1981 2: pl.234-82.

7 Dalman 1942: fig.48, 50-2, 66, 80; Ayoub 1980-81: pl.V; Khammash 1986, house in Hmud; Royal Scientific Society 1995?: 91-4.

8 Kalayan, Leger-Bellair 1966 1: 20, house in Kobayat; el Khouri 1975: 4-6, 10, plan of a village house in the Beq'a; Ragett 1974: 16-35.

9 Thoumin 1932: pl.XVIII, XIX; Boucheman (1930?): 25-31; Weulersse 1940: 240-6; Dalman 1942: fig.43, 67; Yagi 1983: fig. 5, 13.

10 Goodwin 1971: 430-1.

11 Bishop 1891 2: 344-5.

12 Philippides 1977; Philippides 1983 1: figs on 43, 75, 110-13, 128, 200, 207, 208 (Eastern Aegean, Sporades - Ionian Islands); for lavish photographs see Slesin 1990.

13 The elevated surfaces at the 'divan' in the bath-house at Khirbat el-Mafjar may be regarded as an early, but not straightforward, precedent, in Hamilton, Grabar 1959. An elevated platform is found in the *iwan* of one of the houses of Fusṭat, late 10th century, house no. 5 in Bahgat, Gabriel 1921. In a modest pre-1260 house excavated at R'safa, the history of which may go back to the 9th century, elevated platforms were found in the *iwans* of a *qa'a* -like suite, as well as inside a simple room (Saliby 1990). An early *qa'a* with elevated *iwans* is the Qa'a ad-Dardir, Cairo, attributed to the 12th century (Revault, Maury 1975 1: 5). The elevated platform is used in the *qa'a* at the mansion of Sitt Tunshuq, Jerusalem c. 1380.

14 E.g. the pavilions at Qubadabad (Otto-Dorm 1969; Hillenbrand 1994: 418).

15 Petherbridge 1978: 199.

16 Depaule *et al.* 1984; Depaule 1987, 1994; Kuban 1995: 106-14.

17 Maundrell 1703; entry for 13 March, 1697.

18 This is demonstrated particularly well in the Syrian house. See a typological study of Syrian apartments in Depaule *et al.* 1984: 89-123. See also Azar 1985: fig.9, 9a. Entrance zones in the form of a small square were not common in the Cairene house.

19 Goodwin 1971: 433.

20 As suggested by Reuther 1925: 213.

21 On the Palestinian town-house see Harvey 1910; Waddington 1935; Ben-Arieh 1984: 25-30; Hirschfeld 1995: 193-206; Petersen 1995: 95-6; Fuchs, forthcoming a.

22 Canaan 1932-33: 40-1.

23 Canaan 1932-33: 44.

24 Rogers 1862: 47 on a house in Bethlehem: 'in a deep arched recess, opposite to the door a number of mattresses and wadded quilts were neatly piled up; for in genuine Arab houses no bedsteads are used, and consequently no rooms are set apart expressly for bedrooms. Mattresses are spread anywhere in various rooms and courts ... according to the season, or to the convenience of the moment.'

25 Rogers 1862: 262.

26 Hirschfeld 1995: fig.150; Burgoyne 1987: fig. 45.5.

27 Hirschfeld 1995: 195.

28 Waddington 1935; Hirschfeld 1987: 193-206; Burgoyne 1987, apartments over the Awhadiyya, fig.5; the Taziyya, fig.36.4, 29.6, pl.36.17; west of the Ribat al Kurt, pl.7.10, fig.7.6, isometric view, 152.

29 Eldem 1986 2: 234-59; Goodwin 1971: 448, fig. 517.

30 Dar Khalil al-Mulla in Waddington 1935: 5: 'the two bays are divided from each other by a carved wooden screen, and there is a step up into the main bay.' Hirschfeld (1995: 197-8, fig.147,156) found this element in rooms and the two *'alliya*s that he recorded. Canaan (1932-33: 22, fig.5) shows a plan of an apartment with an entrance zone and a raised main space, separated by a 'wooden balustrade'.

31 Hirschfeld 1987, *ibid.* Cf. Rogers 1862: 137, on a house in Shafa 'Omar (Shefar'am): 'On the left there was a broad wooden platform, raised about two feet from the ground, with a low ornamental wooden railing at the edge of it.'

32 For Greece see above note 12; Greenlaw 1995: figs. on 75, 121.

33 On the central hall in Palestine see: Jaussen 1927: 24-7; Kroyanker 1985; Fuchs, Meyer-Brodnitz 1989; Gonen, Kroyanker 1993: 112-15.

34 For essays on various aspects of change in 19th century Palestine see: Ma'oz 1975; Migdal 1980: 9-17; Kushner 1986.

35 Houses with the typical tile roofs or triple arcades are missing in views of Palestinian landscapes, such as those by the painter David Roberts, dating from the first half of the century. Houses in new extra-mural neighbourhoods cannot date before c. 1870. See discussion of dating in Fuchs, Meyer-Brodnitz 1989: n.3.

36 For a study on the new Arab neighbourhoods outside the walls of Jerusalem see Kark, Landman

1980/81. General accounts on the development of Palestinian towns in the 19th century see Schick 1880; Carmel 1975; Ben-Arieh 1981, 1984, 1986; Kark 1990; Kark, Oren-Nordhein 1995.

[37] Oliphant 1887, chapter on 'Domestic Life among the Syrians.'

[38] On the penetration of new technologies and materials into Palestine see Kark 1995.

[39] Rogers 1862: 122. Cf. the similar impact of Western furniture in other regions, paragraph on *objets* in Depaule 1987.

[40] Oliphant 1887 (see n.37).

[41] The standard source on the central hall house in Lebanon is Ragette 1974. See also Weulersse 1946: 262-70; Antonius 1965; Kalayan, Liger-Bellair 1966; el-Khouri 1975; Panerai 1982; Depaule *et al.* 1984: 125-31; Aboussouan 1985.

[42] Weulersse 1940: 282-5.

[43] Fuchs, Meyer-Brodnitz 1989: 417-19.

[44] Schick 1894/95: 271.

[45] Bethlehem suffered much destruction during the Egyptian occupation, but in 1880 it looked like a 'newly built town', Schick 1880. Its, then, mostly Christian population prospered on trade in souvenirs. Some of its wealth originated from the success of emigrant Bethlehemites abroad. Cf. the discussion of the Cappadocian town of Sinasos below. For illustrations see: Farrar 1874: 34; Ninck 1897: 188; Kendall 1949: fig.17; Schiller 1979: 164; Schiller 1980: 234.

[46] For an impressive documentation project see Anon. 1985?.

[47] Depaule 1987: figs. 6-8; David, Grandin 1994: 100f. These authors point out the affinity between central hall arrangements in Egypt, Syria, Turkey and Lebanon.

[48] The study in Pinon 1994 of French embassies in Constantinople designed 'à la turque' suggests that central hall arrangements were known in the capital by the beginning of the 18th century.

[49] Eldem 1984-87; Kuban 1995: 64-78.

[50] 'Ländliches Rokoko in Südost-Europa' in Camesasca 1971: 244; Blaser 1975: fig.78-9, 96-9; Greece: Moutsopoulos 1990.

[51] See also photos of north Iraqi towns in Hamilton 1992.

[52] Hitti 1957: 474-5.

[53] Sinasos: Anon 1985?: 21-2, 53, 127.

[54] Blin 1987 and other papers in the same issue.

[55] E.g. Weulersse 1946: 267 defines the Lebanese central hall house as 'la nouvelle demure imitée de l'Occident', and explains (268) that 'c'est essentialement une demure citadine, conçue et realisée à Beyrouth au contact de l'Orient et de l'Occident.'

[56] The resemblance between Venetian houses and the Lebanese central hall house - both in plan and façade - has been pointed out before - e.g. Ragette 1974: 116, 169-79. Central-hall schemes were common in the *piano nobile* of both palaces and farm-houses of the Venetian lagoon up to the 18th century. It is, no doubt, Venetian influence that brought this scheme to the towns of Eastern-Adriatic shores. It would be difficult, however, to demonstrate direct and dominant Venetian influence on domestic architecture in Anatolia and the Levant in the second half of the 19th century. Pinon 1994: 76 even suggests a common Byzantine ancestor for both the Venetian and Turkish house. Venetian or Palladian models may have been assimilated first in Constantinople and later transmitted to the provinces. It is interesting to note that the Ottoman commercial delegation to Venice occupied one of the oldest Venetian central-hall houses, the Fòntego di Turchi until 1838. There was also a Venetian embassy in Constantinople. On the Venetian house see: Tricanato 1948; Goy 1989.

[57] Describing his Talitha Kumi orphanage in Jerusalem, dedicated 1868, Schick (1894/95: 268) wrote: 'Ebenso war in Hinsicht der Anlage und Vertheilung der Hausräume der Plan des Verfassers bahnbrechend. Dürch die Hausthür kommt man zuerst in eine Halle, an welcher rechts und links die Zimmer liegen.'

[58] Asfour 1993: fig.10.

[59] Asfour 1993: 130-3.

[60] Cf. Carswell 1977: 2: 'The elegant domestic architecture of the whole Levant coast, from Lattakia in the north through Tripoli, Beirut, Sidon, Tyre, Haifa, Jaffa and Acre to Gaza in the south, superficially seems to be occidental; but a closer inspection reveals the true origin to be local, and not imported.'

[61] Ragette 1974: 88.

[62] On the *iwan* house in Lebanon see: Kalayan, Liger-Bellair 1966 1: 42ff.; Ragette 1974: 67-89; el-Khouri 1975: 8; Aboussouan 1985: 151-5, 167-75, 209.

[63] The *Iwan*-house was the better type of house even in poor villages, see e.g. Goodwin 1971: 430: 'The better houses have arched eyvans or loggias but the humbler ones are simply crofts.'

[64] Thoumin 1931, 1932; Yagi 1983.

[65] Kuban 1995: 231.

[66] Herzfeld 1943: 28-9.

[67] I have seen *iwan* houses in Israel in Safed, Shefa, 'Omar, and Haifa. Old photos show examples as far south as Beersheba. For Bethlehem see n.45 above. See also Thomson 1890: fig. on 356. For Jordan see Khammash 1986: 35-7.

[68] See e.g. Kuban 1995: fig.22, 24, 28, 84 drawn from various sources.

[69] Gabriel 1940 1: fig.35, house in Mardin; Kuban 1995: fig.104.

[70] Davie, Nordiguain 1987: fig.11, 12.
[71] See n.70.
[72] A recent reiteration of this interpretation, put forward by S. H. Eldem, is given in Kuban 1995: 47-99.
[73] This was explicitly suggested in Panerai 1982 and Fuchs, Meyer-Brodnitz 1989: 412-14.
[74] On Ottoman painted decoration see Renda 1977 and Renda in this book.
[75] On painted decoration in Palestine see Roman 1996.

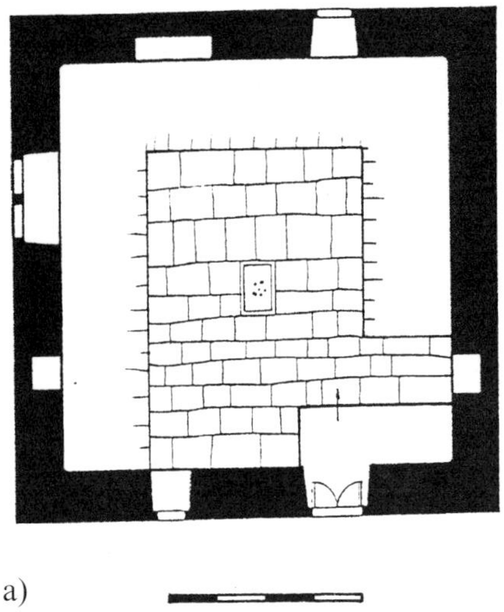

a)

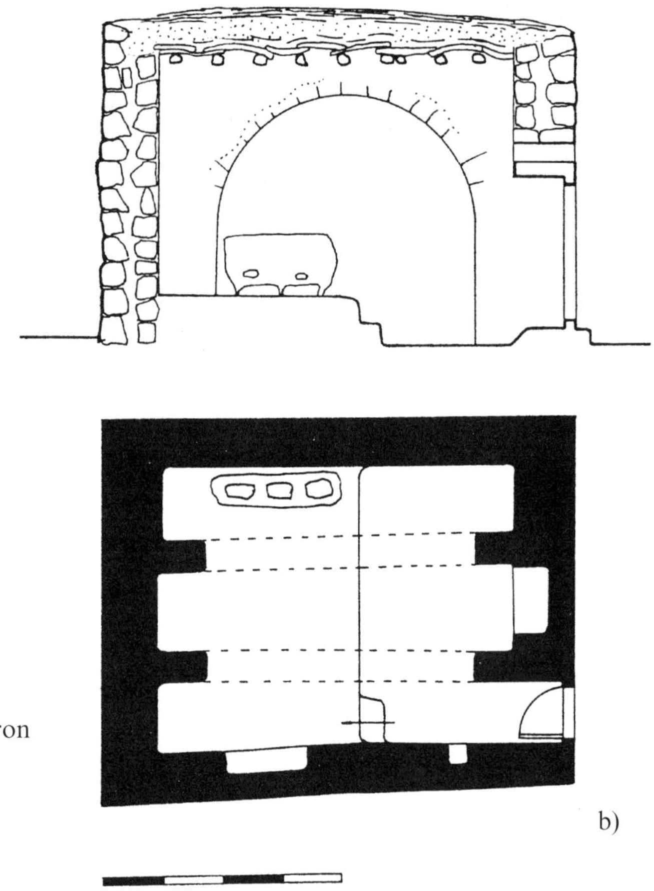

b)

Fig. 8.1. Palestinian village houses
a) Guest house at Bani Na'im, near Hebron
b) House at Dura, near Hebron
c) House at Majd al-Kurum, Galilee

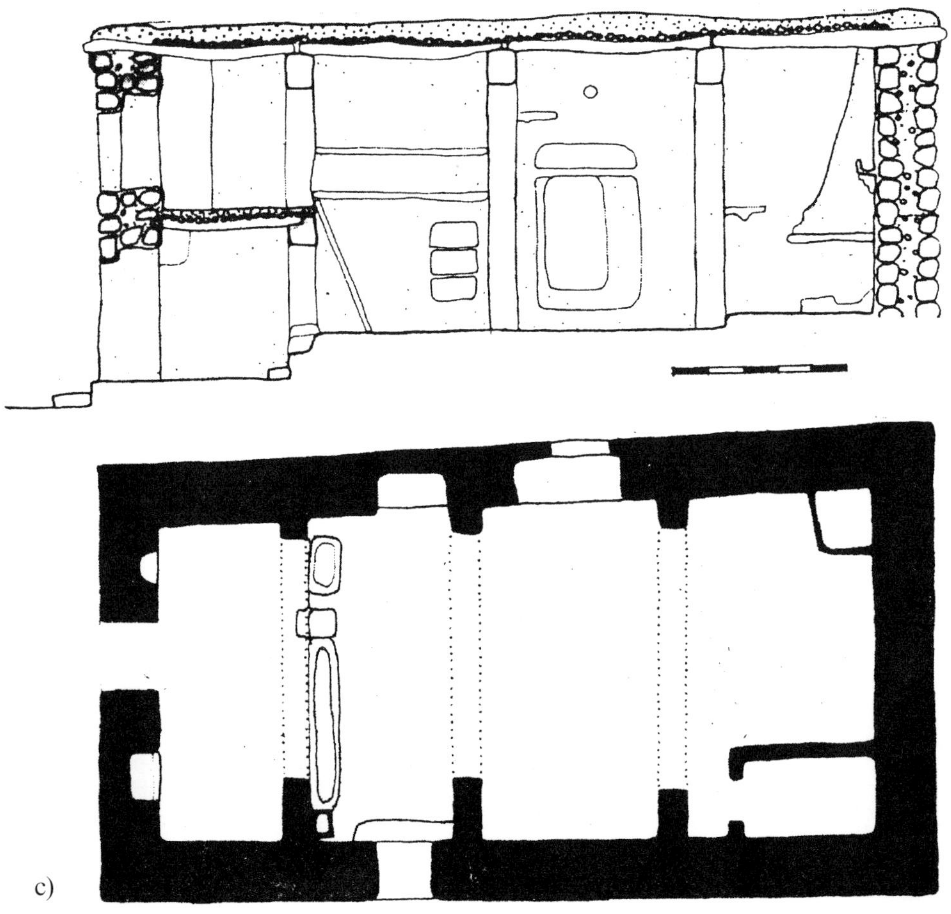

c)

Fig. 8.2. Houses around Hezekiah's Pool, Jerusalem

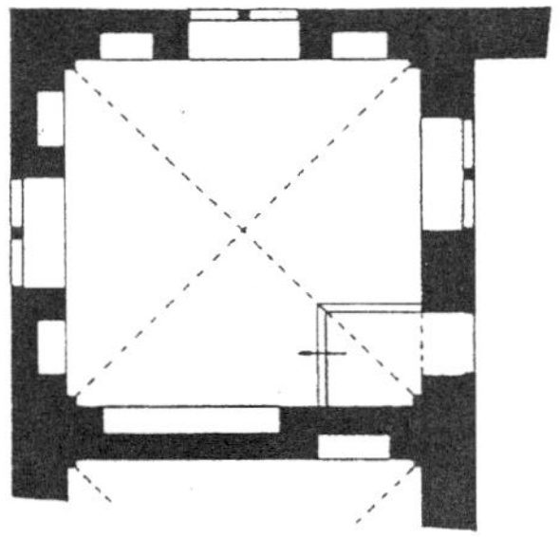

a) Palestinian townhouse

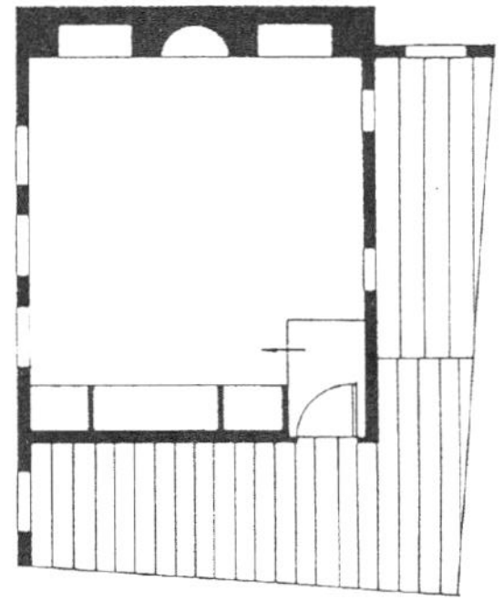

b) Turkish house

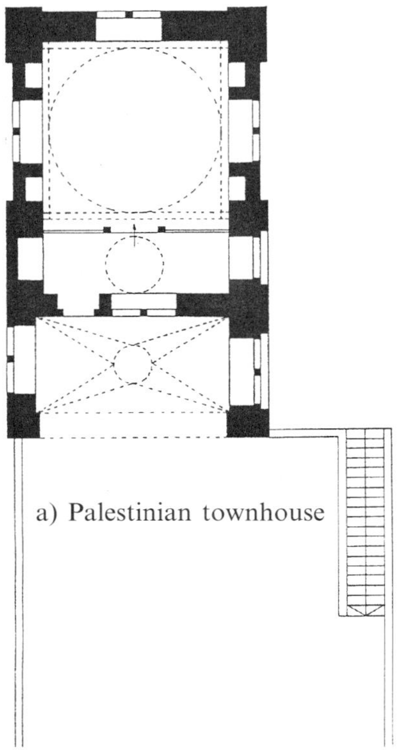

a) Palestinian townhouse

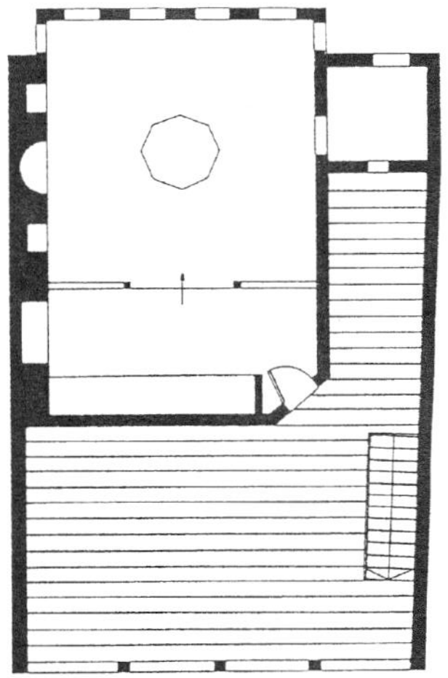

b) Turkish house

Fig. 8.3. Apartments in Palestinian & Turkish town-houses

a) Dar Shahin, Hebron

b) Kayseri

Fig. 8.4. Apartments in Palestinian & Turkish town-houses

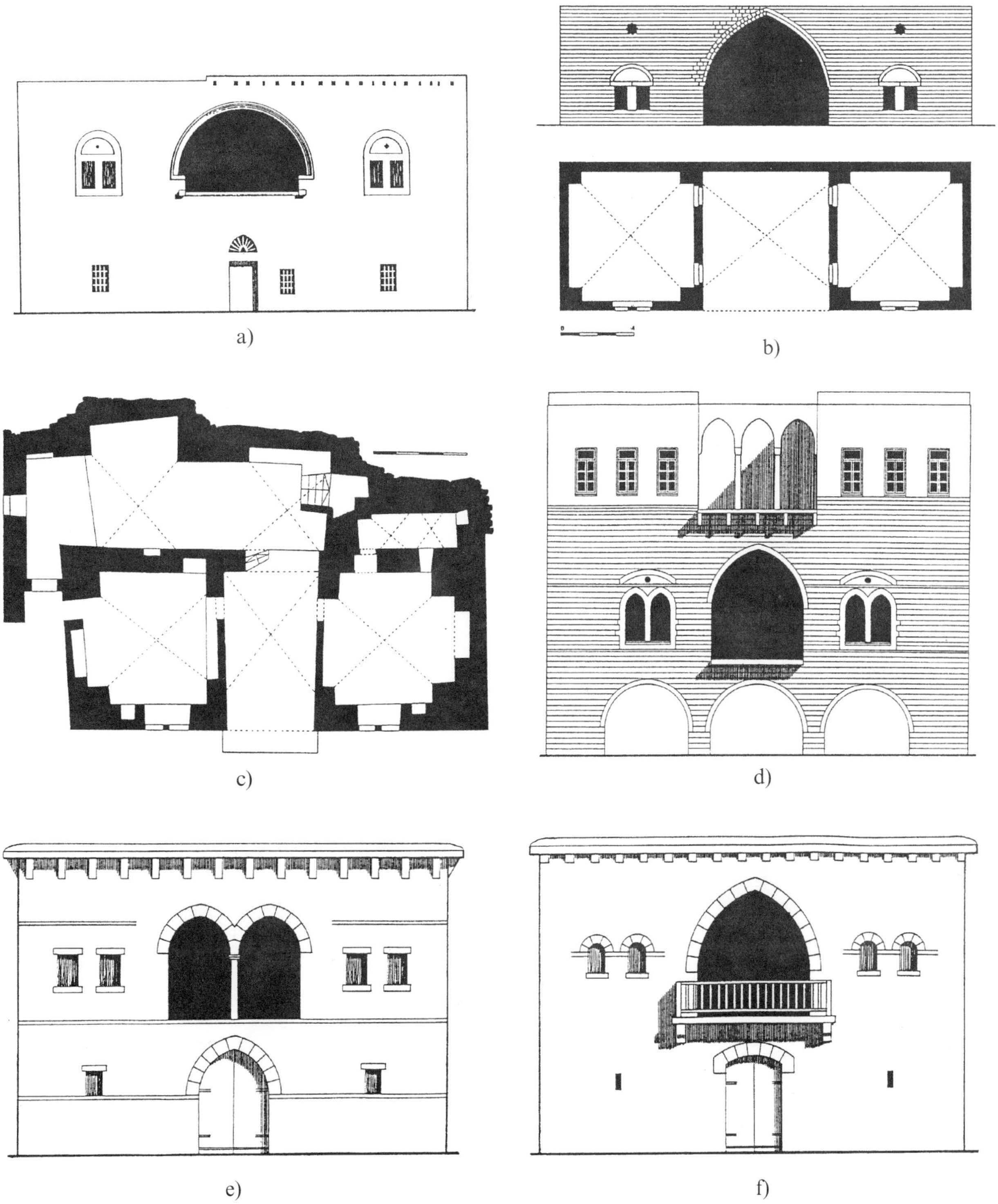

Fig. 8.5. The *Iwan* house
a) House at Bethlehem
b) House at Yafa, near Nazareth
c–d) House HaMeiri, Safed
e–f) Houses at Silvan (Mayyafarikin)

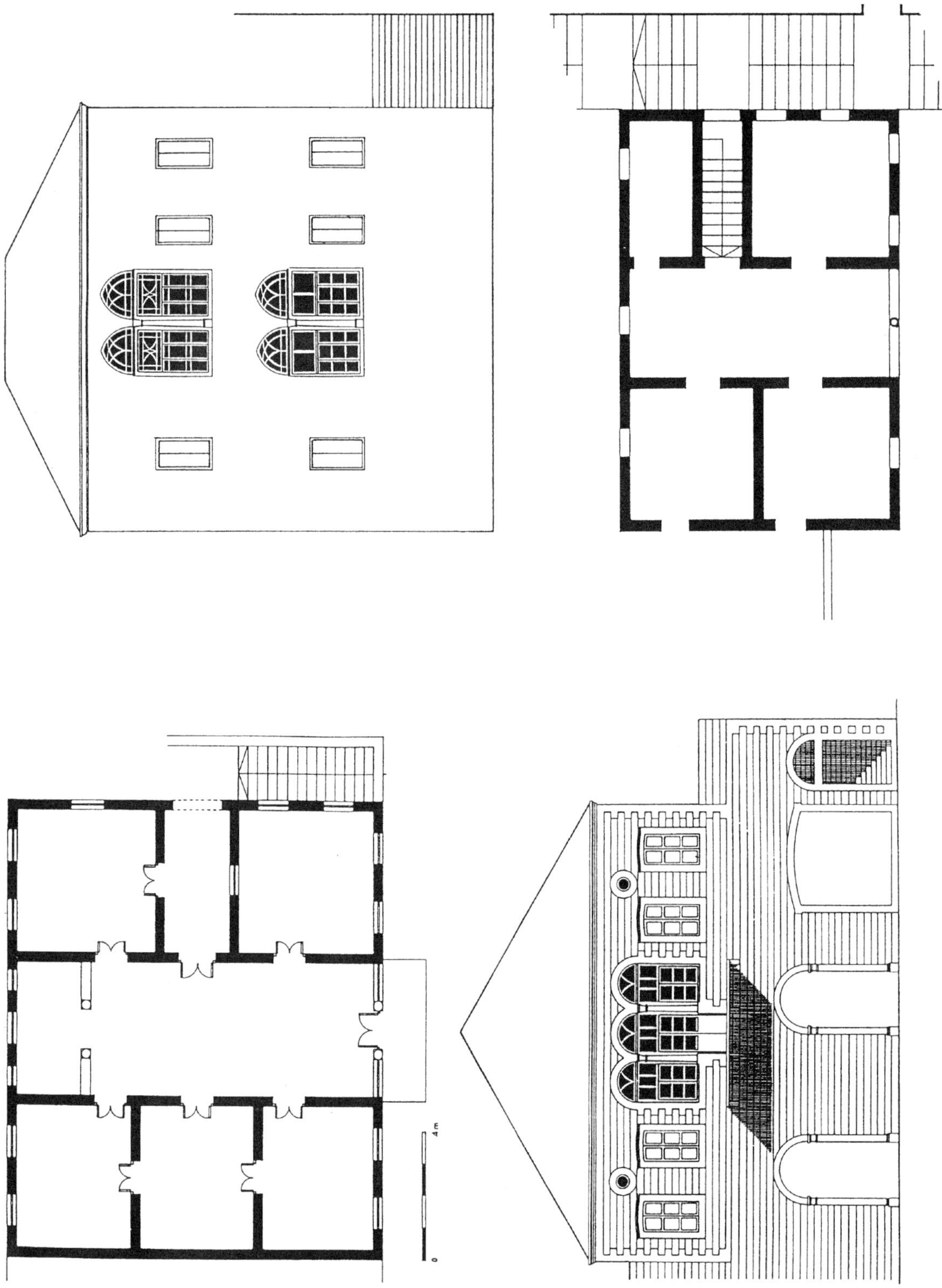

b) House off Shivat Zion St, Haifa

a) House near the Ottoman railway station, Haifa

Fig. 8.6. Central hall houses

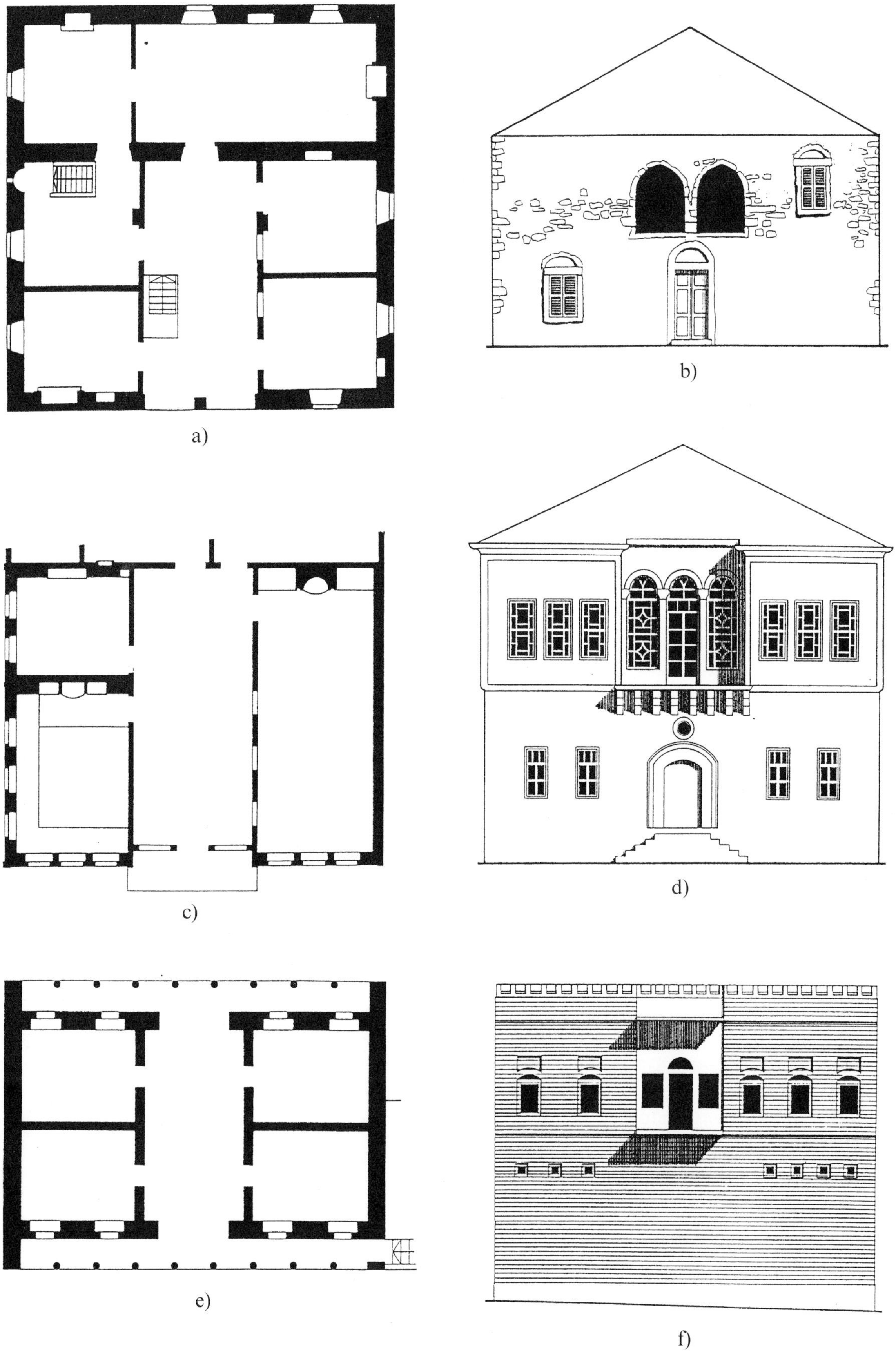

Fig. 8.7. Central hall arrangements in Ottoman domestic architecture

a–b) House at Didyma
c–d) House at Sinasos, near Nevşehir
e) Inn, E. Syria
f) House at Irbil, northern Iraq

9: HOUSES OF THE OTTOMAN PERIOD IN JORDAN

Alison McQuitty
British Institute at Amman for Archaeology & History

I have decided to deviate slightly from the title of the conference – 'The Ottoman House' - at least for the first section, and indulge in a brief survey of the main architectural types of the Ottoman period in Jordan. By doing this I want to give some idea of the variety and range of buildings of this period and the context within which the 'Ottoman House' should be considered. I will then briefly discuss the urban architecture of Jordan and move on to my own research into the Domestic Rural House. This research is based on archaeology and the recording and analysis of standing buildings in conjunction with the use of oral history. I will end with a brief discussion of the use to which this traditional housing in Jordan is now being put. Fig.9.1 is a map of modern Jordan showing the places mentioned in the text.

The point I will make in this paper is that very few of the buildings of the period 1516-1918 show any Ottoman-ness, if such a quality can be defined; their variety matches the fluctuating and regional character of Ottoman control in Jordan. The Ottoman buildings, as opposed to the buildings of the Ottoman period, are not domestic - they were vehicles of the Ottoman state and expressions of their control. There are few surviving, or at least recognised, buildings of the 16th to the early-19th century. This has much to do with the nature of Ottoman settlement and the nature of research into the Ottoman period in Jordan - a study still in its infancy. However, the exception to this statement is found in the Hajj forts. Besides taxation, the major concern of the Ottoman State in Jordan was protection of the Hajj route to the Holy Cities of Mecca and Medina. This route was established in the 16th century to replace the road further west which was prone to suffering from raids. The architecture of these forts has been comprehensively studied and described by A. Petersen (1989, 1995b). What follows is a very brief summary.

There were two main construction phases of the forts - the mid 16th century and the 18th century. Pl.9.1 shows Qatrana Castle which was built in 1531 (and, incidentally, restored with money from the Turkish government). Like forts throughout the ages it has a caravanserai-like plan with an open courtyard surrounded by rooms on the ground floor for stabling animals and *iwan*-plan rooms for living on the upper floor. The exterior of the building and its small entrance is plain apart from three spheres set in triangular arrangement above the gate. Petersen reports that this is an Ottoman symbol derived from an ancient Buddhist symbol for good luck. A more functional addition to the façade was the machicolation over the entrance through which noxious substances would be poured on the heads of the enemy. This machicolation is supported by corbels. The rampart of the fort is decorated with crenellations. Both these latter features are typical of Ottoman architecture in this region. By the eighteenth century the exterior of the forts had changed while the basic plan remained the same. This probably reflected the growing need to counter attacks using fire-arms which were introduced to the local Bedouin tribes at that time. The corbels supporting the machicolations no longer had gaps between them. Rather these acted as platforms protruding from the main wall of the fort which allowed a wider field of fire. Al-Hasa fort which was built in the latter part of the 18th century is a good example of this later type.

For the next examples of Ottoman Imperial Architecture, we leap forward to the late- 19th/early 20th century. As in the 16th century, the Hajj route produces the most Ottoman of constructions. Pl.9.2 shows Qatrana railway station which dates to 1904. The railway was started in Damascus in 1900 and reached al-Madina in 1908. This is a good example of the rural station, a type which is found from Istanbul to Mecca. The pitched and tiled roof supported by iron I-beams is the most telling Ottoman feature (Daher 1995). The simple façade is echoed in the following building of a slightly earlier date, which is again an implant into the local regional tradition. The school in Kerak was built in 1893 during the rule of Sultan Abdul Hamid (pl.9.3). Elements of the façade are very much akin to the urban architecture that was springing up further north in the town of Salt and which really belong to a more general Eastern Mediterranean architectural milieu.

That leads into the topic of urban architecture which is certainly worthy of a paper in its own right. All I propose to do here is to discuss some examples of the styles that entered the urban centres and villages of Jordan in the late 19th and early 20th centuries. The introduction of new styles sparked by fashion and the introduction of new construction materials can be seen in the townscapes of Salt and Irbid. As a generalisation, these new styles appeared 30 years later in Jordan than further west or north in the better established urban centres of Palestine and Syria.

The architecture of the town of Salt stands out in Jordan and has been well-documented by a project of the Salt Development Corporation and the Royal Scientific Society (Royal Scientific Society 1990; Khatib & al-Asir 1995). The revival of Salt and its transformation from a small rural centre to an urban settlement started in 1867 when the *vali* of Damascus re-established order and Ottoman control. A large number of trading families moved east from Nablus in Palestine bringing new ideas and architects with them. Pl.9.4 shows the façade of one of these merchants' buildings built between 1892 and 1906. The building is on three storeys and is sumptuously decorated inside with marble floors and painted ceilings and walls very familiar in the repertoire of Ottoman architectural decoration. By the time Ottoman rule in Jordan had come to an end, some of these architectural styles had spread to the outlying villages. Pl.9.5 shows the complex of Hajj Guweida Suleiman Obeidat built in Hartha, a prosperous village in the North of Jordan, in 1919. This building is unusual in the village and apart from its grand two-storey entrance and 'Alia, the courtyard behind and the buildings ranged around its perimeter are typical of rural architecture.

I think there is no doubt that all students of past human behaviour and settlement would agree that the environment and economy have a great influence on the type of settlement and buildings which a population chooses. The form of the buildings reflects both the construction materials available and the needs of the occupants. This is particularly true when that population is close to the land. For many episodes of history, the majority of the population of Jordan has been engaged in subsistence mixed-farming economy - that is both agriculture and pastoralism. The environment and geography of Jordan is extremely varied, ranging from the basalt and sand deserts of the east, with less than 150mm of rainfall per year, to the plateaus, which support rain-fed grain production, to the olive tree-covered Mediterranean-like hills and the fertile wadi-sides and bottoms which allow irrigated fruit and summer-crop cultivation. The rural architecture reflects this variation, but in detail rather than in general type.

Fig.9.2 depicts a house from the northern hilly area of Jordan and shows the essential elements of rural architecture of that region. The *qa'al bayt* is the main body of the house - the area in which animals were penned at night. In the rural houses of North Jordan it is often at a lower level from the *mastaba* on which the human inhabitants ate, sat and slept. *Mastaba* means bench which is also a frequent installation within courtyards. *Kawair* and *rawiyat* are both structures in which to store agricultural produce. *Kawair* are made from mud, animal hair, pebbles and water covering a reed or branch sub-structure. Food stuffs needed every day, such as lentils and grain for bread-flour, would have been kept in these smaller storage structures. *Rawiyat* are larger storage areas between roof-supporting arches, which act as more permanent storage areas.

These architectural elements within the housing are common throughout Jordan and have been the focus of study by archaeologists, architects, anthropologists, historians and developers (Biewers 1992, Biewers and Kana'an 1993, Fakhoury and Sweiss 1995, Kana'an and al-Rifai 1988, Kana'an and McQuitty 1994, Khammash 1986, Mershen 1992, Noca 1985). As stated before, however, there is considerable variation in the configuration and use of these structures. One variation is between the nucleated villages of these houses with their associated courtyards in the areas where permanently settled communities prevailed e.g. the hilly areas of North Jordan, and the plateaus where grain-production rather than mixed-farming was the focus, such as the Kerak Plateau. The focus of my research has been in this area, around the archaeological site of Khirbat Faris and the modern village of al-Qasr.

Oral history relates that buildings such as shown in pl.9.6 were constructed at the end of the 19th century. There are two standing examples at Khirbat Faris built on the instructions of one Faris Majali. They are extremely large with a floor area of c. 30m^2. The elements of the buildings are the same as those well-known from North Jordan although there is no height-distinction inside the house. The large roof area can be supported since arch-walls have been built out perpendicular to the side walls. The arches spring from these arch-walls rather than the house side-walls themselves. Excavation has shown that while the side-walls had no foundation trench, the arch-walls, being load-bearing, were sunk into deep foundation trenches. The walls and the arches are dry-laid apart from the arch key-stone which was mortared into place. A more complete example of this type of house, built at the same time in the nearby village of al-Qasr, shows how awe-inspiring these structures are when roofed (pl.9.7). The spaces between the arches are filled with *rawiyat* (pl.9.8). These stone *rawiyat* would have originally been plastered over. The *rawiyat* were filled from the roof; ramps survive at the back of these houses, which led up onto the flat roof. Grain and/or straw was poured in through the roof and could be taken out through an opening at the base of the bin, inside the house.

Oral history indicates that these buildings were not used primarily for living in but rather for the safe-keeping of agricultural produce. In this area of mixed-farming where both pastoralism and extensive agriculture are practised, people as often as not lived in tents and stored their crops in these storage-houses. These houses were not nucleated or part of settlements formed by complexes of interlocking courtyards. In later times some of these storage-houses became the focus for newly developing villages, for example at al-Qasr (Kana'an and McQuitty 1994), but their primary use was in a mixed-farming system where both tents and houses were used and where the house was *not* primarily for living in.

The antecedents for this building-type are unclear, and there is at least one example un-excavated at Khirbat Faris. In Northern Syria examples from the 18th century are recorded and in the same area Dr. Mike Fuller has found an example which he dates to the 14th century (Fuller and Fuller 1988). I think it is clear that these buildings have been affected more by the functional constraints of the environment and economy rather than anything Ottoman. In Jordan, the only realm in which one can talk of the 'Ottoman House' is in urban housing.

Finally, and very briefly, I want to mention some of the present-day uses to which traditional housing is being put. Traditional villages are chiefly re-used in the realm of tourism. The 'fashion' for restoring and living in old houses for private use has not really hit Jordan yet, largely because the traditional architecture is in the villages and countryside and not in the urban centres where the employment is.

The entire old village of Tayybet, near the famous World Heritage site of Petra, has been very successfully converted into a luxury hotel-complex (pl.9.9). Each village house has become a hotel 'room' and the labyrinthine pattern of village streets has been maintained. New public buildings, like the restaurant, have been built in the traditional style (Fakhoury and Sweiss 1995). At least one other village in the Petra area is being converted for the same purpose. Umm Qeis in North Jordan is a stunning example of village architecture of the Ottoman period (Shami 1989). Many of the houses here are domed; they form large courtyard complexes and the house façades are decorated with architectural fragments from the local antiquity site. One of the courtyard complexes has been converted into a residence and work area for visiting archaeological teams; one complex is the museum and other buildings have been converted into Department of Antiquities offices. The school has been altered to become a restaurant with superb views sweeping across the Jaulan Heights and Lake Tiberias. Sadly, none of these houses are occupied by the original villagers as they were persuaded to leave in the 1970s and 1980s by the Department of Antiquities because their village was on top of an archaeological site. Buildings in several other villages in Jordan have been converted into restaurants and art and craft shops, but for many, including the fine urban housing in Salt, there is no certain future and they are left to decay.

Bibliography

'Amr, K., Zayadine, F., Zaghloul, M. (eds) 1995: *Studies in the History and Archaeology of Jordan* 5. Amman.

Biewers, M. 1990: *L'habitat traditionnel à 'Aima.* (Thèse de Doctorat, Université Lumière, Lyon 2).

---- 1992: 'Occupation de l'espace dans le village traditionnel de 'Aima: approche ethno-archéologique', in Tell *et al.* 1992: 397-402.

Biewers, M., Kana'an, R. 1993: 'Vernacular Architecture Survey of Kurkuma, 316-319', in G. Palumbo *et al.* (eds), 'The Wadi el-Yabis Survey and Excavations Project: Report on the 1992 season', *ADAJ* 37: 307-24.

Daher, R. 1995: 'The Resurrection of the Hijaz Railroad Line', in 'Amr *et al.* 1995: 341-50.

Denton, B., St. Laurent, B. 1996: 'Early Twentieth Century Architecture', in P.M. Bikai, T.A. Dailey (eds), *Madaba: Cultural Heritage.* American Center for Oriental Research, Amman: 47-89.

Fakhoury, L., Sweiss, R. 1995: 'Tayyiba 'A Thriving Village'', in 'Amr *et al.* 1995: 361-74.

Fuller, M., Fuller, N. 1988: 'Tell Tuneir on the Khabur: Preliminary Report on Three Seasons', *Les Annales Archéologiques Arabes Syriennes* 37: 279-90.

Kana'an, R., al-Rifai, T. 1988: *'Iraq al-Amir wa al-Bardon* (Arabic), University of Jordan, Amman.

Kana'an, R., McQuitty, A. 1994: 'The Architecture of al-Qasr on the Kerak Plateau: An Essay in the Chronology of Vernacular Architecture', *Palestine Exploration Quarterly* 126: 127-51.

Khammash, A. 1986: *Notes on Village Architecture in Jordan.* Lafayette, LA.

Khatib, R.Y., al-Asir, H.S. 1995: 'The Golden Era of as-Salt (1870-1950): Urban and Architectural Development', in 'Amr *et al.* 1995: 351-60.

McQuitty, A. 1986: 'Architectural Study of Bait Ras', *Archiv für Orientforschung* 33: 153-5.

McQuitty, A.M., Lenzen, C.J. 1989: 'An Architectural Study of the Irbid Region with Particular Reference to a Building in Irbid', *Levant* 21: 119-28.

McQuitty, A., Faulkner, R. 1993: 'A Preliminary Report on the Khirbat Faris Project: the 1989, 1990 and 1991 Seasons', *Levant* 25: 37-62.

Merschen, B. 1992: 'Settlement History and Village Space in Late Ottoman Northern Jordan', in Tell *et al.* 1992: 409-16.

Noca, L. 1985: *Smakieh: un village de Jordanie,* (Ecole d'architecture de Lyon: Travail Personnel de Troisième Cycle). Lyon.

Petersen, A. 1989: 'Early Ottoman Forts on the Darb al-Hajj', *Levant* 21: 97-117.

---- 1995a: 'Preliminary Report on an Architectural Survey of Historic Buildings in Ramla', *Levant* 27: 75-101.

---- 1995b: 'The Fortification of the Pilgrimage Route During the First Three Centuries of Ottoman Rule (1516-1757)', in 'Amr *et al.* 1995: 299-306.

Royal Scientific Society 1990: *Salt: A Plan for Action* 3 vols. Salt Development Corporation, Amman.

Shami, S. 1989: 'Settlement and Resettlement in Umm Qeis: Spatial Organisation and Social Dynamics in a Village in North Jordan', in J. P. Bourdier, N. A. Sayyad (eds), *Dwellings, Settlements and Tradition*. New York: 451-76.

Tell, S., 'Amr, K., Zayadine, F., Zaghloul, M. (eds) 1992: *Studies in the History and Archaeology of Jordan 4*. Department of Antiquities, Amman.

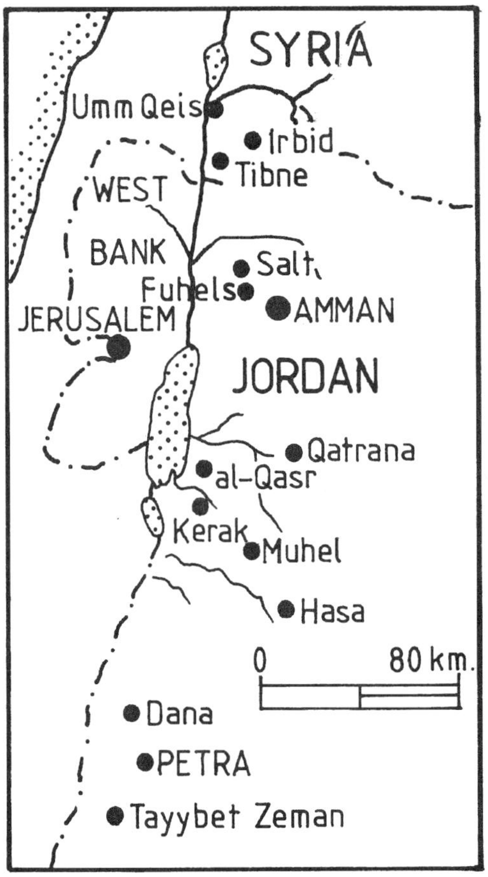

Fig. 9.1. Map of sites discussed

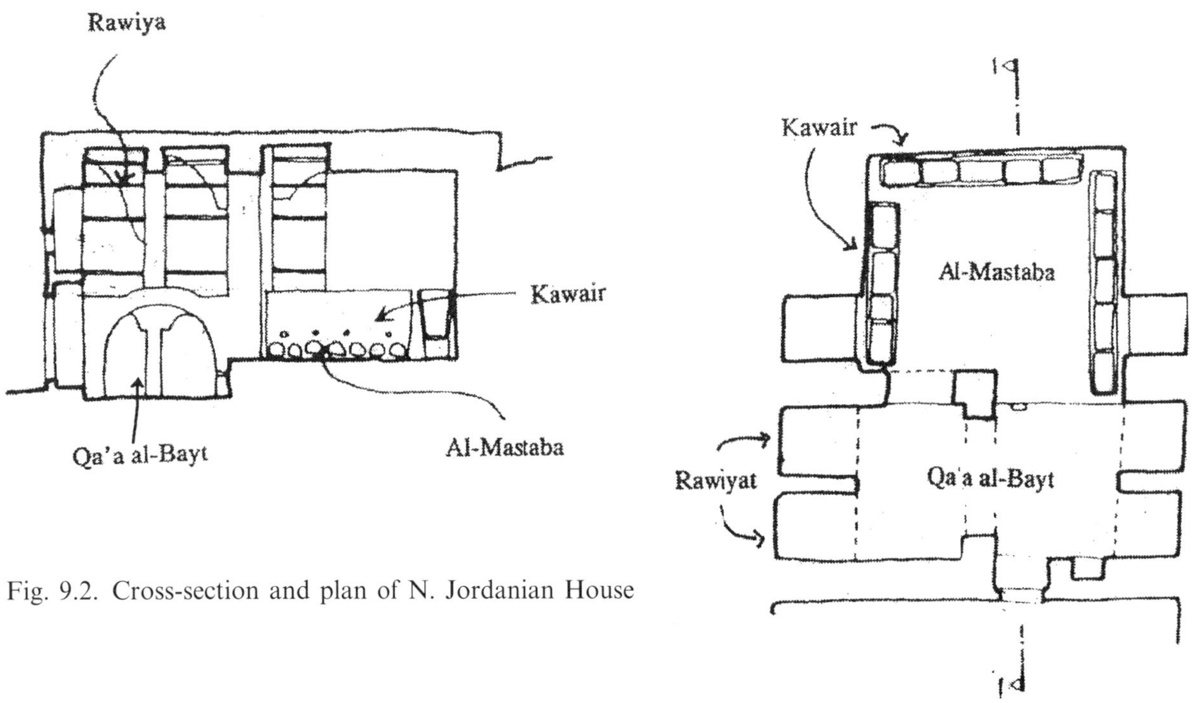

Fig. 9.2. Cross-section and plan of N. Jordanian House

10: OTTOMAN HOUSES IN CYPRUS

Assoc. Prof. Dr. Netice Yıldız
Eastern Mediterranean University, Gazi Magosa, Cyprus

Introduction: A Historical Perspective

Cyprus has a long history. Archaeology has demonstrated that early man came to the island about 7000 BC and settled in the south-eastern part at a place called Khirokitia. The bee-hive houses built by these people are in fact an interesting feature of the Neolithic period. Since then settlement has continued on the island until today and it has witnessed several different cultures associated with the different ethnic origins of those who have lived on the island and those who have controlled it throughout its history. Turkish civilisation on the island, with which this paper is primarily concerned, dates back to the end of the 16th century.

Following the conquest of Cyprus by the Ottoman Empire in 1570/1571, the island saw an influx of Turkish families. The areas reserved for settlement by them were mostly those where the Latins had resided, and Nicosia, the capital city of the island, was divided into 25 quarters, nearly 15 of which were occupied by the Turks and bear Turkish names (Jeffery 1918: 32-3). Famagusta, in contrast, remained closed to Christians living on the island for nearly 300 years following the conquest of the city by the Turks (Jeffery 1918: 104), and only Turkish people lived there. Corneille de Bruyn, who travelled in Cyprus in the 17th century and published an informative description of what he saw, was unlucky not to have been able to enter the walled city of Famagusta during his visit (Bruyn 1702: 266).

There are interesting Ottoman houses that have survived until the present day in every part of the island, and while it can be said that there are parallels between the houses in Cyprus and those of Anatolia, nevertheless they display local variety from both the architectural point of view as well as the living traditions of their inhabitants. The Ottoman houses in Cyprus, in fact, show partly Mediterranean coastal characteristics, and partly those of Anatolia.

There are several examples that reflect a chronological sequence of houses; these mainly occur in the Turkish part of Nicosia and in Famagusta, that is, within the walled cities. The best examples are those which were constructed over Latin foundation walls, either Gothic or Venetian buildings constructed usually by the rich pashas who lived in Cyprus. The travel books give much information about the types and external appearance of these buildings, although there is almost no information on the interior design of an Ottoman house built during the early centuries of Ottoman control. On the other hand, 19th century travellers, particularly Dr. Edward Daniel Clarke, Archduke Louis Salvator of Austria and Mrs. Scott-Stevenson give complete descriptions of 19th century Turkish houses.

Recent restoration projects have enabled some of the houses to be seen to their best advantage, while some projects still await implementation owing to the lack of financial resources in the Department of Antiquities in Northern Cyprus. It is very upsetting to see from time to time that these buildings have undergone deterioration; a detailed study of the characteristics of these buildings must be carried out before restoration can take place. Although personal observation forms part of this paper, its main thrust is based on information given in the travel books, since even the best looked-after buildings have lost many of their original features as a result of the alterations carried out by their owners or unsuccessful restoration projects.

Location of the Ottoman Houses

The Ottoman houses in Cyprus are generally located within the walled cities of Nicosia (Lefkoşa) and Famagusta (Magosa). There are exceptions to this, either where summer residences and farm houses were built in the countryside or in other towns such as Kyrenia (Girne), Paphos (Baf), Lefke, Lapitos (Lapta), Larnaca and Limassol. Giovanni Mariti, for instance, who lived on the island during the years 1760-67, referred to a large house belonging to a Turkish agha in the village of Dicomos (present-day Dikmen) as the only noteworthy monument he had encountered on his way from Nicosia to Kyrenia (Mariti 1909: 49). In general, though, Turkish houses were usually in separate quarters in the town. In Paphos there were three quarters: Turks occupied the centre of the metropolis with nearly 150 houses, whereas the Greek quarter, with about 50 houses, and the marina were in a place called Ktima (Turner 1920 2: 555). The same was true in Episcopi, where there were even some villages in which the Turks and Greeks set up their houses on the slopes of two separate hills (Ali Bey 1816 1: 263, 289), though in such cases research also shows that Ottoman-style houses were actually preferred by the Greeks and foreigners living on the island.

Early Ottoman Houses in the 16th and 17th Centuries

Although many new buildings were constructed on the island as a whole during Turkish occupation, it is interesting to see that in the early years of Turkish rule the Turks themselves preferred to make use of and adapt existing buildings left over from the Latin period, rather than construct new palaces or mansion houses even for people of high rank. For instance, according to a document dated June 13, 1571, it was requested that three houses appropriate for the needs of the *Beylerbeyi* (Governor), *Kadı* (chief judge) and the *Defterdar* (treasurer) be rented for their accommodation within the walled city, the rents and expenses for their repair and decoration being paid by the government.[1] A direct result of this is that several eclectic styles of housing still exist in the old parts of Nicosia and Famagusta, which remained within the city walls. There are, in fact, several interesting examples of this eclectic style, with the doorway and façade walls in Gothic or Venetian style, while the interior design of the houses is completely Turkish.

The cities inherited by the Ottoman Empire in 1570/71 are believed to have had rather beautiful houses and palaces, although it is known that a considerable amount of destruction involving the monuments of Cyprus, particularly in Nicosia, took place in the Venetian period during the construction of the city walls (Keshishian 1990: 64; Jeffery 1918: 88; Januen 1785 2: 1074-5). According to the accounts of several European travellers such as Wilbrandi von Oldenburg, Jacobus de Verona, L. Von Suchen and John Maundeville, there were in Nicosia beautiful large houses which were finely decorated and painted, and which were reminiscent of the houses in Antioch during the Lusignan period (Cobham 1908: 13). In addition, travellers such as John Locke and Elias of Pesaro, who travelled in Cyprus during the Venetian period, also described the houses of Nicosia and Famagusta as being fine and well built (Cobham 1908: 71, 73).

Arif Dede, the Turkish historian, in his *Chronique of Cyprus,* confirmed this fact by describing Nicosia and Famagusta as being rather fine cities, with large beautiful houses, palaces, and gardens within the fortresses, which were masterpieces created by a famous architect from Italy. He added that there were 7000 houses, and several palaces in Nicosia which were rather comfortable and richly decorated (Arif Dede 1991: 40)

In the memoirs published by several European travellers we can see that the early years of Ottoman rule are marked by a continuation of this refined environment in the large cities. Fynes Moryson, an English traveller who visited Cyprus in May 1596 during his travels in Europe and the East, described the houses of this island as built after the manner of Asia, using not much stone, one storey high, and plain at the top, which was plastered, and where the inhabitants ate and slept in the open air (Cobham 1908: 185). Another traveller, Stochove, who visited Cyprus in May 1631, described Nicosia, in his travels entitled *Voyage du Sieur de Stochove, Efait en Années 1630, 1631, 1632,* as having grand houses built of cut stone, with fine wide streets, and he added that there was nothing Turkish about these nor the buildings, since the majority of them were Venetian work (Cobham 1908: 216). Noel Dominique Hurtel of Arras in Artois, who visited Cyprus in 1670, described the Turkish palace and houses in Nicosia in his work entitled *Du Voiage de Jerusalem,* in the following words:

> There is a palace to be seen where the Pasha had his residence; it stands opposite to a large square, wherein is a pyramid, and every Friday the Turks learn horsemanship. We were told that the kings of Cyprus lived in this palace; in size and height it is a fine structure. Above the entrance are the arms of the House of Lusignan, and those of Savoy, set in many fine devices. The other houses in the city inhabited by the Turks are generally of good cut stone, built, we were told, by the Venetians, and the streets are wide and handsome. The houses are set in beautiful gardens, well planted, chiefly with the palms which bear dates. (Cobham 1908: 233)

A study of the old houses also proves the accounts given by these travellers. There are some fine examples of houses with outer walls built in well cut stone, some even having Gothic tracery or rosette windows, and with the arms of the Latin families carved on their walls, while on the other hand the projecting bay (*cumba*) of the halls (*sofa*) on the first floor of the houses, the windows and the interiors completely altered to Turkish style are proof of adaptation.

It was the same with the Turkish *seraglios* (palaces) both in Nicosia and Famagusta. As has been stated above, the Turkish palaces in both cities were Venetian buildings which were renovated and decorated according to Turkish traditions. The budget book from the period of Cafer Pasha, the governor, dated 1589-99, gives information on two palaces reserved for the Governor, one in Nicosia, and the other one in Famagusta.[2] Giovanni Maritti (1909: 43) remarked upon the alterations seen as the caprice of successive Pashas and Governors which left nothing worthy of notice. Mrs. A. Batson Joyner (1878: 29) mentioned in the case of the palace in Nicosia that it was built in the Norman Gothic style. She added that with the exception of an archway and outer walls little remained of the original building and now it had balconies with wooden latticework and wooden roofs. It was a large building with many apartments since Clarke (1812: 346) referred to several passages they passed along in order to reach the Governor's apartment for an audience with the Pasha. The palace was not of course in good condition in the 19th century, since the governor of Cyprus was a Muhassıl[3] who was renting the island for a while and in return paid a certain amount of tax to the Sultan every year. Ludwig Ross (1910: 24) described the place as a building in the Turkish fashion, with a poor crumbling lumber chest, hanging doors, rotten floors and paper window panes. This building was pulled down during the early years of British rule in Cyprus at the beginning of this century in order to build new government offices, but the area is still popularly known as Saray Önü. The Gothic stone ornamentation, particularly the flamboyant archway and probably one of its wooden doors, which is in the eclectic style and the middle part of which is decorated in early Turkish classical style of the *kündekâri*[4] technique, are exhibited in the Lapidary Museum opened in 1905.

There was another large residence of the Turkish Governors in Famagusta, which was also originally a Latin building, i.e. a Gothic building with a Renaissance portal, part of which still remains today.

Pococke refers to the palace in Famagusta in the following words: 'The ancient piazza seems to have been very beautiful; the house of the governor with a portico before it is on one side, and the western front of the church of Saint Sophia on the other.' (Cobham 1908: 255). He also stated that in Nicosia there were several very magnificent houses still remaining which dated from the time of the kings of Cyprus; some of them had been repaired by the Venetians according to the rules of contemporary architecture, while there was a most beautiful Corinthian doorcase belonging to a house which, they said, belonged to the Venetian general. Pococke was surprised to see that in Famagusta the existing buildings did not take up even half the space within the walls, and a great part even of those were not inhabited (Cobham 1908: 255, 260).

It is clear from the description of the late 16th and 17th centuries that the Turks utilized the existing buildings in the island rather than pulling them down. In particular three beautiful houses (two in Nicosia, the other one in Famagusta) prove the idea that the Turks made use of the existing Latin buildings by altering the interior design, or even rebuilding them internally to meet the needs of Turkish families, leaving only the outer walls of the building unchanged. A rather beautiful house from this early period exists in Nicosia at Kirlizade Street (pl.10.1), with the Lusignan arms still extant on it, while the windows, and the projecting bay (*cumba*), facing west like the main entrance of the house, show the Turkish alteration of the place. The building has by now lost its originality and beauty, but a description of it is given by Archduke Louis Salvator of Austria (1983: 24, 26) as follows:

> There are very few houses worth seeing at Levkosia. However, an old stone house in the Yegni Djami street, called Kaloiro al Effendi Konak, is worth mentioning, which is inhabited now by two Turkish families. It has a Gothic arched gate, the outer cornice of which is crowned by finials and a shield of arms over them; there are also arms at both sides. Some traces of Byzantine windows and gargoyles at the corners of the cornice are still visible. The Turkish inhabitants have erected a wooden pavilion in front. The interior of the edifice was once richly decorated in Oriental fashion; now, we are sorry to say, the whole of it is sadly neglected and half in ruins. The balcony shows elegantly-shaped stone ornaments, different grotesque figures, and tiny carved windows. Entering the house itself we find in the first place a large divan-room, with soft, inviting seats all round; the fine ceiling, elaborate shutters on the latticed windows, and a neat inlaid cupboard by the side of the door, remind us of best Moorish works; there are also little hanging stairs or shelves, on which the thousand little nothings of a harem are neatly arranged. On one side we enter a smaller room with a wooden ceiling, divided into squares, and a low balustrade in front of the latticed windows. Some steps lead up to a higher platform with divans, separated by another balustrade from the rest of the room. Neat shelves are visible everywhere. The doors are partly of square design with Turkish fretwork, partly carved in the elaborate style of the Renaissance, or else arched. There are rooms with groined arched ceilings, others simply covered with flat beams, which are supported by small consoles. On the second floor there is an exceedingly fine room, the ceiling of which is composed of Turkish wood-work. Over the door-posts is a small latticed balcony which rests on the slender columns of the balustrade separating the upper divan from the rest of the room. Ornamental shelves with turrets in the middle give the room a lively aspect, which seems to have been opened in olden times for the family feasts and dances.

This house is under restoration at the moment. As stated by Louis Salvator, it has lost its magnificence owing to neglect. The fine, beautifully painted and gilded ceiling in one of the rooms mentioned by Salvator is at present covered with dust and smoke (pl.10.2), while the fireplace, lattice windows, inlaid cupboard and shelves no longer exist. The ceilings of the other rooms also are the only parts that remain in good condition up to the present day.

A second example is the house which was believed to have been built by Menteş Efendi, the kadı of Cyprus in the earlier years of Turkish rule (pl.10.3-5). This house, which had been once the palace of the Latin Archbishop, was restored and used by Küçük Mehmet Agha, who was appointed governor of Cyprus in the period 1816-1821 (Gürkan 1982: 106-7). The Gothic hood-mouldings over the Turkish-style windows, which have replaced the Gothic ornamental stone traceries, the projecting bay (*cumba*) in the middle of the building, and the arms of the Frankish families carved on the southern façade of the building show the eclectic character of the house. The upper main room also has an elaborate wooden ceiling with geometrical decoration and an attached square-shaped central panel with elaborate geometrical decorations. One of the rooms on the upper floor also has Turkish-style niches on the side of the cupboards.

There is also another remarkably beautiful example of this kind of house in Famagusta (pl.10.6). The size of the house, the interior arrangements, and a piece of tile remaining in the Turkish bath, which is in the courtyard of the house, suggest that it was once occupied by an important person of high rank, either a kadı or the treasurer of the city. The entrance of the house is surrounded with rather high walls built of well cut stones. The other three sides have Venetian walls with chimney pieces that reflect its original Venetian character, while the glazed top windows and shutters show the Turkish additions. The building consists, in fact, of two large houses which were built at different times, although the outer walls show a unique character. The part of the house on the right hand side of the entrance seems to be the earlier and better one. The stone staircase with its wooden balustrades leads into a *hayat* (veranda or open *sofa*) off which are two rooms. One of these rooms still retains the raised wooden platform with its wooden balustrade, which divides the sitting area from the lower floor level *(sekialtı)* immediately adjacent to the entrance. This, together with the decorated shelves on the walls along three sides of the room occupied by the platform, is the only part of the house to reflect the original interior arrangement of a Turkish room. The rooms below the stone staircase are entered through a pointed arched door, which is a local characteristic found in many houses. There is a fountain just near the staircase. The Turkish bath in the courtyard has beautifully shaped niches and traces of tiles that once covered the whole interior. Only one piece of blue and white tile, most probably made in Kütahya, and now in a rather defaced condition, remains in this bath today.

In all three houses the entrance is through a Gothic gateway into a courtyard. The houses in Nicosia have in addition a *sofa* or hallway off which the rooms are situated, while in Famagusta the house is entered directly via the courtyard. The flight of stone stairs also leads to a *hayat* (veranda) around which the rooms are grouped. Therefore, all the rooms open onto the courtyard.

Ottoman Houses in the 18th and 19th Centuries

It can be assumed that the type of houses started to change in the 18th century, perhaps as a result of a terrible earthquake that took place in 1718. Similar earthquakes had been reported between the years 1567 and 1583, which caused slight damage to the cities. It is said, for instance, that an earthquake which took place in 1583 threw down a house in the Limassol area. The terrible earthquake of 1718 and those in later years might well have affected the building style, as has been stated by many sources (Jennings 1993: 174-5).

Alexander Drummond, who visited Cyprus in 1745, described the houses in Larnaca, another city in the southeastern part of the island, as follows:

> All houses here, as well as in other places, are of large bricks, dried in the sun; these are neat enough. They never build higher than one floor, in order to avoid some part of the dreadful effects of earthquakes, and these houses last longer than one could imagine, though the architects, joiners, and carpenters are the most bungling artificers that ever were seen. (Drummond 1754: 140)

Giovanni Mariti, who lived in Cyprus between the years 1760-1767, described Nicosia as possessing wide streets to set off the palaces and buildings which adorned them, but adds that in many places they had been altered, and new houses built of unburnt bricks had been inserted, breaking the regular line and making a poor impression (Mariti 1909: 44). He expresses his sorrow at the houses in Famagusta, saying (1909: 67) that

> The ancient houses are being constantly sold; men buy them to pull down and carry off their woodwork, especially beams and rafters. But it is strictly forbidden to take away a single stone, so that everywhere you see great heaps.

According to Mariti, buildings were rarely more than two storeys high, a ground and first floor; the roofs were made of earth mixed with clay. During the summer cracks appeared in this as a result of the heat, but during the winter these were plugged by the action of the rain. These roofs were half a *braccio*[5] thick, supported by stout beams, with cross rafters and a double reed mat. If the rains were long and continuous, the inhabitants were obliged to make frequent repairs. However, he says that houses so built and roofed would resist the shock of earthquakes, which stone houses did not, as quite recent experience showed. The floors were paved with a very soft white marble, which flaked off very rapidly; this too was a product of the island. The windows were all glazed, and every house had its own garden. Maritti (1909: 30-1) also added that the best and largest houses owned in Larnaca usually belonged to the European consuls, the largest being that of the English consuls, while there were both Greeks and Turks who owned fine and spacious houses, though not such as need particular mention, for they were of a wholly different and irregular shape.

According to Louis Salvator (1983: 19), there were very few houses built of stone in Nicosia at the end of the 19th century. Those which existed were adorned with Gothic arched windows and flowing tracery, but nobody seemed to pay much attention to them. Most of the houses were made of large clay bricks, as they said, for fear of earthquakes.

The change in building material and architectural techniques was described as wretched and ugly by some travellers, while others, in contrast, described them as cheerful, tasteful and beautiful.

After the middle of the 19th century the plan of the houses changed. Instead of opening into a courtyard, the entrance led directly into the *sofa* (hallway) of the house, around which were the rooms. The number of windows also increased, but some traditional characteristics like the projecting *sofa* on the upper floor was used in almost every large house. This change can be attributed to the increase of European influence on society, since it also occurred in Turkey.

Several houses were constructed in the neo-classical and neo-gothic style during this period. The conservative, religious families sought to maintain the privacy of their houses by retaining the courtyard plan with the entrance of the house having a simple door, while those influenced by the then modern style had outer doors opening directly into the *sofa* of the house.

Some of the Turkish houses built in the last decade of the 19th century and the first half of the 20th century have dated inscriptions, while a few of them also have prayers, these being mostly in Arabic numerals and characters, or star and crescent motifs inscribed on their doorheads, a result of increasing patriotic feelings in the British period.

An interesting description that we may mention for the late 18th or 19th century Ottoman houses is given in the memoirs of Esme Scott-Stevenson. Mrs. Scott-Stevenson lived in Cyprus for a while with her husband, Captain Andrew Scott, who was appointed the Civil Commissioner of Kyrenia and also worked as the assistant Commissioner to Sir Garnet Wolsey. They stayed in Kyrenia during their residence, where they lived in a little Turkish house at the harbour. The description of the house given by Mrs. Scott-Stevenson in her memoirs is rather interesting since we have no remains of such houses any more in Cyprus. The description runs as follows:

> Our house in Kyrenia was the quaintest little dwelling imaginable. It was only one storey high, and built in the shape of a hollow square. In the centre was a court filled with orange, lemon, quince, and mulberry trees. The roof was flat and covered with mud, and became in the spring time a perfect garden, full of iris and anemones grown from the seeds sown by the birds and the wind. The back of our house faced the sea, and our drawing room was built on piles right over it, so that on looking out of the windows I could see the fish swimming. We had a Turkish bath attached to the house but this was never used, as none of our servants knew how to manage it. By the side of the building was a stone tank, always kept filled with water. Our dining room was a long chamber, having six windows looking onto the sea, with low divans round the walls. These served as the most comfortable couches, and were very convenient for all the tray newspapers. Above the divans in Cypriot houses there is always a wooden shelf, on which the inmates arranged their china plates and bowls, whether for use or ornaments I could never decide. Instead of plates, we placed a row of gourds, for gourds grow to perfection here, and my husband got some very fine specimens, even better ones than some he brought home from Ashantee. Our sitting room was painted in true Turkish style: stars and crescents in every colour round the top of the walls, below this, verses from the Koran and different proverbs. Some of these were translated to me as follows:
>
> 'Let God keep away from the man who has the face of a friend, but the heart of an enemy.'
>
> 'Wine and women turn a wise men into a tyrant.'
>
> 'He who knows how to keep his tongue silent saved his head.'
>
> 'At Constantinople fire devours your goods, plague takes your wife, and women your wit.'
>
> At the end of the room was a gaudily painted recess, to hold a basin and ewer for washing the hands. We filled this with flowers, thinking a lavatory unnecessary in an English drawing room. The ceiling was the quaintest part of all. It was divided by a raised trellis of plasters all over the surface and in each almond-shaped space was a

separate daub of colour, all in graduating shades: canary, amber, gold, orange, brown, and the same with the blues, reds, and greens. Strange to say it is not hideous, and in some odd way seemed to harmonize the room. The floor was covered with cool Turkish matting, while a few pieces of English furniture gave quite a comfortable appearance to the little apartment. Opposite the entrance of our dwelling stood the mosque, a square building with a graceful minaret. (Scott-Stevenson 1880: 94-7)

It was not only the Turkish nobility or rich men who used the typical Turkish-style houses. The dragoman who represented the non-Moslems' legal rights at the Ottoman Porte and some other rich non-Moslems, together with the European consuls, lived in large, luxurious, Turkish-style houses. Dr. Clarke gives us a clear description of the dragoman's house together with the palace of the Pasha:

> We went to the house of Mr. Sekis (the English Dragoman as he is vulgarly called), a rich Armenian merchant, who enjoys English protection for transacting whatsoever business their nation may have with the Governor. His house was in all respects a palace, possessing the highest degree of Oriental magnificence. The apartments were not only spacious, but they were adorned with studied elegance, the floors being furnished with the finest mats brought from Grand Cairo, and the divans covered with satin, set round with embroidered cushions. The windows of the rooms, as in all Oriental houses, were near the roof, and small, although numerous, and placed close to each other. They had double casements, one being of painted glass, surrounded by carved work, as in the old Gothic palaces of England. These perhaps derived their original form from the East, during the crusades. So many instances occur to strengthen the opinion, that I may be liable to unnecessary repetition, when allusion is made to this style of building. The custom of having the floor raised in the upper part of the chamber, where the superiors sit, as in our old halls, is strictly Oriental; it is the same in the tents of the Tartars. We were permitted to view the Harem. This always consists of a summer and a winter apartment. The first was a large square room, surrounded by divans; the last an oblong chamber, where the divans were placed parallel to each other, one on either side, lengthways; and at the upper extremity was the fire-place, resembling our ancient English hearths. Soon after he proposed that we should accompany him to the Governor's. As we descended, he showed us his beautiful garden, filled with standard apricot trees laden with ripe fruit, and our wine, as he said, our dinner, already cooling in marble fountains, beneath the shade of orange, citron, lemon, fig, vine, and pomegranate trees. (Cobham 1908: 386-7)

General Characteristics of the Ottoman Houses

1. Construction techniques

It is through the travel books of the European travellers that we get information about the construction techniques and the basic materials of Ottoman houses. Giovanni Mariti (1909:30-1) gives a rather detailed description of house construction in Cyprus, and almost the same description is given by Fred H. Fisher (1878: 42-4), who published a book on Cyprus in 1878. Salvator too gives much information about construction techniques, materials, decoration and the prices of houses.

According to them, houses were generally built of bricks made of clay, chopped straw and moist earth which were then dried in the sun, their shape being similar to those made in Italy. The size of these bricks was nearly two feet long and six inches wide. The same mixture was also used to bind the bricks together during construction. The walls were then plastered with the whitest possible gypsum, which was found abundantly in the hills near Larnaca. The foundations of these buildings were in most cases of stone, and usually of ancient origin. The remains of old walls were in fact frequently found under later houses, some of them leaning half over, the same in the case of old arcades with rough arches (Salvator 1983: 19). Internally such houses were paved with very soft marble, which was found in the island mainly in the place called Eğlence.

The great majority of the roofs of these houses, especially in those districts where Greeks and Turks lived side by side, were covered with clay mixed with chopped straw. This kind of mortar was simply poured over mats made of reeds, which were placed over the beams (themselves supported by marble cornices) and provided a surface to support the clay. Roofs so constructed were about nine inches thick (Fisher 1878: 42). Sometimes the beams were left sticking out under the roof instead of cornices; in other cases they were covered with simple boards. With clay roofs of this kind the gutter consisted of a clay or wooden pipe running along the edge of it (Salvator 1983: 19). As the Rev. Nathaneal Burton (1838: 166) observed, the roofs of the houses were somewhat sloped, and had a more cheerful appearance than those in the towns of Syria. An opening covered with two marble slabs leaning at a sharp angle against one another formed the chimney of these houses (Salvator 1983: 19-20).

According to Salvator, building was done with great rapidity. First a brick was laid; then some mortar, composed of earth and straw, was poured from a mason's tray with two handles over the brick, another brick, half crumbled and dusty, was put on the top, some more of the mixture followed, another brick was placed in position and so on, so that the house was finished in less than no time, and had the advantage, moreover, of drying soon after it was finished. Because of this, as Louis Salvator noted, the houses were exceedingly cheap. He also noted that the price of 1,000 of these bricks was 100 piastres, or about a pound sterling (Salvator 1983: 19). One advantage of houses built in this fashion was the capacity they possessed of resisting earthquakes, and sad experience had brought the Cypriots to prefer them to houses of stone (Fisher 1878: 42-4). Clay houses would last a hundred years, but they had frequently to be repaired, as the straw with which the bricks were plastered up became rotten and left holes in the wall (Fisher 1878: 19).

According to Louis Salvator, most of the Turkish houses had prominent pavilions with lattice-work windows. Others, to the number of about 150, mostly in the Turkish and Greek districts, were surmounted by wooden gables; the roof projected far out and had a sort of wooden casement under a prominent part of it, made in the Turkish fashion. The water was allowed to run down from it into a wooden gutter running all round the eaves (Fisher 1878: 19).

2. Plan of the houses

The plan of Ottoman houses was always based on the privacy of family life as well as climatic conditions. They do not show much difference in this respect from most Anatolian Ottoman houses. As has been indicated by Fred H. Fisher and many other travellers, not to mention the evidence provided by existing examples, the majority of houses had only one upper storey, though some of those belonging to the Greeks and Turks were fairly large and spacious, even if built in a unique and somewhat whimsical style and laid out in a very irregular manner (Fisher 1878: 42-4). In contrast, many houses, particularly in the villages, had only a ground floor.

Thus, archival records, travel books and also the existing examples show that only one or two storeyed houses were built in Cyprus during the Ottoman period. Further information about Turkish houses which were included in the register of charitable foundations is provided by records in the *Sheriye Sicilleri* (judicial records) dating back to the early years of Ottoman rule. Several such *vakıfs* (pious foundations) possessed houses, other residential buildings, fields and gardens which they rented. (Hadım) Cafer Pasha Foundation had a house which was rented for five *akçe* a month, while Mustafa Paşa had five two-storeyed (*fevkani*) and four single-storeyed (*tahtani*) houses which were rented for 80 *akçe* (Jennings 1993: 59).

This kind of record, like the travel accounts and currently existing examples, all combine to show that the houses were generally of one or two storeys, and that *tahtani* was the term used for single-storeyed structures, while *fevkani* was the name given to the larger, two-storeyed, houses. An engraving showing Ottoman houses in Nicosia (pl.10.7) provides good evidence of what once existed in the city, though many of these within the last two decades have been replaced by modern buildings.

a. Size. At the beginning the size of Ottoman houses was moderate, but since the Turks had a preference for living within the walled towns, land available for house-building became scarce and this led to an actual reduction in house-size within the walled towns of Nicosia, Famagusta and Kyrenia in the 19th century and the beginning of the present century. Ioannes Cotovicus described the dwellings as little and low, though the reason he gave for this was the frequent occurrence of earthquakes on the island (Cobham 1908: 89). Basil Stewart (1908: 108), in turn, referred to Turkish houses in the villages as being larger and better built.

b. Façade and entrance. The front of the houses mainly faced the street, and it was on this side that the different periods of the building could be best understood. As Salvator (1983: 20) mentions, in the old parts of walls Gothic arches, hood-mouldings, and projecting turrets were often encountered. Sandys (1658: 172) and Ioannes Cotovicus (Cobham 1908: 89) described the entrances of the houses as being small and lacking height, for the most part reached by steps for a more difficult point of entry.

As remarked by Salvator, the doors of the houses usually had only a wooden frame, which was sometimes inserted into a Gothic arch. Over the entrance-door of Turkish houses there was often a wooden motif, in the shape of the star and crescent, or only a star, with little wire hoops to hold the oil cups for illumination on the anniversary of the Sultan's accession and other festivals. The entrance-doors were generally made of thin strips of wood, each fastened by what were usually three rows of nails running horizontally, one row at the top, one in the middle, one at the bottom. Some of the doors are found made in a similar manner but with lozenge-shaped panels. The cross-bars of the doors were very elaborate in some Turkish houses. With the Greeks they were usually in the shape of a cross. The doors also had knockers, which were either arabesque-shaped or simple rings. These rings, if provided with a chain and lock, would also serve to fasten the door. As a rule a plain bolt on the outside was the only protection against intruders. A bit of wood stuck through it from the inside prevents it from being opened from the street. Here and there horse-blocks with steps at the side of the door were to be seen (Salvator 1983: 20).

Usually, entry inside is through a simple doorway which opens into a *sofa* or portico, oriented towards a courtyard or garden, or opens directly into a courtyard. Such courtyards were often planted with orange or lemon trees and jasmine plants. The rooms of the early Ottoman period were mostly arranged in an 'L' shape plan along an arcaded *sofa* (portico), or a *hayat* (veranda) around the courtyard, and usually there were two floors, with the bedrooms mainly on the first floor. Late 19th century Turkish houses in contrast opened directly into a large hall, around which the principal rooms were located, and facing the entrance door was the flight of stairs, usually made of wood, that led to an upper *sofa* around which were the bedrooms. The kitchen was usually opposite, at the back of the house. There was often also a small courtyard, access to which was through the kitchen door, and which was used as a service area for the kitchen and for drying laundry or housing animals and pets. In many cases it was also filled with a variety of plants.

According to Louis Salvator, the doors of most Turkish houses were carefully locked, and a screen stood immediately behind them, so that when the door was opened no one could see the interior. Having passed the screen the visitor entered the paved *sofa*, usually facing a garden or a courtyard. The roof of the *sofa* frequently rested on Gothic arches with round pillars and square capitals. In the absence of arches the roof was supported by round columns, and the cross-beam was then adorned with carved consoles. All the windows opening into the *sofa* were provided with Moorish lattice-work. From the entrance the stairs led to the upper floor either by a regular staircase, or steps on the outside of the wall. Pretty little doors with carved Moorish arches formed the entrance to the interior (Salvator 1983: 20-2). Usually, there was a water tank with its fountain under the staircase.

c. Doors and windows. The houses had several windows either on the front, opening onto the street, or into the *sofa* or courtyard. The windows were small and high in early houses, while in later periods the number and the size of the windows increased. Ali Bey compared the houses in Cyprus to those of Africa, and he said that the way they were built was exactly the opposite to those in Africa, which had no windows and received light only from the door - even in the largest houses - while in Cyprus on the other hand they had two rows of windows placed one above the other. He remarked with surprise that although the room he stayed in was only 24 feet by 12, it had fourteen windows and a door (Cobham 1908: 394). The windows of both Turks and Greeks had lattices on the sides; and often blinds as well. Many of these windows were also protected by carved wooden shutters hinged at the top of the window and which operated in much the same way as awnings (Salvator 1983: 20).

d. Rooms. The Turkish inhabitants of the richer class had a reception room on the upper floor, richly furnished with divans along the walls, and shelves decorated with various objects of glass and china. There were sometimes two living rooms in rich houses for the use of the women. The living area of these rooms was arranged on raised wooden platforms *(sekiüstü)*, around which were the divans (*sedirs*), on two or three sides of the room. These rooms opened into other rooms with broad divans and pillows; sometimes in the corners there were small shelves or niches containing flower pots, lamps, and ornamental glasses such as slender scent bottles or silver items. Rich Turks had large latticed pavilions, which were delightfully cool in summer if there was the slightest breeze. They also enjoyed, as a cool resting-place, the flat roofs of the houses (Salvator 1983: 24).

Large houses belonging to people with an important official position usually had *selamlık* and *harem* as separate apartments.[6] This was even present in the houses of rich Greeks, as has been mentioned above in the case of the dragoman's house. The doctor Delaroiere, who visited Cyprus accompanied by M. and Madame Lamartin, described the house of the sheikh of Hala Sultan. After they had been entertained in his room, which had no other furniture than a divan and a fine closely woven mat covering the floor, and where the walls and ceiling were decorated with verses from the Koran written in Turkish, he was requested by the sheikh to visit his *harem*, where his wives were sick. Delaroiere described the *harem* as being exactly the same as the living room of the sheikh, with the exception that here the windows were closely grated, which made the room rather dark (Cobham 1908: 460).

The ceilings of the large rooms were usually supported by groined arches resting on brackets, or by simple beams. Smaller ones were supported simply by flat beams under which lay Egyptian mats and these were supported by small consoles. The floor was covered with mats from Egypt, and in the middle of the room stood the copper fire pan which held glowing charcoal. In the houses of poorer people the rooms on the ground-floor were also used as living space, and the light came in through handsome-looking little windows, made by apertures in the thick stone walls, and with glass panes on the inside like those usually found in the mosques (Salvator 1983: 22).

Ornamented shelves were installed all round the rooms. Curtains hung down from the ceiling and could be drawn up or let down by strings. Chairs with carved backs and low seats, and other more or less common pieces of furniture were also to be found. Often a basket, called *tabayia*, was suspended from the ceiling to keep the bread in, and there was a piece of board in a corner with the water-jug standing on it (Salvator 1983: 22).

Mrs. Lewis (1894: 222) also mentioned the finely carved ceilings and doors she had seen in the Turkish house occupied by the Rev. J. Spencer, Inspector of Schools, in Nicosia. The photographs showing the entrance door and the decorated ceiling in the house of Kamil Pasha published by Sir Harry Luke (1957: 97, 160), and some existing examples confirm this. The ceilings in the Lusignan house and a wooden ceiling in the Bedesten are fine examples of these. These ceilings are wooden, richly painted in the *'kalem işi'* (pen work) technique and finely gilded. Unfortunately, the ceiling in the Bedesten has lost its originality (through the enthusiasm of painters who have attempted to restore it from time to time), while the ceiling in the Lusignan house is threatened with similar treatment.

e. Kitchen. The kitchen was situated on the ground-floor, with the fireplace in the corner, or in the middle of the wall, after the Turkish fashion. Many houses had a perfectly round baking-oven with a marble floor and stone sides, covered on the top with clay and straw. Most of the houses had their own wells; otherwise water was brought in by donkeys which had two pitchers hanging on either side (Salvator 1983: 24).

f. Garden or courtyard. Almost every house had a courtyard or a garden in the inner part of the house where orange and lemon trees, gigantic palms towering over the fruit-trees, and flowers were grown, and where there was usually a fountain. These were the places where the women generally spent their days. The large mansion houses also had their baths and toilets in the courtyards of the house. Besides these private enclosures there were extensive public gardens within the boundaries of the city, occupying more than half of the available space. All the private gardens were bounded by walls on the street-side; in contrast the side adjoining the open *sofa* of the house was fenced only by a low wooden balustrade. They were watered either from cisterns or directly from the aqueducts and produced all manner of fruits (Salvator 1983: 22-4, 26). Some of them even had large pools. A document signed by Mehmed, the kadı of Nicosia, and dated 20 July 1766, tells about the death of a gardener while swimming in the pool of the house of a Turkish gentlemen who was the son of Ibrahim, the deceased, in the Yenicami quarter of Nicosia.[7]

Conclusion

The houses that we inherit today mostly date back to the last decade of the 19th century and the first half of this century. The Arapahmet Quarter in Nicosia, which is included in the restoration and preservation project of Unesco is in the process of being partially restored. But the fate of one of the largest and most magnificent examples, the *konak* (mansion) in the Karamanzade district, has yet to be decided upon. The *konak*, which is two storeyed, has a beautiful balcony, and most of the rooms on the first floor had beautiful wooden ceilings with geometrical decorations. There is no information about this house at the moment. All we know is that an old lady living in this area referred to it as the *konak* of the Yeniçeri Agası. A beautifully restored *konak* is at present serving as the main Ethnographical Museum of the city. This is the mansion house of Derviş Paşa, who published a newspaper entitled *Zaman*. Although the building has been finely restored, it is my own opinion that some parts of it, such as the ceilings and the Turkish bath, have in fact been altered for the worse owing to the lack of technical facilities in the Department of Antiquities in North Cyprus. Another important building, Kadı Menteş Efendi Konak (pl.10.3-5), which was mentioned above, has also been recently restored and is used as the Office of the Union of the Municipalities. But it would be a good idea to arrange this as the city museum since it is in the most important tourist centre of the city. Worthy of note is yet another house in the Selimiye district which has recently been restored (pl.10.8). Some of the houses of Famagusta, one of which was mentioned above, and the façade of which was built mostly of stone, together with the brick houses in Lefke, are included in restoration projects but are still awaiting attention for financial reasons. Two important examples in Famagusta are two archway houses which constitute quite interesting examples of Ottoman housing.

The houses within the walled cities which remained intact until recently show varying characteristics and demonstrate the evolution of domestic architecture in Cyprus. Their survival was in fact due to the financial problems in the Turkish parts of Cyprus until 1974. The increase in prosperity within Turkish Cypriot society since 1974 on the other hand has actually led to the destruction of many of them within a short space of time in order to build either new houses or, more particularly, offices and commercial centres within the walled cities. As a result several beautiful houses have been pulled down within the last 20 years. Unfortunately too, the preservation and restoration projects involving most of the houses that have received attention have not been effectively carried out.

It is in fact rather upsetting to see today that all those old houses which were the large, luxurious *konaks* of the late 19th century and the first quarter of this century are abandoned by their owners, and mostly rented to poor families, mainly labourers. It remains the task of my colleagues and myself, therefore, to ensure their proper preservation as a vital part of Cyprus' Ottoman heritage.

Bibliography

Ali Bey 1816: *Travels in Morocco, Tripoli, Cyprus, Egypt, Arabia, Syria and Turkey.* London.

Arif Dede 1991: *Kıbrıs Tarihçesi* (ed. and trans. by H. Fedai). Ankara.

Batson Joyner, A. 1878: *Cyprus, Historical and Descriptive (adapted from the German of Franz Von Löher with much additional matter by Mrs. A. Batson Joyner, And Two Maps).* London.

Bruyn, C. de 1702: *A Voyage to the Levant or, Travels in the Principal Parts of Asia Minor, the Islands of Scio, Rhodes, Cyprus, etc.,* (English tr. by W.F.). London.

Burton, Rev. N. 1838: *A Narrative of a Journey From Liverpool to Alexandria ... in the years 1836-37.* Dublin.

Clarke, E.D. 1812: *Travels in Various Countries, Asia and Africa,* Part the Second, (Greece, Egypt and the Holy Land), Section I. London.

Cobham, C.D. (ed. & tr.) 1908: *Excerpta Cypria, Materials for a History of Cyprus,* London, (repr. 1986).

Drummond, A. 1754: *Travels Through Different Cities of Germany, Italy, Greece and Several Parts of Asia As Far As the Banks of the Euphrates.* London.

Fisher, F.H. 1878: *Cyprus, Our New Colony and What We Know About It.* London.

Gürkan, H.M. 1982: *Kıbrıs Tarihinden Sayfalar.* Nicosia.

Januen, D. (Le Chevalier) 1785: *Histoire Générale Des Roiaumes de Chypre, de Jerusalem.* Leiden.

Jeffery, G. 1918: *A Description of the Historic Monuments of Cyprus.* Nicosia (repr. London, 1983).

Jennings, R. 1993: *Christians and Muslims in Ottoman Cyprus and the Mediterranean World, 1571-1640.* New York.

Keshishian, K. 1990: *Nicosia, Capital of Cyprus Then and Now.* Nicosia.

Lewis, Mrs. 1894: *A Lady's Impression of Cyprus in 1893.* London.

Luke, Sir H. 1957: *Cyprus, A Portrait and an Appreciation.* London, (repr. 1973).

Maritti, G. 1909: *Travels in the Island of Cyprus* (tr. C.D. Cobham). Cambridge (reprinted London, 1971).

Ross, L. 1910: *A Journey to Cyprus, (February and March 1845)* (tr. C.D.Cobham). Nicosia.

Salvator, L. (Archduke of Austria) 1983: *Levkosia, The Capital of Cyprus, with 15 engravings by the author. Reprinted from his original account of a visit to the island in 1873.* Trigraph, London.

Sandys, G. 1658: *Travailes, Containing a History of the Original and Present State of the Turkish Empire, Their Laws, Government, Policy, Military Force, Courts of Justice and Commerce; The Mahometan Religion and Ceremonies; etc.* (6th ed.). London.

Scott-Stevenson, Mrs. 1880: *Our Home in Cyprus.* London.

Stewart, B. 1908: *My Experiences of Cyprus.* London.

Turner, W. 1920: *Journal of a Tour in the Levant.* London.

Yıldız, N. 1992: 'Ottoman Period in Cyprus, A Glance at Turkish Architecture', *New Cyprus* Feb-Mar.

---

[1] Bş. Bk. Ar. (Prime Ministry Archive, Istanbul) *Mühimme No:13, No: 1127;* Yıldız 1992: 23.

[2] Bş. Bk. Ar., *Maliyeden Müdevver Defterler, D.No:423, Ruznamçe Defteri,* fols.9, 22, 35; Yıldız 1992: 23.

[3] Technically a tax-collector appointed to govern the island instead of a governor proper.

[4] In this pieces of wood in various geometric shapes and decorated with plant motifs are fitted together without either glue or nails in such a way that even if the wood later dries out and shrinks, the pieces will not fall out.

[5] A *braccio*, an Italian measure of length, equals nearly two English feet. *The Compact Oxford English Dictionary,* New Edition, Oxford, 1987 (1992), 166.

[6] The *selamlık* is a reception room reserved for men. The *harem* is used by all members of the family, but is also the part of the house where the womenfolk can entertain their female guests.

[7] *Topkapı Palace Archive,* E.11011/1.

PART THREE: THE OTTOMAN HOUSE IN DETAIL

The papers in the previous section discuss Ottoman houses in general typological terms, and often provide documentation of construction methods, building components and decorative motifs. However, the sharper focus of the four papers in this third group reveals a more intimate picture of the houses. Indeed, the closer one looks, the more one understands the degree to which Ottoman houses are documents of social dynamics as well as autonomous works of art.

Ali Kamil Yalçın's investigation of construction techniques in the historic river front neighbourhood in Amasya provides insight into traditional methods. His glossary of terms is extensive; comparison with terminology used in other papers points out that certain words are used consistently throughout the country, while others have regional variations, suggesting directions for future research. Yalçın also notes two categories of houses on the Amasya waterfront: late Ottoman houses influenced by styles from Istanbul, and earlier more vernacular houses. Beginning in the 18th century Istanbul houses consciously adopted European features, and these naturally made their way to more provincial locations. Hatice and Okay Kuşçu analyse one mansion in Amasya, showing how it changed over time. In particular, the use of western-style furniture, the replacement of fireplaces with stoves, and the introduction of modern plumbing caused transformation of the house. The house may be understood as a document of changing lifestyles.

The theme of Westernisation appears again in the paper by Günsel Renda about 19th century interior wall paintings. The paintings are landscapes using perspective and shading in a Western manner; however, figures are absent, reflecting religious sensibilities. The use of realistic painting is itself a European device, reinforcing other Western fashions that were effecting the transformation of traditional houses.

Wooden façade decoration is the subject of the paper by H. Örcün Barışta. The examples from central and south central Anatolia that she presents reveal a multiplicity of design sources that are a consequence of the location of towns on trade routes. Itinerant craftsmen and population migrations would spread ideas and provide a rich vocabulary of motifs. Once again, Ottoman houses display the same richness in detail that they demonstrate in typological development and variation.

11: OTTOMAN HOUSE CONSTRUCTION IN THE OLD TOWN OF AMASYA

Ali Kamil Yalçın
Amasya

Ottoman houses in Anatolia were built to take advantage of available materials and to respect the local climate and topography. For this reason their architecture varied from region to region. But there were also differences within regions or towns that reflected the wealth and social standing of their owners.[1]

A few towns, such as Amasya in north central Turkey, have houses that remain from their Ottoman past, and some of them are as old as 300 years. But they have lost much of their documentary value because of their continual use. Their original forms and decorations have been re-configured, and even if the intention was a simple repair, the expertise required, or even the appropriate materials, may have disappeared over time. Many of the structural changes were made when large families subdivided a house and portioned out the now smaller spaces to their grown children and their new families. This type of remodelling meant not only new walls and smaller rooms, but the addition of new stairways and new entrances and often the loss of open balconies. But by far the worst damage to these old houses has been done by leaving them partly or wholly empty and subject to deterioration by vandalism or the weather.

İçerişehir: the Ottoman settlement in the ancient town of Amasya

Amasya has been a thriving city since pre-Roman times. In fact, until the twentieth century, the densest residential area remained the wall-protected enclave that sat below the steep slope of Harşene Mountain where it meets the Yeşil Irmak river, the ancient River Iris. This part of Amasya was the home of its oldest palaces which, with the residences that were built at its feet, is still called the 'Inner City', the *Enderun* of the Seljuk period and the *İçerişehir* of the Ottomans.

Yalıboyu (river-front) houses along the Yeşil Irmak

The *içerişehir* houses that line the waterfront were built in the Ottoman period, either using the *bağdadi* technique, i.e. a wooden frame supporting walls of lath and plaster, or the *hımış* technique of a wooden frame infilled with mud bricks. The foundation of the houses, in contrast, is regularly cut stone (*kargir*). This stone foundation encloses a basement room. In fact, many of these river-front houses use the ancient stone walls of the Romans as a part of their foundation element. These houses that face the river are called *yalıboyu houses*, and are one of the few remaining series of river-front houses left in Turkey.

Although one wall of the house may overlook the street which runs behind the riverfront, to preserve privacy the main entry into the living quarters of the house is never directly from the street itself but from a central courtyard usually reached via a corridor which passes though that part of the building fronting onto the street. The ground floor of this outer section of the house is often windowless and mainly used for storage; above it and reached by a set of stairs is usually the *selamlık*, the area reserved for use by the men of the family and their (male) guests. This *selamlık* area on the first floor has windows facing onto the street, but not onto the courtyard, which forms part of the area reserved for the family as a whole, its servants, and female guests, the *haremlik*. Beyond the courtyard is a further suite of rooms on two floors (with usually also a basement given over to storage) fronting onto the river itself and completing the *haremlik*. Since the rooms here are afforded greater privacy, they have windows facing onto both the river and the courtyard. Within such an arrangement the ground floor, which is the warmest, is called the winter area or *kışlık*, even though it may be used throughout the year. Above this is the area reserved for summer, the *yazlık*; while at the very top, just under the roof, one often finds a small room open to views of the town, with windows on three sides, called a *şahnişin* or *şahnişirin*. Within the *haremlik* suite rooms were generally arranged around a common area or *sofa*, which might be enclosed or open, like an *eyvan* (*açık sofalı*), on one side to the courtyard. Over all the most highly decorated room of the house was the main room (*baş odası*), where the head of the house would sit in a corner, with windows facing in two directions. This room could also double as the *selamlık*. The *harem*, however, might also be decorated.

In Amasya, the *yalıboyu* houses seem to be divided into two styles: one which reflects Istanbul and the other that is more local or vernacular. The houses that line the river to the east of the Mağdenus bridge are in the Istanbul or late Ottoman style; the ones to the west are more vernacular. It is not clear whether this has to do with repair work. However, the oldest houses today are to be found in the western area of the *yalıboyu* and the *içerişehir* houses. The central area of the *içerişehir*, that is away from the water and towards the mountain, used to house Amasya's oldest mosque which had a low and broad minaret, the 12th century Enderun Cami, but it was lost to the earthquake of 1938 and is now a playground for children. This western area also has a public bath from this period, the Yukarı Hamam as well as the Hatuniye mosque built in 1509 by Bülbül Hatun, the wife of Bayezid II, who was the son of Mehmet the Conqueror.

In the 19th century, the important area of the *içerişehir* shifted to the east, toward the Hükümet Bridge, and it may be for this reason that we see the larger, Istanbul-style houses in this area. But by the second half of the 20th century, the Ottoman life style that called for separate areas for men and women had ceased, and the house interiors began to be changed. The economic and social life of the town moved to the south, across the river. Many wealthy families from this area moved away, and the old people who stayed locked the *selamlık* parts of their houses and lived on the ground floor of the *harem* which was easiest to heat and was also open to the garden or courtyard. Today, the beautiful houses in the *içerişehir* are important only to tourism and many of these gardened homes are rented out.

The İçsokak (inner street) of the İçerişehir

Behind the *yalıboyu* houses is another row of houses, separated from them by a narrow street (pl.11.1). Both sets of houses have their front entrances facing this street. Where the mountain allows space, there are additional houses behind these, or the row of houses is divided by a cul-de-sac (*çıkmaz*) that ends at one of these set-back houses. Today, there are additional, squatter, houses (*geçe kondu*) built along the slope of the mountain.

The original street structure of the *içerişehir* is largely intact, although some of it was destroyed when a railway track was cut into the mountain in 1928. The street itself was paved with uncut stones, and curved according to the topography. The stones in the centre of the street were angled to make a water course and to provide drainage for rainwater. In 1940 this street was paved in a parquet style, with dark green stones brought from the nearby town of Suluova and glass-green ones from Doğantepe, and also with dark yellow andelit stones. These would shine in the sunlight and glisten after the spring rain. But with the laying of a new sewer system in 1980, all these stones were buried, replaced by drab asphalt paving.

The houses that do not face the river, but are built along the inner street on the north side of the *yalıboyu* riverside plots differ from the *yalıboyu* mansions in a number of respects. First of all, instead of having one side that faces the street and another that faces the river, they have one side that faces the street and another that backs onto the Harşene mountain's steep slope. Internally too they display greater variation of layout. In the case of some, for instance, the street door leads directly into the house, behind which is a garden or courtyard; in others the garden/courtyard is at the front; in others still, those situated off a cul-de-sac perpendicular to the street, the entrance is via the cul-de-sac into a central garden/courtyard which has rooms on either side. This arrangement, furthermore, has been used to advantage, the builders having put their kitchens to the north, to the back, in order to provide insulation from the cold. In the kitchen they have built stone (*kargir*) walls and they put the fire place (*ocak*) and cupboards (*yüklük*) to the north side of the rooms as well. In one or two instances, where the area between the street and the mountain is wide enough, the blind end of the cul-de-sac is itself occupied by a house with a courtyard entrance, or covered *sofa* entrance, under an overhang (pl.11.2). The entrance is identified by double doors decorated with nails (*çift, çakma kapılar*).

House plans

The plans of these houses can be described in some detail:

1. Ground floor (yer-katları). The southern elevation of many of the inner street houses, that is, the side that faces the entrances to the river front houses, is occupied by a *sofa* or covered courtyard called an *evaltı örtülü sofa*, above which are the *selamlık* rooms or an open balcony. The kitchen is also open to this courtyard, and generally there is no basement below.

2. The upper, living area, floor (ev-katları). Whereas the street-level floor adjusts to the curves in the street, or to the topography of the ground, the floors above conform to a general programme that allows the living space to become cantilevered projections (*çıkma*) over the street, forming rooms with two right angled corners for windows (pl.11.3). Cantilevers never project into a neighbour's space, and if two neighbours have a shared wall, the view from bay windows incorporated into upper rooms will always be directed away from the neighbouring house. Set into the roof of the top floor there may also be a further cantilevered room called *şahnişirin* projecting beyond the line of the main roof and with windows on three sides (pl.11.4).

The supports that hold the cantilevered rooms are constructed in a variety of styles: vertical columns, horizontal beams, diagonally placed braces, and braces covered with lath & plaster (see below). The more intricate and developed were often richly decorated with geometric motifs and a variety of colours similar to the *edirnekarı* motifs on interior wood elements, or, with the advent of Rococo, with gold and silver.

Parts of the house common to all old Amasya houses

1. Bathing areas. Many rooms had a *gusülhane*, which was a small closet-like space in the room wall where one could sit and wash with hot water from a copper kettle. The *gusülhane* was built into the wall next to the fire place (*ocak*), which heated both the water and the air of the room. The *gusülhane* was covered in zinc to insulate and waterproof it. In a few residences there was a Turkish bathing room (*hamam*). These *hamams* had also a cool place both to change clothes and to rest. Within the first ten years of the Republic, the *gusülhane* went out of fashion, and a larger room was used for bathing, although the traditional way of sitting and pouring water from the large kettle remained popular.

2. Cantilevers (çıkmalar). The upper floors of Amasya's *içerişehir* houses cantilever over the river or the street to extend the floor space of the building and take advantage of the view. The consoles that support these cantilevered rooms, or *çıkmas*, take the following forms.

a. Because vertical columns occupy ground space and would therefore restrict street access, they are usually found only along the river front itself, supporting cantilevers over the riverbank (pl.11.5). Cantilevers created in this way often provided protection for a river-front entrance to the basement of the house, the windows of which would be protected by wooden or iron grilles.

b. Extensions of upper floor supports project at right angles to the house wall and serve as the base for further beams that run parallel to the wall (*bindirmelik* or *desteksiz bindirme*, pl.11.6-7).

c. Diagonal props springing from the house wall (*eliböğründe*, pl.11.7-8). This simple method of support seems to be something of a local style.

d. The space between the diagonal props and the wall is covered with lath and plaster (*bağdadi*, pl.11.9-10), which is sometimes either further embellished with decoration or given additional support. This seems to be a late-Ottoman style.

3. Windows and their lattices. The upper floor windows that allow views of the river and the street are made in a 1:2 proportion; their width is 90cm with a 180cm length. Each window has two guillotine sliding sashes, and these sash windows each have four equal glass frames, not fixed with putty but with wooden nails and constructed to fit into each other (pl.11.5). The lower windows have a different proportion, usually 2:3, so that they are wide but not low to the ground.

In order to protect the privacy of the room from outside view, a wooden latticework screen (*kafes*) was set over the window (pl.11.11). Some of these extended from the window as an open-work box so that women could look down onto the street or lean out to look along it without being seen (pl.11.12). Most of these, however, have been removed since they are no longer felt to be necessary. Sliding lattice work also protected *sofas* or *eyvans* or verandas that might be seen, above and behind a garden wall, from the street.

In the local style small semi-circular non-opening windows (*kafa penceresi*) constructed on a frame of either of wood or plaster of Paris (*alçı pencere*) were added to the tops of more normal windows fronting onto the street. These were often filled with coloured glass or at times incorporated a design of Islamic calligraphy or flowers and were designed to admit more light into those rooms. The late Ottoman style and Baroque-influenced houses, however, tended to restrict such windows to the *şahnişirin*.

The embellishment of the façade (dış bezeme)

Structural elements became important decorative elements only in the later Ottoman period. Thus the vertical wood beams at the corners of the house (*köşe dikmesi*), and the projecting wooden string courses that separated floor levels, (*kat silmesi*, locally referred to as *yaşmak*) were used as aesthetic elements on the façades of the houses (pl.11.5). In Amasya there is often also a wooden decoration in the form of a triangle under the gable of the roof (pl.11.2).

The eaves (saçak) and the roof (çatı). The wooden urban houses of the vernacular style have pitched roofs covered with tiles which extend beyond the walls to form eaves protecting the exterior walls from the rain. These eaves stretch as wide as possible over the street or courtyard resulting in triangular gable ends (*kalkan duvar*). Along the river-front houses the direction of the pitch is north-south and as a result the eaves actually join those of neighbouring houses, forming what appears to be a row of attached houses. On other houses, those not attached to their neighbours, the eaves might turn up at the corners in the shape of a fan (*yelpaze*). This shape was not used in the late Ottoman period because on the main roof (*ana beşik dam*) was now the small roof (*yavruk beşik*) on the *şahniş*, which sloped in the opposite direction to that of the main roof. On the façades of the *şahniş*, or if there were no *şahniş*, along the short façade of the house, a triangular gable wall (*alın duvarı*) would be built to cover the empty space under the two sides of the sloping roof. This wall would be the one to carry any decoration, either floral motifs in wood, the calligraphic seal of the Ottoman sultan (*tuğra*), or a bird house in the shape of a small model house. The most frequent decorations were apotropaic writings to protect the house itself; thus one can find *Maşallah u kane* (*With God's Protection and Mercy*) or *Ya hafiz* (*Oh Protector*) in black or dark red (*aşı kırmızı*) on the white surface of the walls and surrounded by a painted frame. These protective sayings worked their wonders until the middle of our own century. But today, these beautiful houses, with their distinctive decoration, must depend on all of us for their protection.

Glossary Of House Terms

Abdesthane: A cupboard-like area next to the fireplace where one can bathe with water heated by the fireplace. Used for general hygiene and for ritual washing (*abdest*), as before prayers.

Ahır: Stables that form the ground floor of a house.

Alatürka kiremit: Clay roofing tiles shaped like slightly less than half a cylinder, but with one end wider than the other so it can fit snugly over the narrow end of the one next to it.

Alçı pencere: Non-opening upper windows that are made of stained glass in a frame of wood or plaster (*alçı*) moulding.

Alınlık, Alın duvarı: A triangular or semi-circular decorative area above the door or window, or below the roof.

Avlu: A courtyard

Bağdadi: A lath and plaster wall or ceiling, made by smearing plaster (*sıva*) onto wood laths (*çıtalar*) that are nailed or tacked onto wooden beams (*direkler*).

Baş odası: The best room in the *selamlık* section of the house, used for the senior male members of the family or for entertaining.

Bindirme: A corbel or supporting log.

Bindirmelik: A row of supports of stone or wood in the form of a console used to carry the part of the building that extends out. The *bindirmeliks* transfer the load.

Boğumlu ahşap sarkıt: Articulated stalactites or *muqarnas*-shaped supports made of wood and often in a Baroque onion shape.

Bulgurlama: Insulation made of lime and straw, placed among the floorboards.

Cumba: The general Turkish term for that area of a room jutting out like a bay window. In Amasya it is more normally called *şahniş*.

Çakma kapı: A wooden door whose hinged leaves are made of flat boards laid vertically side by side and braced with two horizontal boards, one at the top and one at the bottom, that are joined by a diagonal board, the entire leaf held together with screws or nails.

Çatkı: The framework of a house.

Çeşme: Fountain, often a public fountain on the street side of a house.

Çift kanat çakma kapılar: Double wooden doors.

Çıkma: Overhang or projection, a room that juts out from the upper floor of a house (see *cumba* and *şahniş*).

Çıkmaz: A cul-de-sac in a residential neighbourhood.

Çıta: A wooden lath.

Destek: A support.

Desteksiz bindirme: Corbelling that is the sole support of a projecting room, that is, there are no additional elbow-like *eliböğründe* supports.

Devesırtı (Camel-back): A sloping under-surface of eaves.

Dış bezeme: The external decoration of a house.

Dökme: Joist or rafter.

Edirnekarı: Designs painted on wood, usually doors, ceilings, walls or cupboards, in oil paint.

Eliböğründe: A wooden buttress or diagonal prop that extends from the façade wall of the house to support the *çıkma* or cantilevered room.

Ev: House.

Eyvan: A room that is completely open on one side, for example to the courtyard, or a part of a room that is open on one side to a central room.

Gusülhane: A cupboard-like area next to the fireplace where one can bathe with water heated by the fireplace. When it is used for ritual washing, as before prayers, it is called *abdesthane*.

Hamam: A building for public bathing by use of hot water from taps and steam, or a room in a house made for bathing.

Haremlik: The area of the house reserved for the family, its servants, and its female guests.

Havuz: A pool in the garden.

Hayat: In the Balkans and Northern Anatolia the *hayat* is the ground floor area first entered on opening the gate from the street. It is usually covered with earth, but if it is covered with stone, it is called the *taşlık*. It is here that daily life goes on. In Amasya the *hayat* includes the open *sofa*.

Hımış: The construction technique employing a wooden frame infilled with sun-dried mud bricks.

Hücre: Wall niche used as a decorative shelf, sometimes called *göz* or *tembel gözü*.

İçerişehir: The part of the city that is surrounded by the ancient walls.

Kafa penceresi: In the vernacular style of Amasya houses these are upper windows that do not open.

Kafes: Wood lattice that covers the exterior of windows for privacy.

Kargır: Building material of cut stone and brick.

Kalkan duvar: The exterior wall of a house or building that takes on a triangular shape due to the steep pitch of the roof that is edged by a ridge or ridge tiles.

Kerpiç: Sun dried mud brick.

Kireç: Lime; *Kireç harcı* - mortar made of lime and sand; *kireç sıva* - lime, fine sand and hemp.

Kiremit: Clay roofing tile.

Kışlık: The part of the house, usually a lower floor, that keeps warm and is used in winter.

Konak: mansion.

Köşk: A small room in a garden, or a comfortable, semi-enclosed, raised seating area at the end of the veranda, or a penthouse.

Mahya: Roof ridge.

Ocak: A fireplace on the wall of a living room, the hearth inside the kitchen, or the stove that is often found in the courtyard.

Payanda: An internal support within a house-frame; a prop or buttress for supporting a leaning wall.

Saçak: The wide eaves of the roof.

Saman: Straw.

Samanlık: Ground floor room for storage of straw.

Saraybağı: The horizontal underneath section of eaves (as such it is to be distinguished from *devesırtı*).

Sedir: Seating benches that line the window walls of a room (the Amasya word is *makat* or *divan*).

Selamlık: The area of the house reserved for men and their male guests.

Silme: Moulding or projecting string course.

Sıva: Plaster.

Sofa: An enclosed or open central room on any floor onto which open all the other, more private, rooms.

Sundurma çatı: A single-sided sloping roof.

Şahniş: In Amasya, a *cumba*, a cantilevered room.

Şahnişin, Şahnişirin: A projection on the top floor of the house, with windows on three sides, that overlooks the street or the inner courtyard.

Taşlık: When the *hayat*, or entry area of the house is covered with stone (*taş*) it is called the *taşlık*.

Tuğla: Brick.

Yalı: A mansion along a shore.

Yalıboyu: The shore of a river.

Yaşmak: The Amasya vernacular word for decoration constructed of wood.

Yazlık: The part of the house, usually an upper floor, that is open to the breezes and thus used in the summer.

Yüklük: Wooden storage cabinets, with doors, that are built into the walls of the rooms.

---

[1] When we examine the architecture of the houses in the countryside around Amasya, we find that most of the villages that subsisted by animal husbandry had flat-roofs (*düzdam*) and the walls were constructed out of wooden beams (*hazen*) and sun-dried mud bricks (*kerpiç*). In the settlements that depend on handicrafts and agriculture the houses resembled urban ones with a wooden frame filled with sun-dried mud bricks covered in plaster (*hımış*). In the forest villages, of course, we can see the greater use of wood, both for structure and covering the façades. The storage buildings, used for crops (*tahıl ambarın*), are always built of wide wooden boards in a manner where they can fit into each other and therefore not use nails.

12: THE MANSION OF HASAN KURTOĞLU IN AMASYA

Hatice Kuşçu and Okay Kuşçu[1]
Ankara & Istanbul

Introduction

The period of the Ottoman Empire's decline began in the 18th century and coincided with the period of 'Westernisation'. At that time connections with Europe were established at the level of foreign envoys, and commercial relationships increased. To achieve progress in the military field, foreign experts were called upon, and high-ranking government officers were sent to Europe. As a result the Ottoman Empire faced changes in social, cultural and technical fields.

The close relationships established with western countries led to European styles exerting an influence on Ottoman art and architecture. The first western influences in architecture are mainly to be seen in the realm of decoration and details of embellishment rather than in the actual structure of buildings. Western motifs and fashions were accorded the highest priority, and were employed on the interior surfaces of buildings as wall and ceiling decoration. The overall pattern of construction on the other hand did not face fundamental changes in terms of building size or layout. Yet this westernisation, which manifested itself in the form of changes to the decoration of buildings during the 18th century, led the way in the 19th century to a radical transformation of the traditional layout of buildings. In the case of residential buildings, the changes that occurred in the development of form and space within houses lay rather in the realm of alteration than total reshaping. For instance, the basic concept of room-to-*sofa* relationship, with rooms leading off the *sofa*/hallway remained the same, yet the traditional spatial function and daily use of rooms did undergo changes. In addition, in the second half of the 19th century the upper levels of society in the period of the Tanzimat reforms encouraged the construction of large-scale buildings in order to reflect the magnificence of the Ottoman Empire. This was also true in the case of residential buildings, and in this period many great mansions were constructed.

These changes, seen predominantly in the architecture of the capital, also had a degree of influence upon the buildings of Anatolia. Religious, military and residential buildings were all affected by these new styles, and thus, beginning with Istanbul, many cities in Anatolia underwent changes to their overall appearance. The mansion that we have examined in our study was built in this period, and thus we believe it will serve as a good example to demonstrate western influence upon Anatolian structures.

The mansion, located beside the Kunç bridge, which unites Zübeyde Hanım and Mehmet Paşa streets, is situated on the banks of the Yeşilırmak river in the northeast sector of Amasya (fig.12.1). Compared to other buildings on the riverfront, the mansion is constructed on a more expansive and better protected plot. In terms of its planning and architectural structure, it is in fact very deserving of detailed study.

Three families still live in the mansion, but some parts of the building are kept closed. For this reason it should be noted that there have been sections of the building in which we have not been able to obtain measurements or conduct a detailed survey.

History of the mansion

The construction date of the mansion, which was built for one of the first members of the National Assembly of the Turkish Republic, the late Hasan Kurtoğlu, is not known for certain. According to the information provided by his granddaughter, who is still alive, one could surmise that the building dates to 1890 at the latest. In time the mansion passed from Hasan Bey to his son Tahir Bey, and today belongs to Tahir Bey's daughter Semahat Hanım.

An important factor that needs to be borne in mind is that though the building was constructed within a single period and as a single entity, it has undergone piecemeal alteration on a number of occasions and thus has changed over the years. As a result of these additions and alterations we have unfortunately been prevented from understanding completely the original structure and layout of the mansion. This is why we have found it useful in our study to divide the building up into the units that define its present state.

Although there has not been any important alteration of space in the part of the building we consider as the original house, it is certain that the structure facing the southwest has suffered great changes to the ground floor, and this is also the case with the middle section, which was originally used as the stable and warehouse. The central section has in fact been separated into units to serve as living quarters for three families, and a part of the ground floor of the house in the southwest section has been changed for use as a shop.

Description of the mansion

The mansion is a two-storeyed building, and only near the river side is there a basement in the original house. Originally the ground floor of the building would not have had as many entrances and windows as it now possesses, and it is most probable that the mansion at first had an inward-looking layout. The upper floor of the building is at the moment not being used, and some of the rooms on the ground floor are only used during certain months of the year by Hasan Bey's granddaughter and her family. The back garden is provided with a high wall to separate it from the alley and the river, and thus provide privacy.

From the information we have gathered from the older generation in Amasya the original house, where the present owner resides, was a place where guests from the Palace would be entertained.

The original house has entrances both on the Mehmet Paşa Street and on the side facing the bridge. The house, which also has an entrance from the garden, shows an interesting use of split-level development. The entrance from the side facing the bridge has two steps leading up to it, and this, together with with the projecting bay that is formed by the *sofa* on the upper floor, makes us believe that it once served as the main entrance (pl.12.1). Three steps from the entrance lead us to the hall from which rooms lead off (fig.12.2). Next to the main entrance, on the left as one enters, is a small door which cannot be opened. The present inhabitants inform us that it leads down to a lower storeroom. The room to the left of the entrance hall, which is reached by three steps up, we are told was the coffee-room. It has a lower ceiling than the others and contains a divan 40cm. in height which continues from wall to wall in front of the window. A fire place is set into the wall facing the door.

The two rooms which open off the hall and face the river have façades that are angled, resulting in trapezoidal plans. As this angle is not due to the nature of the site, the reason for it must be aesthetic: to enjoy more sunlight and more varied outlooks. There is also an entrance with three steps leading from the back garden into this part of the building and opening into a secondary hall, which is separated from the main hall by a wall and door. From this secondary hall, where the main staircase leads to the upper floor (and under which a WC has been installed), a third room of trapezoidal plan leads off. This is now used as the kitchen. Also leading off the secondary hall is a bathroom built during one of the periods of alteration and, next to it, an empty space with a high ceiling to which four steps lead down. This space is actually the entrance of the mansion from the side facing Mehmet Paşa Street. The house occupants have indicated that meals were prepared in the kitchen next to this space and were served there, so that as well as an entrance it also acted as a dining room. Another rather small room with a low ceiling is situated off this same space. The reason for the low ceiling is that the entrance from Mehmet Paşa Street and the present (side) entrance are at slightly different levels and since the room lies directly beneath the coffee room the low height of the ceiling in both rooms reflects the change in entrance level, creating a kind of mezzanine effect (see fig.12.2,3, section A-A). Although the wooden doors, with which the room ends, allow light to enter, and lead us to believe that the doors open onto the outside, we know that there is no such opening actually on the outside. This is why we believe this space is linked with the space at the left of the entrance facing the bridge, which we were not able to enter. From the space with the low ceiling there is a passageway to the basement proper. It is obvious that this passageway was opened up at a later date by removing the wall. Unfortunately, as the basement was dark and was used as storage space for wood and other objects, measurements were not made. However, we did notice a door which we understood was sealed off at some stage. In front of this door, which we surmise leads to the garden, is built a hen house that is still in use.

On the upper floor there is a *sofa* or large hallway from which five large rooms lead off (fig.12.4). The *sofa* has bays projecting from both that side of the house facing the bridge and the side facing the garden (pl.12.2, 3). The windows of these bays are wider than those in the rest of the mansion, and in front of each window is placed a divan for seating. The bay facing the bridge also extends further out than the other. From all the rooms facing the river, as well as from the windows of the *sofa*, there is a magnificent view. At the left of the staircase there is a sixth room which does not open onto the *sofa* but which faces the river. In the cupboard of this room is a water tap which we understand was installed at some time after the mansion was built. It is not in use at the moment. As a matter of fact, the form of the cupboard itself does not have the traditional features one associates with Turkish houses. From this room three steps lead to a space which we were told gives access to the attic.

The next house, which we shall refer to as No. 1, has its entrance in the 4th span of the façade facing Mehmet Paşa Street (counting from the north end of the mansion, fig.12.2, 5); in the same section is located a door that opens into the back garden. At the right of the entrance is a room and at the left is a kitchen and WC which were built as part of the alterations. A staircase of 18 steps leads to the small *sofa* on the upper floor. The room at the right of the *sofa* is actually the third room of the original house and faces the street. It is most probable that this room had two entrances in its original form.

The entrance to house No. 2 is situated in the central span of the façade, which is wider than the others. This part of the house, which is right in the middle of the entire building, was originally used as an entrance for animals and carriages to reach the back garden. In all probability this space was open at the rear; at present it has a small door that opens onto the back garden, and it has no other function than to contain a staircase leading to the upper floor and a WC under it. From the oven located in the second of the dilapidated rooms next to the garden we understand that this was once the kitchen. At the left, there is only one room. Although very much destroyed, square floor tiles are still visible in some of the corners of this room. The floor is 34cm. higher than the entrance and in one corner there is a drinking basin and faucet. On the upper floor the middle room is located right over the entrance of this house and forms a projecting bay over the street. It can be considered a kind of small *sofa*. As a matter of fact, it is very common in Turkish houses that middle rooms which have windows on only one side are provided with such projecting bays in order to obtain more daylight. The windows of this room mirror the dimensions and style of those we have seen in the main *sofa* of the original house. This space is actually divided in two by wooden doors with glass panels, and in this way a room and a hall are created, from which two rooms open off.

In house No. 3 the entrance is also provided at the centre, and rooms are located at either side. The entrance is divided into two with an arch and has a small door opening onto the back garden. It is interesting that the room fronting onto the street to the right of this entrance belongs to the neighbouring house and not to this one. This intersecting planning is generally the case with this building. The room to the left of the rear entrance, among those near the garden, has an oven and this suggests that this was once used as the kitchen. At present, it is divided into two and is being used as the store room. It is not known whether these rooms in houses 2 and 3 were also originally constructed as kitchens or whether they were turned into them during alteration. We believe these parts were later additions.

The corresponding area over the entrance on the upper floor is separated into two with wooden doors with glass panels. The space facing the street is used as a room. The rooms at either side open onto this middle space or room. The space overlooking the garden combines with that occupied by the staircase and can be considered a kind of wide *sofa*. It is into this that the room now used as the kitchen opens.

The main entrance to house No. 4 is from the alley, with another entrance via the back garden. Not all the rooms on the ground floor in this part of the building belong to this house. The space between the four spans on the side facing the street, for instance, is separated off as shops. As we could not enter this part, we have not been able to indicate on our drawings whether there are interior partitions or not.

The side facing the alley is not perpendicular to the front of the building. We have been told that once there was a stream where the alley now runs; i.e. probably the reason for the angled façade here is the original presence of the stream.

On the ground floor beyond the entrance, there is a fireplace that is said to be original, together with a WC which we understand was built afterwards. The space next to the fireplace is used as a storage room, and from the staircase at the right of the entrance we reach an intermediary floor or landing. On this we find a WC, bath tub and sink which are all later additions. From this landing we reach the upper floor by means of twelve steps. The central space here is divided into two by wooden doors which have glass panels. The part facing the main street has a projecting bay and from it two rooms lead off, one at each side. Of these the room which occupies the corner of the building is considered more prestigious and in consequence is larger, just like the corresponding room at the other corner of the mansion. On this first floor the external wall facing the alley is not set at an angle like the ground floor. Instead, a triangular projection built out over the ground floor wall produces a roughly square room. The same is true for the corresponding room facing the back of the building. These corner projections are supported by decorated braces. Such decorated projections to houses are, in fact, a common feature of traditional Turkish houses.

The ground floor of the side facing Mehmet Paşa Street is constructed out of stone masonry. The rest of the walls are built of timber frame, infilled with brick. The columns at both ground and first floor levels on the street façade are constructed out of 33cm. wide stones placed on top of each other and carrying capitals measuring 23 x 60cm. Between the columns are 13 arches. The joists of the first floor are extended to form cantilevered projections that are covered with lath and plaster (*bağdadi*). On these joists a sill plate is placed, which becomes the base for the timber structural columns and the wall framing of the upper storey walls. The distance between structural columns and vertical framing members is kept wide and horizontal connections and props are placed between them. This structure is maintained throughout the height of the building. Only consoles supporting bays intersect the horizontal line of the first floor. The brick infilling to the walls is entirely covered with stucco, with only the first floor joists and vertical supports at the corners of rooms left bare. The eaves of the house follow the indentations and projections of the building façades, and the roof is covered with guttered clay tiles.

Throughout the building three standard types of windows have been used. The windows of the *sofa* of the original house, and those of the projecting bay in the middle of the side facing Mehmet Paşa Street measure 120 x 216cm. Most of the other windows in the house, like the the side windows of the *sofa* of the original house, measure 100 x 216cm. A standard dimension cannot be given for the side windows of the bays in general since this depends on their overall width. Doors and ceilings are extremely plain and we see no use of the intricate wood carving as decoration that is so common in Turkish houses. There are, however, gilded curtain cornices which do provide us with a clue to western influence.

Conclusion

So far we have studied the units of the mansion separately, but when we consider the building as a whole, we see that the relationship of the various spaces within it suits the basic traditional Turkish concept, though each unit does now show considerable differences in use from its original traditional function. Rooms which are actually condensed living units in the Turkish house have now lost these characteristics. For instance, there is no lower level (*seki altı*) in the rooms any more. We find no divans in most of the rooms; in fact, we only find two in the *sofa*. We understand from the few pieces that are left that western style furniture was used. Fireplaces have been taken out of the rooms, and stoves are used as heaters. There are no bed storage cupboards (*yüklük*) and no washing facilities (*gusülhane*) such as were placed in cupboards.

The social and cultural structures that have changed as a result of western influence have influenced the daily life of buildings like the mansion, and without doubt it is these residential spaces that have been most influenced by the changes. When we examine the situation from this viewpoint, we see that houses are not just places for shelter; they also are sources which give information about a society's whole social, cultural and economic structure. This is why it is very important to protect such examples of our cultural heritage, to enable us to follow directly society's change and progress.

Our cultural heritage is important not only in order to be able to trace past values, but also to allow them to act as a source to create our future. For a society not to lose its cultural identity and not to become alienated from its own personality in the modern world, it has to integrate its identity into the conditions of present day life. This will not be done by erasing all traces of the past, but can be achieved by protecting and improving them. The main purpose of protection is to prevent the demolition of old houses and old districts in the urban context which face the danger of obliteration, to renovate them and to offer them to contemporary life. To achieve this, more importance should be given to educating and influencing people's consciousness of their environment and thus to establishing their cultural identity. In addition, it will be wise to overcome the various bureaucratic problems that exist in order to allow us to achieve results in a proper and scientifically based manner.

Bibliography

Arel, A. 1992: *Osmanlı Konut Geleneğinde Tarihsel Sorunlar*. Ege Üniversitesi Güzel Sanatlar Fakültesi Yayınları 11, Izmir.

Cezar, M. 1971: *Sanatta Batıya Açılış ve Osman Hamdi*. Türkiye İş Bankası Kültür Yayınları, Istanbul.

Denel, S. 1982: *Batılılaşma Sürecinde İstanbul'da Tasarım ve Dış Mekanlarda Değişim ve Nedenleri*. ODTÜ Yayınları, Ankara.

Eldem, S.H. 1955: *Türk Evi Plan Tipleri*. İTÜ Mim. Fak. Yay., Istanbul.

Kafesçioğlu, R. 1955: *Kuzeybatı Anadolu'da Ahşap Ev Yapılar*. İTÜ Mim. Fak. Yay., Istanbul.

Kazmalıoğlu, M., Tanyeli, U. 1978: 'Anadolu Konut Mimarisinde Bölgeler Farklılaşmala', *Yapı* 38: 28-41.

Küçükerman, Ö. 1973: *Anadolu'daki Geleneksel Türk Evinde Mekân Organizasiyonu Açısından Odalar*. T.T.O.K. Yay., Istanbul.

Küçükerman, Ö., Şemsi, G. 1995: *Anadolu Mirasında Türk Evleri*. T.C.Kültür Bakanlığı Yayınları. 177-7, Sanat-Sanat Tarihi Dizisi 177-9. Istanbul.

Multu, A. 1975: 'Türk Evleri', *Sanat Dünyamız* 1/3: 3-13.

Sözen, M., Eruzun, C. 1992: *Anadolu'da Ev ve İnsan*. Creative Yay., Istanbul.

---

[1] We are grateful to Oya Talı Kuyumcu for her generous help in producing the drawings that accompany this paper. We would also like to thank Semahat Hanım, a granddaughter of the late Hasan Kurtoğlu, and her daughter, Berrin Kılınç for all their help in providing detailed information about the history of the family and the mansion.

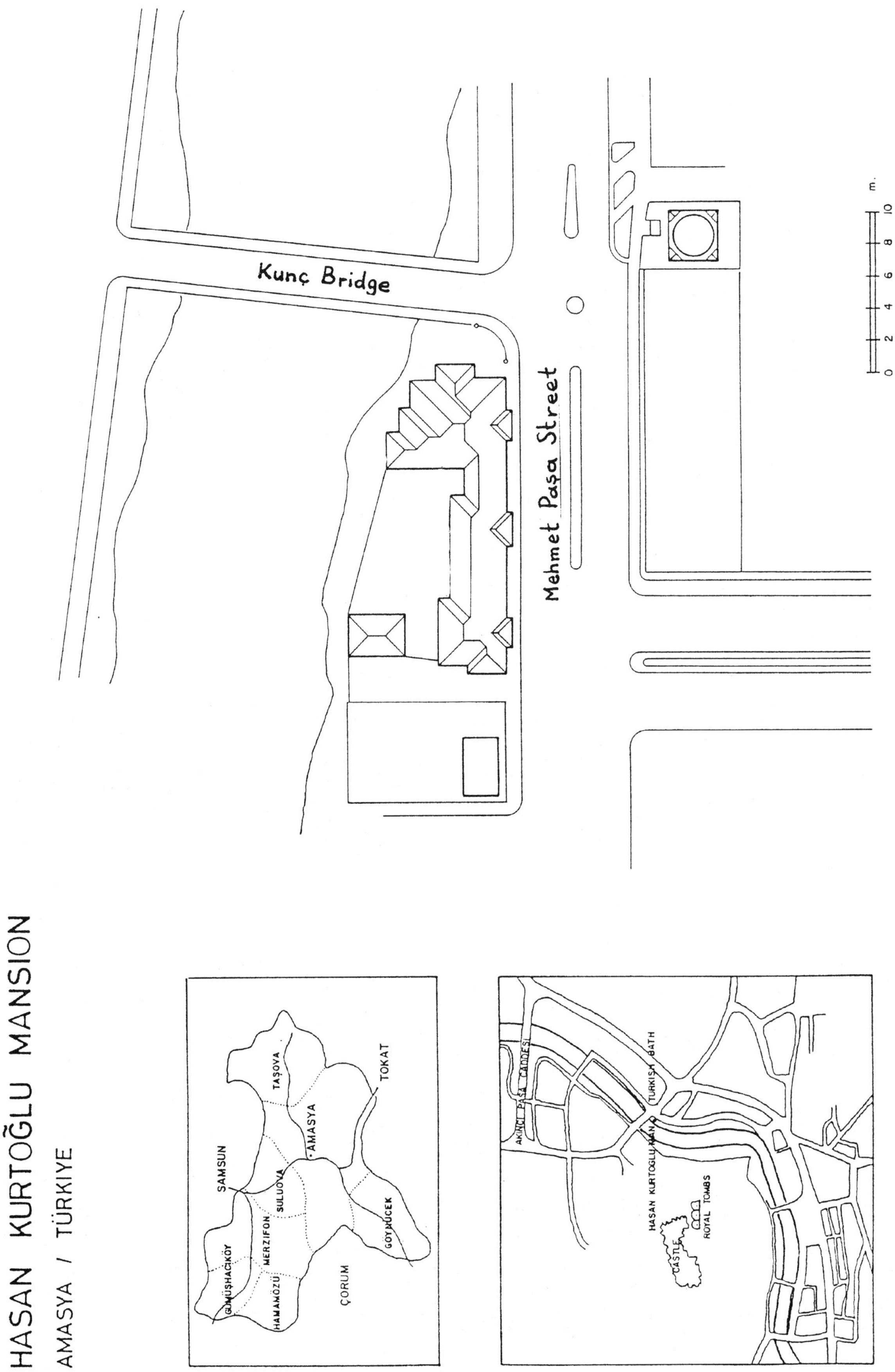

Fig. 12.1. Location plan

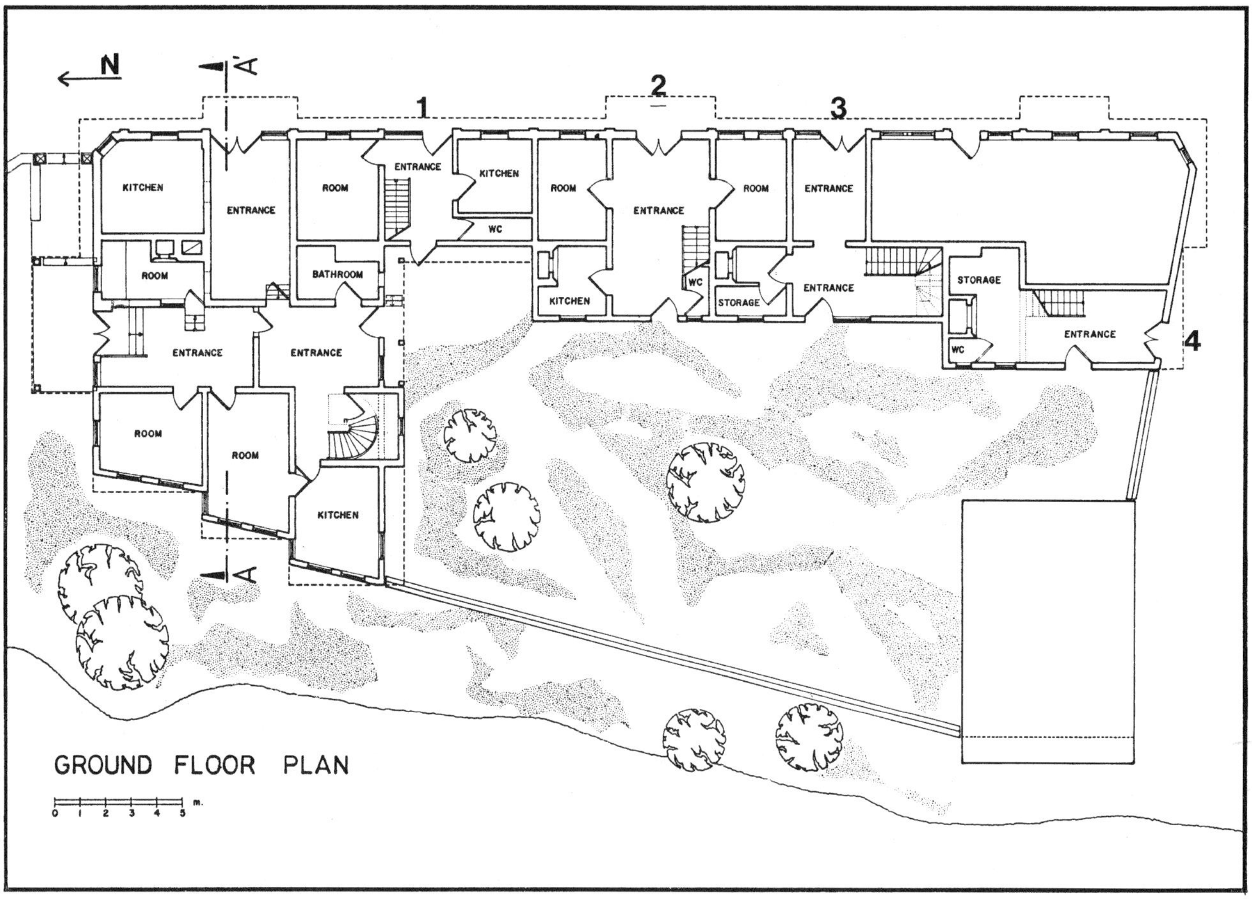

Fig. 12.2. Ground floor plan

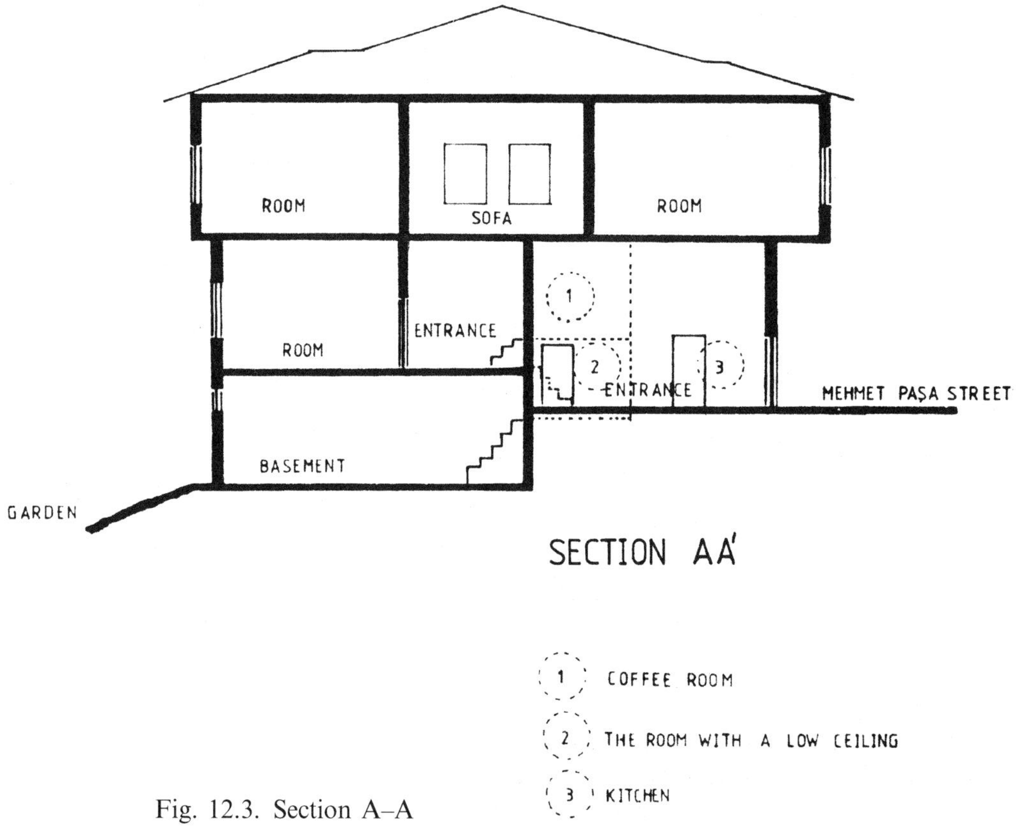

Fig. 12.3. Section A–A

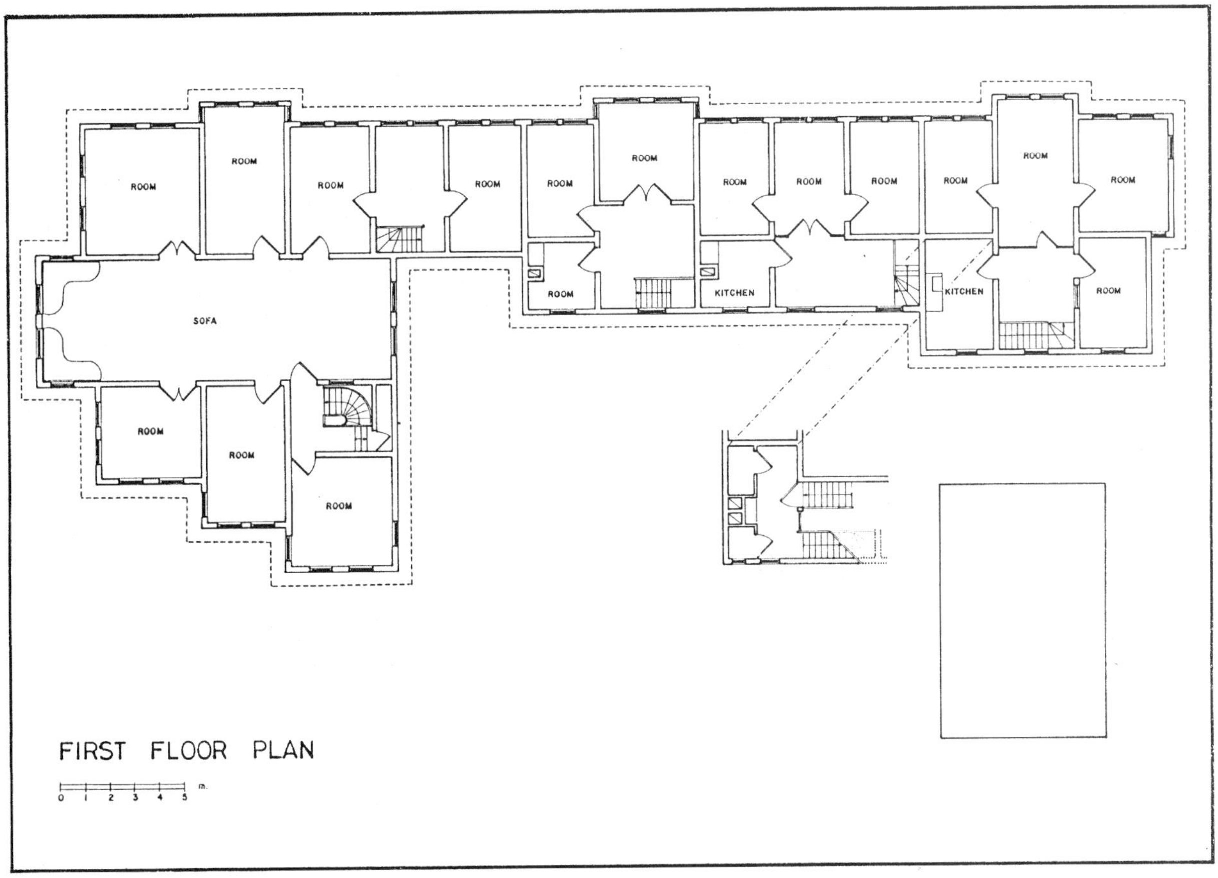

Fig. 12.4. First floor plan

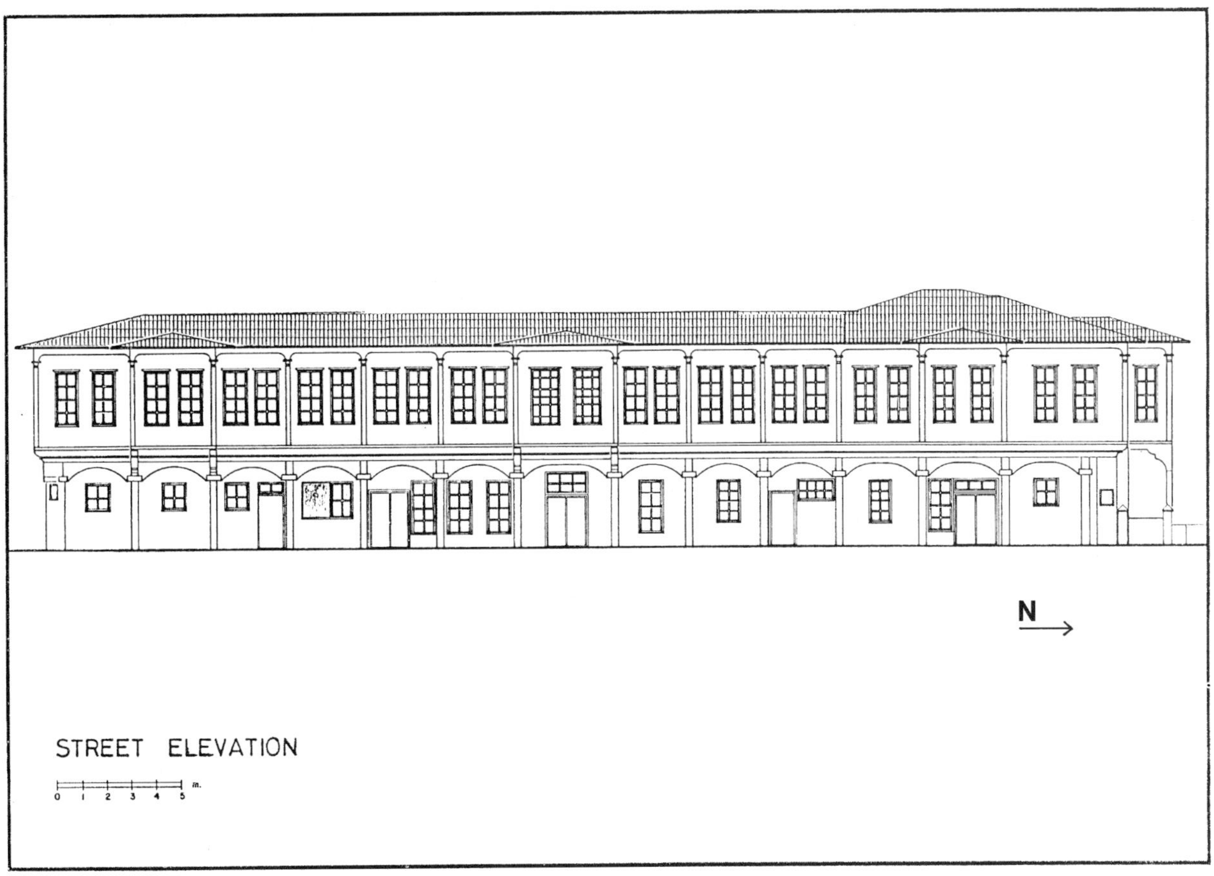

Fig. 12.5. Street elevation

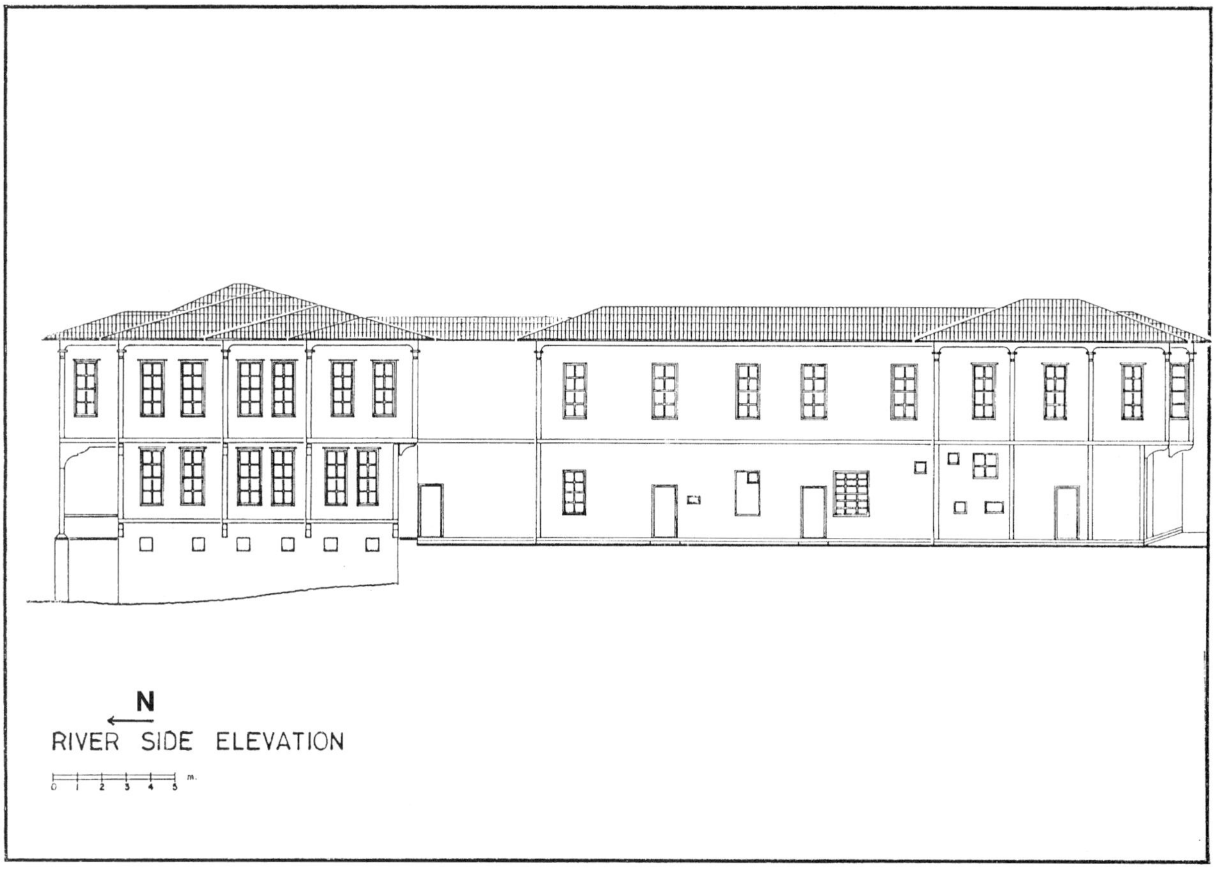

Fig. 12.6. Riverside elevation

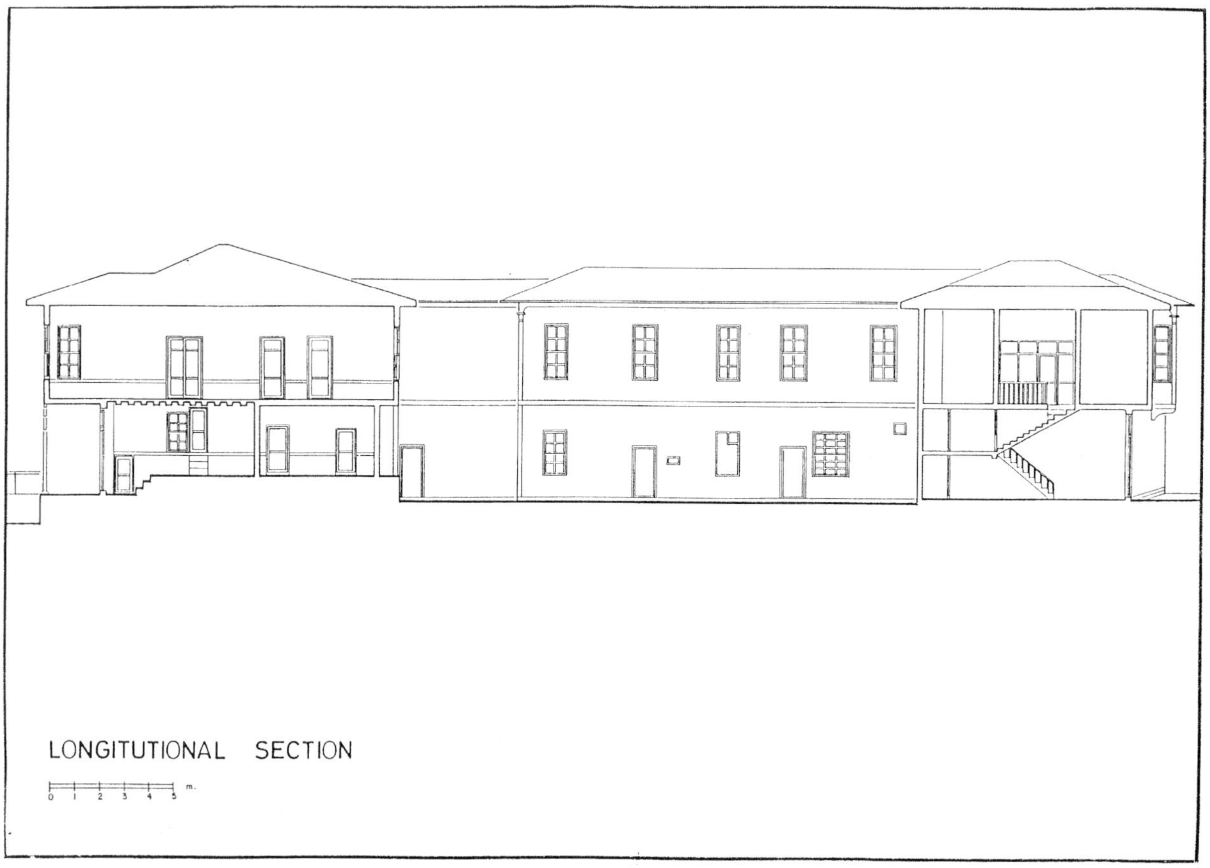

Fig. 12.7. Longitudinal section

13: WESTERNISMS IN OTTOMAN ART: WALL PAINTINGS IN 19TH CENTURY HOUSES

Prof. Dr. Günsel Renda
Hacettepe University, Ankara

In spite of the rich heritage of domestic architecture in Turkey, art historians' interest in the subject is relatively new. It is fortunate, though, that through growing efforts directed towards 1) the production of architectural surveys made in the last twenty years and 2) the conservation of monuments, we are now able to define the distinctive characteristics and regional styles of vernacular architecture in a vast territory once controlled by the Ottoman Empire. However, the painted decoration in houses has not been the subject of a separate study until recently, despite the fact that it is often the decoration itself, much more than the architectural design, that reveals the different phases of artistic currents within the Ottoman Empire and reflects the social and cultural changes that occurred, especially in the later centuries.

The last two centuries of Ottoman history mirror the process of westernisation in the Empire as a whole. It is during this period that interest in European cultural life resulted in a western-oriented affectation in life-style and the arts among court circles and the elite. A new flavour was brought to Ottoman art in the 18th and 19th centuries, marked by an interesting blend of European elements with traditional style. Studies of late Ottoman buildings reveal a marked change in architectural decoration. While newly imported architectural elements appeared on the exteriors of buildings, painted decoration in the interior took a new form. The traditional brushwork technique using paints mixed with water and glue, the *kalemişi* decoration of geometric and floral motifs, now developed into wall paintings of landscapes and still life. Wall paintings, in fact, became an essential part of the decoration in many Ottoman buildings of the 18th and 19th centuries including mosques and even *türbes* (monumental tombs), but they are most especially found in houses and palaces.

In the Turkish house decoration is a programme of the interior. Every Turkish house has a *başoda*, the main room that serves as the guest room and which is always decorated with much care. The distribution of the decoration in this room is closely related to its spatial organisation, which has remained unchanged over the centuries from the simplest dwellings to the larger town houses or even royal residences. The room has two levels, the *seki üstü*, the sitting area which is a platform usually raised one step above the entrance and the *seki altı* which is on the same level as the entrance. On the entrance wall there is usually a built-in cupboard and niches placed on the two sides for lamps or other articles. This wall and the ceiling usually display elaborate woodwork, sometimes painted or even gilded. Painted decoration or wall paintings are found as narrow friezes or panels on the upper sections of the wall between the cupboards or wooden panelling and the ceiling. The wall paintings are usually views from Istanbul or other major provincial towns. Sometimes they are just idyllic landscapes with imaginary palaces and pooled gardens. Human figures, however, are excluded from these paintings until the very end of the 19th century.[1]

It was the natural outcome of westernising efforts in the Ottoman court circles that the imperial residences were decorated in the new manner. The Harem section of the Topkapı Palace not only serves as an exquisite example of Ottoman domestic architecture but also displays the development of a distinctive programme in painted decoration in the 18th and 19th centuries. The Gözdeler wing built in 1770, for example, carries on the exterior all the characteristics of an 18th century Ottoman house, and in the interior it is decorated with baroque cartouches and landscape panels. The quarters added by Selim III in the 1790s similarly display fanciful baroque and rococo carvings enframing views of Istanbul. In these landscapes waterside houses on the Golden Horn or the Bosphorus are set against a background of soft hills and a blue sky with all the architectural details accurately rendered. There is an awareness of perspective and tonal variations in colour marking a new trend in Ottoman painting, away from traditional manuscript illustration based on two-dimensional imagery and omitting light and shade (pl.13.1,2).

This new type of painted decoration spread rapidly from the capital to the provinces in the east and west by the end of the 18th century and is found mainly in houses commissioned by the provincial notables, the governors and the wealthy merchants. The 18th century marks the decentralisation of the Ottoman administration when, with the decline of the *sipahi* organisation, the military that was granted land by the sultan for services, there was instead an increase in the power of the local mercenary forces. The notables now had the right of inheritance and they became more powerful not only as military leaders but also as local financial authorities. They certainly led a life-style similar to that in the capital and they built and decorated their houses in the new westernising style prevailing in Istanbul[2] (pl.13.3).

There are several houses still surviving in the western part of Anatolia displaying this new type of decoration. The Hadımoğlu House in Bayramiç near Çanakkale, built in 1796 by a family of notables, has two main rooms with exquisite painted decoration. In one of the rooms a view from the Bosphorus is placed above the cupboards; in the second room there is a landscape depicting a nearby port (Renda 1978, 715, 726; Tayla 1978; Renda et al. 1988, Fig. 72). Other similarly decorated houses are found in the neighbourhood. A house in Edremit belonging to the Kabakçi family dating from 1805 has two rooms decorated with landscapes. Not far away from this is the Mehmed Ali house in Adatepe with several rooms displaying views of neighbouring towns (Renda, Erol 1980, Fig. 45, 61; Süslü 1978, 99; here pl.13.4). The Mehmed Ali Ağa house in Reşadiye near Datça in the southwest has more provincial views painted on its walls but the general decorative programme is the same (Renda 1974). The better known Çakıroğlu Konak in Birgi has two main rooms decorated with views of Istanbul and Izmir, with additional wall paintings in the halls painted in the 1830s[3] (pl.13.5). The painted houses are not confined to western Anatolia but they are found in further provinces as well. Many houses in central Anatolia are decorated in the same manner. A house in Göreme built by an official guard at the court of Mahmud II has several landscapes displaying a masterly hand on its walls, including a view of the Tophane section of Istanbul (Renda 1985) (pl.13.6).

Houses in the Balkan provinces followed the same programme in painted decoration. The regions of Macedonia, Kastoria, Ambelakia, Verria, Selitsa and the Aegean Islands have a number of houses with wall paintings. Houses in other Balkan towns such as Plovdiv, Scopia, Tetovo, Koprivshtitsa etc., and even further provinces such as Albania, were similarly decorated whether they were owned by Turkish families or local Christians. Many of them belonged to local merchants who had trade relations with Istanbul and various European towns. Therefore, views of Istanbul as well as other Mediterranean ports including Venice are very common in these paintings. For example, the Pultidis House in Siatista has a view of Istanbul painted on the wall in its main room; so does the Georgios Schwartz House in Ambelakia dating from 1798 and the Nanzi House in Verria, thus proving that the new decorative programme spread into the provinces especially during the period of Selim III[4] (pl.13.7).

The new style of painted decoration travelled to the eastern provinces as well, and several houses in Syria and Egypt are marked by their interiors richly decorated with wall paintings. Although the houses in these regions are the Mamluq-type courtyard house, their main rooms are painted in the new Ottoman manner. The Nizami house in Damascus dating from 1803 has two rooms with views of towns painted on the walls, one of them easily identified as a view from the Bosphorus (pl.13.8). The Mujallad house in Damascus is decorated in the same manner. The decorative details and the paintings in these houses remind us of the decoration in the Selim III wing in the Topkapı Palace Harem.[5]

Similarly painted houses in Cairo show that the westernised Ottoman style replacing the Mamluq type of decoration expanded through the patronage of Mehmed Ali who was recognised as governor of Egypt in 1805. His Europeanising ideology accorded with the reforming Ottoman sultans of the time; therefore the spread was very rapid in his period. His own palaces were all decorated in the new Euro-Ottoman style. Although some of the buildings he built no longer exist, the Kasr-al Gawhara (Bijou Palace) in the citadel in Cairo, built in 1814, is a surviving example of this type of decoration. The wall paintings placed in narrow friezes or niches are very similar in style to those in the Topkapı Palace Harem, dating from the same period[6] (pl.13.9).

A survey of the Ottoman house in the provinces at the end of the 18th century and the first decades of the 19th century shows that wall painting became an essential part of the decoration in houses and was spread widely in the Empire by patrons who were in one way or another politically tied to the capital. Even if the styles varied, the same elements were shared by the artists painting them. For example, in all the city-scapes upright trees are set among red-roofed buildings along with gardens, pools and flocks of birds; carefully drawn boats sail on the water, but human figures are never included except in some houses belonging to Christians. These elements seem to have become stylised motifs used by local artists to whom this new type of decoration was undoubtedly introduced by artists coming from the capital.

In the second half of the 19th century painted decoration in Ottoman houses took a new form. This is the period in Ottoman history in which westernisation was institutionalised in the empire. The series of reform movements aimed at a more western pattern of organisation, which was proclaimed in the decree of 1839 known as Tanzimat, the new order, basically reformed governmental institutions and brought new regulations on administrative matters. With these regulations urbanism took a new form. New districts were established in Istanbul and the provinces, in which urban notables continued constructing luxurious houses, but these were now joined by wealthy merchants who led a European lifestyle and built mansions in the new manner. This is because the number of rich merchants increased in both the capital and all the provinces as a result of the empire's liberal trade policies. New districts were developed for this new bourgeoisie in all the towns, bringing further European influence and a more eclectic style to domestic architecture and decoration using new techniques. The new life-style they led brought European furniture into the houses necessitating a new type of spatial organisation in the rooms. Wall paintings now moved much higher up the walls and onto the ceilings. Oil painting was now the preferred form, replacing the traditional *kalemişi* paintings, which used paints mixed with glue or egg yolk. There was also more variety in theme including exotic landscapes, European vistas, hunting scenes, boats, animals, birds and elaborate still-life scenes.

This new decorative style was undoubtedly initiated by the 19th century sultans themselves who built a series of massive European-looking palaces along the Bosphorus in the second half of the 19th century, reflecting the eclectic architectural styles prevailing in Europe at the time. In the Dolmabahçe, Beylerbeyi, Göksu and Yıldız Palaces in Istanbul the interiors display a variety of European furniture, mirrors, and chandeliers resulting in painted decoration being placed much higher on the walls and onto the ceiling. The repertoire in wall painting now includes landscapes with towers and castles resembling European postcard illustrations or exotic views of tropical lands, various hunting animals and some human figures, but these only at the end of the century (pl.13.10). Houses of the elite in Istanbul were also decorated in a style similar to the palaces. For example, Abutlar Yalı on the Bosphorus, dating from the mid-19th century, has European-looking interiors with exotic landscapes of Egypt (pl.13.11-12). A house in Beşiktaş belonging to an official working for Abdülhamit II has painted on its walls and ceilings views from Istanbul and some still life scenes very similar in style to easel painting produced at the time. A *konak* in the Vefa district built in 1893 has several rooms painted with views of Istanbul, one even displaying the newly built railway and bridges (pl.13.10). Towards the end of the century the human figure in small size is included in the wall paintings found in some of the rooms in the Dolmabahçe and Yıldız Palaces. Such figures are also included in landscapes painted in the Edip Efendi Yalı on the Bosphorus dating from the same period[7]. In all these buildings built in the second half of the 19th century, the repertoire is very similar and shows that the wall paintings are the work of the same ateliers in Istanbul. Undoubtedly there were now groups of artists living in Istanbul painting in the European manner, who decorated buildings as well. All the views of Istanbul show great similarities. They draw the city from the same angles, usually from the Çamlıca Heights or Pera and depict certain popular districts such as the Göksu plain with its fountain, the Tower of Leander or the Fenerbahçe bay and its lighthouse. These views were also popular in the same period in easel paintings executed by Turkish and European artists in Istanbul, showing that the artists probably used engravings or photographs as models (pl.13.13-15).

A look at the provinces in the second half of the 19th century reveals that the houses built by the bourgeoisie in the newly developed districts compete in luxury with one another and with those in the capital. Since they are furnished with European-type furniture, the painted decoration is mostly on the ceiling or in panels near the ceiling. Oil painting is preferred and a more European repertoire is used similar to those in the capital. A house in Safranbolu dating from 1890 has on its ceilings oil paintings of views set in medallion frames reminding us of European postcards. Gaziantep has several houses lavishly decorated. In the Güllüoğlu house, belonging to a wealthy merchant family, the views of Istanbul painted on its ceilings are very similar to those paintings found in Istanbul houses dating from the same period (pl.13.14).[8]

Damascus is one of the provincial towns that witnessed a considerable increase in the construction of houses by urban notables in the second half of the 19th century, especially in the newly developed extramural districts of the town. The wealthy Damascenes brought a type of occidental urbanism to Damascus introducing a new life-style, using European furniture and having their houses lavishly decorated.[9] Their houses, faithfully following the latest trends in Istanbul, demonstrate the extent of political and cultural ties between the capital city and this significant provincial town. In these houses large panoramas of Istanbul are very common, some placed on the ceilings depicting the urban setting of the capital city at the end of the century. In one such panorama, now removed to the Damascus museum, the two bridges on the Golden Horn are very carefully depicted and a balloon hovering above the Sea of Marmara indicates that it must have been painted after the 1880s (pl.13.16). The current developments in Istanbul must have interested house owners in the provinces, as such panoramas were common in houses in other provinces too. A house in Acre belonging to a Greek merchant family has on its stairwell a vast panorama of Istanbul, again with the two bridges on the Golden Horn, the newly built Sirkeci railway station, and steamboats on the Sea of Marmara.[10]

The new techniques and repertoire were adapted in the western provinces as well. The panorama of Istanbul found in the Makris house in Selitsa is strikingly similar to those late panoramas in the Damascene houses showing the two bridges as landmarks of the city and modern ships on the sea (Makris 1986, pl.40). These are all bird's-eye view drawings of the city as seen from the heights of Pera. This brings to mind, once again, the possible use of photographs or postcards of the city, which were very popular at the end of the century.

A study of the new decorative programme that seems to have spread so widely in houses in the Ottoman empire in the 18th and 19th centuries brings out certain significant facts. Late Ottoman houses and their decoration mirror the significant political and economic ties between the capital and the Ottoman provinces. Secondly, they bring out the extensive administrative and economic power held by the provincial notables after the 18th century, and thirdly, they point to the emergence of a wealthy merchant class in the 19th century resulting in an increase in luxurious private dwellings in the newly developed districts. The study also shows that the patrons fall into two categories. The first are the officials appointed by the Ottoman government, that is the notables, who not only administered but also faithfully followed the westernising ideas and tastes developing around court circles in Istanbul. The second category, the local merchants, also kept close ties with the central administration, often serving as agents of the monopolies held by the sultans for their personal advantage. The examples studied here show that in the second half of the 19th century there was a shift of patronage from local notables to the rich bourgeoisie.

One other issue concerns the identity and provenance of the artisans and craftsmen producing these wall paintings, their training and working methods. Documents concerning similar work in Istanbul indicate that they were painted by the *nakkaş*, a term that is used for illustrators of manuscripts, designers of motifs for the minor arts, and for decorators of walls as well. The *nakkaş* could be a part of the palace school or an outsider who could be employed for royal commissions when needed. This was also true of wall decorators. Those not working permanently for the court had their own workshops and belonged to guilds. We know enough about the guild system in the Ottoman Empire to tell that the construction guild is where masons and plasterers belonged. Although A. Raymond published several documents about the construction guilds, there is no mention of wall painters in these; however, documents from various court books about construction work in Ottoman Cairo published by N. Hanna record facts about painters and their guilds.[11] These documents reveal that the painters had been under the authority of the *mimarbaşı*, the chief architect, just like the construction guilds. The construction of houses was undoubtedly carried out as private commissions but court registers show that an inspection by the *mimarbaşı* could be secured if the patron was dissatisfied with the work and made an official legal complaint (Hanna 1984, 64).

As to the identity of the artists producing these wall paintings the study of wall paintings in the royal residences in Istanbul and archival documents relating to them reveals that they were executed by local artists, Muslim or Christian. There is no evidence for foreign artists employed at the Topkapı Palace in the 18th and 19th centuries. On the other hand recent documents have revealed that the Selim III wing was possibly decorated by a Greek painter from Kapıdağı who took on several other commissions from the sultan.[12] Stylistic similarities between wall paintings in the Topkapı Palace and those in other houses built and decorated at the time, indicate that it must have been the same workshops in Istanbul that took commissions of this sort.[13] Their styles have great affinity with the works of European artists such as Hilair, Cassas, Mayer, Melling, etc. working in Istanbul at the time, showing once again their impact on the local artists in the formation of a new artistic milieu within the capital city.[14] In the second half of the 19th century, however, European artists themselves took commissions from the sultans for work in the royal palaces. Records of payments made by the court indicate the names of artists working in the Dolmabahçe and Beylerbeyi palaces and various kiosks in the Yıldız complex. Some European names are mentioned such as Chelebowsky, Aiwazovsky, Lemnio, Masson, Zonaro as well as local artists such as Karayanis, Bafolos, Garbis, Ahmet, Ali Haydar. These documents indicate that it was a cosmopolitan group of artists who produced these wall paintings.[15] This heterogeneous nature of the artists accounts for the variety of subject matter and technique appearing in wall paintings in the second half of the 19th century.

The evidence for workshops or ateliers in Istanbul since the mid-18th century is a significant matter because local artists, Muslim or Christian, working in these ateliers were influenced by visiting European artists and perhaps taught others as well. Istanbul, therefore, was the centre initiating this type of painting and also fulfilling commissions for provincial patrons, at least for major projects. These artists from the capital in turn must have influenced local craftsmen who carried on a similar line of work in local workshops. Moutsopoulos (1967, 102-3) talks about the travelling guilds of construction in Macedonia fulfilling commissions in other towns. There is further evidence for artists travelling to different provinces. Sources tell us that Mehmed Ali commissioned several Turkish and Greek artists from Istanbul to decorate his palaces in Cairo.[16]

The survey of wall paintings within the empire shows that they are expressions of a period in Ottoman culture in which westernisms affected royal circles in the capital as well as urban notables and merchants in the provinces who had international ties. These paintings form a separate genre because they represent a period of transition from manuscript illustration to painting in the western sense. Although certain western elements such as perspective or light and shade are adapted in these paintings, the iconography is Ottoman. They are landscapes, yet they exclude figures. They do not intend to illustrate life and people in these towns but only to draw the setting. These views still retain the topographic approach which appeared in town views in Ottoman manuscript illustrations. This is partly because the first Turkish institutions in which drawing was taught were the military schools, where only topographic drafting was needed. Secondly, for the Ottoman artist landscape was the most suitable medium for applying western modes of expression. It also suited the tastes of the patrons because these landscapes made their homes look like European interiors and at the same time avoided the religious objection to figural representation on a monumental scale. It is evident that both the patrons and the artists working for them shared the aesthetic values of a westernising society in transition.

Bibliography

Anon 1995: 'Beit Miyalled', *The World Interiors* (June): 78-84.

Arık, R. 1976: *Batılılaşma Döneminde Anadolu Tasvir Sanatı.* Ankara.

Boppe, A. 1989: *Les Peintres du Bosphore au dix-huitième siècle* (2nd ed.). Paris.

Carswell, J.1977: 'From the Tulip to the Rose' in *Studies in Eighteenth Century Islamic History.* Southern Illinois University Press: 328-58.

Deherain, H. 1931: 'L' Egypte turque', *Histoire de la Nation Egyptienne* 5. Paris.

Diamantopoulou, A. 1987: *Ambelakia.* Athens.

Duda, D. 1971: *Innenarchitektur syrischer Stadthaüser.* Beirut.

Eldem, S.H. 1977: *Birgi Çakırağa Konağı.* Istanbul.

Ergenç, Ö. 1981: 'Osmanlı şehirlerindeki yönetim kurumlarının niteliği üzerinde bazı düşünceler', *VII. T. T. K. Bildiriler* II. Ankara: 1265-74.

Hanna, N. 1984: *Construction Work in Ottoman Cairo.* Cairo.

İbrahim, M. 1995: 'Makedonya'da Türk İslam Mimarisinde görülen duvar süslemeleri', *9. Milletlerarası Türk Sanatları Kongresi Bildirileri.* Ankara: 287-98.

İnalcık, H. 1977: 'Centralization and Decentralization in Ottoman Administration', in *Studies in 18th Century Islamic History.* Southern Illinois University Press: 27-52.

Kiel, M. 1978: 'Aspects of Ottoman Turkish Architecture in Albania', *Fifth International Congress of Turkish Art.* Budapest: 541-8.

Koumbas, V. 1984: *Lesbos.* Athens.

Labeyrie, I. 1991: 'Quelques réflections à propos de la maison Nizam à Damas', *L'Habitat traditionnel dans les pays musulmans autour de la Méditerranée* III. IFAO, Cairo: 828-46.

Lezine, A. 1972: *Trois palais ottomanes à Caïre.* Cairo.

Makris, K. 1986: *The Wall Paintings of the Houses of the Village of Eratira-Selista.* Thessaloniki (in Greek).

Moaz, A.S. 1995: 'Domestic architecture, notables and power. A neighbourhood in late Ottoman Damscus', in *10th International Congress of Turkish Art, Geneva, 17-23 September, 1995.*

Moutsopoulos, N.K. 1967: *The Popular Architecture of Verria.* Athens.

Özkaya, Y. 1977: *Osmanlı İmparatorluğunda Ayanlık.* Ankara.

Pauty, E. 1933: *Les Palais et les maisons d'époque musulmane au Caïre.* Cairo.

Peev, Ch. D. 1943: *Alte Haüser in Plovdiv.* Berlin.

Raymond, A. 1973: *Artisans et commerçants au Caire au xviiie siècle.* Damascus.

Renda, G. 1974: 'Datça'da Eski bir Türk Evi', *Sanat Dünyamız* 2: 22-9.

---- 1977: *Batılılaşma Döneminde Türk Resim Sanatı 1700-1850.* Ankara.

---- 1978: 'Wall Paintings in Turkish Houses', *Fifth International Congress of Turkish Art.* Budapest: 711-36.

---- 1985: 'Göreme'de Korunması Gereken Bir Ev', *III. Araştırma Sonuçları Toplantısı.* Kültür Bakanlığı Eski Eserler ve Müzeler Genel Müdürlüğü, Ankara: 103-32.

---- 1996: 'Ressam Kostantin Kapıdağlı hakkında yeni görüşler', in *19. yüzyıl İstanbul'unda Sanat Ortamı.* Sanat Tarihi Derneği Yayınları 2, Istanbul: 139-62.

Renda, G., Erol, T. 1980: *Çağdaş Türk Resim Sanatı Tarihi.* Istanbul.

Renda, G., Erol, T., Turani, A., Özsezgin, K., Aslıer, M. 1988: *A History of Turkish Painting.* Seattle & Washington.

Revault, J., Maury, B. 1975-83: *Palais et maisons du Caire du XIVe au XVIIIe siècles* (4 vols). Cairo.

Roman, Y. 1996: 'Overhead Art', *Eretz* 49 (Nov.-Dec.): 23-35.

Roshkovska, A. 1973: 'The Arie's painted houses in Samokov', *Annual Social Cultural and Educational Association of the Jews in the People's Republic of Bulgaria* 5: 119-53.

Rouanet, A., Piponnier, D. 1985-6: 'Etude iconographique et technique d'un ensemble decoratif: la maison Nizam à Damas', *Bulletin d'études orientales* 37-38: 1-159.

Sarcia & Curatola, G. 1981: 'Perferia ottomane e laicismi decorativo' in *Il Mondo Islamico Interazione e Acculturazione*, I. Rome: 128-64.

Schilcher, L.S. 1985: *Families in Politics; Damascene Factions and Estates of the 18th and 19th Centuries*. Stuttgart.

Soikov. 1977: *The Architecture of the Town of Koprivshitsa*. Sofia.

Süslü, Ö. 1978: 'Adatepe'de Hacı Mehmet Ağa Konağının Süslemeleri', *İstanbul Devlet Mühendislik ve Mimarlık Akademisi Dergisi* 2.

Tayla, H. 1978: 'Hadımoğlu Mansion in Bayramiç', *Turkish Treasures* 1: 99-114.

Vacalopoulos, A.E. 1973: *History of Macedonia 1354-1833*. Thessaloniki.

Weit, 1949: *Mohammed Ali et les Beaux-Arts*. Cairo.

Yum,Ş. 1995: 'Son Dönem Osmanlı Saray Yapılarındaki Bazı Tasvirler Üzerine Gözlemler', in *9th International Congress of Art, Proceedings* 3. Ankara: 543-52.

---

[1] Research carried on by Turkish scholars in the last twenty years has produced a number of publications on wall paintings The art of wall painting is discussed within the framework of late Ottoman painting with an extensive catalogue of works from Istanbul and other parts of the empire in Renda 1977. Wall paintings in buildings in Anatolia are taken up in detail in Arık 1976. For a specific study on wall paintings in houses see Renda 1978. A number of wall paintings in the Topkapı Palace have been published in various books and articles. For a comprehensive survey and catalogue of the material see Renda 1977: 79-108, 231-5; Renda *et al.* 1988: 69-86.

[2] For more information on the local notables and their status see Özkaya 1977, İnalcık 1977, Ergenç 1981.

[3] Eldem 1977; for a new dating of the paintings see Renda 1977: 145-9.

[4] Information about painted decoration in houses in the Balkans can be found in a number of publications: For Bulgaria: Peev 1943; Soikov 1977: Roshkovska 1973; Scarcia, Curatola 1981. For Macedonia and Greece: Moutsopoulos 1967; Vacalopoulos 1973; Koumbas 1984: Diamantopoulou 1987; Makris 1986; İbrahim, 1995; Kiel 1978.

[5] For publications by the Institut Français de Damas after the restoration work carried out by the Institute see Rouanet, Piponnier 1985-6; Labeyrie 1991. For illustrations of the Mujalled house see 'Beit Mujalled', *The World Interiors*, June, 1995: 78-84. For other houses in Syria with wall paintings see Duda 1971; Carswell 1977.

[6] Deherain (1931: 84-6) mentions that at the end of the 18th century there were several palaces in Cairo belonging to the notables in which the walls were decorated with landscapes, inscriptions, friezes and floral motifs. Weit 1949 quotes several travellers in Egypt remarking on these Ottoman style paintings, also giving some information about artists fetched from Istanbul. For painted decoration in other houses in Cairo dating from the end of the 18th and 19th centuries see Pauty 1933: 7-64; Lezine 1972; Revault, Maury 1983.

[7] For some examples in Istanbul dating from the second half of the 19th century see Renda *et al.* 1988: 79-85.

[8] Some of the wall paintings in the Anatolian houses dating from the end of the 19th century are illustrated in Renda *et al.* 1988: pl.80-83.

[9] The Damascene élite and its factions are discussed extensively by Schilcher 1985. For Damascene society in the second half of the 19th century see Schilcher 1985: 211-18. Several houses have been brought to light by scholars studying the urban development of the city. I am grateful to Dr. Abdal Razzaq Moaz for information about some houses with wall paintings and for providing me with his papers on the subject, Moaz 1995.

[10] Roman 1996. I am indebted to Dr. Ron Fuchs for sending me this article on painted ceilings in Ottoman Palestinian houses of the 19th century. The Galata and Unkapanı bridges on the Golden Horn which had been built in wood earlier in the century were reconstucted in 1872 and 1877 respectively.

[11] Raymond 1973: 520, 577; Hanna 1984: 57-60. Moutsopoulos (1967: 102-4), talking about guilds in the Greek mainland in the Ottoman period, presumes that the *nakkaş* belonged to the group of plasterers.

[12] Kostantin Kapıdağı, a well known artist in Istanbul at the end of the 18th century, painted several portraits of Selim III as well. For his work see Renda 1996.

[13] Sadullah Paşa and Bostancıbaşı yalıs in Çengelköy have wall paintings very similar to those in the Topkapı Palace Harem dating from the beginning of the 19th century (Renda 1977: 113-16).

[14] For information on these artists and their work see Boppe 1989.

[15] Some of these documents are dealt with by Yum 1995.

[16] Weit (1949: 113-19) narrates several travellers' accounts commenting on the wall paintings in the Mehmed Ali Palace on the citadel in Cairo, that these were naive paintings painted in 'Euro-Turkish' or 'Euro-arabesque' style by Turkish and Greek artists

from Istanbul. Pauty (1933: 63-4) mentions that Mehmed Ali's palaces built and decorated by Turkish and Greek artists from Istanbul brought a new idea of palatial architecture and decoration to Cairo.

14: WOOD DECORATION ON THE FRONTAGE OF LATE OTTOMAN HOUSES IN CENTRAL AND SOUTH CENTRAL ANATOLIA

Prof. Dr. H. Örcün Barışta
Gazi University, Ankara

Ottoman architecture is very rich in religious, social, military and residential buildings. Within the wide borders of the Ottoman Empire domestic architecture, consisting of country, town, and village houses from central and south central Anatolia and dating from the 19th and early 20th centuries, attracts our attention. Their structural and decorative elements show variety owing to their location, and generally some interesting regional features can be observed[1]. It is noticeable that the houses built on the transit highways were instrumental in carrying central Anatolian tastes to south-central Anatolia as well as passing on some elements in the opposite direction - from the Mediterranean coast to central Anatolia. These houses were constructed and decorated with several materials. One of these materials is wood.

My aim here is to provide information about the wooden decoration on the front of some houses located in central and south-central Anatolian towns and cities, and to include in these some interesting examples of country houses which took city or town houses as their models. The subject of Ottoman private town and city houses in central and south-central Anatolia is a complicated one; for there is a variety of arrangement and decoration; generalisation can be deceptive, and it is not possible here to deal with the whole spectrum of variety reflected in different forms encountered. Apart from country houses that differ fundamentally from city and town houses, this paper will be based on observations at (in alphabetic order) Afyon, Alanya[2], Antalya, Arvallı[3], Bademli, Bolvadin, Burdur, Döşemealtı, Emirdağ, Hadım, Hoyran, Karaboynuzlar, Kaş, Kayseri, Konya, Mersin, Seydişehir, Sille, Yahyalı, and Yeşildağ (fig.14.1, 2).

In attempting to throw some light on the use of wood on the frontages of houses from the area mentioned above by means of selected examples, the paper wil! deal with decorative elements rather than structural ones, and greater emphasis will be given to specific examples from central Anatolia, in conjunction with south-central Anatolia, rather than stating common or characteristic features for each region.

Nature, climate, lifestyle, customs and beliefs, not to mention aesthetic factors, have all had a role in the formation of the Ottoman house. For instance, in the positioning and planning of houses we soon become aware of factors dependent upon landscape and climate. Thus, in terms of landscape, some houses face onto gardens and other greenery (the overall preferred outlook); others, such as those in Alanya and Antalya, face towards the sea or, in the case of Arvallı, front onto a river. In the majority of cases, however, a functional integration of the house with gardens or private areas such as a courtyard is evident (pl.14.1). For other houses, which front onto roads, the provision of courtyards and gardens on other sides of the building is clearly important.

As regards climate, houses with separate parts for use in summer and winter are well exemplified by instances from Alanya. From the point of view of lifestyle, houses with separate women's and guest quarters constructed either as a single unit under one roof or as separate suites are worthy of note. Generally the frontage of these houses is emphasised by the presence of a greater quantity of decoration in a variety of materials. Prominent here is the use made of wood. Bay windows, *sofas*, doors, blind (i.e. false) windows, vaults, pillars, posts, brackets, eaves, bowers, trellises decorated with various motifs, all indicate the importance of wood and are important features because they reflect the aesthetic values of the later Ottoman period in the 19th and early 20th centuries.

The use of solid wood facings is rare in central Anatolia owing to the shortage of supply. Instead, wood combined with stone, brick or clay seems to predominate. Very often we find it used either with ashlar masonry or with masonry of a rougher texture, or with regular or irregular shaped stone and brick. While cedar of Lebanon (turpentine tree) is a typical wood employed in south-central Anatolia, the use of red pine is also widespread. As for stone, commonly found types are either sandstone or travertine. Some people, in contrast, preferred to use rubble walls studded with stones and bricks of irregular shapes as external facings. Others used a mixture of rough stones and roughly broken pieces of brick mixed together haphazardly, or at times ashlar masonry and brick in alternating layers together with wood. There are good examples of such combinations in both Alanya and Antalya. Another intermingling of materials was achieved by using clay and stone together with wood. For the combined use of clay and wood we can point to examples in the region of Konya and Afyon. For the combined use of regular-shaped stone and wood as decorative elements the houses of Kayseri present interesting examples (pl.14.2). On the other hand, for the use of irregular-shaped stone we can point to houses in Hadım and Seydişehir.

The bulk of the houses involved are in general two-storeyed, though sometimes a third storey is added either in the centre of the house-front or at one corner. On the upper storey there is a fondness for bay windows, *sofas* and balconies. The windows on the ground floor are placed high enough to preserve privacy, while those on the upper storey have various shapes and sizes. The openings or projections such as bay windows, *sofas* and balconies on the front of houses are generally covered with shutters and balustrades which are made in various styles depending on the use intended for that part of the building.

In one group the frontage is divided into two halves. An important feature of this group are bay windows projecting from the frontage. These bay windows are either unobstructed or they are covered with latticework. They are usually crowned with a pediment and are carried on brackets or pillars. Some of them have decorated eaves. While houses from Konya, Hoyran and Afyon may be cited as examples of unobstructed bay windows, houses from Sille, Hadım and Seydişehir provide evidence for the inclusion of lattice grilles or balustrades over bay windows (pl.14.3, 4). There are also some interesting examples in the town of Yeşildağ where the bay windows on the front of the building are offset from the centre (pl.14.5).

Sometimes balconies are placed in the centre of the façade. Arvallı is remarkable in this respect with examples reminiscent of the balconies at Kaş. These balconies are also supported by brackets or pillars and covered with a roof with eaves. There are also examples of balconies in Alanya reminiscent of those in Konya.

In another group the centre of the buildings is given little prominence. In this group two-storeyed houses in Alanya and Antalya are worthy of note. In these houses the frontage is divided into two halves horizontally. One corner is occupied by a staircase which leads on one side to an open or closed narrow room reminiscent of a *sofa*, or there is an open colonnade on the first floor which has all the appearance of a long narrow balcony.

Generally the houses open onto a courtyard bounded by outer walls, and family life goes on in the privacy provided by these walls. Balustrades, shutters, and latticework are also constructed with the same aim of providing privacy, as well as the more mundane function of giving protection from the sun. Some of the houses have a porch which leads to a garden. Such porches generally feature decorated door posts, coverings and balustrades, and some have a bower or trellis which leads from the entrance to the porch into the courtyard and includes a well in its visual aspect. There are some good examples of such garden architecture at Alanya.

The bulk of the houses are either 'fully roofed' or have some addition to the roof. In the case of 'fully roofed' houses, sometimes the façade is emphasised with a pediment together with sloping and gabled roofs with decorated eaves in various shapes. Examples may be cited from Konya, Sille, Hadım, Seydişehir, Hoyran, Yeşildağ, Antalya and Alanya. There are interesting examples in Afyon province at Emirdağ and Bolvadin, where the junction of the upper parts of the walls creates a deep recess crowned with a triangular pediment. A remarkable system of roofing is found in Afyon province at Bademli. Here a semicircular dome is placed under the pediment (pl.14.6).

A group worth mentioning in the case of 'fully roofed' houses are those flat-roofed instances which incorporate garden terraces. Within this group one finds variation in the design of the roof gardens included, with often a partly covered and portable construction employed. At Konya, Sille, Antalya and Alanya there are elegant examples of trellises and bowers consisting of wooden posts, where the side walls are composed of grapevines. Antalya and Alanya exhibit a difference from central Anatolia in their use of begonias.

Judging from surviving examples great attention was given to wooden elements on the front of buildings, especially to shutters, doors and balustrades. In terms of window shutters houses at Kayseri which incorporate these are worthy of note, while fine latticework grilles in a variety of designs curtaining the windows are found at Alanya, along with window shutters (pl.14.7, 8).

Undoubtedly the most important element on the front of houses which incorporate wooden features are the doors consisting of either one or two leaves. The front door of the building is not always the only means of entry; there is often also a service door on the ground floor and sometimes a gate in the wall surrounding the garden, besides service windows opening onto the street on the ground floor. While doors of various forms are to be found in both central and south-central regions of Anatolia (pl.14.9), service windows are rare. There are a few examples in Antalya and Yeşildağ. On the other hand there are good examples of balustrades and balconies in different shapes from Arvallı, Yahyalı, Döşemealtı, Konya and Alanya (pl.14.10). While only a few examples exist, wooden ceilings crowning porches are also found. We also find a tendency to emphasise the entrance by means of elaborate porticos, as on the front of some houses at Alanya (pl.14.11, 12).

However, sometimes a richness of woodwork is gained on some of the frontages by projections from other buildings, which incorporate balconies like *sofas* and latticework trellises, as in examples at Alanya and Karaboynuzlar (pl.14.13).

The techniques applied in woodwork are carving, fretwork, tongue and groove, nailing and lattice work. The most widespread technique seems to be carving together with variations such as angular bas-relief, where the cut into the wood is at right angles to the surface, or rounded relief, which presents a more flowing effect. A multiplicity of types is visible on door and window panels as well as balconies and balustrades. Around Kayseri and Alanya in contrast the preference is for tongue and groove. There are also delicate window balustrades in which the bars carved from red pine trees are placed edge to edge within grooved frames made of the same material. Fretwork carving, in turn, seems to find favour around Konya; there are also elegant examples at Hoyran (pl.14.14). The decorative use of nails is to be found around Konya and Antalya (pl.14.15), while from Seydişehir and Alanya instances of lattice work attract attention. Here the outer frame of the lattice is formed using a vertical and horizontal series of laths. Sometimes the gaps between these are filled with diagonally placed interweaving laths to form octagonal, diamond or star shaped decoration (pl.14.16, 17).

The subject matter depicted in such woodwork includes floral patterns such as roses, clover, poppies, dahlias and a variety of leaves and stems, as well as geometrical patterns such as triangles, circles, semicircles, stars and diamonds. There are also examples decorated with calligraphy and animal figures. While geometric motifs were often selected in central Anatolia, with the exception of Kayseri, floral patterns seem to be more popular in south-central Anatolia. Generally floral patterns were used to decorate door or shutter panels. There are rare examples in Alanya where door posts and the ceilings of the porches were decorated with carved floral patterns. Among the objects on display in Antalya and Alanya Museums, for instance, are doors decorated with floral patterns which add a richness to the overall effect. In the Archaeological Museum at Alanya there are also examples of window-shutters constructed in geometrical patterns as well as a unique door post made of a wooden block inscribed with 'Year 1237 H' (1821) and decorated with a floral border.

At Konya and Alanya there are also some interesting examples of decoration in the shape of animals on some houses. At Konya we can point to a bay window decorated with bird figures (pl.14.18), while at Alanya there are two houses where weather-cocks in the shape of birds can be seen.

In forming and laying out the motif-patterns craftsmen adopted a free style. They depicted their motifs either in an objective or non-objective manner. Among the examples where an objective manner was followed, sometimes a stylised and sometimes a naturalistic approach to nature is observed.

Among the non-objective arrangements geometrical units were skilfully used to form a detailed composition. The layout of the compositions can be divided into two main groups: compositions formed by one motif-design or pattern, and compositions formed by using more than one motif. Sometimes both are used in one piece.

In conclusion, a richness in the use of woodwork on the frontage of houses located in central and south-central Anatolia is evident. This is exemplified by porches with pillars, balconies, bay windows, trellises, bowers, doors, window shutters and latticework. The location of towns on the transit highways, together with itinerant Turkish craftsmen working in this field, seems to have been an effective factor in the transmission of influences from central Anatolia to south-central Anatolia or in the opposite direction, from the Mediterranean coast to central Anatolia. Undoubtedly, migrations played an important role in this influence starting from the Seljuk period. Turkish people who migrated seasonally, as well as immigrants through the centuries, were instrumental in carrying some features from one region to another. As regards balustrades, parallels can be drawn between Afyon, Konya, Sille, Hadım, Seydişehir and Alanya, while similarities in carving can be noted between Kayseri, Yahyalı, Antalya, Alanya and Kaş Arvallı. Careful observation in these regions directed towards the later Ottoman period will doubtless reveal more examples for comparison in the future. In addition, houses located in summer pastures which incorporate examples of woodwork made by unknown artists and craftsmen will throw light on the transit areas on the high plateaus.

Bibliography

Barışta, H.Ö. 1966a: 'Alanya'da Bazı Evlerde Gözlenen Taş İşçiliği', *Alanya Tarih ve Kültür Seminerleri*. Alsav, Alanya Belediyesi: 161-8.

---- 1966b: 'Antalyanın Kitabeli Evleri', *Sanatsal Mozaik* 5.16: 34-7.

---- 1966c: 'Alanya Evlerinde Görülen Ağaç İşleri Üzerine', *Alanya Tarih ve Kültür Seminerleri*. Alsav, Alanya Belediyesi: 393-8.

---- 1966d: 'Burdur Çeltikçi Arvallıdan Damat Giyimi', *Erdem*, Atatürk Kültür Dil ve Tarih Yüksek Kurumu, Atatürk Kültür Merkezi, Aydın Sayılı Özel Sayısı 11, V.9, N.26: 491-8.

---- 1991: 'Düz Damlı Konya Evlerinde Görülen Küp Bacalar', *Türk Halk Mimarisi Sempozyumu Bildirileri*. Kültür Bakanlığı, Halk Kültürünü Araştırma Dairesi Başkanlığı and Selçuk Üniversitesi Rektörlüğü, Ankara: 35-44.

---

[1] In Barışta 1991, which is about the flat-roofed houses with earthenware jar chimneys, see p.36 for the use of wood in forming the roof in central Anatolia and p.39 for a photograph of a roof from Seydişehir. In Barışta 1966a, which is about masonry at Alanya, the construction of the walls of houses is explained with examples. For the use of wood see p.163f. In Barışta 1966b, which is about some houses at Alanya with marble, sandstone or travertine inscriptions, see p.36 for stone and pp.34-36 for photographs of some houses with doors, window shutters, bay windows, porches and balconies.

[2] In Barışta 1966c, which is about woodwork on the houses at Alanya, see pp.394-5 and 397-8, with photographs on pp.393, 396 and 397, for information about the houses.

[3] In Barışta 1966d, which is about the broom-ware at Arvallı, see. p.492 and photographs 2-5 for information about woodwork in Arvallı.

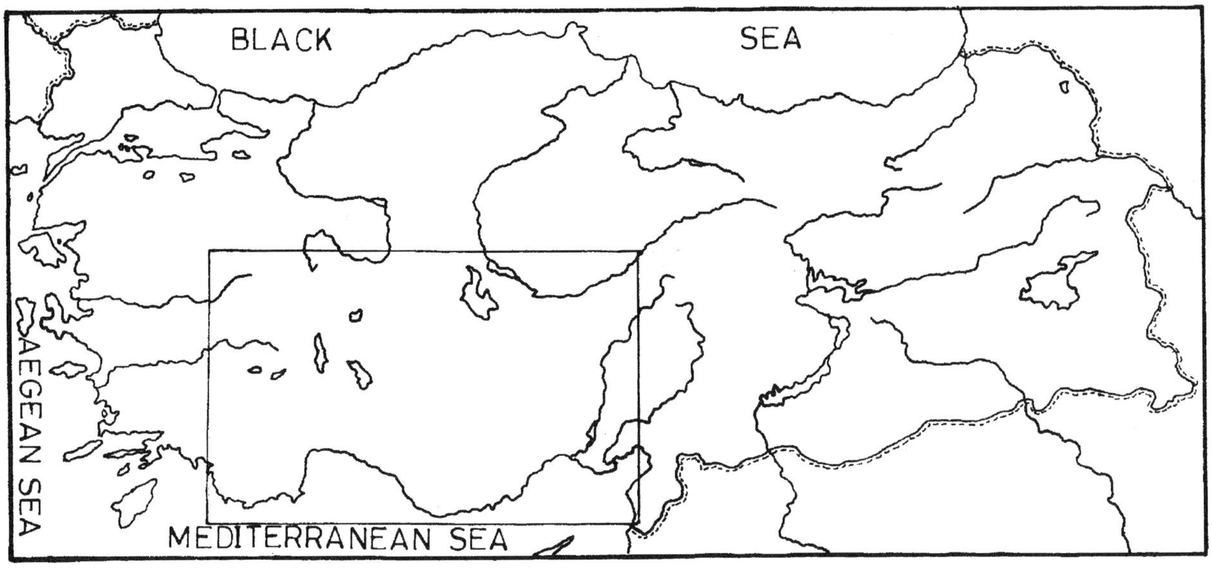

Fig. 14.1. Map of Turkey showing area of fig. 14.2

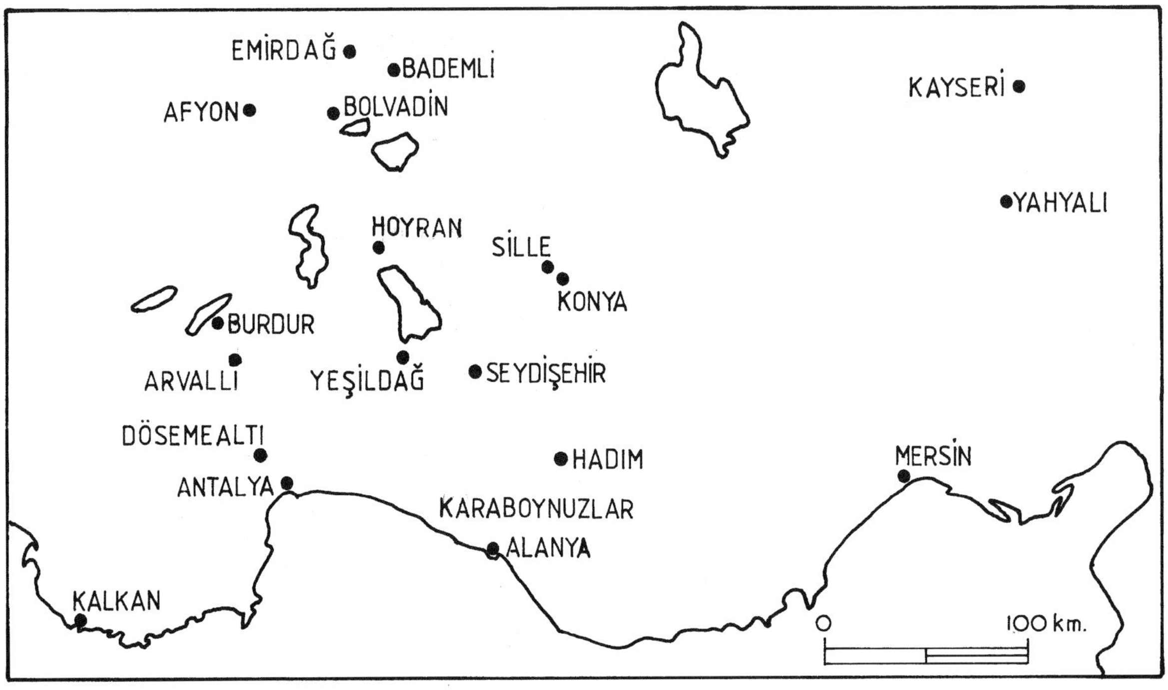

Fig. 14.2. Map of the area discussed

PART FOUR: THE FUTURE OF THE OTTOMAN HOUSE

The symposium papers amply illustrate the rich cultural heritage embodied in surviving examples of Ottoman houses. Westernisation, deterioration due to neglect, weather, and an influx of poorer populations from the countryside to towns and cities have combined to place this heritage at risk. Efforts at preservation are hindered by lack of financial resources and sufficient administrative mechanisms for conservation. These are among the issues addressed by Haşim Karpuz in his paper about the houses of Konya. While Konya is a specific example, the points he makes have general applicablility. In particular, the education of people to the value of the historic houses and the provision of financial incentives for conservation are cited as critical courses of action.

Candan Ülkü provides a case study in restoration, describing how a traditional house in Mersin was transformed for contemporary use. Indeed, one of the keys to successful preservation is the economic viability of new uses. Whereas certain buildings might be frozen in time as museums, the majority are best seen as adaptable and desirable places to live and work. For this reason, preservationists must constantly address issues about the extent and authenticity of restoration to undertake. If the Ottoman house is to provide a living tradition, it must be carefully understood and its potentials exploited to create continuity from past to present to future.

Finally, William Bechhoefer discusses characteristics of Ottoman house and urban form, using Amasya as a case study. He describes the historic development of Amasya, including its success in the designation of an entire neighbourhood, as well as individual houses and monuments, as historic properties to be preserved. Amasya is shown to be exemplary in terms of its expression of public and private institutions and in terms of the harmony established between built form and nature, suggesting that principles of Ottoman urban form constitute a living tradition to inspire and guide new development. Indeed, the historic continuity of ideas that has been responsible for the fundamental humaneness of Ottoman houses and urban environments might be the most important legacy of the examples presented in this volume.

15. THE ARCHITECTURAL CHARACTERISTICS OF TRADITIONAL HOUSES IN KONYA AND THEIR CONSERVATION PROBLEMS

Prof. Dr. Haşim Karpuz
Selçuk University, Konya

Introduction

Konya is a city which possesses some of the oldest and the most important examples of housing in the history of architecture. In addition to factors of geography that shaped the environment, an architectural heritage stretching from the Neolithic Age to the present day, and the accumulation of culture and art within the city, which was once the capital of the Seljuk state, have all played a significant role in the city's development.

The houses of Konya occupy, in fact, an important place in the architecture of Turkish housing. It is here, for instance, that the typologies of the oldest houses of central Anatolia are to be found. For instance, houses with a *hayat* (courtyard) provide exemplars for Turkish houses planned without a *sofa* (hall). Similarly, houses that incorporate a *mabeyn* (a kind of *sofa*) with a *sundurma* (an open porch) in front and two rooms remind us of Hittite constructions, and it was the *mabeyn* that developed into the inner *sofa*, characteristic of so many houses. In addition to their overall design Konya houses possess characteristics of façade and ornamentation peculiar to themselves.

The first detailed work on Konya houses was produced by Celile Berk (1951). Following from this Sedat Hakkı Eldem illustrated examples of Konya houses in his well-known work, *Türk Evi Plan Tipleri* (*The Typology of Turkish Houses*) 1961. In these works it was mostly the examples of older houses that were examined. In contrast, the co-authors, M. Sözen and O.N. Dülgerler (1991: 79-100) chose to deal with examples of more recently dated urban and rural houses. Yılmaz Önge (1991: 137-45), in turn, is the first researcher who worked on the ornamentation of Konya houses. There are also a number of academic theses devoted to the subject of Konya houses (e.g. Uğurlu 1983, Ulusoy 1992).

Architectural Characteristics of Konya Houses

A. Building materials

The building materials of Konya houses may be summarised as follows: The main building materials are stone, mudbrick (adobe) and timber.

Stone: This was used for the foundation and base of house walls up to a height of 50-60cm. Two types were used. One of them is stone from Gödene used for the walls. The other is stone from Sille, seen mostly as flag-stones covering the ground of courtyards and the *mabeyn*.

Mudbrick: This is a traditional building material and has two types: *ana* (the larger size) and *kuzu* (the smaller). It was used both in walls of pure adobe construction and in walls of adobe infill within a wooden frame.

Timber: Poplar, willow and juniper were the three types of timber basically used on roofs. In contrast, pine tended to be used more for interior carpentry (pl.15.1).

Brick & tile: Brick was used in the sections of some walls and for corbelled eaves under roofs. Clay roof tiles were used on hipped roofs.

Earth: This was the main traditional covering material of roofs. Over the timber rafters, firstly *hasır* (rush matting) or *kındıra*, *saz* (reeds) or *pardı* (twigs) and grass were laid, and then over them was spread specially kneaded soil. For the floors a similar material was used. For the partitions of interior walls various types of *hımış* and *bağdadi* (lath and plaster) were employed.

B. Important spaces forming the house-plan (fig.15.1,2)

1. Rooms: Within the traditional house there exist different types of rooms, e.g. main rooms, storerooms, summer rooms (the *köşk*/penthouse on the roof), and winter rooms. As part of the overall structural entity wood provides a dominant element. Closets for bedding (*yüklük*), flower niches (*çiçeklik*) and cupboards are almost exclusively made of carved and ornamented wood. Very large storage spaces were actually set into the thick mudbrick walls of some rooms (pl.15.2).

2. Mabeyn: This, in the context of Konya, is an area rather like a passageway between the rooms on the ground floor; in other words it is what in a different context would be a kind of small hall or *sofa*. In Konya, the main hall (*sofa*) on the first floor is also called a *mabeyn*. In some villages, a stove was set into the wall directly opposite the door of the *mabeyn*.

3. Sofa: In Konya houses the *sofa* is generally enclosed because of the climate (pl.15.3). In these areas are found sitting divans (*sedir*) and corner windows. There do exist also, however, covered exterior *sofas*.

4. Courtyard (hayat): In Konya houses, the courtyard and garden are both called *hayat* in single or two-storeyed houses.

5. İzbe: This is a kind of basement in which foodstuffs are stored.

6. Kitchen/oven-room, Stable-Straw storage (Mutfak/Tandırdamı, Ahır-Samanlık): All these are located in the courtyard, and separate from the house.

7. Çereş: This is a room used for making boiled grape-juice.

8. Hariciye: This is a room kept for guests, or a welcoming room for male guests (*selamlık*), separated from the main house. There were also some houses which had a separate section for the womenfolk and for welcoming their guests (*haremlik*).

C. Typology of houses

As mentioned in the introduction the typology of Konya houses shows a development from those without a *sofa*/hall to those with an interior *sofa*/hall.

1. Houses with a Hayat (courtyard) (fig.15.3a): These are houses composed of one or two rooms placed around the courtyard or garden. They can exist as either one or two storeyed structures, the latter being rarely found today. Examples have been discussed by Cecile Berk (1951: 46).

2. Houses with Mabeyn (fig.15.3b,c): These houses incorporate a single hall-passageway (*mabeyn*) and surrounding rooms at ground level (a storeroom is at times placed at basement level). In such one-storey constructions the *mabeyn* performs many of the functions of the *sofa*. However, it did not develop completely into the *sofa*. Therefore, it may represent a transitional stage between the houses without *sofa* and those with an interior *sofa*.

3. Houses with Sofa: Such houses developed from the houses incorporating a *mabeyn*. From the *mabeyn* at ground level, one could climb to the *sofa* upstairs by means of a staircase. In Konya such houses can be divided into three types depending on the position of the *sofa*:

a) Houses with External Sofa (fig.15.3d): The outer hall/*sofa* was closed with a glazed partition. Open types of exterior *sofa* are also to be found in Akşehir.

b) Houses with Internal Sofa (fig.15.3e,f,g): These houses present an aspect of the *sofa* which is different from that of the classical exterior *sofa*. By placing one room on one side and two rooms on the other side of the *sofa*, a variable arrangement was produced. There are plenty of examples of these.

c) Houses with Central Sofa (fig.15.3h): The only example of this type of house in Konya is Tartan's House in Karaman dating from the end of the 19th Century. It is one of the rare Turkish houses which has landscape pictures of Istanbul as part of its internal decoration.

The development of the houseplan may be summarised as follows: The simplest form is the house with *hayat* (courtyard). While most of these exist as single-storey houses, it is possible to find two-storeyed examples of them and by means of a staircase one can climb from the timbered terrace (*tahtaboş*) on the ground floor up to the first floor. The second stage are the houses with *mabeyn*. From this develops ultimately the house with either interior or central *sofa*, both of them very common and popular house plan types in 19th century Anatolia. As development took place, changes occurred not only in the structural plan of such houses, but also in their façades and decoration.

D. Characteristics of the Façade (fig.15.4, 5)

The arrangement of the façade demonstrates considerable variety. The important components of the façade are timbered terraces/balconies (*tahtaboş*), projecting bays (*çıkma*), and eaves (*saçak*) (pl.15.4). The bays sometimes project over the street and sometimes over the courtyard. Any projection formed by extension of the *sofa* beyond the confines of the ground floor may be rectangular, reflecting the shape of the *sofa* within, or it may be triangular in shape, or it may be given additional variety of its own and take on the shape of a pentagon or oval. Generally, though, the *sofa* projects beyond the ground floor to its full width (i.e. the bay is the full width of the *sofa*) and is carried on two or three timber columns (pl.15.5).

As well as timber columns the projecting bay may be carried on lath and plaster (*bağdadi*) corbels, or on timber or metal struts. For protection from the evil eye, there is an old custom of locating a piece of porcelain or a glazed plate on the façade of houses, often just below the roofline.

On the houses with flat earth-roofs, rush (*kındıra*) and corbeled brick eaves were used. With such eaves long wooden gutters are found; some waterspouts actually take on the shape of a stylised dragon. On those houses with a hipped roof covered with traditional tiles, which were very common at the end of the 19th century, triangular and rectangular window heads made of wood and plaster are found (pl.15.6).

In the 19th century, the number of windows increased and their dimensions became larger. Windows built in baroque style were given a thick stone and plaster surround, rectangular in shape, at times incorporating a low or pointed arch with keystone. On the façades of the *sofas* of some great houses triple arched windows were built. The windows have external shutters and lattices. The windows of the later period were built with iron balustrades.

As in the case of windows, doors of the earlier period were in the traditional rectangular form; later they were built within an arch and with western-style glazing.

E. Decoration

Konya houses are fairly rich in terms of decoration. Although in the case of earlier houses decoration is seen only on the doors and window lattices, from the middle of the 19th century onwards decoration became much used on the façade. With time it increased also on windows, the latticework balustrades of timbered terraces/balconies (*tahtaboş*) and on eaves. There are cornices on sofa-bays and the eaves of some houses which are formed from fretwork figures and plant motifs. Geometric decorations particularly were used on the underneath of bays and timbered terraces. Nails used to decorate gates and door knockers also draw our especial attention as decorative features.

In rooms and *sofas* three different decorative techniques were used depending on the material used (Önge 1991: 140f):

1. Decoration in the form of wood carving and fretwork: These decorations were used on door panels, on flower niches, the tops of cupboards, on ceilings and on ceiling roses (fig.15.6). Some door panels on the other hand were arched and generally without decoration. Doors decorated with sun-motifs are found in the neighbouring settlements such as Karaman, Akşehir and Beyşehir. Almost all of the wood-carved motifs are in the baroque style using small pieces of wood to build up geometric patterns. The motifs found in the central parts of ceilings are usually in the shape of stars with eight, ten or twelve points, or undulating wheels of fortune (pl.15.7).

The most important decorative elements of such houses are the flower niches and mirror settings. Their frames and tops are decorated with geometric and plant motifs with colouring being especially used on the upper sections (pl.15.8,9).

2. Nail Decoration: This decorative technique dates from the Seljuks and is seen on ceilings and on cupboards (Önge 1991: 141). Nail decoration was used in such a way as to supplement the main decoration.

3. Painted Decoration: Particularly after the middle of the 19th century, landscapes and other forms of decoration using plant motifs were painted onto lath and plaster ceilings. On the ceiling of the Deveciler house in the Kuzgun Kavak District, for instance, there are geometric and plant motifs characteristic of the 19th century. There are also calligraphic texts on the upper panels of doors (Önge 1991: 141). Similarly, on the ceiling of the house at No.18 Şehri Ayin Street, the main composition is formed by imaginative landscapes (pl.15.10). Similar decoration can be seen on the ceiling of Meydanı Şerif of Mevlana Dergah and in the *sofa* of Çelebi's flat.

F. Western Influences seen in Konya Houses of the 19th Century

Towards the end of the 19th century, an enormous upsurge of economic activity was experienced in Konya. The cause of this was the arrival in the city of the Bagdad railway, and the remarkable investments made by Maruni and the wealthy inhabitants of Konya. Grand houses and hotels were built beside the road along which ran the horse-drawn tram from the station to the tomb of Mevlana. The differences in such new houses can be seen in terms of material, design and decoration. On the façades the windows are constructed in a baroque rectangular or curved form; and one is struck by the elaborate carving, the decorated windows and eaves, as well as onion-shaped motifs over the hallways or *sofas* (pl.15.14).

The most important components of the houses of this period are the köşk (penthouse) rooms and the timbered balconies (*tahtaboş*) placed in front of these rooms. These, in fact, together with their decorated wooden balustrades, provide a major element of variation in façades (pl.15.11, 12). Further instances of intricately carved balustrades and other forms of timber ornamentation reflecting western baroque styles can be seen in the use of balconies elsewhere on buildings (pl.15.13). In Konya, though, we also find examples of the köşk built as separate structures in the form of pavilions. The most beautiful examples were built in the Millet Garden and the Dede Garden by the municipality (pl.15.15). Unfortunately, none of them has survived to the present day.

Western baroque influence seen on the façade of houses is also reflected in interior design and decoration. Within the *sofa* the cupboard over the stairs grew in importance and in some houses we find at the side of the *sofa* an area raised on a few steps. In particular the divans placed in the bays of *sofas* as seating (*sedir*) were raised above the normal level and separated as a private section. Similarly, there was a tendency to incorporate niches for flowers or mirrors in the side walls of the *sofa*. Also as part of this process the *pabuçluk* (the place for leaving shoes in rooms) was removed, and the number of cupboards decreased. Arched and embellished doors to rooms were discontinued and plain doors were introduced. By way of decoration, flower niches and ceilings were given increased importance and elaborate motifs were added (fig.15.7).

Conservation problems of Konya houses

In photographs of Konya from the end of the 19th century, the unity of its urban form and texture can be seen in the scale of its streets and the layout of its districts. Since then, because few efforts have been made to preserve this historic form, neither the city walls dating from the Seljuk period nor the original fabric of the districts belonging to the Ottoman period have survived to the present day. At best certain streets that still bear the characteristics of the 19th and early 20th centuries have been made conservation areas. These streets are Nakipoğlu-Seyyit İbrahim Street, Celal Street, Sedirler and Köprübaşı Streets.

The first city improvement plan of Konya was introduced by Eyüp Kömürcüoğlu in 1946. This plan was in force until that produced by Yavuz Taşçı as part of a competition in 1967. In both plans, however, insufficient weight was given to the preservation of the historical environment and monumental buildings; even the preservation of houses was not taken into consideration. As a result of this great difficulties arose in subsequent years in carrying out conservation. Extensive listing work relating to Konya houses was carried out in 1982, but in this the historic core and the development of the city were neglected and not investigated with sufficient care or attention. The listing was, in fact, carried out cursorily by simply touring the streets. As a result of this process, though, 65 individual examples of private architecture were listed. Of these ten have subsequently been demolished as the result of either not being registered by means of a title deed or for some other reason. Subsequently, however, the task of listing buildings in the city has been continued by specialists of the Commission for the Conservation of Cultural and Natural Heritage in Konya, and 125 individual houses have been designated for conservation.

The problems of conserving listed houses may be summarised under the following headings:

1. As mentioned previously, improvement plans and the compilation of listed buildings were not carried out with the aim of conservation. As a result some houses were left within the street rights-of-way and therefore, left to be demolished.

2. The survival rate of listed houses has been meagre. They are either left to go to rack and ruin as a result of being abandoned by their owners, or have to be demolished as the result of damage caused through renting them to poor people.

3. The ignorance of house-owners is an important additional problem in this respect since they usually do not know what to do with respect to conservation or where to gain such information. The difficulty of repairing and restoration is, in fact, the most important problem in conservation that we encounter. It is very difficult for owners to get surveying and restoration projects prepared and submitted. Some restoration work is actually carried out in a way that results in the house being almost reconstructed. In other cases the historic houses in important areas of the city are left simply to crumble away.

Conclusion

The traditional houses of Konya are the oldest and the noblest houses of Anatolia. Unfortunately the examples surviving to the present day in Konya itself, the oldest of which date from the 19th century, do not represent the richness of the past; certain examples do remain, however, in Akşehir and Karaman. After the 19th century traditional styles gave way to examples influenced by the west, and gradually the western characteristics of façade and decoration grew in importance.

As a result of large-scale migration from the country to the town the historical identity of Konya, which once possessed an important architectural heritage, has vanished under the onslaught of unchecked urbanisation and industrialisation, something that has happened to many other cities. As a matter of urgency plans for conservation and improvement embracing all the conservation areas of the city should be prepared and put into effect.

The houses, streets and the conservation areas should be restored by providing enough resources, and they should be preserved as living entities by giving them a proper function.

The people living in old houses are generally poor people. Therefore, they should be helped by being provided with detailed plans for restoration, and financial support during the various stages of restoration.

New organisations should be instituted for the conservation of old houses. Ministries, universities, local authorities, volunteer organisations and society in general should co-operate, ensuring as wide a participation as possible.

Conservation efforts related only to the houses themselves are not sufficient. It is also necessary to educate the people, to support house-owners financially, and to encourage people towards conservation.

Bibliography

Berk, C. 1951: *Konya Evleri*. Istanbul.

Eldem, S.H. 1967: *Türk Evi Plan Tipleri*. Istanbul.

Önge, Y. 1991: 'Konya Evlerinin Tezyinatı', *Türk Halk Mimarisi Sempozyumu Bildirileri*. Ankara.

Sözen, M., Dülgerler, O.N. 1991: 'Konya Evlerinden Örnekler', *ODTÜ Mimarlık Dergisi* 5.1. Ankara.

Uğurlu, K. 1983: *Anadolu Selçuklularinda Mesken Tiplerinin Gelişmesi* (doctoral thesis). Konya.

Ulusoy, M. 1992: *19. Yüzyıl Konya Ev Mimarisinde Avrupa Mimarisinin, Etkileri* (master's thesis) Konya.

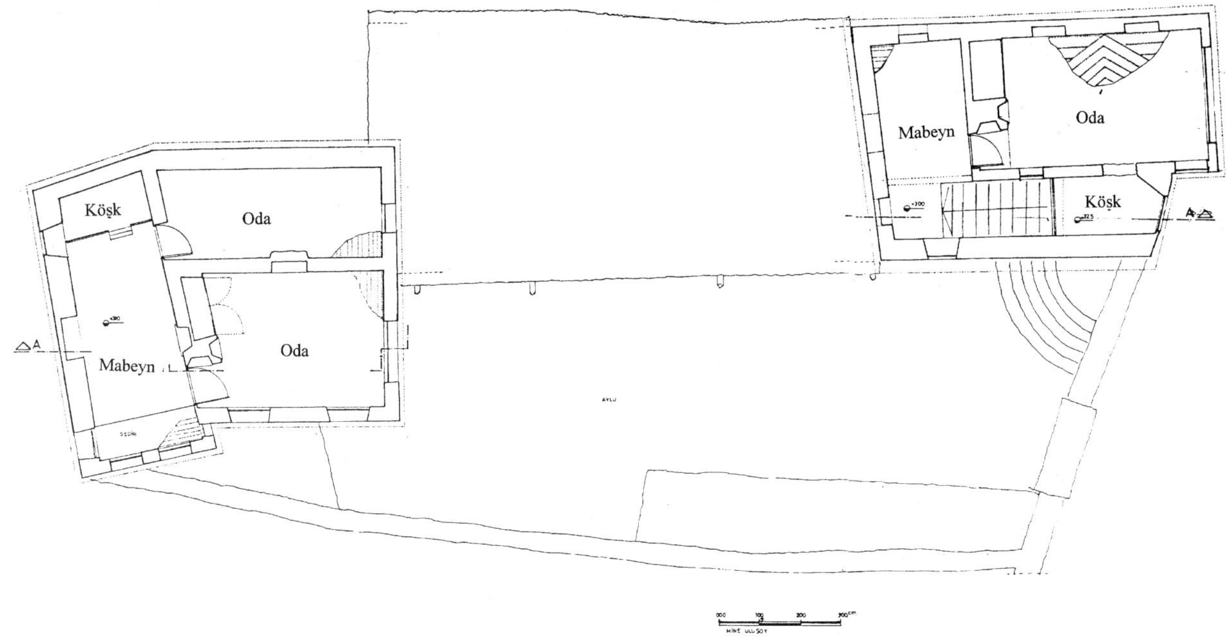

Fig. 15.1. House of Mehmet Kışla, first floor

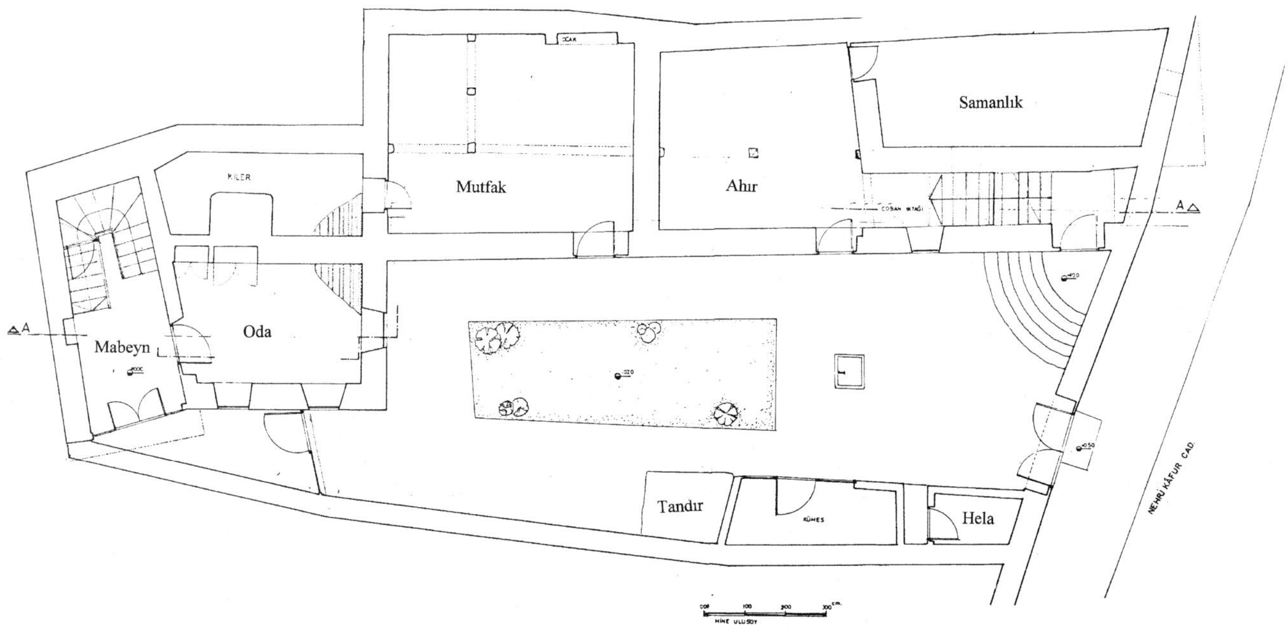

Fig. 15.2. House of Mehmet Kışla, ground floor

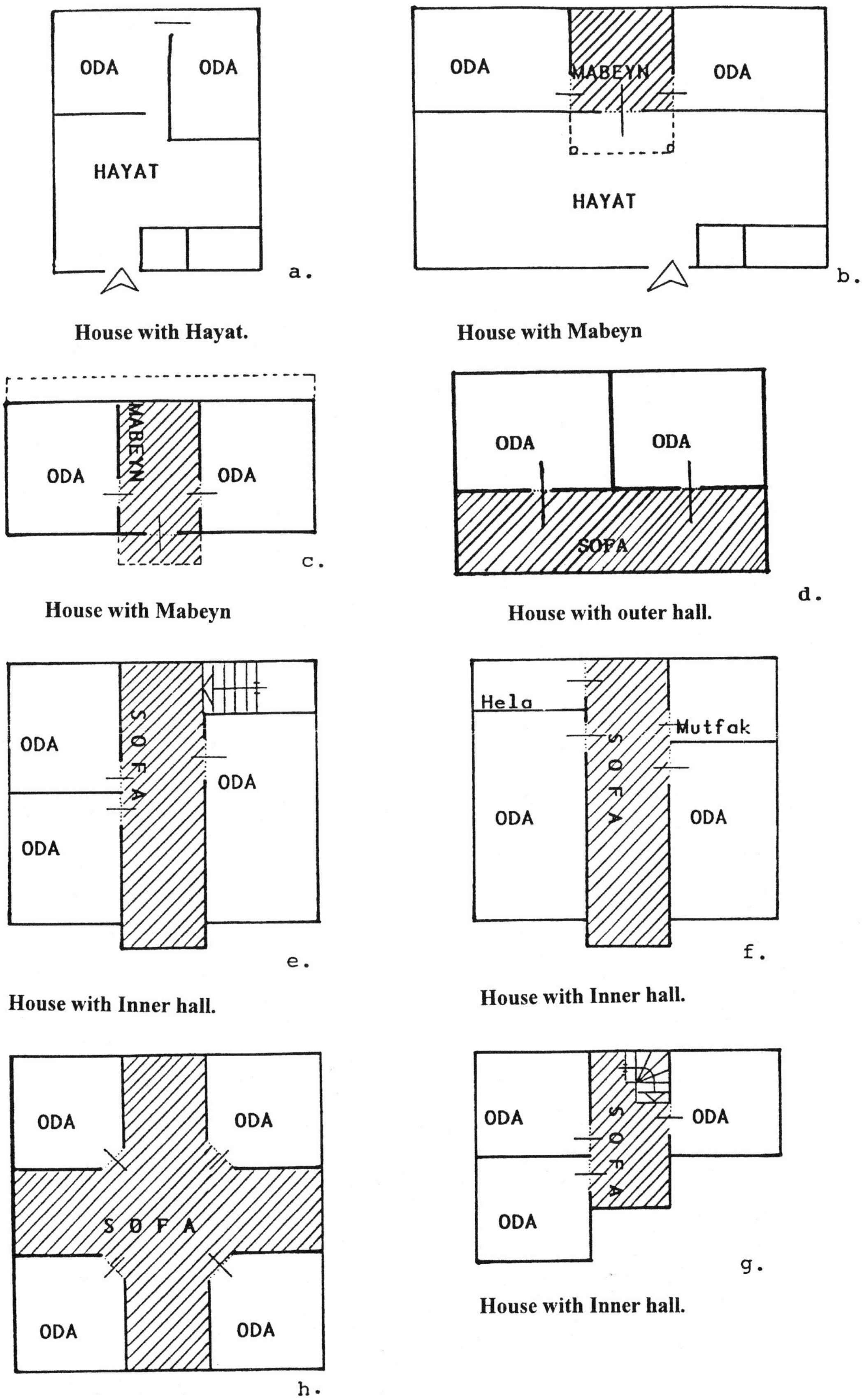

House with Hayat. (a.)

House with Mabeyn (b.)

House with Mabeyn (c.)

House with outer hall. (d.)

House with Inner hall. (e.)

House with Inner hall. (f.)

House with central hall. (h.)

House with Inner hall. (g.)

Fig. 15.3. Typology of houses

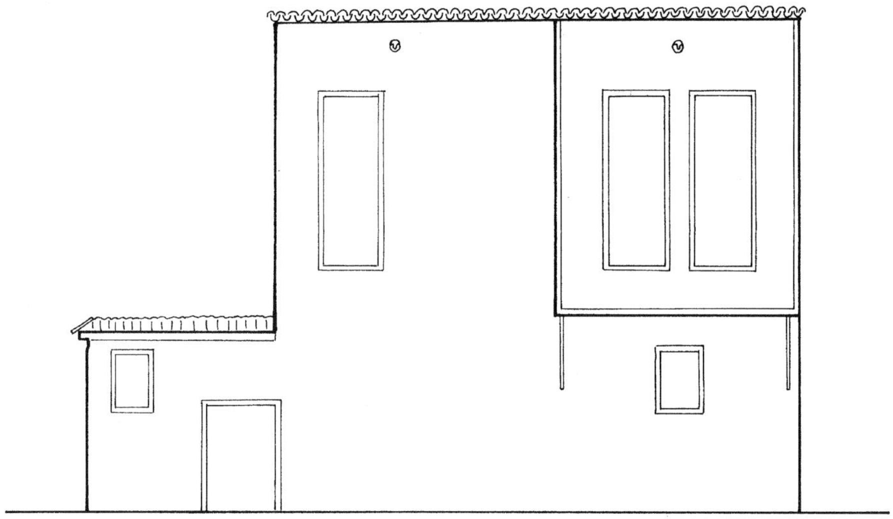

Fig. 15.4. The entrance façade of 17 Seyyit İbrahim St.

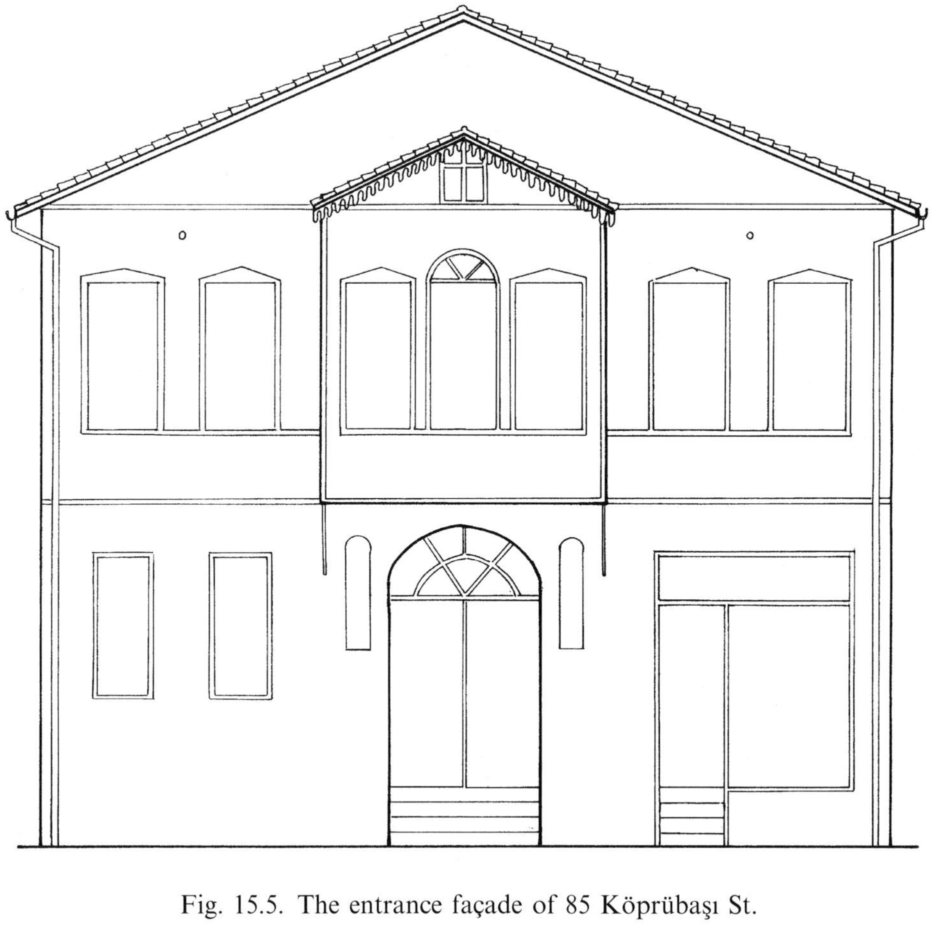

Fig. 15.5. The entrance façade of 85 Köprübaşı St.

Fig. 15.6. Examples of ceiling ornament from Konya houses

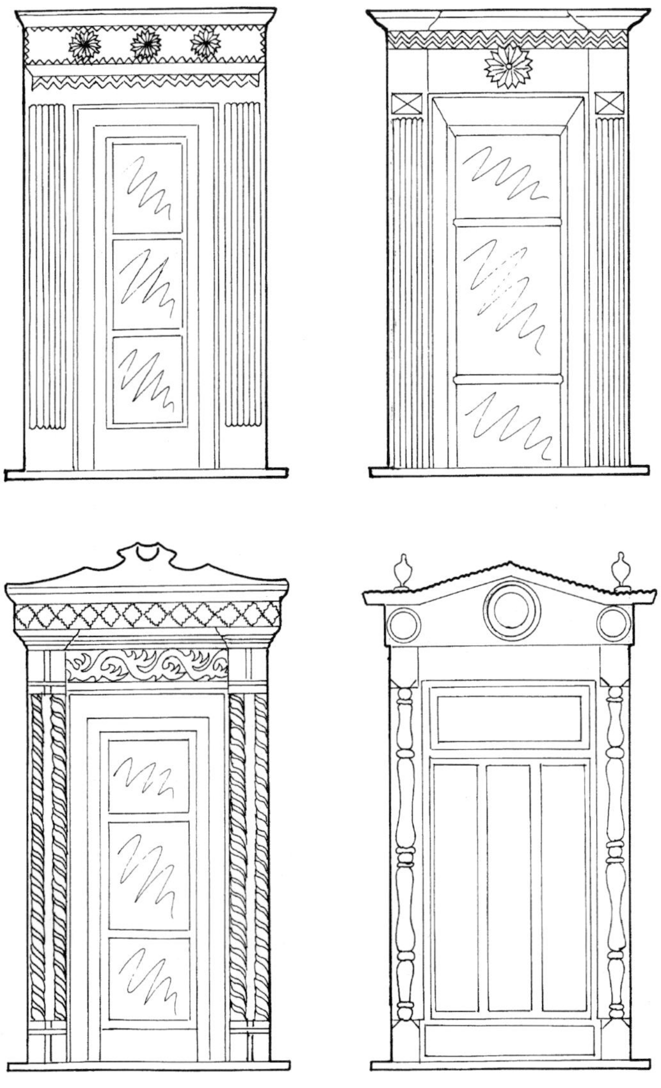

Fig. 15.7. Examples of niche surrounds

16: ADAPTING A TRADITIONAL BUILDING FOR CONTEMPORARY USAGE IN MERSIN

Dr. Candan Ülkü
Mersin University

Setting the Scene

İçel Art Club is an important centre that houses many significant artistic activities. It is in fact composed of three buildings, two of which form the subject of this paper: the so-called 'Estate Depots', which date back to the beginning of this century and were restored in the years 1992-1993. The Green Building (pl.16.1), named after the green of its windows, houses the Teoman Ünüsan Exhibition Hall, and the other, the Yellow Building (pl.16.2), houses the Nevit Kodallı Concert Hall, which is used for gatherings as well as for training musicians.

This paper tries to introduce to the wider public these two buildings and their contemporary use by focusing on the restoration process. Ultimately, the paper will present a short view of the history of Mersin's architectural heritage as exemplified by these buildings. Finally, the paper will argue that similar buildings and streets in Mersin must be preserved and be used by the people.

The city of Mersin bears many of the features of a typical 19th century city, and therefore we cannot find traces of a truly typical Ottoman city texture within it. The district of Cami-i Şerif and its environs constitute the main residential area and it is here that İçel Art Club is located, facing the so-called Art Street, which is one of the streets connecting Mücahitler Street and Uray Street, and hence completes the boundaries of the district. When one walks in this part of the city, one can easily see that the streets are set out in a grid pattern, and a number of these lead to the harbour.

The first city plan of Mersin was made in 1932, while efforts towards the protection of traditional buildings in the city were first initiated in 1974, and later in 1992 protection areas were added to the zoning and construction plan of the city (Renda 1995; Yenişehirlioğlu et al. 1995: 42).

The Buildings

It has been claimed that the buildings under consideration, which occupy a plot of 380 sq. m. and comprise what was originally a stone house and storage area, were erected in the 1890s by Mavromati, a wealthy inhabitant of Mersin at that time. Şinasi Develi (1996: 19) gives the following information about him: 'He was a Greek of Turkish citizenship and one of the foremost businessmen of the area. He owned factories in Mersin and Tarsus and large real estate in Mersin. He was the Russian Consul'. In fact, though, it has been impossible to find either an inscription or a document to date the buildings exactly. As a result, the master craftsmen who worked on the construction and adornment of these buildings are not known. An iron plaque bearing the date 1810 and belonging to an insurance company is once claimed to have been on one of the walls of the first building, thus suggesting an early date of construction, but its present location is not known. A picture depicting a similar insurance company plaque can be seen in the book, *The Houses of Mersin*.

The buildings are situated in an area which has been closed to new construction since 1976, in line with Şevki Vanlı's planning in 1974. They were last used to house offices of the Ministry of Finance and Customs, though currently the building is registered in its title deeds as belonging to the General Directorate of the National Real Estate of the Finance and Customs Ministry.

The garden shared by both buildings is quite small, and the buildings also share a stone staircase which rises on a steel T-beam system between them. Having reached a common landing the staircase then forks off left and right to the two buildings (fig.16.1). The stairs leading to the floor above the exhibition hall of the Green building (on the left) join a small balcony at this upper level. The Volta floorings, made of brick or stone and supported by steel joists, are distinctly visible under the balcony (pl.16.3).

At first glance, the buildings resemble each other on the outside. The reason for this is that similar elements, for instance a high entrance door, bay windows etc. are found in both. In order to reduce the heating effect of the sun, the walls have been faced with large dressed stone blocks and the windows are small and few in number. In common with many houses fronting onto the street, a door common to both buildings opens onto a small garden. Here we would have expected to find the water pump that commonly existed in such houses, but traces of it have proved impossible to locate on what is now the concrete floor of the garden. Like most buildings in the area, however, the existence of a *belvedere*, the so-called *cihannüma*, is a characteristic feature. Inside the buildings the rooms are large and have high ceilings, and both the floors and ceilings are made of wood. The rooms, though, have no ornamentation.

These buildings resemble each other not only in their outside appearance but in their plan as well. The ground floors, for instance, lack partitions and are high ceilinged; the plan of the upper floors in contrast shows rooms leading off a central hall or *sofa*. Both buildings also have their downstairs entrances on the street itself, and although the exact function of the ground floor is difficult to ascertain as the result of later restoration, analogies from other buildings, such as No. 15, 67 Street, suggest that this was used for storage while the upper floor served as living quarters. This is partially confirmed by the fact that the ground-floor entrances have double doors, and that in order to facilitate the loading and unloading of goods (especially cotton) these were made high and do not incorporate projecting shades.

a. Building I: The so-called Green Building. The monumental entrance doors of this building have been further beautified with ornamented corner supports, and iron cornices. Similarly, on the doors of the upper entrance rectangular side columns and iron sectional lintels have been used (pl.16.4). The plan of the interior, in contrast, is quite plain.

Upstairs, the hall/*sofa* (fig.16.1d) incorporates a projecting bay above the entrance door which has windows on three sides. A section of this hall, including the bay, has been divided off from the rest by means of a glass partition, thus providing an extra room (pl.16.5). The bay itself is supported by fine cast iron brackets (pl.16.6) and its roof is covered with tiles from Marseilles (pl.16.7). The building also has a roof terrace, but this has been left without a present-day function. The rooms themselves lack ornamentation and are all lighted by shuttered windows. The shutters are attached to the outside of the window cases by means of special hinges.

The original kitchen (fig.16.1a) is situated in the southwest corner overlooking the court. The bathroom and the toilet are on the west side of the building facing the garden.

As for upstairs flooring, closely spaced 20 x 40 cm. cedar-wood joists are mounted on sectional steel I-beams set into the cut stone walls of the building, and on this is set the wooden flooring itself. A 10 cm. skirting-board goes all the way round. Also on the upstairs floor, French-style Volta flooring can be seen.

The underlayment of the roof is made from pinewood easily obtained from the immediate vicinity. The ceilings themselves are made of wooden panelling set into frames. No adornments such as a central ornament, carving or other decoration have been used here.

b. Building II: The so-called Yellow Building. Sharing the same garden with the Green Building, the Yellow Building is a two storey, plain fronted structure where simple stonework has been used, while the upstairs bay window has been built on a wooden frame using lath and plaster. The walls have been white-washed with lime and coloured with yellow oxide paint.

Internally the plan of this building is similar to the Green Building. The upper floors were used for living space, and the hall/*sofa* extends through the building and has rooms leading off on both sides. The bay window is an extension of the hall/*sofa* itself with windows on three sides. On the upper floor oilcloth resembling linoleum has been used.

In terms of both buildings we are faced with plain but tasteful decoration to the ground floor entrance doors, especially in the case of the Green Building, which has small stone columns on both sides of the door and the upstairs windows, and toothed and oval ornamentation on the lintels of the rectangular windows, which matches that on the eaves (pl.16.6). Wooden decoration on the front of the building is in fact centred on the doors, windows and eaves of the roof. One might have expected the lights above the entrance doors and the windows of the hall/*sofa* of both buildings to incorporate stained or cut glass. However, any that may have existed probably disappeared owing to its poor quality. The Green Building also incorporates fine cast-iron work in the form of window brackets already referred to and plaster moulding under the bay windows. Internally decorated plasterwork is confined to plant motifs around the water-tap on the first floor (pl.16.8).

The Restoration Process

a. Prior to Restoration. The ground floor of both buildings had rubble stone walls, on the exterior and interior of which ashlar was used; this was then given a lime wash. The Green Building itself had, in fact, undergone adaptation about 40 or 50 years ago in that two new service doors had been opened up and the two windows overlooking the street were made into double-windows.

b. The Restoration Process. At the restoration stage, the aim was limited to simple repair. Essentially, the plan was to renovate the worn-out sections, and to replace what was damaged or decayed with the same material, in order to avoid spoiling the general characteristics of the buildings. The process was intended to give the buildings architectural integrity meeting the requirements of the new functions while carefully preserving the original features.

c. After the Restoration Process. Both buildings gained new functions following restoration. The first, the Green Building, became the exhibition hall and includes administrative units. The art gallery it incorporates was named after Teoman Ünüsan, a previous governor, who contributed to the cultural and artistic organisations in Mersin. The second building, the Yellow Building, which was first used as a storage area and then as a depot for documents, has been transformed into a concert and conference hall which can seat 126 people and is named after Nevit Kodallı, the famous musician and composer. The rooms on the floor above the Nevit Kodallı Hall have been converted to practice rooms for music.

Evaluation and Conclusion

The buildings discussed in this paper have been named after the colours of their windows (yellow, green) and are interesting examples of the house architecture that constitutes a considerable portion of Mersin's architectural heritage. They represent indeed buildings that are typical of Mersin domestic housing: ashlar walls at ground level, no direct connection between floors, the ground floor originally given over to storage of material such as cotton, and the first floor providing living quarters are representative features. In addition we find a *belvedere* (Yenişehirlioğlu et al. 1995: 45f).

When we consider the plan of the buildings in the typology of Mersin houses, we find that they belong to the class of houses with inner hall/*sofa* extending through the building at right-angles to the road, and rooms leading off on both sides. From the viewpoint of their street frontage under the heading of 'houses without garden' they come into the category of two storeyed buildings with a centrally placed entrance (Yenişehirlioğlu et al. 1995: 47-8).

In terms of frontage, they can be compared with Buca houses. Erpi classified such houses into two groups: those of 'Chios style' and 'Mansions' (Erpi 1987: 52). Among the houses built in Chios style, those classified as 'A bay window type' resemble the buildings we have been discussing (especially, example nos. 34 and 35). In these buildings the bay windows on the front face the main road and the entrances are on the same axis (Erpi 1987: 75, 69).

In his book *Protection, Restoration*, Cengiz Bektaş notes that freezing the past and the present and making buildings uninhabitable for people is not 'protection' (Bektaş 1992: 11). 'The human dimension should not be forgotten in the buildings to be protected. Any effort not protecting life cannot be a positive effort for humanity ... the shell of the tortoise creates only sadness if its inhabitant is not alive' (Bektaş 1992: 12). Therefore, what the purpose of protection should be is described by Öymer Gür (1995: 64) as follows: '(The purpose) should not be to protect the 'beautiful' and 'important' itself, but should aim to create a 'context', and 'function''.

The İçel Art Club buildings can be shown as examples of restoration / transformation projects placing the human element in the foreground. At the same time, they remind us that there are other buildings in the city waiting to be restored and to assume new functions.

One of the suggestions made in connection with the restoration and transformation of old buildings in Mersin concerns the 'city museum'. City museums, where the historical past and cultural heritage of cities are exhibited, attract our attention. Among the buildings where such a museum could be established in Mersin one can include the English Oil Factory dating from the 19th century, or a house in the city centre dating from the beginning of the 20th century. It is known that those British scholars who researched the history of Mersin, beginning with Yumuktepe, lived in these buildings for some time. Among these Veli Sevin cites John Garstang, Seton Williams, Richard Barnett, Seton Lloyd, Oliver Gurney, William Brice and Gordon Childe (Sevin 1996: 17).

The complex of buildings we have described here is counted among the successfully completed restoration projects in Mersin (Renda 1995). The restoration of these two buildings with their newly acquired functions has shown that similar buildings and even whole streets that have survived to the present day in and around Mersin can be preserved by proper measures of protection.

Bibliography

Bektaş, C. 1992: *Koruma Onarım*. Y.E.M., Istanbul.

Develi, Ş. 1996: 'Aya Yorgi Kilisesi', *İçel Sanat Kulübü Aylık Bülteni* 47: 19.

Erpi, F. 1987: *Buca'da Konut Mimarisi (1834-1934)*. ODTÜ, Mimarlık Fakültesi, Ankara

Korucu, A. 1993: *Mersin Nazım İmar Planları Raporu*. Mersin.

Öymen Gür, Ş. 1995: 'Koruma ve Çevresel Estetik Üzerine', *Yapı* 163 (Haziran): 63-7.

Renda, G. 1995: 'Giriş', *Mersin Evleri*. Kültür Bakanlığı, Ankara.

Sevin, V. 1996: 'Dünyanın Yaşanan En Eski Beldesi Mersin'e Bir Kent Müzesi Düşlemek', *İçel Sanat Kulübü Aylık Bülteni* 47 (Mayıs): 17.

Ülkü, C. 1995:. 'Mersin Kent Müzesi', *İçel Sanat Kulübü Aylık Bülteni* 40: 32f.

Yenişehirlioğlu, F., Müderrisoğlu, F., Alp, S. 1995: *Mersin Evleri*. Kültür Bakanlığı, Ankara.

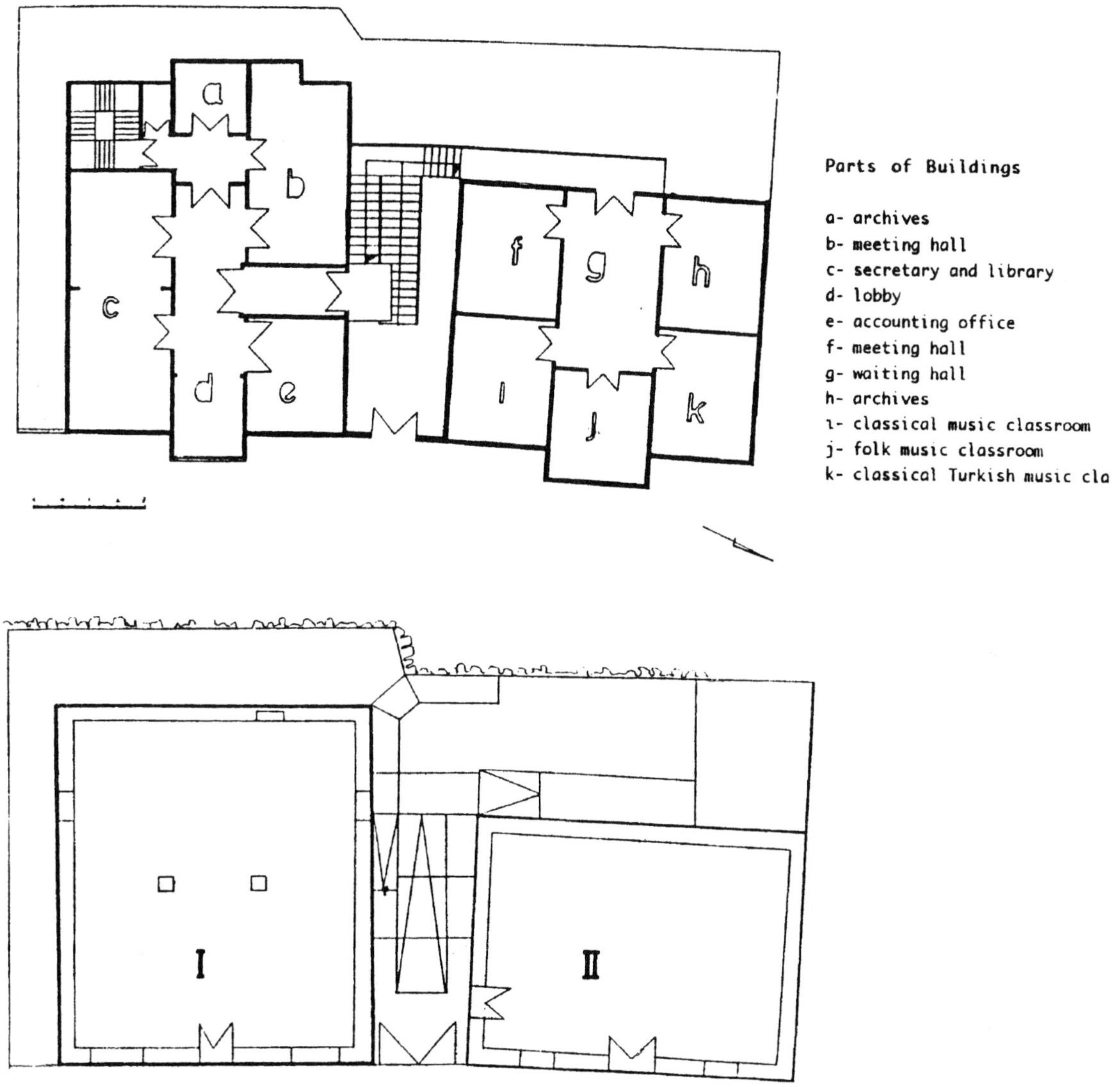

I. The so called "Green" Building
II. The so called "Yellow" Building

(From the İçel Art Club Archive)

Fig. 16.1. Plan of the Art Club

17: HOUSE AND URBAN FORM IN AMASYA, TURKEY: A PARADIGM FOR NEW NEIGHBOURHOODS

Prof. William Bechhoefer
University of Maryland

> Some old forms are so honest, so completely logical and native to the environment that one finds - to his delight and surprise - that modern problems can be solved and are best solved by the use of forms based on Tradition.
>
> (John Gaw Meem, cited by Bunting 1983: 24)

Vernacular architecture has been a significant inspiration for architects and designers of the last half of the twentieth century. Modernists such as Walter Gropius and Le Corbusier found justification for their own design philosophies in the utilitarian use of materials and technology, the functional adaptation to site and climate, and the beauty of apparently simple manipulations of space and form. Furthermore, in 1964 the exhibition and book by Bernard Rudofsky, *Architecture Without Architects,* emphasised the humane quality of vernacular built environments, and provided numerous examples of rich settings for social interaction. The fit between cultural context and architectural form further reinforced the social agenda of modern architects. More recently, practitioners of 'The New Urbanism' have extolled the virtues of traditional neighbourhoods and towns. Their design processes extract principles from existing urban places that can be used to create codes and guidelines for new development.

One source of vernacular building traditions is Turkey, which has a long history of contact with Europe and America. Le Corbusier, Bruno Taut, and other Western or Western-trained architects were appreciative of the qualities of architecture in Turkey, which they saw as reinforcing their own architectural intentions. The 'Turkish House', in particular, was noted for its clarity of form and structure, its functional integration, its garden, and its role in making urban streets (see further Bozdoğan 1996). Nonetheless, much of modern architecture in Turkey has been lacking in the very qualities of vernacular building that it is supposed to emulate. Particularly in the realm of housing there has been a world-wide proliferation of standardised apartment blocks that do not adjust to landscape, climate, and existing architectural and social conditions. Whereas vernacular builders were able to create almost infinite variation within a relatively limited palate of architectural components, the repetitious and anonymous qualities of the modern housing block are rarely relieved. The contrast is most vivid when modern construction replaces or is inserted into traditional neighbourhoods. More often than not the new construction is insensitive to its context, possessing neither the aesthetic richness nor the social viability of the original.

Understanding this condition, the Turkish architect, scholar and teacher Sedad Hakkı Eldem was prompted to write (1987: 269):

> It is generally true that Turkish cities were unprepared to face the demands of the twentieth century, with the net result that as modern cities encroached on traditional Ottoman structures, they destroyed whatever was valuable or worth preserving in them.

Nonetheless, traditional architecture and urbanism can still be observed in Turkey, albeit often in fragments. In the writing of Sedad Eldem, three general themes in Ottoman urbanism emerge (Eldem 1987: 265-90). The first theme is the intimate relationship of building and the natural landscape. Even when building is intense, the pre-existing topographic character of the site is apparent at the urban scale. Furthermore, gardens perforate an otherwise dense urban fabric, providing relief to streets and to public and private structures. Indeed, an Ottoman town has a sense of existing intimately with the landscape, an extension, perhaps, of nomadic sensibilities that are considered to be among the generators of Turkish house form (Küçükerman 1985: 27-30, 87).

The second theme is the generally informal character of the Ottoman city. Ottoman urbanism was never based on the kind of strong formalism characteristic of western cultures. There are no formal public spaces or monumental axes to be found in the cityscape. Rather, places in front of significant buildings or in neighbourhood streets acquire meaning through the spontaneous meetings and gatherings of people over time. The sultans provided important centres of cultural, religious and commercial activity, allowing residential development to fill in between these complexes. Monuments are not joined by boulevards or united by public squares as, for example, in Paris or Rome. Rather, there is an organic equilibrium characterised especially by pedestrian-oriented gardens and streets organised more with respect to topography and social relationships than to political spectacle.

The third theme is the equilibrium of expression of community values and the values of government. The rule of a centralised authority is clearly seen in monumental building, whereas great personal freedom is exhibited in neighbourhoods. Cities grew naturally and incrementally, with considerable attention given to public amenities such as a safe water supply, mosques and commercial structures. On the other hand, the efforts of numerous private builders in residential districts were guided only by a few simple rules of civility, assuring individuality within the neighbourhood as well as community identity apart from the works of government. It is a remarkable lesson that every house in a Turkish city is different, even as there is an overall consistency in building technique, scale and character. Sedad Eldem ascribes this quality of the Turkish city to be the result of a deeply rooted 'democratic way of life' that could assert itself within the larger Ottoman empire.

Taken together, the three themes outlined above provide a generalised framework for looking at an Ottoman city. At a more intimate scale, response to physical and cultural particularities of place differentiates one city from another. Amasya, in Northern Anatolia (pl.17.1), provides an example of Ottoman urbanism which is paradigmatic in its clarity of urban structure and in its persuasiveness of urban amenity. Amasya demonstrates that the principles that guided its historical development are as vital and valid today as they ever were. As a detailed model of urbanity, Amasya teaches lessons that go beyond its city limits.

Amasya

The centre of Amasya flanks the Yeşil Irmak river (pl.17.2). On the north bank Ottoman houses cling to the older fortified wall at the base of the steep mountain that rises to Pontic tombs and the ruins of a citadel at the top. The houses form the most important remaining assemblage of urban waterfront houses in Anatolia, comparable to some waterfront neighbourhoods which can be seen on the Bosporus near Istanbul. Cafés, promenades, and important Selçuk and Ottoman monuments occupy the south side of the river. The urban riverscape is architecturally and symbolically the heart of Amasya, the linear centre for layers of buildings and gardens that parallel the river (fig.17.1). Understanding of the principles by which their poetic urban experience is organised can aid in assuring that future development continues long-standing urban traditions.

As a site for a fortress Amasya's mountain is ideal, for a vast area may be surveyed from the top, and the slopes are so steep as to be easily defensible. Furthermore, the south face of the mountain at the base is ideal for the construction of a fortified wall on the river. The south orientation is desirable for house construction and the river provides a water supply. The river wall which is now seen dates from the Pontic period and its remains are found in the basements of the later houses. The earliest settlement was built behind this wall; higher up are the rock-cut tombs which are the only important vestige of the Pontic Kingdom in Anatolia. It was at this level, too, that the king's palace was built. The citadel at the top protected the entire valley.

Amasya was taken over by the Romans and later by the Byzantines, serving as an important military headquarters. The Selçuk Turks moved in during the 11th and 12th centuries, initially occupying the south river bank to fight the residents on the other side. At the end of the 13th century Amasya was conquered by a Mongol dynasty and in 1386 it was taken by Sultan Yıldırım Bayezid and incorporated into the Ottoman empire.

Political stability under the Ottomans brought prosperity to Amasya. The city continued its strategic role as a military headquarters. Two sultans were born there and Sultan Bayezid II was one of a number of sultans who, as crown princes, were to serve their apprenticeships in government there. Because of its natural amenities and political importance Amasya was one of the favourite cities of Suleyman the Magnificent for entertaining foreign guests and for his own personal visits. Architectural and urban development in the Ottoman period was consequently significant, building on long-established foundations.

The North Bank of the Yeşil Irmak

The residential neighbourhood on the river was recognised by the Ottomans as ideal in satisfying their love of sun, gardens and view (pl.17.3). Because of the security of the empire, the defensive wall no longer served its original function and became foundations for houses which view the river. As late as the mid-sixteenth century the houses were made of earth and had flat roofs, built in a timeless manner that can be seen in Anatolian villages today (Goodwin 1987: 429-30). The sultan's palace was at the level of the Pontic tombs, supported by a massive retaining wall.

Other than a few modern houses, the houses to be seen today are primarily from the nineteenth century, with some from the eighteenth and even seventeenth centuries. They incorporate fragments of earlier construction and follow earlier street paths. Although many houses are dilapidated, the neighbourhood is exceptional in conveying the scale, character and amenity of an Ottoman town. Indeed, this neighbourhood was considered the best in Amasya and was, therefore, occupied by Muslim landowners. Although the builders were primarily Armenian Christians, and although other groups were part of Ottoman society, it was the landed aristocracy which held privileged positions in the empire. Thus, wealthy landowners lived with the best river view and, just behind them on the slope, middle class landowners established themselves. The palace was higher up, with servants' quarters built precariously on adjacent extremely steep land below the Pontic tombs. Only fragments of the palace remain and the sites of servants' quarters are now occupied by squatter settlements.

The Ottoman houses are in many respects typical of many houses in northern Anatolia where abundant forests fostered a rich tradition of woodworking for structural framing, cabinet work and surface panelling to develop. They are constructed of timber frame, with infill of earth or brick covered in plaster; windows are numerous, and roofs are sloped and covered with tile. Lower floors generally are constructed of masonry so that the plan can easily follow the irregular contour of streets. Timber above is used to create the regular rectangular rooms preferred by Ottoman builders, a consequence of which is cantilevered projections over the streets. Likewise the response to the temperate climate has been to create rooms which can be opened to breezes in the summer and closed for warmth in the relatively mild winters; fireplaces are usual features of living rooms. Abundant rainfall sustains a garden for every house.

Topography and social responsibility conditioned urban form. The terrain in northern Anatolia is extremely irregular and it is typical that houses follow and adjust to contour. There were few rules governing the siting of houses, but it was imperative not to block a neighbour's view or access to summer breezes. Likewise it was unacceptable to overlook the privacy of a neighbouring garden. In general, houses were free-standing, connected to other houses only by garden walls; streets were defined by house and garden walls (pl.17.4).

However, at Amasya the extremely limited amount of space for building on the river front gave rise to attached houses with a particular plan organisation framed by parallel walls (fig.17.2). To the south are the more private living quarters, with views of the river; these are separated from rooms on the street behind by a garden. The rooms closest to the street are shops and guest quarters for visitors. To the north of the main neighbourhood street is another row of attached houses. The layering of the house plan in relation to the river, to the street, to the south sun and to degrees of privacy within the house reinforces the layering of the overall urban plan (fig.17.3). The tightly packed assemblage of house and gardens gives urbanity to the neighbourhood while maintaining the substantial amount of planting that is characteristically humane in Ottoman towns.

The South Bank of the Yeşil Irmak

Unlike the predominantly residential north bank, the south bank of the river has a history of orchards, gardens and public buildings. The earliest construction in Amasya had to be defensible and was, therefore, clustered on the north bank. At the same time, orchards were planted on the south bank where there was an expanse of relatively level ground. A road was built along the river edge connecting Amasya to other major settlements. Thus, from at least as early as the Pontic period the land use pattern for the river banks was established, complementing the dense construction of the north bank with the open space of the south bank.

Although there are fragments of Roman and Byzantine construction on the south bank, the first major building activity took place under the Selçuks, who built mosques, schools, markets and other public buildings. The road along the river and the orchards were maintained, and new buildings were sited in the next layer of land to the south. The Selçuk period also saw increased residential development behind the new public buildings. The orchards were, therefore, no longer part of a larger agricultural terrain, but became isolated and used as public gardens. The use of the open space for food production became less important than its use for relaxation and as a promenade. The increasing density of Amasya was focused on the river front as the functional and symbolic centre of the city.

The dramatic growth of Amasya under the Ottomans followed the same patterns of urbanism. Although the Ottomans built in the strip of garden space, they only allowed buildings compatible with public access to gardens. Exemplary is the mosque complex of Sultan Bayezid II, 1485, whose courts and gardens open toward the river and are available to all, complementing the urban promenade with its important cultural presence.

With the governor's palace and residences of leading citizens on the north side of the river and public buildings and gardens on the south, Amasya possessed a linear urban centre around which increasing numbers of new neighbourhoods were built. The new neighbourhoods were built to the south and especially to the east where the valley of the Yeşil Irmak broadens.

Amasya Today

The north bank of the river retains much of its character, due to its relatively difficult terrain and, therefore, restricted automobile access. A railroad track hugs the mountain and has relatively little visual impact. Squatter housing occupies sites previously occupied by palace servants and does not disrupt the character of the neighbourhood; contemporary construction is not always so sensitive. The Pontic tombs are a major tourist attraction, and the retaining walls of the palace have been restored to provide easy access by foot.

Furthermore, in 1978 the Turkish Ministry of Culture declared the neighbourhood a National Cultural Area and the houses were designated Historic Buildings. One house has been restored as a museum. The establishment of the Riverside Housing Rehabilitation Project (YABEP) in 1994 was a positive step in co-ordinating public and private efforts to preserve and give new life to the historic district.

On the south side of the river, the city functions much as it always has, while accommodating a building density considerably greater than in the past. The road is in most places a boulevard with trees. On weekends the road is closed to traffic and becomes a popular promenade. The mosque complex of Bayezid II continues to offer its tranquil spaces to passer-by and worshipper alike.

On the other hand, the site of the Bayezid mosque is the only remnant of the larger garden strip that had survived through most of the Ottoman period. The rest has been filled with largely undistinguished buildings that make little gesture to the river or to the idea of a garden promenade. The worst buildings are facelessly bureaucratic, while the best make serious attempts to relate to the pattern, scale and character of Amasya in contemporary ways. A new civic square to the east is intended to be the new centre of town, but cannot compete in amenity with the older river promenade (pl.17.5).

Conclusion

The study of Amasya reveals inherent urban ideals, structures and principles that are characteristic of Ottoman cities in general. In the urban design of Amasya there is a delicate balance of built form and nature, of formal buildings and informal urban places, and of public authority and individual autonomy. At the same time the particular geographic, historical and cultural circumstances of the city have given it its own distinctive character.

The visitor to Amasya today cannot fail to be struck by the beauty of the river and the elegant equilibrium of buildings and gardens that contribute to the quality of life of the city. Equally striking and obvious is the assault on these qualities. Like many traditional environments, the centre of Amasya is fragile in the face of contemporary development, since images of modernity too often do not respect or reflect local climate, topography and culture. Amasya, however, provides a model for urban development that might shape the future. Far from being a static artefact of history Amasya demonstrates specific principles and attitudes about urbanism that should be used for its own benefit.

Amasya should also be instructive to those involved in the intense urbanisation of contemporary Turkey. In that regard, the Congress for the New Urbanism met in Charleston, South Carolina, USA, in May 1996, and adopted a new CNU Charter. It begins by stating:

> The Congress for New Urbanism views disinvestment in central cities, the spread of placeless sprawl, increasing separation by race and income, environmental deterioration, loss of agricultural lands and wilderness, and the erosion of society's built heritage as one interrelated community-building challenge.
>
> We stand for the restoration of existing urban centres and towns within coherent metropolitan regions, the reconfiguration of sprawling suburbs into communities of real neighbourhoods and diverse districts, the conservation of natural environments, and the preservation of our built legacy....
>
> We advocate the restructuring of public policy and development practices to support the following principles: neighbourhoods should be diverse in use and population; communities should be designed for the pedestrian and transit as well as the car; cities and towns should be shaped by physically defined and universally accessible public spaces and community institutions; urban places should be framed by architecture and landscape design that celebrate local history, climate, ecology, and building practice...

Clearly, Amasya's historic neighbourhoods offer abundant and inspiring evidence of the wisdom of these contemporary pronouncements. The historic continuity of ideas that has been responsible for the fundamental humaneness of Amasya's urban environment might give new meaning to a definition of what it means to be 'modern'.

Bibliography

Arık, R. 1976: *Batılılaşma Döneminde Anadolu Tasvir Sanatı*. Ankara.

Bozdoğan, S. 1996: 'Vernacular Architecture and Identity Politics: The Case of the 'Turkish House'' *Traditional Dwellings and Settlements Review,*

7.11 International Association for the Study of Traditional Environments, Berkeley: 7-18.

Bunting, B. 1983: *John Gaw Meem: Southwestern Architect*. Albuquerque, NM.

Eldem, S.H. 1984-7: *Türk Evi Osmanlı Dönemi* (3 vols). Türkiye Anıt Çevre Değerlerini Koruma Vakfı, Istanbul.

Goodwin, G. 1987: *A History of Ottoman Architecture*. New York.

Küçükerman, Ö. 1985: *Turkish House: In Search of Spatial Identity*. T.T.O.K Yay., Istanbul.

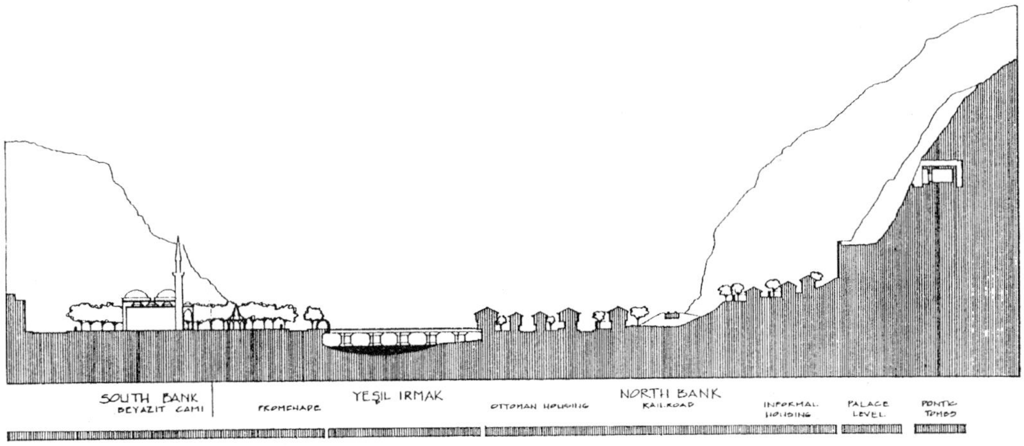

Fig. 17.1. Diagrammatic section of Amasya showing layering of buildings and open spaces along river

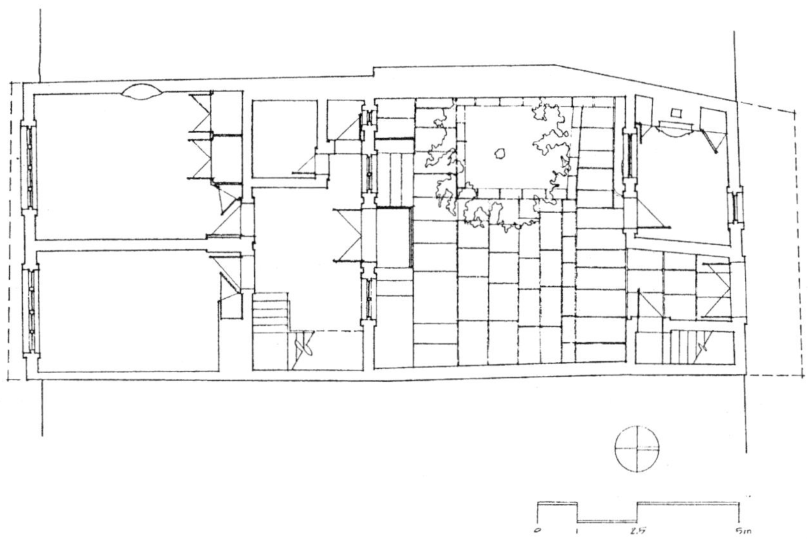

Fig. 17.2. Ground floor plan of a typical Amasya house

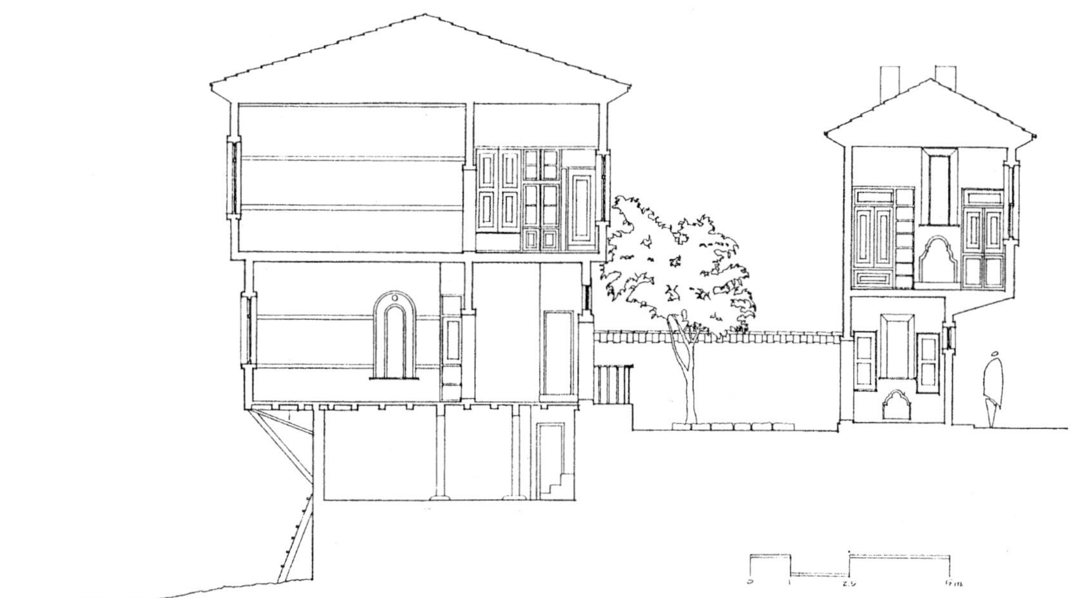

Fig. 17.3. Section of a typical Amasya house

Pl. 1.1. Street in Tokat, 1993

Pl. 1.2. Rural house in Bosnia

Pl. 1.4. Market area in Sarajevo, late 19th century

Pl. 1.3. Street in Izmir 1838

Pl. 1.5. Amasya after the 1915 fire

Pl. 1.6. Village room in Yoruk

Pl. 1.7. History of Amasya

Pl. 1.8–10. Posters of Amasya

Pl. 1.11. Child's drawing of Istanbul

Pl. 1.12. Le Corbusier's 'Turkish Wooden House'

Pl. 1.13. Drawing of Amasya in 1811

Pl. 1.14. Vignette of Amasya's Hatuniye mosque

Pl. 1.15. Hatuniye mosque & Hazeranlar mansion

Pl. 1.16. Amasya, c. 1900

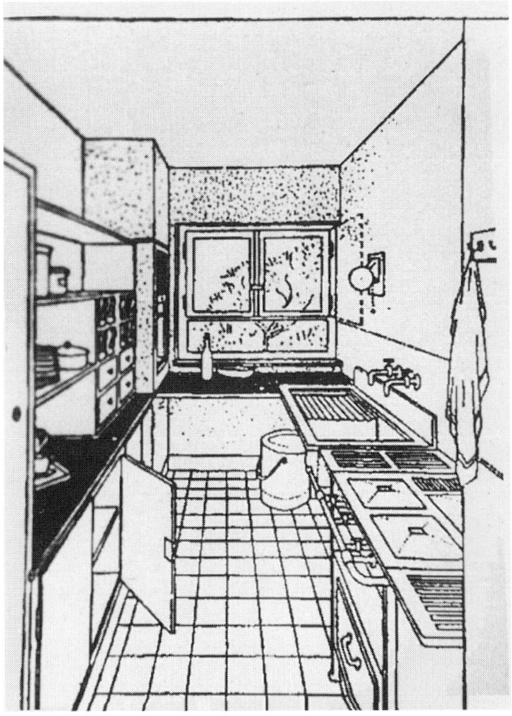

Pl. 1.17. 'The Modern Kitchen' 1933

Pl. 1.18. Reconstruction of tray-meal, Safranbolu

Pl. 1.19. Early apartment building in Amasya, 1950s

Pl. 1.20. 'Turkish Model Home' 1938

Pl. 1.21. The Oriental Café 1948

Pl. 1.22. Room interior, Konya

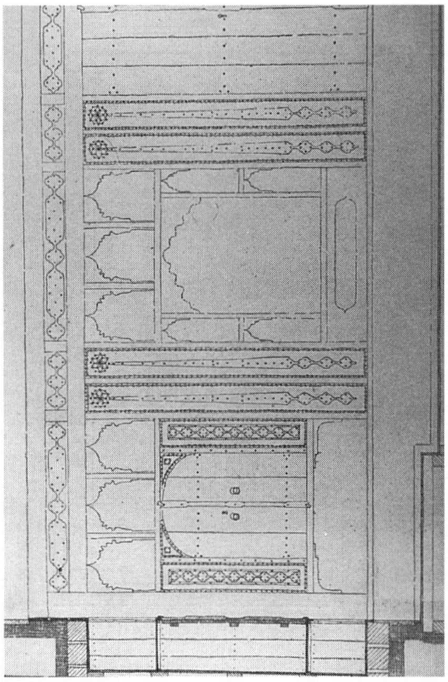

Pl. 1.23. Room interior, Konya

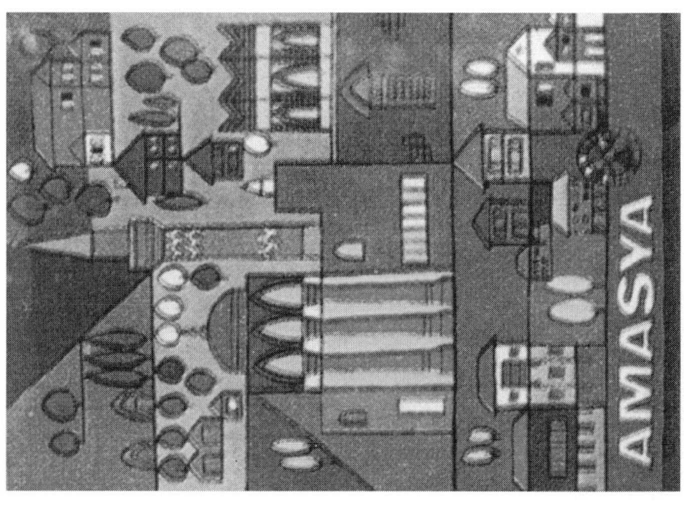

Pl. 1.24. Poster of Amasya

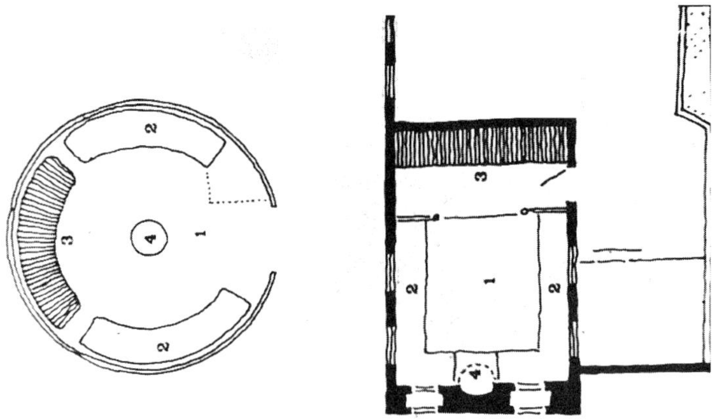

Pl. 1.25. Turkish room & tent compared

Pl. 1.26. Room in Akyaka, Gökova 1970

Pl. 1.27. Hazeranlar mansion, Amasya, 1993

Pl. 1.28. Hazeranlar mansion, Amasya, 1970s

Pl. 1.29. Soğuk Çeşme St, Istanbul, 1950s

Pl. 1.30. Soğuk Çeşme St, Istanbul, rebuilt

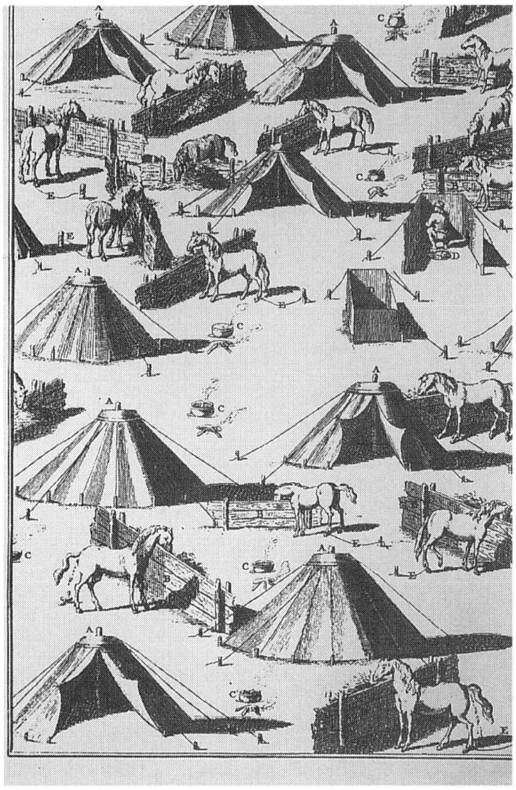

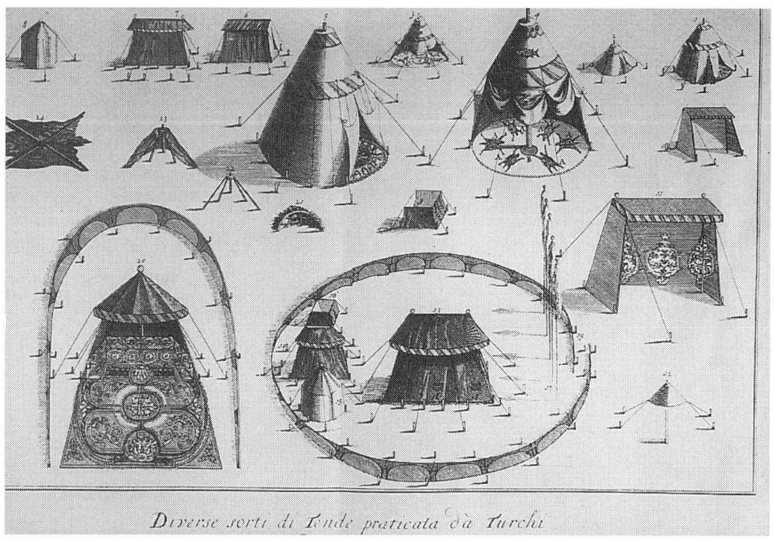

Pl. 3.1–2. Ottoman military tents

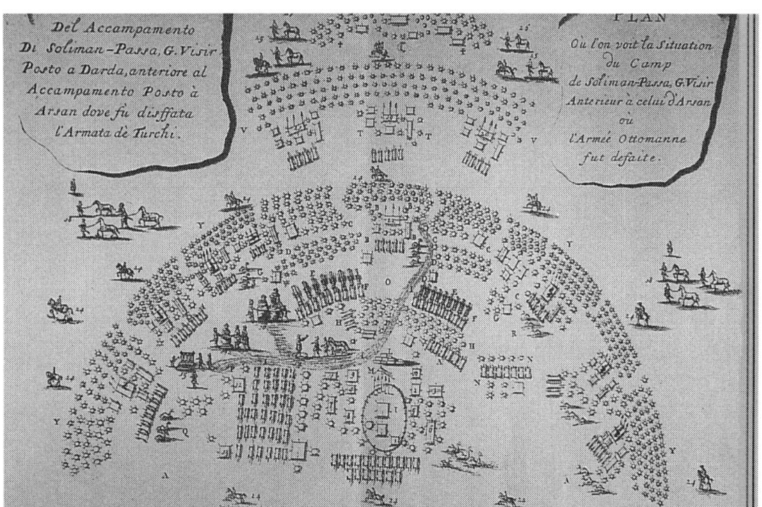

Pl. 3.3. Ottoman encampments

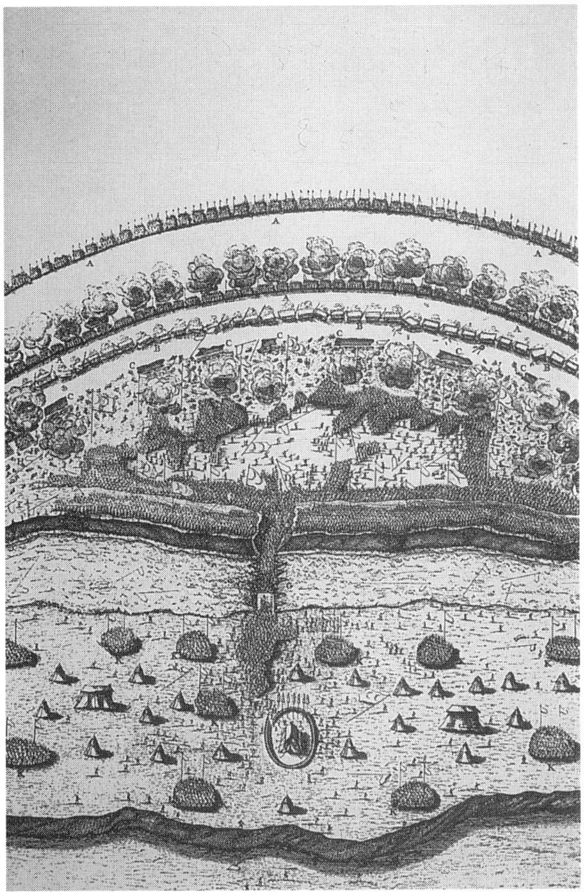

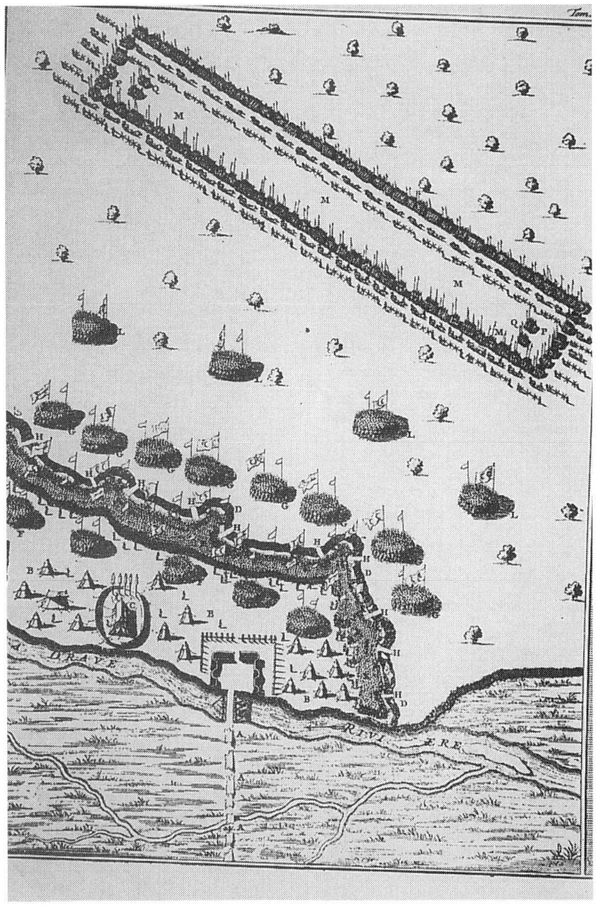

Pl. 3.4–5. Ottoman encampments

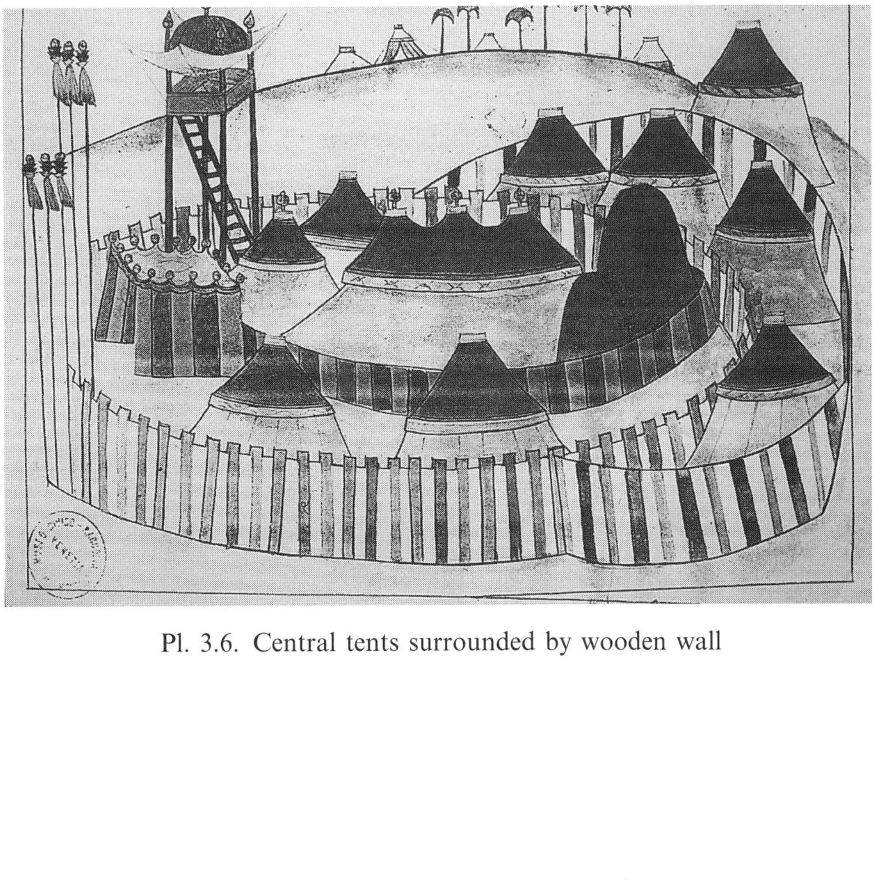

Pl. 3.6. Central tents surrounded by wooden wall

Pl. 4.1. General view of Safranbolu 1991

Pl. 4.2. Timber and mud-brick construction

Pl. 4.3. Timber & baked brick construction

Pl. 4.4. *Tokmak* on door

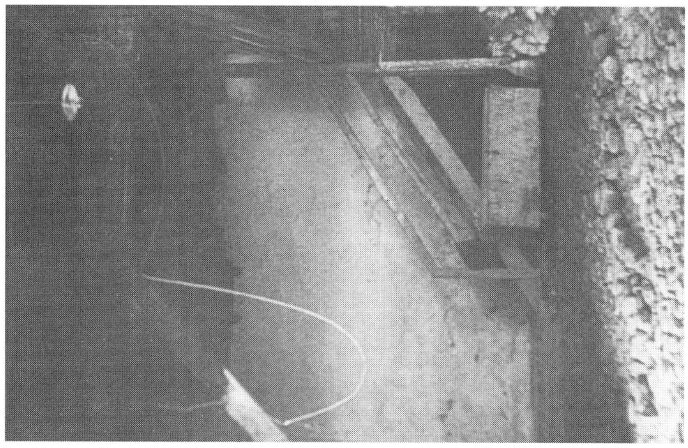

Pl. 4.5. Courtyard in Safranbolu, 1992

Pl. 4.6. Cinci Hanı

Pl. 4.7. Calligraphy on fountain

Pl. 4.8. Lacework from Safranbolu, 1994

Pl. 4.9. Projecting *sofa*

Pl. 4.10. Projecting *sofa*

Pl. 5.1. View of Tire from Toptepe

Pl. 5.2. House of Ali Hodimli

Pl. 5.3. House of Zühre Kızılkara

Pl. 5.4. House of Seha Gidel

Pl. 5.5. House of Ayşe Bideh

Pl. 5.6. House of Sabit Appan, entrance door

Pl. 5.7. House of Bayraktar Ağa, main room

Pl. 5.8. House of Ali Hodimli, first-floor door

Pl. 5.9. House of Ali Okuroğlu, window & lattice

Pl. 5.10. House of Bayraktar Ağa, clerestory windows in the main room

Pl. 5.11. House of Ahmet Giritlioğlu, corner pilaster

Pl. 5.12. House of Ahmet Karcı, east side

Pl. 5.14. House of Bayraktar Ağa, cupboard in the main room

Pl. 5.13. House of Bayraktar Ağa, ceiling ornamentation

Pl. 6.1. Balaban, general view

Pl. 6.2. *Selamlik* under house of Emin Erdoğan

Pl. 6.3. *Selamlik* entrance to Balaban Bey St.

Pl. 6.4. Bridge between house of Hacı Ali Yılmaz

Pl. 6.5. Bridge between houses

Pl. 6.6. 17th century fountain at house of Duran Önder

Pl. 6.7. Interconnection of houses at roof level

Pl. 6.8. *Eyvan* on house of Naci Bayram

Pl. 6.9. *Cumba* in house of Naci Bayram

Pl. 6.10. *Örtmelik* of house of Hasan Göncü

Pl. 7.1. One-roomed house in Asarcık Kayalı village

Pl. 7.2. Two-roomed house in Yukarı Arım village

Pl. 7.3. Two-roomed house in Asarcık Kayalı village

Pl. 7.4. *Sofa* of two-roomed house in Yukarı Arım village

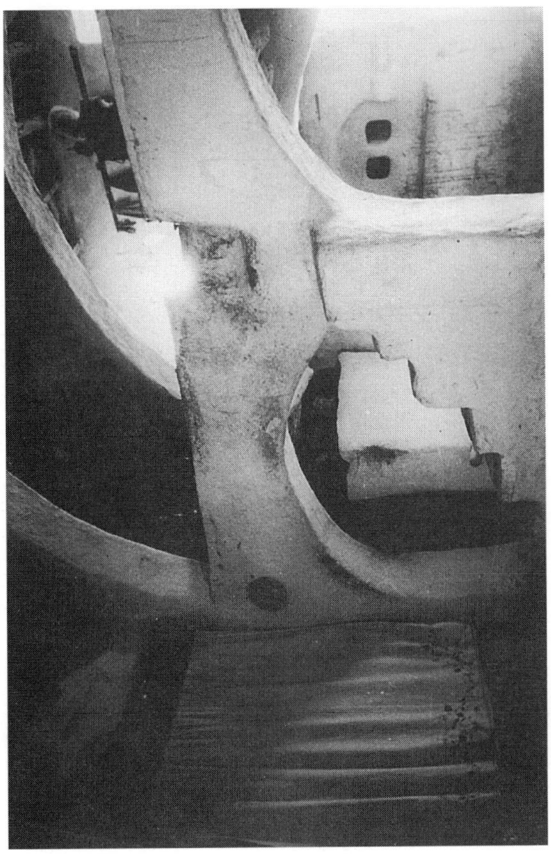
Pl. 8.1. A house in Majd al-Kurum, Galilee

Pl. 8.2. Ladder leading to the gallery level, Majd al-Kurum

Pl. 8.3. Courtyard of a house in Kafr Kana, Galilee

Pl. 8.4. A house in Majd al-Kurum, interior view

Pl. 8.5. The living quarters of a house in Jerusalem

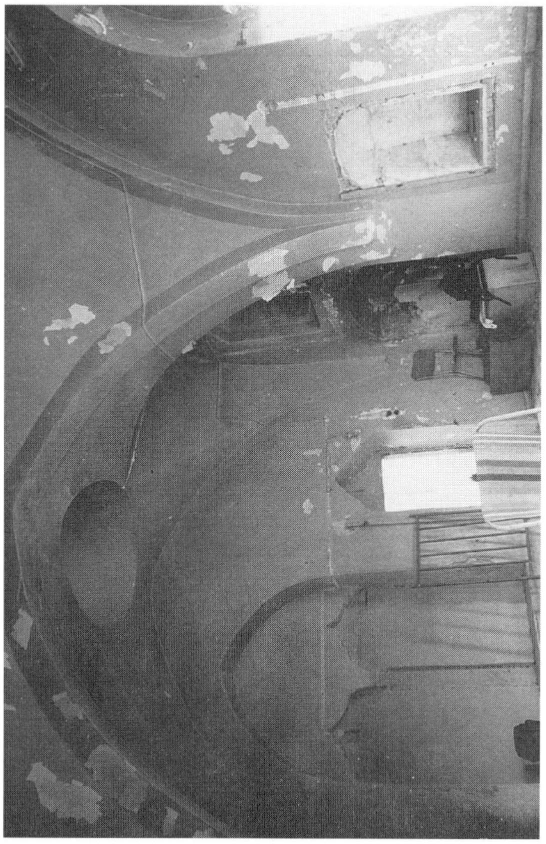

Pl. 8.6. 18th century house in Ramla

Pl. 8.7. House complex, Ramla

Pl. 8.8. Dome of an upper apartment in the house complex, Ramla

Pl. 8.9. A house in Bethlehem

Pl. 8.10. A house in Bethlehem

Pl. 8.11. The house HaMeiri, Safed, interior of *iwan*

Pl. 8.12. The house HaMeiri, Safed

Pl. 8.13. A house in Shivat Zion St, Haifa

Pl. 8.14. Yefet St, Jaffa

Pl. 8.15. Houses with arcades, Haifa

Pl. 8.16. Interior of a house in Acre

Pl. 8.17. Painted ceiling over the central hall in a house near the old saray, Nazareth

Pl. 8.18. Painted ceiling in the same house

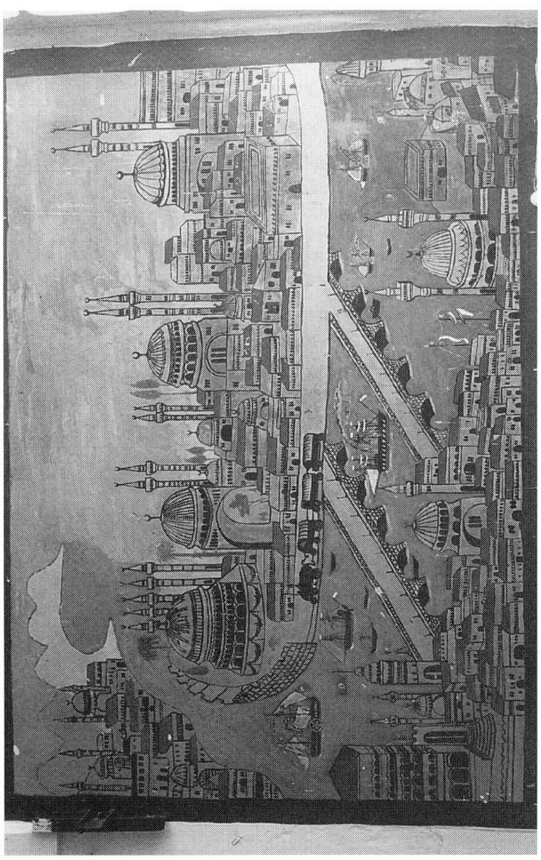

Pl. 8.19. Wall painting showing Constantinople, Acre

Pl. 8.20. Painted ceiling, Nazareth (Pl. 8.17), detail

Pl. 8.21. Frieze showing Sidon in a house in Nazareth

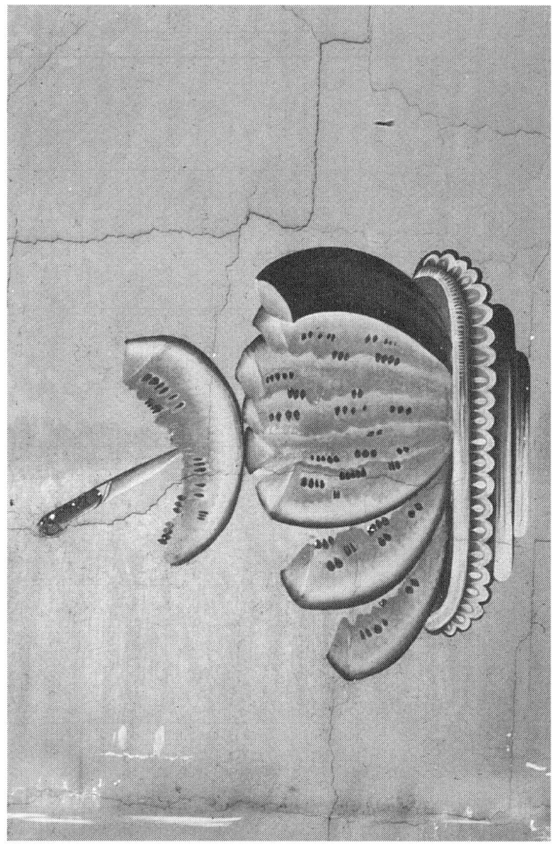

Pl. 8.22. Painted ceiling, Nazareth (Pl. 8.17), detail

Pl. 8.23. A house on Prophets St, Jerusalem

Pl. 8.24. Triphoric aperture on a house in Bethlehem

Pl. 8.25. House in Antalya

Pl. 8.26. House in Antalya

Pl. 9.1. Qatrana Castle

Pl. 9.2. Qatrana railway station

Pl. 9.3. Abdul Hamid School, Kerak

Pl. 9.4. Merchant house in Salt

Pl. 9.5. House of Hajj Guweida Suleiman Obeidat, Hartha

Pl. 9.6. 19th century house at Khirbat Faris

Pl. 9.7. Interior of house at al-Qasr

Pl. 9.8. *Rawiyat* at Khirbat Faris

Pl. 9.9. Tayybet Zeman

Pl. 10.1. Lusignan-Ottoman house, Nicosia

Pl. 10.2. Ceiling in Lusignan-Ottoman house, Nicosia

Pl. 10.3. Konak of Kadı Menteş Efendi (Küçük Mehmet Efendi), Selimiye district Nicosia

Pl. 10.4. Konak of Kadı Menteş Efendi, southern view

Pl. 10.5. Konak of Kadı Menteş Efendi, courtyard & hall

Pl. 10.6. Venetian-Ottoman house, Famagusta

Pl. 10.7. Houses in Nicosia 1878

Pl. 10.8. Restored Ottoman house in Selimiye district Nicosia

Pl. 11.1. The road between the river front houses (left) and the inner city

Pl. 11.2. A cul-de-sac

Pl. 11.3. A projecting cantilever

Pl. 11.4. A *şahnişirin*

Pl. 11.5. A riverside mansion with a column-supported cantilever

Pl. 11.6. *Bindirmelik* supports

Pl. 11.7. *Bindirmelik* supports with *eliböğründe* props

Pl. 11.8. *Eliböğründe* prop

Pl. 11.9. *Bağdadi*-style cantilever supports

Pl. 11.10. *Bağdadi*-style cantilever supports

Pl. 11.11. Window lattice

Pl. 11.12. Projecting window lattice

Pl. 12.1. Main entrance to the house

Pl. 12.2. View from the river

Pl. 12.3. View from Mehmet Paşa St.

Pl. 13.1. Gözdeler wing, Topkapı palace Harem, 1779

Pl. 13.2. Rococo carving & landscapes, Topkapı palace Harem, 1789

Pl. 13.3. Hadımoğlu Konak, Bayramiç, Çanakkale, 1796

Pl. 13.4. Mehmet Ali house, Adatepe, c. 1830

Pl. 13.5. Panorama of Izmir, Çakırağa Konak, Birgi, c. 1830

Pl. 13.6. Tillioğlu house, Göreme, 1825

Pl. 13.7. Schwartz house, Ambelakia, 1798

Pl. 13.8. Nizami house, Damascus, 1803

Pl. 13.9. Kasr-al Gawhara, Cairo, 1814

Pl. 13.10. Kayserli Ahmet Paşa Konak, Vefa Istanbul, 1893

Pl. 13.11. Abutlar Yalı on the Bosphorus, mid. 19th century

Pl. 13.12. Sarı Köşk, Beylerbeyi, 1865

Pl. 13.13. Şale Köşk, Yıldız palace, late 19th century

Pl. 13.14. Güllüoğlu house, Gaziantep, late 19th century

Pl. 13.15. Dolmabahçe palace, late 19th century

Pl. 13.16. Panorama of Istanbul, Damascus, late 19th century

Pl. 14.1. House and garden in Alanya

Pl. 14.2. Wood & stone frontage in Kayseri

Pl. 14.3. Bay window in Hadım

Pl. 14.4. Bay window in Seydişehir

Pl. 14.5. Off-centre bay in Yeşildağ

Pl. 14.6. Pediment dome in Bademli

Pl. 14.7. Window-shutters in Kayseri

Pl. 14.8. Window balustrade in Alanya

Pl. 14.9. Doorway in Alanya

Pl. 14.10. Balustrade in Yahyalı

Pl. 14.11. Decorated porch ceiling in Alanya

Pl. 14.12. Decorated porch in Alanya

Pl. 14.13. Trelliswork in Alanya

Pl. 14.14. Fretwork decoration in Hoyran

Pl. 14.15. Nail decoration on a door in Konya

Pl. 14.16. Balcony in Arvallı

Pl. 14.17. Latticework in Seydişehir

Pl. 14.18. Decorated bay in Konya

15. Haşim Karpuz: Traditional Houses in Konya

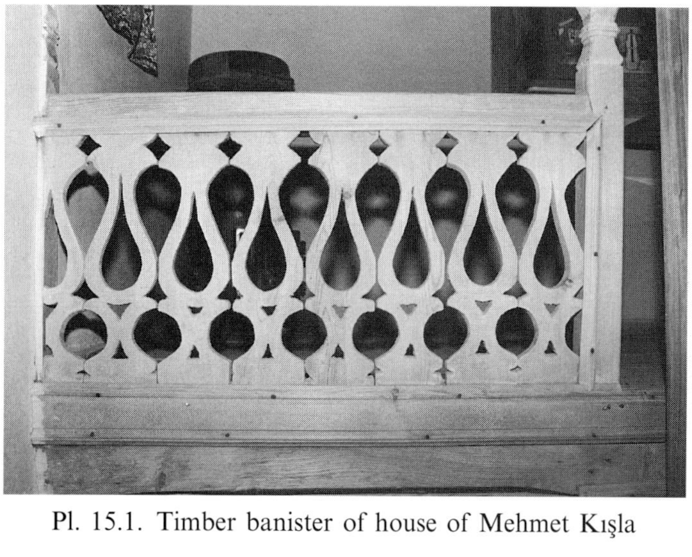

Pl. 15.1. Timber banister of house of Mehmet Kışla

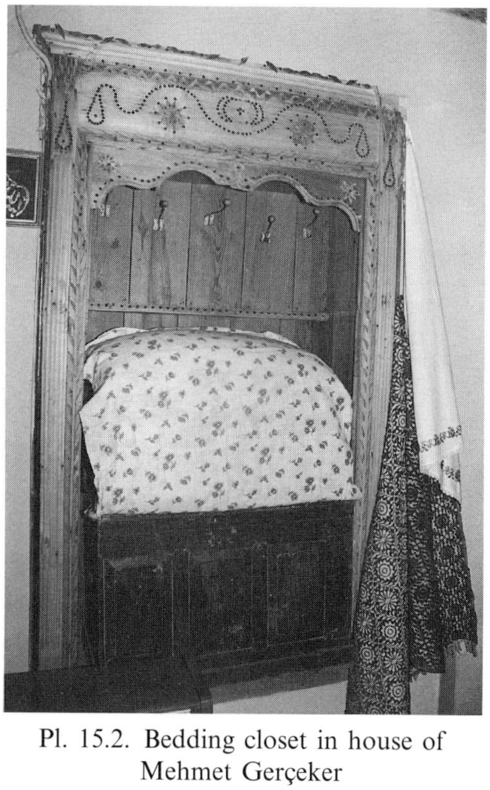

Pl. 15.2. Bedding closet in house of Mehmet Gerçeker

Pl. 15.3. *Sofa* in house of Mehmet Gerçeker

Pl. 15.4. Bays on house at 21 Sırçalı Mescid St.

Pl. 15.5. *Sofa*-bay at 10 Seyit İbrahim St.

Pl. 15.6. Decorated window tops

Pl. 15.7. Ceiling ornament in house of Mehmet Kışla

Pl. 15.8. Flower niche in house of Mehmet Kışla

Pl. 15.9. Flower niche in house of Mehmet Gerçeker

Pl. 15.10. Painted ceiling decoration at 18 Şehri Ayin St.

Pl. 15.11. Penthouse at 43 Tacül Vezir St.

Pl. 15.12. Penthouse at 45 Sedirler St.

Pl. 15.13. Balcony at 51 Mimar Muzaffer St.

Pl. 15.14. Decorated eaves at 89 Köprübaşı St.

Pl. 15.15. Pavilions in public gardens

Pl. 16.1. The Green Building

Pl. 16.2. The Yellow Building

Pl. 16.3. Volta flooring under the balcony

Pl. 16.4. Upper entrance to Green Building

Pl. 16.5. Upper *sofa*

Pl. 16.6. Bay supports & decoration

Pl. 16.7. Roof of the Green Building

Pl. 16.8. Decorated water tap

Pl. 17.1. General view of Amasya, looking north

Pl. 17.2. The linear centre of Amasya with the Bayezid mosque & Pontic tombs

Pl. 17.3. Ottoman river-front houses built on earlier fortification walls

Pl. 17.4. The humane scale of Amasya's historic neighbourhood

Pl. 17.5. The new civic square, looking south-east: the integration of the old and new